Children and Young People Who Sexually Abuse Others

ldren and Young People Who Sexually Abuse Others provides a detailed and coherent
ount and analysis of the current state of research, policy and practice in relation to this
vice user group, providing an invaluable resource for those new to the field, as well as for
se with more experience. This latest edition – which includes both new and revised
oters – addresses context and systems issues, assessment and planning, interventions and
ctitioner issues. Topics covered include:

- policy, law, organisational contexts and service provision in the UK;
- developing a comprehensive inter-agency system of response;
- the management of sexual behaviour problems in schools and in placements;
- assessment issues and resilience based approaches;
- the use of information technologies such as mobile phones and the Internet;
- methods of intervention with children and young people and their families;
- unconscious processes in therapeutic work and practitioner support.

Written in a rigorous and accessible manner, *Children and Young People Who Sexually
Abuse Others* addresses key aspects of working with children and young people with sexually
harmful behaviours. It will be useful to a wide audience, including students, experienced
professionals at front-line and managerial levels, and academics with an interest in this area
of work.

Marcus Erooga is Area Children's Service Manager for the NSPCC in Calderdale and
Lancashire, UK.

Helen Masson is a Reader in Social Work at the University of Huddersfield, UK.

Children and Young People Who Sexually Abuse Others

Current developments and practice responses

2nd edition

Edited by Marcus Erooga and Helen Masson

Foreword by Professor Nigel Parton

Routledge
Taylor & Francis Group

LONDON AND NEW YORK

First edition published 1999
This edition published 2006 by Routledge
2 Park Square, Milton Park, Abingdon, Oxon OX14 4RN

Simultaneously published in the USA and Canada
by Routledge
270 Madison Ave, New York, NY 10016

Routledge is an imprint of the Taylor & Francis Group, an informa business

Typeset in Times by
Keystroke, Jacaranda Lodge, Wolverhampton
Printed and bound in Great Britain by
MPG Books Ltd, Bodmin

British Library Cataloguing in Publication Data
A catalogue record for this book is available from the British Library

Library of Congress Cataloging in Publication Data
Children and young people who sexually abuse others : current developments
and practice responses / edited by: Marcus Erooga and Helen Masson ;
foreword by Nigel Parton.–2nd ed.
p. cm.
Includes bibliographical references and index.
1. Teenage sex offenders–Great Britain. 2. Teenage sex offenders–Rehabilitation–Great
Britain. 3. Teenage child molesters–Great Britain. 4. Teenage child molesters–
Rehabilitation–Great Britain. 5. Social work with juvenile delinquents–Great Britain.
6. Social work with sex offenders–Great Britain. 7. Child sexual abuse–Great Britain–
Prevention. I. Erooga, Marcus, 1957– II. Masson, Helen C.
HV9067.S48C55 2006
364.36–dc22
2005027546

ISBN10: 0–415–35412–9 (hbk)
ISBN10: 0–415–35413–7 (pbk)

ISBN13: 978–0–415–35412–7 (hbk)
ISBN13: 978–0–415–35413–4 (pbk)

To Caroline

Bill, Sam and Tom

Contents

Illustrations

Figures

Tables

Contributors

Nick Bankes is an independent social work consultant, trainer and counsellor. He has worked as a child protection specialist since 1989. Dr Bankes is currently Director of ACT (Ireland): an assessment, consultation, therapy and training service in the field of sexual abuse in the Republic of Ireland. Previously he has developed assessment and therapeutic services for adolescent and adult perpetrators of sexual abuse in the UK. Nick's interests are in the area of staff care and supervision. His PhD research thesis explores the impact of this work on practitioners. He is a reviewer for the *Journal of Sexual Aggression*.

Richard Beckett is a Consultant Clinical and Forensic Psychologist, and Head of Oxford Forensic Psychology Service. Involved with the accreditation of the English Prison Sex Offender Treatment Programmes, he is the author of many associated publications and is currently developing measures to systematically evaluate the impact of treatment on adolescent abusers.

Linda Butler and **Colin Elliott.** *Linda Butler* is a Principal Child Therapist and registered Cognitive Behavioural Psychotherapist. She has undertaken post-graduate training in Child Sexual Abuse at the Institute of Child Health and worked extensively with abused children and their families. *Colin Elliott* is a Consultant Clinical Psychologist and Head of Child Psychology Services in North East Wales. Linda and Colin work in Wrexham Child and Adolescent Mental Health Service, specialising in individual and group cognitive-behavioural therapy, and have considerable experience in running parents' groups for the treatment of conduct disorder and children's and carers' groups for children with problems of impulse control, including sexual aggression.

Carol Carson is an independent trainer and consultant who also works as a Child Protection Co-ordinator for Leeds Social Services. Carol has worked in voluntary, residential and field social work and as a Child Protection Co-ordinator for Leeds Education Department. She has experience of direct work with children and young people who display sexually problematic/harmful behaviours and of supporting staff who work with these children. She has developed guidelines on understanding and managing sexually problematic/ harmful behaviours for foster carers, staff working in residential and education settings and for staff involved in working with children under 10 years old.

Joan Cherry and **Deirdre O'Shea.** *Joan Cherry* is a founder and Director of the Northside Inter-Agency Project, a community-based treatment programme for young people who sexually abuse, in Dublin, Ireland. She participates in the provision of individual, group and family work to young people and their families and offers training and consultation to other professionals and organisations. She is the author and co-author of a number of journal articles. *Deirdre O'Shea* is a Systemic Psychotherapist based in Dublin. Deirdre has been involved in undertaking individual, group and family therapy with children who have been sexually abused and their families, both in Ireland and in the UK. Deirdre has also worked with young people who have sexually abused and their families for a number of years. Deirdre currently undertakes family therapy at the Northside Inter-Agency Project.

Kevin Epps is a Consultant Forensic Clinical Psychologist. He is currently in private practice and works in collaboration with Positive Experiences, an independent therapeutic residential resource for young people. Dr Epps is also an Honorary Lecturer in Forensic Psychology at the University of Birmingham. He has spent most of his clinical career working with children and young people exhibiting extreme forms of antisocial behaviour, including serious sexual aggression. His PhD research involved a comparative study of adolescent sexual offenders, and he is often asked to act as an independent consultant and expert witness in legal proceedings involving sexual offending.

Marcus Erooga is Area Children's Services Manager for the NSPCC in Calderdale and Lancashire and for a number of years has had experience of practice and management of services relating to sexual abuse and sexual offending. He is author of a number of publications on related issues and, with Helen Masson, was co-editor of the *Journal of Sexual Aggression* from 1998 until 2003. He gained his Masters degree at the University of Manchester, his Advanced Award in Social Work at the University of Leicester, and he is a Visiting Honorary Research Fellow at the Centre for Applied Childhood Studies at Huddersfield University and current Vice-Chair of NOTA.

Hilary Grant is a Consultant Forensic Child and Adolescent Psychiatrist. Dr Grant is also Lead Clinician for the West Midlands Forensic CAMHS service (Birmingham and Solihull Mental Health NHS Trust). Her clinical works involve inpatient and outpatient assessment and treatment of young people who present a serious risk to others, including serious violence and serious sexual aggression. She also acts as an expert witness in legal proceedings, involving violent and sexual offending.

Simon Hackett is Professor of Child Welfare at the University of Luton. With Helen Masson and Sarah Phillips, he has recently completed a two-year research project across the UK and Republic of Ireland into the state of policy, theoretical approaches, service responses and user perspectives in relation to young people who have sexually abused others. Simon's practice base in this field extends back to the early 1990s. He was previously Programme Director of G-MAP and continues to be involved in clinical practice with children and young people at the NSPCC Kaleidoscope project. Simon is the author of many publications on sexual abuse by children and young people and related subjects and he is editor of the *Journal of Sexual Aggression*.

Helen Masson is a Reader in Social Work at Huddersfield University and a founder member of the University's Centre for Applied Childhood Studies. Since 1994 Dr Masson has been researching policy and practice developments in relation to young sexual abusers and she is the author of a number of book chapters and journal articles on this and related subjects. With Marcus Erooga, she was co-editor of the *Journal of Sexual Aggression* from 1998 until 2003 and is now co-editor of the *British Journal of Social Work*.

Tony Morrison and **Julie Henniker.** *Tony Morrison* is an independent social care trainer and consultant and a Visiting Honorary Research Fellow at the Centre for Applied Childhood Studies at Huddersfield University. He works with agencies on inter-agency development, supervision, the management of young people with sexual behaviour problems, with a particular interest in family work and attachment-based approaches. He has acted as external consultant to several programmes, including the AIM programme. He is also author of a number of journal articles and books on these subjects. *Julie Henniker* is a social worker with a background in the field of sexual abuse. She is the manager of the AIM project which works across the 10 local authorities and key agencies within Greater Manchester in respect of developing consistent responses, assessment and interventions to children and young people who sexually harm. In addition the project provides training and consultancy on a national basis.

David O'Callaghan, Jeremy Quayle and **Bobbie Print.** *David O'Callaghan* was involved in work with young people who sexually abuse from 1988 until his untimely death in 2004. He held a research grant in this area and published extensively on this topic. He was a Programme Director with G-MAP, an independent therapeutic service to sexually aggressive young people based in Greater Manchester. David was a frequent presenter at national conferences and provided training for probation, health and social services. *Jeremy Quayle* is a Senior Forensic Psychologist working for G-MAP in Greater Manchester. He worked as a university lecturer for a number of years, publishing research papers focussing on biases in human reasoning, before moving to the Prison Service where he assisted in the development and accreditation of the Substance Treatment and Offending Programme (STOP). Dr Quayle is currently developing risk prediction and assessment tools, and researching the outcomes of treatment for adolescents who sexually abuse. He also delivers individual and group interventions and training in this area of work. *Bobbie Print* is Director of G-MAP, an independent organisation based in Manchester that specialises in therapeutic work with young people who sexually harm. Bobbie has worked with G-MAP since its inception in 1988 and has presented and published widely in this field. She was a founding member of NOTA and served on its executive committee for seven years.

Ethel Quayle and **Max Taylor.** *Ethel Quayle* is a lecturer in Applied Psychology at University College Cork, Ireland, and researcher and project leader with COPINE. Dr Quayle trained as a clinical psychologist and has extensive experience working with sex offenders. She is director of a postgraduate MA in cognitive behaviour therapy. *Max Taylor* is Professor of Applied Psychology at University College Cork, Ireland. He has extensive research experience in the area of Forensic Psychology, particularly with respect to terrorism and the role of the new technologies. He is the founder and director of the COPINE Project.

Jane Scott and **Paula Telford.** *Jane Scott* is a Children's Services Practitioner at Kaleidoscope (NSPCC), providing direct services to children and young people who display sexually harmful behaviour and to their carers. Jane has worked at the service for four years and before that worked in statutory child protection with a local authority for nine years. *Paula Telford* is the Children's Services Manager at Kaleidoscope (NSPCC), a service based in the North East of England offering assessment and intervention for children and young people who display sexually harmful behaviour (SHB) and their families. Prior to joining Kaleidoscope, Paula worked for 19 years in statutory child protection, holding a post-qualifying award in this area. She has written contributions to other SHB publications, including an account of Kaleidoscope's parents' group.

Eileen Vizard and **Judith Usiskin.** *Eileen Vizard*, Consultant Child and Adolescent Psychiatrist, is Clinical Director of the Young Abusers Project, an assessment and treatment service within Camden Islington Primary Care Trust and supported by the NSPCC, which has seen over 350 children with sexually harmful behaviour between the ages of five and a half and 21 years. Dr Vizard has published and taught widely within the field of child care and child abuse and is currently undertaking Home Office funded research into the early origins of sexually abusive behaviour and emerging severe personality disorder in childhood. *Judith Usiskin* is a Child and Adolescent Psychotherapist, also based at the Project, whose special area of interest is in learning disability and sexual abuse. She has lectured widely as well as contributing to relevant publications.

Foreword

This is an important and very timely book. While it builds on the earlier edited book by Marcus Erooga and Helen Masson *Children and Young People who Sexually Abuse Others: Challenges and Responses* (Erooga and Masson (eds) 1999), it is much more than this. Not only does it reflect the changes in thinking, policy contexts and practice responses to this highly challenging issue, the book makes a substantive contribution to these developments in its own right. As well as including updated and revised material, this book is more comprehensive, with a number of new, substantive chapters providing an extended range of ideas, theoretical frameworks, and a range of assessment and intervention strategies which can be drawn upon by practitioners, managers and policy makers in the field.

An area of practice which is seen as quite specialist, work with children and young people who sexually abuse others nevertheless sharply illustrates many of the current issues, tensions and complexities which pervade contemporary child welfare practice. In particular, ways to integrate concerns and legal frameworks informed by the criminal youth justice arena with those with a more explicit child welfare orientation are highlighted here and are central to the work. There is no doubt that this area is highly complex and clearly illustrates the need for both sensitive practice guidance and highly skilled practitioners who are able both to work in a context of uncertainty and to respond with clarity and sensitivity. What this book clearly demonstrates is the importance of working in a multi-disciplinary context where the various professionals respect and recognise both their own particular contributions and orientations and those of others, in order to ensure that the young people who engage in sexually abusive behaviour and those who are the victims and survivors receive a response which meets the needs of all concerned. This is a major challenge. Both the needs of the children and young people who pose a risk and those who are at risk of being abused, together with their respective views and experiences, lie at the centre of the book.

There is no doubt that thinking and practice responses, together with some elements of the legislative and policy context, have moved on considerably since the first edition was published in 1999. Not only has there been a raft of new guidance, legislation and organisational change in the UK and the Republic of Ireland in the intervening years, which is very helpfully summarised and discussed by Helen Masson in Chapter 2, but also, particularly in England, it is clear that we are now embarking on yet another major period of change following the publication of *Every Child Matters* (DfES 2003) and the passing of the 2004 Children Act. Their emphases on the importance of multi-disciplinary work, focusing on the needs of children and young people, and holistic assessment which attempts to intervene at an early stage, now permeate what we are trying to do for all children and young people.

In other respects, however, the initiatives and developments discussed in this volume are somewhat different from the mainstream. What is very clear is that practice in relation to children and young people who sexually abuse others has been developed by practitioners on the ground, who are trying to develop their thinking and practice in response to the particular demands they are addressing on a day-to-day basis. Unlike the more wide-ranging 'top down' changes we are currently witnessing, the developments described in this volume are largely practitioner-led. It demonstrates what practitioners are able to do in very complex and demanding situations and that their knowledge and skills should be respected and built upon. In this respect, much of the local policy development and practice initiatives illustrated here provide an exemplar for what can be developed in other areas of child welfare and protection practice.

The book also illustrates how work in this area has moved forward in the intervening six years. Perhaps an underlying theme of the 1999 publication was a plea that this was an issue that should be recognised and for which policy and practice needed to be developed. In this context much of the emphasis was on the need for thoughtful and systematic assessments relevant to the needs and challenges of this particular client group. While issues around assessment and the development of different assessment frameworks continue to be a major theme of this book (Part 2), there is now a much greater emphasis on the range of interventions that can be applied, with six of the seventeen chapters having intervention as their focus. Similarly the importance of 'practitioner issues' is more central and is explicitly the focus of the two chapters which make up Part 4.

Perhaps the central message that comes through from this book is that work in this area needs to explicitly recognise that the people being worked with are primarily children and young people with their own needs rather than 'incipient sex offenders', and that whilst they may pose particular challenges which should not be underestimated, the essential principles of all work with children and young people are central to this area of practice. It has become clearer that forms of intervention and treatment developed specifically for adult sex offenders are not always appropriate with children and young people, and that not everyone coming to the attention of services will necessarily need treatment. It is not the case, either, that every child or young person who engages in sexually abusive behaviour will necessarily develop into an adult sex offender but, once again, practice is ahead of official guidance in this understanding (Department of Health (1999), and see also the July 2005 consultation on the new *Working Together*). Essentially, these are rarely 'little demons' who always require pre-emptive intervention, they are children and young people whose needs and behaviours have far more in common with other children and young people than they have differences. It is much better to assume that they are typical and normal, rather than abnormal and thus requiring an exceptional and punitive response.

Marcus Erooga and Helen Masson must be thanked for bringing together such a distinguished group of people to contribute to this book. Not only does it take our thinking and practice forward, the book raises a number of issues for policy makers and managers, as well as providing an invaluable resource book for anyone, whether experienced or coming to this field for the first time. While the contributors come from all parts of the UK and the Republic of Ireland, there is also no doubt that the book will provide a major contribution to the international literature on this topic.

Professor Nigel Parton
Director
Centre for Applied Childhood Studies
University of Huddersfield
UK

Preface

During the 1990s there was developing awareness of the fact that children can exhibit sexually problematic behaviours and that young people can also be sexual abusers of others. Consequently, this recognition also led to a gradual increase in services to meet their needs. The scale of the problem was illuminated when studies of incidence and prevalence in the United Kingdom and elsewhere led to estimates that between a quarter and up to a third of reported sexual abuse was committed by under 18-year-olds (National Children's Home 1992).

The original edition of this book, published in 1999, reflected this greater recognition of the problem and comprised a natural development from another Routledge publication on (adult) male sexual abusers (Morrison *et al.* 1994). *Children and Young People Who Sexually Abuse Others: Challenges and Responses* comprised thirteen chapters written by leading experts in the field in the UK, the whole comprising a 'home-grown' publication designed to complement much of the existing literature which, at that time, was of North American origin.

The first edition of the book clearly met a need, with buoyant sales both in the UK and, somewhat to our surprise, in the rest of the world. Since 1999, however, research and practice understanding about children with sexual behaviour problems and young people who sexually abuse have continued to develop and so we decided that the time was right to work on a second edition. Thus this revised and much expanded volume aims both to update the contents of the first edition, and also to widen the focus to include topics and areas of discussion which were either not being aired six years ago and/or about which very little was then known. Although still committed to commissioning chapters largely from within the UK, with contributions from nationally respected practitioners, clinicians, academics and researchers, we are also delighted to include, in this volume, four chapters written by leading practitioners, academics and researchers based in the Republic of Ireland. In total, there are seventeen chapters in the book, nine of which are substantially updated versions of chapters that appeared in the first edition and eight that are newly commissioned.

The book is, as before, intended for a number of audiences across a range of agencies and organisations involved in child protection, criminal and youth justice, psychiatry, psychology and counselling. Practitioners who have continued to be at the forefront of formulating responses to children and young people with sexual behaviour problems, will, it is hoped, find this volume relevant and helpful in developing their understanding and practice. Similarly, their managers and those responsible for policy will find the book useful in illuminating the practice complexities and dilemmas which their staff face and in outlining the issues which organisations and systems need to resolve, offering detailed guidance on best policy and practice. The book will also be of value to students studying in the health and social care fields and to educators involved in professional training.

The authorship reflects the book's firm commitment to the importance of multi-agency and inter-disciplinary collaboration and the content addresses work in both community and residential settings. Although there are differences in perspective and emphasis between chapters, we see this as healthy and inevitable given the relative youthfulness of this area of work and its complexities and given the diversity of the population which comprises children and young people who sexually abuse others. Indeed, it is hoped that the rich mix of theoretical and practical perspectives, from, for example, cognitive behavioural to psychodynamic approaches, contained within the book will offer stimulation and food for thought for readers with both more and less experience in work with this service user group.

In view of its increased size and scope this second edition, *Children and Young People Who Sexually Abuse Others: Current Developments and Practice Responses,* is divided into four parts covering *Context and Systems; Assessment and Planning; Interventions* and *Practitioner Issues.* This is to provide, we hope, a logical ordering of chapters, starting with the broad contexts within which practice in this area is conducted, through to the detail of assessment and intervention work with children and young people with sexually problematic or abusive behaviours and concluding with some consideration of the impact of the work on practitioners and practitioner needs.

In the *Context and Systems* section, Chapter 1, by the co-editors, provides an overview of issues of incidence and prevalence; a summary of the characteristics of children and young people with sexually problematic or abusive behaviours; recommended principles of and approaches to work; an outline of relevant knowledge and key theoretical models; and an overview of the state of service development currently in the UK and Republic of Ireland. The chapter aims to provide a backdrop for subsequent chapters and so it is suggested that this should be a useful starting point for most readers, before exploring the remainder of the book. The other chapters in this section are new commissions. Chapter 2, by Helen Masson, focuses on the broad policy, guidance and legislative frameworks which inform practice and outlines service development at national and local levels across the UK, drawing on recently completed research (Hackett *et al.* 2003). This broad sweep is then complemented by Chapter 3, written by Tony Morrison and Julie Henniker, which discusses the development of their nationally recognised model for the local systems of response: The AIM project. Finally, in this section, Chapter 4, written by Carol Carson, addresses an often neglected area: how teaching staff, within schools and as part of wider multi-agency networks, can recognise and work with children and young people with sexual behaviour problems who, after all, spend the majority of their time in school settings from at least five to up to 18 years of age.

The section on *Assessment and Planning* starts with Chapter 5, newly written by Hilary Grant, which covers the purposes, content and process of assessment work with young people who have sexually abused others or who are displaying sexually problematic behaviours. Chapter 6, a revised chapter prepared by Nick Bankes, provides an overview, at a broad, macro level, of issues relating to placement provision for these children and young people. Included here is consideration, from a systemic perspective, of the formal and informal processes which impact on decision making about choice of placement.

Chapter 7, a revised chapter written by Kevin Epps, addresses the difficult balancing act involved in minimising the risk of further acts of sexual abuse and victimisation, whilst also ensuring that the developmental, educational and therapeutic needs of young people with sexual behaviour problems are addressed. Chapter 8, newly written for this edition by Simon Hackett, describes the key concepts of newly emerging resilience theory and explores how they can inform interventions with young people with harmful sexual behaviours. Such an approach provides an important adjunct to more traditional models of assessment and intervention, which tend to be risk and problem based. By contrast, a resilience approach is an inherently strengths-based model, which seeks to focus on, and enhance, young people's developmental competencies. Finally in this section, in Chapter 9, Ethel Quayle and Max Taylor, who work in the Republic of Ireland, discuss developments in new technologies which were not even a consideration at the time of the previous edition but which are now of frequent concern in relation to this population. Thus the chapter explores online adolescent sexual behaviour and the ways in which sexual harassment and victimisation can take place. In this context, literature that relates to adolescent use of the new technologies is drawn on, along with work on the Internet and problems with self-control.

The third section, on *Interventions*, includes six chapters, five of which are substantial revisions of chapters which appeared in the first edition. Chapter 10, written by Eileen Vizard and Judith Usiskin, covers a range of topic areas in relation to individual psychotherapy with young people who have sexually abused others. Chapter 11, written by David O'Callaghan, Jeremy Quayle and Bobbie Print, offers a model for working in groups with young men who are sexually aggressive and ideas for setting up such groups. The original chapter, in the first edition, was co-authored by Bobbie Print and her colleague, David O'Callaghan, whose sad and untimely death in 2004 is an enduring source of sadness both to those who knew him but also those who benefited from his skill and knowledge, both service users and professionals. Chapter 12, written by Jane Scott and Paula Telford, addresses the relatively neglected area of work with young women who sexually abuse and Chapter 13, by Linda Butler and Colin Elliott, describes and analyses the *Stop and Think* model for work with younger children. In Chapter 14, newly written by Joan Cherry and Deirdre O'Shea, who work in a specialist project in the Republic of Ireland, the importance of working with the families of children and young people with sexual behaviour problems is stressed and ideas for such work are provided. Finally in this section, Richard Beckett, in Chapter 15, critically reviews the complex areas of risk prediction and evaluating treatment outcomes in relation to young abusers and provides an overview of the result of his national study of adolescent treatment programmes.

The final section of this second edition, on *Practitioner Issues,* comprises two chapters, one of them newly commissioned. Chapter 16, revised by Simon Hackett, analyses the many aspects which make up empowered and empowering practice in this area of work, both from the perspective of practitioners and from the perspective of service users, in all their diversity. Finally, Chapter 17, written by Nick Bankes, describes the findings from his research which examined unconscious processes in practitioners who were working therapeutically with children and young people who had sexually abused others. Having concluded that processes such as countertransference and projective identification do occur, he discusses the implications of his findings for the training and supervision of practitioners.

As with the first edition, the balance of content in this second edition reflects current understanding of the known population exhibiting sexually problematic or abusive behaviour, hence the primary focus on interventions with and the management of young males from about 10 years of age and older and their families. However, it has also been a priority to include revised chapters on work with sexually aggressive young females (Chapter 12) and on younger children who have sexual behaviour problems (Chapter 13). Throughout the book, authors of chapters also refer, as appropriate, to the particular issues and aspects requiring consideration which arise when working with children and young people with sexual behaviour problems who are also from a minority ethnic background or who exhibit a degree of learning difficulty.

We have also been very much aware of the need to try and maintain consistency in terminology given the range of phrases used to delineate children and young people who are sexually aggressive or abusive towards others, phrases which have fallen in and out of favour since the early 1990s and which remain contested today (Hackett *et al.* 2003). In the hope of providing clarity for the reader the phrase 'sexually aggressive child or children' is used to denote younger children, those usually under the age of criminal responsibility in a given nation. A number of similar descriptors, for example, young sexual abusers, adolescent or juvenile sexual abusers, and young people who sexually abuse refer to children and young people typically aged above the age of criminal responsibility. Unless specifically addressing young female sexual abusers the pronoun 'he' is used throughout, in recognition of the fact that the bulk of sexually aggressive children and young people who sexually abuse others are male.

At the conclusion of this introduction to this second edition we record our grateful thanks to all our chapter contributors for their expertise and their forbearance in the face of our enthusiastic editing. Our thanks, too, to Sue Hanson, who has provided invaluable secretarial support during the preparation of this volume. Finally we would want to acknowledge our respective long-suffering partners who have, once again, provided all the hidden support, without much complaint, whilst we were absorbed in 'that book'.

Part 1

Context and systems issues

1 Children and young people with sexually harmful or abusive behaviours

Underpinning knowledge, principles, approaches and service provision

Marcus Erooga and Helen Masson

Introduction

Sexually harmful or abusive behaviour by children and young people first emerged as a matter of concern in the United Kingdom during the early 1990s (see, for example, National Children's Home 1992) and now, a decade or so later, is firmly established both within the professional community and with policy makers as a problem which requires a response (Masson and Hackett 2003). This introductory chapter provides an overview of the current state of knowledge about such children and young people and of the developing consensus about principles of work and preferred intervention approaches. A brief description of the state of service provision in the UK and the Republic of Ireland is also offered, based on the most recent research findings available (Hackett *et al.* 2003).

Incidence and prevalence of sexual harm and abuse by children and young people

The latest available criminal statistics for England and Wales, those for 2003/4 (Home Office 2004), give the recorded level of all sexual offences as 52,100, a 7 per cent increase on 2002/3 but still comprising less than 1 per cent of all recorded crime, a very similar picture to that in 1999, when the first edition of this book was published. Interestingly, 11 per cent fewer individuals (5,700) were subsequently cautioned, reprimanded or found guilty of sexual offences in 2003/4 than in 1999, when 6,400 were cautioned or found guilty. Of the 2003/4 total of 5,700, 1,300 (23 per cent) were cautioned or reprimanded, of whom (based on approximate figures contained in the Home Office statistics) up to 8 per cent (less than 100) were aged 10–11 years, up to 19 per cent (less than 250) were aged 12–14 years, up to 19 per cent (less than 250) were aged 15–17 years and up to 19 per cent (less than 250) were aged 18–20 years. The vast majority of these cautions and reprimands were of males. So, it would appear that children and young people aged between 10 and 20 years accounted for up to approximately 65 per cent of all cautions or reprimands for sexual offences in 2003/4. In the same year, 4,300 individuals (again almost all male) were found guilty in a court of a sexual offence, of whom up to 1 per cent (less than 50) were aged 10–11 years, up to 3.5 per cent (less than 150) were aged 12–14 years, up to 8 per cent (less than 350) were aged 15–17 years and up to 8 per cent (less than 350) were aged between 18 and 20. Thus a much smaller percentage of children and young people (up to 21 per cent) accounted for findings of guilt as a result of court process.

These statistics, which refer only to offenders over the age of criminal responsibility and only to recorded crimes, represent just a small proportion of sexual harm or abuse committed by children and young people, particularly as much abuse goes unreported or is not recognised or dealt with as such. Various other kinds of studies have, therefore, tried to estimate the prevalence of sexual abuse or harm by young people within a population.

In an early major retrospective study of adults concerning their experiences of abuse in childhood, for example, Finkelhor (1979) found that 34 per cent of women and 39 per cent of men who recalled having a sexual encounter during their childhood with someone five or more years older than themselves reported that the older partner was aged between 10 and 19 years. Twenty years later, in a prevalence study of child maltreatment in the UK, Cawson *et al.* (2000) surveyed a representative sample of 2,869 young people aged 18–24 years and found that 11 per cent (three-quarters of them female) had been sexually abused, this involving contact either against their will by parents/carers or by other people when they were 12 or under and the other person was five or more years older. Ninety per cent of this abuse had been unreported. Interestingly, in relation to intra-familial sexual abuse (which comprised only a very small proportion of the total sexual abuse reported), the most likely relative to abuse was a brother (mentioned in 31 per cent of cases where relatives were involved, compared to a prevalence rate of father/daughter incest of 0.3 per cent). As regards the much larger category of extra-familial sexual abuse, the perpetrators were usually people known to the respondents and were often their peers: boy or girlfriends, friends of brothers or sisters or fellow pupils or students. In another study, in Scotland, Wight *et al.* (2000) surveyed 7,395 14-year-olds. Eighteen per cent of the boys and 15 per cent of the girls reported having had sexual intercourse – in 20 per cent of these cases the respondents indicated that there had been some level of coercion. Considering the findings of these and other studies over the years (see, for example, Ageton 1983; Fromuth *et al.* 1991; Glasgow *et al.* 1994) overview reports (for example, National Children's Home 1992; Openshaw *et al.* 1993; Lovell 2002) conclude that there appears to be a consistent finding that between about one-quarter and one-third of all alleged sexual abuse or sexual harm involves children and young people.

Groups within the population – attending to diversity

In the early 1990s pioneering literature (see, for example, Ryan and Lane 1991) tended to focus on the white, male adolescent aged between 14 and 17 years as the modal type of juvenile sexual offender. Whilst criminal statistics continue to demonstrate that reported young sexual offenders are predominately males in their middle to late teenage years, what we have come to appreciate is that sexually harmful and/or abusive behaviour is not only exhibited by this sub-group of young people.

In their survey of 186 service providers in the UK and Republic of Ireland Hackett *et al.* (2003) found that approximately 27 per cent of services were working with children who were under 10 years of age, although most of the young people worked with were either in the age range 10–13 years or, in the case of English and Welsh youth offending teams, in the 14–18-year age range. In terms of gender, 76 or 41 per cent of the 186 services had worked solely with males. The remaining 110 services (59 per cent) had some experience of working with female service users but only four services (2 per cent) across the five nations worked only with females.

Focusing on ethnicity, only one service out of all of Northern Ireland, Scotland and the Republic of Ireland had worked with service users from a minority ethnic background. However, in England and Wales, 31 or 28 per cent of youth offending teams and 23 or 40 per cent of the other services surveyed reported having worked with young people with sexual behaviour problems who were from an African-Caribbean, Asian or other ethnic background. It would appear that most young adolescent male sexual abusers in treatment are white but this finding may, as with black adult sex offenders (Cowburn 1996), reflect the racist bias inherent in the criminal justice and other systems which result in young black offenders being dealt with more punitively and having less access to treatment facilities. Research by Feilzer and Hood (Youth Justice Board 2004a) into the operation of the criminal justice system, for example, found that a young person of mixed parentage was three times more likely to be prosecuted than a young white offender and that young men from minority ethnic groups tended to receive more restrictive community sentences or longer terms of custody than their white counterparts.

What was of particular interest in the Hackett *et al.* study (2003) was that, with the exception of Northern Ireland, over half of the services in the various nations studied reported working with significant proportions of children and young people with sexually problematic behaviours whom they considered to be learning disabled. However, it appeared that few such young people had been formally assessed as such. Other studies of young people with sexually harmful behaviour have found similar over-representation of people with learning disabilities (Dolan *et al.* 1996; Hawkes *et al.* 1997). Lane with Lobanov-Rostovsky (in Ryan and Lane 1997) have commented in relation to this group:

> Clinical observation indicates numerous similarities but also some unique differences between sexually abusive behaviour of disabled and non-disabled youth. The range of behaviours, the types of sexually abusive behaviours, and the elements of the behaviour appear similar, while the associated cognitive processes, the context of the behaviours and the level of sophistication exhibit some differences.
>
> (p. 342)

What little research has been undertaken seems to suggest that there may be a more repetitive, habitual quality to the behaviour of these youngsters in terms of victim choice, location and frequency of behaviour, they may have greater difficulty understanding the abusive nature of their activities and may justify what they have done against what they perceive to be normal male behaviour. They may also exhibit more impulsivity and a more childlike need for immediate gratification. Stermac and Sheridan (1993) suggest that they are significantly more likely to display inappropriate, non-contact 'nuisance' behaviours such as public masturbation, exhibitionism and voyeurism and that they are less discriminating in their choice of victim, choosing male and female victims equally. Their behaviour also has to be understood in the context of societal prejudice towards such disability, a general lack of attention paid to issues of sexuality in relation to this group and their increased vulnerability to being the victims of sexual abuse themselves. Clearly management and treatment of these young people have to be planned in the light of careful assessment of their cognitive and social functioning so that, for example, treatment delivery attends to issues such as shortened attention spans, more experiential styles of learning and the need for careful use of language and repetition of messages (O'Callaghan 1999).

Given what has been outlined already in this chapter about incidence and prevalence, it is unsurprising that the survey by Hackett *et al.* (2003) also found that 105 or 56 per cent of services across all five nations, including Youth Offending Teams (YOTs), had worked with children and young people with sexual behaviour problems who had not been charged with any offence. On the other hand, all 186 services had also worked with young people charged with a range of offences, right through to small minorities of young people who had been charged with the most serious sexual offences, involving physical contact and violence.

What emerges is that the total population of children and young people with sexually harmful or abusive behaviours is a very heterogeneous group, not only in terms of age, gender, ethnicity and disability, but also in terms of the levels of personal and social vulnerabilities they experience and demonstrate and in terms of the risks they present to others. In this regard, they are no different from other children and young people in trouble, some of whom may have relatively modest needs (for education, support and more acceptable outlets for their energies) whilst a few exhibit serious deficits in personal functioning and social skills and present a serious risk to others' wellbeing. *Childhood Lost* (The Bridge Child Care Development Service 2001), the report of a serious case review into the death of an 11-year-old boy, WN, is a tragic account of the life and circumstances of DM, an 18-year-old who murdered WN. It catalogues the long history of DM's sexually harmful and then abusive behaviours, culminating in his conviction at the age of 14 on 12 specimen charges of sexual abuse against a number of children and his removal from his highly problematic family circumstances into local authority accommodation.[1] DM represents the extreme end of risk (to self and others), at the other end of which are the majority of children and young people whose problematic behaviours are not evidence of deep-seated and intransigent difficulties.

Issues of recidivism

Understanding has developed across time about the likelihood of children and young people with sexually harmful or abusive behaviour continuing with their problematic behaviour into adulthood, whether or not they are ever the focus of professional interventions. Early thinking, as reported in the National Children's Home inquiry report (1992) and implicit in the central government guidance *Working Together* (Department of Health 1991b) was that, unlike other juvenile delinquents who typically grow out their offending, young sexual abusers were more likely to continue in their abusive behaviour unless treated, preferably under some kind of civil or criminal legal mandate. Thus the notion developed that young sexual abusers were likely to become the adult sex offenders of the future unless subject to early, and often substantial, intervention.

Since the mid-1990s, studies and associated literature have cast doubt on the NCH Committee conclusions (for example, Will 1994; Glasgow *et al.* 1994; Weinrott 1996; Becker 1998b) and it would appear that such views might have, in part at least, resulted from misinterpretations of studies of the development of offending careers in adult sex offenders. Nevertheless, *Working Together* (Department of Health 1999) still reflects this earlier thinking:

> Work with adult abusers has shown that many of them began committing abusing acts during childhood or adolescence, and that significant numbers have been subjected to abuse themselves. Early intervention with children and young people who abuse others, may therefore, play an important part in protecting the public by preventing the continuation or escalation of abusive behaviour.
>
> (p. 70)

Their survey of experienced practitioners by Hackett *et al.* (2003) indicates, however, a very different attitude to the issue of recidivism and the likely continuation of youthful sexually abusive behaviours into adulthood, with 90 per cent of respondents strongly agreeing that:

. . . the vast majority of young people do not go on to become adult sex offenders, but that an identifiable, small sub-group are at high risk of so doing.

(p. 14)

However, the survey revealed respondents' concerns about a continuing uncertainty around this issue at the local, inter-professional level and Hackett *et al.* (2003) reported that it was noticeable how often a version of the paragraph from *Working Together* (Department of Health 1999) or something like it was included in inter-agency documentation. As Masson and Hackett comment (2003):

> This is, of course, problematic in a number of ways. On the one hand it may lead to some young people with low-level sexually problematic behaviours being subject to extensive and intrusive levels of intervention unnecessarily. On the other, it may divert resources away from those young people in higher risk groups who are in need of a more intensive intervention response.

(p. 115)

As later chapters will reinforce, local service providers should consider establishing a differentiated approach to intervention, in order to address the different levels of needs and risks presented by these children and young people, needs and risks which can only be identified as a result of a sensitive and thorough assessment of individual cases.

Characteristics

Having established that we are discussing a heterogeneous population, there has, nevertheless, been work undertaken over the years to analyse the general characteristics of the various sub-groups identified on the basis of age and gender. Thus male adolescent sexual abusers are often characterised as having a number of psychosocial problems and social skills deficits, often being socially isolated, lacking intimacy skills and sexual knowledge, and experiencing high levels of social anxiety (Becker and Abel 1985; Fehrenbach *et al.* 1986; Awad and Saunders 1989; Richardson *et al.* 1997; Långström and Grann 2000; Way 2005). Marshall *et al.* (2000) and Cortoni and Marshall (2001) have suggested that problems of early emotional attachment contribute to low emotional intelligence, low empathy for others, low self-esteem and emotional loneliness and a failure to establish intimate relationships in later life. Ward *et al.* (1997, 2000) have also attempted to identify the developmental processes by which experiences of attachment may relate to interpersonal sexual violence for some males. Most recently Smallbone (2005) has proposed a model which suggests that attachment insecurity may be both a predisposing and precipitating factor for sexually abusive behaviour by young people.

   Young male sexual abusers may well be doing poorly at school both in terms of behaviour and educational attainment (Kahn and Chambers 1991; Kenny *et al.* 2001), some may be abusing substances (Hunter 2000; Campbell and Lerew 2002) and some may be using pornography (Hunter 2000). Like adult male sexual offenders relatively high proportions of young male sexual abusers (between 25 and 60 per cent depending on the study cited) report having been victims of sexual abuse themselves (O'Callaghan and Print 1994). A number of studies, therefore, also suggest that the families of such youngsters may have a number of difficulties in terms of their stability and intra-familial dynamics (Ryan and Lane 1997).

Within the total group of adolescent sexually abusive males there may well be other sub-groups. Epps (1999), for example, supports the work of James and Neill (1996) who suggest that there may be three distinct sub-groups: those who target children, those who offend against female peers and women and those who offend against both children and adults. Epps also suggests that whilst the majority of victims of juvenile sex offenders are female (69–84 per cent), as the age of the victim decreases, the victim is more likely to be male. Hunter *et al.* (2003) and Worling (2001) have also conducted studies into different sub-groups of sexually abusive male youth, looking at differences in, for example, victim characteristics, offence and behaviour patterns, social and criminal history, and personality profiles. There is clearly more to be learned in these respects which may inform future intervention approaches. In addition, as already indicated, other factors need to be taken into account in work with minority ethnic young people with sexual abusive behaviour, including factors of language, culture and religion, the experience of racism and so on (see, for example, Abassi and Jamal 2002) and in work with young people with a learning disability (see, for example, O'Callaghan 1999).

Female adolescent sexual abusers

In their overview of female youth who sexually abuse, Lane with Lobanov-Rostovsky (in Ryan and Lane 1997) comment on the very disturbed backgrounds of the young female abusers with whom they have worked, noting high levels of both sexual and physical victimisation, problematic relationships with parents, family separation, problems at school and with peers in particular. They suggest that young female sexual abusers may well benefit from the same kinds of treatment approaches as young male sexual abusers, although they comment that issues of autonomy and the consequences of female socialisation experiences may well be useful additional foci.

Robinson (2005) echoes many of the above comments but in her analysis of the assessment of female sexually abusive youth, she emphasises the importance of attending to differences between female and male development. These include the importance of relationships and connections with others in the development of female identity, in contrast to males who tend to develop identity through independence and autonomy; how females are expected to manage (and usually) internalise their feelings; how, in contrast to males, self-confidence tends to decrease with age in females and how socio-cultural scripts exert different and powerful influences on the development of female sexuality. Chapter 12 in this volume also discusses the similarities and differences between male and female adolescent sexual abusers and one project's approach to work with these young women.

Pre-adolescent sexual abusers

As regards younger children, one of the earliest descriptions of sexually aggressive children in treatment (47 boys aged 4–13 years) was provided by Cavanagh-Johnson (1988). Forty-nine per cent of these boys had themselves been sexually abused and 19 per cent physically abused by people they knew. The boys all knew the children they abused: in 46 per cent of cases the victim was a sibling and 18 per cent were members of the extended family. Compared to adolescent sexual abusers it appeared that these sexually aggressive children used less coercion and more enticement to secure the compliance of their victims. The mean age of the boys at the time of their sexually aggressive behaviour was 8 years 9 months; the mean age of their victims 6 years 9 months. There was a history of sexual and physical abuse in the majority of the families of the boys, as well as a history of substance abuse.

In one of the few studies of female sexually aggressive children, also by Cavanagh-Johnson (1989), it was found that all of the sample of thirteen girls (aged 4–12 years, with a mean age of 7.5) who were in treatment had been subjected to prior sexual victimisation of a serious nature, often with close relatives, and had usually received little support and validation from other family members when they had disclosed their abuse. Thirty-one per cent had also been physically abused. All had used force or coercion to gain the compliance of their victims and 77 per cent had chosen victims in the family. The mean age of their first known sexually aggressive behaviour was 6 years, 9 months and the average age of their victims was 4 years, 4 months.

In a larger, more recent study of 287 sexually aggressive children aged 12 years and under (Burton *et al.* 1997) 79 per cent of the children were male and 21 per cent were female, with the average child living in a two-parent home. In 70 per cent of their families at least one caretaker was chemically dependent; 48 per cent had at least one parent known to have been sexually abused; and 72 per cent of the children were sexually abused themselves (60 per cent by a carer). The children with known sexual abuse histories were younger at the first sign of sexual aggression than those without known sexual abuse histories. Lane with Lobanov-Rostovsky (in Ryan and Lane 1997) have surveyed the issues and concerns raised by young children with sexually aggressive behaviour problems. They have worked with some 100 young children whom they divided into two treatment groups (7–9 years and 10–12 years). The majority of these children were male and two-thirds were white. Nearly half of the children were living at home at the point of referral and over two-thirds had a history of sexual, physical or emotional victimisation or abandonment experiences. One-third exhibited psychiatric, learning or medical problems and about a quarter had been involved in what would be considered other delinquent activity if they were older. Similar findings have been described subsequently by Cavanagh-Johnson and Doonan (2005) in their overview of the current state of work in relation to children with sexual behaviour problems.

Lane with Lobanov-Rostovsky (Ryan and Lane 1997) reported that the treatment approach they adopted with children was eclectic, drawing on a modified version of the abuse cycle concept outlined later in this chapter, complemented with work on the children's own childhood traumas and involving collaborative work with family and other caretakers. The authors of Chapter 13 describe a somewhat similar treatment approach in a UK context, based on cognitive development theory, in their 'Stop and Think' group for young children exhibiting sexually aggressive behaviour.

The development of sexually harmful or abusive behaviour

Estimates of the extent of sexual victimisation amongst those young people who go on to sexually abuse others vary from 30–50 per cent, although other experiences, of physical and emotional abuse or exposure to violence and/or neglect, appear to be much more common (Ryan *et al.* 1996; Skuse *et al.* 1997; Bentovim and Williams 1998; Manocha and Mezey 1998; Beckett 1999).

The traumegenic model developed by Finkelhor and Browne (1985) on the dynamics of the effects of sexual abuse on children and young people gives some clue as to the mechanism by which some abused children go on to abuse others as part of their response to their own abusive experiences. They suggest that as part of the *traumatic sexualisation* following abuse, inappropriate sexual behaviour and sexualised responses may be 'rewarded', either literally by the abuser, or psychologically or physiologically. Thus closeness, intimate relationships and power may become sexualised. The sense of *powerlessness* which may form part of the abuse can lead to a need to control or dominate events or people, and so lead to the re-enactment of the abusive behaviour itself in order to deal with the feelings associated with their own experiences. Feelings of *betrayal*, which may also be a consequence of the abuse, may diminish the ability to form appropriate relationships and may engender feelings of hostility and distrust and possibly a desire for retaliation. Finally *stigmatisation* resulting from abuse can further corrode the self-image and generate a sense of isolation which increases the effect of the other factors.

However, being abused is far from being a predictive factor in becoming abusive. Other issues, therefore, also appear to be significant. Back in 1988 Becker proposed a model that is still seen as very relevant today, a model which includes a broad range of factors which may contribute to the development of sexually abusive behaviour: at an *individual* level, social isolation; impulse conduct disorder; limited cognitive abilities; and a history of physical and/or sexual abuse; *familial* factors: carers who engage in coercive sexual behaviour; family belief systems supportive of such behaviour; and carers who have poor interpersonal skills and lack empathy; and *societal* factors: society which is supportive of coercive (male) sexual behaviour; society which supports the sexualisation of children; and peer groups who behave in anti-social ways. Thus chapters later in this book will discuss assessment approaches which aim to identify and analyse these various interacting factors that contribute to the development of youthful sexually harmful or abusive behaviours.

Principles and goals of work with children and young people who have sexually harmful or abusive behaviour

Part of the UK-wide study conducted by Hackett *et al.* (2003) involved a study of experienced practitioners in the field who were asked about the principles and goals of work which influenced their approach to work with children and young people displaying sexually harmful or abusive behaviour. It became apparent that, as compared with a decade earlier (National Children's Home 1992), there was now an emerging consensus on these matters. Thus the study found high levels of respondent agreement with the following statements:

- Children and young people who display sexually harmful or abusive behaviours are, first and foremost, children and should not be regarded as mini adult sex offenders (p. 14).
- There are multiple pathways to sexually abusive behaviour. It is not simply to be explained by a young person's victimisation experiences (although there must be sensitivity to the possibility and impact of such early experiences) (p. 14).
- The aim of work is to help young people understand and accept responsibility for their behaviour and develop strategies and coping skills to avoid abusing or offending again (p. 15).
- (In addition to victim and community safety) the goal of work is also to promote the physical, sexual, social and emotional well-being of children and young people who have sexually harmed or abused others (p. 15).

Thus these practitioners were approving a model of work which addresses all of a young person's age-appropriate developmental needs, as well as addressing their problematic or offending behaviour. Complementing work with the young person, these practitioners also saw engaging and working with families or other carers as crucial to successful intervention. Thus, there was also strong agreement with the statement:

- The goal is for carers to acknowledge what their child has done, believe in and support change and to take on responsibility for changing the context of the family (p. 15).

In similar vein, there was a clear recognition that the young person's wider environment including, for example, peer relationships, achievements or otherwise at school and societal influences on attitudes to gender and sexuality needed to be the subject of assessment in order to develop packages of care or intervention tailor-made to the individual needs of each child or young person.

Relevant knowledge, theoretical models and concepts

Given the emphasis placed on the need to work with children and young people in a holistic manner, it is not surprising that a range of knowledge and theory are drawn on by practitioners in the field. These include, for example, knowledge about normal child development; learning theory and cognitive behavioural approaches; attachment theory; family systems theory; trauma and post traumatic stress theories; solution-focused work; and motivational interviewing (Hackett *et al.* 2003). However, there are also two models for understanding the processes whereby sexually abusive behaviour occurs, which were developed in North America in the early 1980s and which remain influential today. These are the Four Preconditions Model developed by Finkelhor (1984) and the Sexual Abuse Cycle developed by Lane and Zamora (1982, 1984) and subsequently developed further by Sandy Lane (1991, 1997). This section reviews these models and outlines some of the key concepts that both assist in understanding sexually abusive behaviour and are often components of an intervention programme.

Finkelhor's four preconditions model

A researcher and academic, Finkelhor was seeking a comprehensive theory that addressed the range of knowledge about sexual abusers without being specific to a particular school of thought. He proposed a model which related primarily to adult male abusers but which is frequently adapted in practice for use with younger people.

In summary the model suggests four *preconditions* which must be met before sexual abuse can occur. The potential abuser needs to:

1   Have some *motivation* to abuse – this may be because the victim meets some important emotional need and/or sexual contact with the victim is sexually gratifying and/or other sources of sexual gratification are not available or are less satisfying.
2   Overcome any *internal inhibitions* against acting on that motivation – commonly this is by way of 'cognitive distortions', self-serving distortions of attitude and belief, whereby the victim, either individually or as a 'category' becomes seen as in some way consenting to or responsible for their own abuse.
3   Overcome *external impediments* to committing sexual abuse – gaining the opportunity to have access to the potential victim in an environment where the abuse is possible. In the case of child victims this may relate to the supervision the child receives from others. Those interested in pursuing further the issue of non-abusing carers and their significance

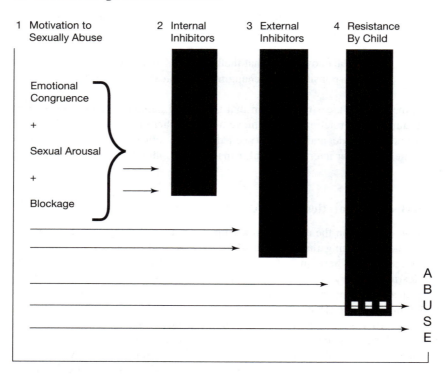

Figure 1.1 Finkelhor's four preconditions model of sexually abusive behaviour.

Source: Finkelhor 1984.

as deterrents to abuse are commended to Gerrilyn Smith's chapter 'Parent, Partner, Protector', which includes an adaptation of the Four Preconditions Model (Smith 1994) and to the current authors' own description of running groupwork programmes for mothers of sexually abused children (Masson and Erooga 1989).

4 Overcome or undermine a *victim's possible resistance* to the abuse – writing in relation to child victims Finkelhor emphasises this is not an issue to be regarded simplistically but may relate to a complex set of factors involving personality traits which inhibit the targeting of a particular child as well as more straightforward resistance to the abuse itself. These concepts are equally applicable to peer or adult victims.

What can be seen, therefore, is that there are a number of potential barriers to abuse, the first two relating to the abuser and the third and fourth relating to factors external to the abuser. The model offers a way of beginning to understand something of the dynamics of the abuser as well as the abuse process, also a feature of the next model to be discussed.

Compulsive behaviour cycles of sexual abuse

Prior to the development of models of compulsive sexual offending in the early 1980s a common view of such behaviour was that it resulted from uncontrollable urges. Practice experience with adolescents (Lane and Zamora 1982, 1984) led to the development of the concept of sexual abuse cycles involving dysfunctional responses to problematic situations or interactions. In these models responses are based on distorted perceptions relating to power and control which then become sexualised. This framework is now regarded as generally applicable irrespective of age or intellectual or developmental functioning and is reported to be in use, with appropriate adaptations to meet individual circumstances or need, in the majority of treatment programmes (Lane 1997).

This widespread use of the concept both for young people and, a separate but similar model independently developed for adults (Wolf 1984), clearly indicates the intuitive and practice-based appeal of this concept for exploring and understanding patterns of sexually abusive behaviour – a tool which is experienced as helpful both to those trying to understand and change their behaviour and those trying to help them to do so.

The sexual abuse cycle for adolescents (Lane 1997) represents cognitive and behavioural progressions prior to, during and after sexually abusive behaviour. When applied to an individual, the details of the components of the cycle will vary, but common elements of the overall pattern are still apparent, with common abusive behaviour patterns, types of gratification and styles of thinking which support the behaviour. However, in using the model it should be noted that it describes a process of events, not a causal representation. It is represented cyclically because of the repetitive compulsive nature of the behaviour sequence and because of indications that previous offence incidents often parallel and reinforce the subsequent offence pattern.

As shown diagrammatically in Figure 1.2, the young person's life experiences, outlook and beliefs predispose them to respond to an event, interaction or problem with feelings of helplessness (the event), experienced as stressful and now anticipated as unsafe (negative anticipation). Feelings of hopelessness are accompanied by a desire to avoid the issue, the feelings and the anticipated outcomes (avoidance). Not being successful in this leads to feelings of resentment and defensiveness and attempts to exert power over others in a non-sexual way as compensation (power/control). Whilst effective, the duration of the effect is temporary, leading to thinking about further power-based behaviours and other behaviours

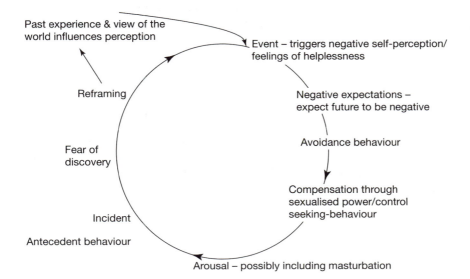

Figure 1.2 The sexual abuse cycle.
Source: Lane 1997.

which might feel good, such as sex (fantasy). The exertion of control or dominance is eventually expressed sexually (sexual abuse). There is then a need to cope with the knowledge of the behaviour and fear of external consequences of being caught (fugitive thinking). Inability to tolerate this anxiety or discomfort leads subsequently to the behaviour becoming assimilated through a series of cognitive distortions or 'thinking errors'. The cycle therefore represents a series of maladaptive coping mechanisms that temporarily alleviate discomfort but do not resolve the problem.

Progression through the cycle is not necessarily consistent, thus an individual will seldom progress through the whole cycle a step at a time, nor will each trigger of the cycle lead to a sexual offence. Lane describes interruptions or delays in the cycle as plateaux, suggesting that in response to repeated triggers the young person may progress to the same plateau several times, not moving on to the next until the current one is not effective in relieving anxiety or countering negative self-perception. She points out that whilst the stress may seem to dissipate temporarily, in fact it accumulates over time. The rate of progression will also vary, though it does appear that the more frequently the maladaptive response pattern is used, the faster the rate of progression becomes. Thus the more habituated to the use of the cycle the lower the individual's tolerance to precipitating events or problems and the further into the cycle the progression of the initial response. An assessment implication may therefore be that the speed of progression may be indicative of the length of time the maladaptive behaviour patterns have been used, though this is not synonymous with the length of time that abusive behaviour has been perpetrated.

Associated concepts

The treatment implications of the models will be apparent. By becoming aware of their pattern of thinking, and emotional and behavioural responses through use of these models, the young person can then consciously develop other methods of coping with stress or abusive stimuli and thus decrease the likelihood of further abusive behaviour.

In coming to understand the dynamics of sexually abusive behaviour, however, a number of other concepts need to be understood and often addressed as part of a programme of intervention.

Minimisation, denial and projection of blame

Inasmuch as the abusive behaviour itself is a dysfunctional response which serves to avoid emotional discomfort so minimisation and denial of the existence of a problem or, at the point of detection that the behaviour occurred at all, is a logical response. Denial is a dynamic, rather than a static state, thus the nature and level of denial is likely to change with the anticipated consequences, emotional and external, of being disclosive. Similarly, there is not a single phenomenon which can be labelled denial, rather there is a continuum of minimisation or denial on which the young person may place themselves at various times. Thus the response may range from outright denial of the abusive act(s) through denial of responsibility for the behaviour: 'I was drunk'; denial of intent: 'I just got carried away'; to minimisation of harm or seriousness: 'It wasn't anything bad I did'.

Cognitive distortions

Distorted cognitions, also described as thinking errors, refer to pro-offending beliefs or attitudes that justify, rationalise or support the sexually abusive behaviour. They commonly distort the role of their victim in the abuse, portraying them as in some way responsible for encouraging or initiating sexual contact.

> Some . . . support a . . . belief in the victim's willingness or need to engage in the sexually abusive behaviour, some shape the perception of the victim as obligated to meet the needs of the perpetrator, some construe the (abusing) behaviour as helpful and still others allow the youth to objectify or depersonalise the victim.
>
> (Lane 1997: 89)

They may also serve to reassure the abuser that they have done nothing wrong and certainly not something harmful. Typical examples would be:

- She must have wanted to – she never said no
- I liked it when it happened to me
- I did no more than what happened to me
- I wouldn't have forced him but he didn't try and stop me so it was OK
- I paid for her Coke so she owes me
- Women are all the same and I know what they want

Once again, whilst the patterns of distortion may be similar to many abusers the specific details will vary according to individual experience and personality, though clues to individual distortions may be heard in explanations offered by the abuser 'I knew he wanted to by the way he looked at me' or echoed by victims in their statements 'he said he was only doing it because he loved me'.

Deviant sexual arousal

The first of the Finkelhor preconditions *motivation to sexually abuse* may relate to deviant sexual arousal for some individuals. Whilst this is an important factor in consideration of adult sex offenders, this is less well established in adolescents. Hunter and Becker (1994) found less correlation between adolescent sexual offenders' measured sexual arousal and their offence histories than has been reported in the literature of adult offenders, and cautioned against interpreting adolescent sexual arousal patterns in the same way as one might interpret adult data. Nevertheless, it is likely that as research progresses, the presence of deviant arousal to children or to non-consenting sex may emerge as an important factor in work with adolescent abusers. For example, there seems to be some association between frequent deviant sexual fantasies in juveniles and the selection of young boys as their sexual abuse victims (Marshall *et al.* 1991; Murphy *et al.* 2001).

Victim empathy and victim awareness

For many offenders a lack of empathy with the experience of their victims will be an important element in becoming sufficiently disinhibited to abuse and there is therefore a significant relationship between lack of victim empathy and cognitive distortions, as it is the latter which contribute to the absence of understanding, cognitively and emotionally, of the impact of their abusive behaviour. The two main components of victim empathy training focus upon developing the service users' intellectual appreciation of the impact of sexual abuse and applying this to their own victim, and, second, developing their capacity for emotional sensitivity and responsiveness to victim distress (Beckett 1994a).

Whereas victim awareness is an intellectual process of understanding, victim empathy describes the emotional connection with the victim experience. It is important not to confuse the two, as whilst awareness may soon be learned, there may be considerable emotional investment on the offender's part to resist making the more difficult connection. These separate aspects may be most effectively addressed in different ways. Awareness may require a didactic approach whereas empathy may be best achieved through experiential techniques.

Relapse prevention

Whilst avoiding relapse is a goal of intervention from the outset, the young person's active participation in that process can increase as their understanding of their own process increases. When an offender understands his own cycle, he should then be able to share this knowledge with relevant others, by developing his own alert checklist (North West Treatment Associates 1988). To do so requires a high level of accountability for thinking and personal choices, recognising internal and external high risk factors (Ryan and Lane 1997). He needs to understand all aspects of his cycle and the implications for his feelings, thoughts and behaviour, as well as the relevant implications for his victim and his partner at the time. He should be helped to develop a relapse prevention plan with identified triggers, danger situations and strategies to cope with these prior to concluding any programme of intervention. Pithers and Gray (1996) have suggested that motivation to learn and use relapse prevention strategies increases once victim awareness and empathy work has been completed.

Service provision in the United Kingdom and the Republic of Ireland

A range of services, statutory, voluntary and private are currently working with children and young people with sexually harmful or abusive behaviours. Hackett *et al.* (2003) surveyed 186 services in all, comprising 111 youth offending teams and 58 other services in England and Wales, two services in Northern Ireland, 10 services from the Republic of Ireland and five from Scotland. Apart from the youth offending teams, whose composition and funding are statutorily determined, the other services in the various nations often described complex, multi-agency organisational arrangements and (sometimes uncertain) funding. They also varied in their size from a one-person service to services with 10 or more professionally qualified staff, often from a number of professional backgrounds.

In terms of policies and procedures most services in the various nations were aware of the relevant legislation and central government guidance available in their respective nations (which will be outlined in Chapter 2) about the principles which should inform practice with children and young people with sexually problematic behaviours, although these principles were not always followed. Thus, in all the nations surveyed, evidence emerged which showed that, in some local areas at least, there was considerable inconsistency as regards when formal meetings such as child protection conferences or multi-agency meetings or their equivalents might be convened to consider the needs and risks presented by a child or young person alleged to have sexually abused someone.

Between them, the 186 services offered a range of assessment and intervention packages although, in contrast to adult sex offender work, group-work programmes were offered by only a very small number of services. Just 32 services (17 per cent), in fact, offered a community-based group-work programme, while 26 services (14 per cent) also reported that they provided a residentially based intervention service. Various assessment frameworks were being drawn on, some of a general nature, such as the ASSET offence-focused model (Youth Justice Board 2000) and the *Framework for the Assessment of Children in Need and their Families* (Department of Health 2000). Other services were using the AIM model which has been specifically designed for the assessment of children and young people with sexually harmful or abusive behaviours, a model which will be the subject of further discussion in Chapter 3, as well as more specialist risk assessment scales such as J-Soap (Prentky *et al.* 2000) and ERASOR (Worling and Curwen 2001), both of them empirically based scales for use in the assessment of adolescent sexual abusers/offenders.

However, when asked to rate the availability and quality of local assessment services, 72 or 39 per cent of services rated their availability as 'inadequate' or worse and 33 or 18 per cent of services rated the quality of available assessment services as 'inadequate' or worse. When asked to rate the availability and quality of local intervention services, much larger proportions of services, 88 or 47 per cent, rated their availability as 'inadequate' or worse. However, smaller numbers of services, 41 or 22 per cent, were concerned about the quality of the intervention services which did exist. Across the five nations there was particularly widespread concern about the availability of good quality placement provision and secure accommodation – almost three-quarters of all services across the five nations rated their availability as 'inadequate' or 'entirely unsatisfactory'. Again, all these issues will be the subject of further discussion and analysis in later chapters, together with an analysis of training, supervision and consultation issues, which also exercised various of the services surveyed.

Conclusion

Whilst sexually aggressive behaviour is experienced by both those who commit it and those who encounter it as confusing and disturbing, during recent years there has been considerable progress in coming to understand the extent of such abusive behaviour, those more at risk of perpetrating it, the dynamics which lead to the behaviour and enable its progression; and ways of responding effectively. Regrettably, although there have been positive developments in terms of service provision since the early to mid-1990s (see by way of comparison the report by the National Children's Home 1992 and Masson 1997/8), there is still an urgent need for further progress. The chapters which follow address this by considering the enabling contexts required for effective responses, in terms of policy, legislation and service provision, as well as the specifics of assessment work; intervention approaches with individuals and groups, as well as work with families; additional considerations in work with young women and younger children who abuse; evaluation strategies and empowerment issues for workers.

The 1990s have seen progress in this area of work that few expected 10 years ago. It is our hope that, by use of the knowledge and expertise reflected in this second edition, sexual harm and abuse by children and young people can be identified, managed and addressed more effectively and the endless ripples of distress and suffering such behaviour causes can be diminished.

Notes

1   For a summary of *Childhood Lost* (The Bridge Child Care Development Service 2001) and discussion of issues raised by the case, see various articles in the *Journal of Sexual Aggression* (2003) Volume 9, Issue 2.

2 Policy, law and organisational contexts in the United Kingdom

Ongoing complexity and change

Helen Masson

Introduction

Work with children and young people who sexually abuse others or who display sexually harmful behaviours is conducted in a context of complex and often changing policies, legislation and organisational arrangements. This chapter is intended to convey something of this complicated and evolving scene. In order to understand the present, a brief discussion of relevant history is provided, together with signposts as to the direction of current developments. Although the main focus is on policy, law and organisational arrangements in England and Wales, reference is also made to differences pertaining in Northern Ireland and Scotland, the other two nations making up the United Kingdom (UK).

The chapter begins with some thoughts on how notions of childhood and competing attitudes to children influence developments in policy, law and systems of response. International conventions and associated legislation are then introduced which provide a backdrop to national legislation and semi-statutory guidance in the UK. The respective policy, legal and organisational arrangements in England and Wales, Northern Ireland and Scotland are then described and analysed, before a concluding section to the chapter summarises key messages for practitioners and managers in the field.

It is hoped the chapter will provide managers and practitioners with an outline map of macro-level features, which it is important to be aware of when responding to this service user group. In comparison with later chapters that focus explicitly on, for example, local responses, direct assessment and intervention work and staff care issues, the content may appear to be rather abstract and removed from immediate day-to-day concerns. However, the reader is encouraged to persevere, as what is discussed is central to the working environment and practices of all welfare agencies and professionals, providing both a mandate for and delineating the boundaries of their work.

Children who sexually abuse others: children in need *and* children in trouble

It has been argued elsewhere (Masson and Morrison 1999; Masson 2004), that young sexual abusers challenge many adults' conceptions of normal childhood sexual development as well as our tendency to hold on to simplistic and dichotomous notions of children, whereby children are categorised as either 'innocent victims' or 'depraved individuals or hooligans' but not both at the same time (Jenks 1996). Such 'splitting' is less apparent in the case of children under the age of criminal responsibility, who are usually deemed to be not responsible for what they have done or for what has been done to them, and hence 'just' in need of care and safeguarding. In the case of those who are considered to be criminally responsible, however, the impact of adults' ambivalent and often intolerant attitudes becomes apparent. This is exemplified in England and Wales where the separation of child welfare systems from youth crime systems, each with their respective and diverging philosophies of intervention, has become increasingly evident in recent years and the subject of ongoing critical analysis (see, for example, Hendrick 1997 and 2003; Tutt 1999; Smith 2003; Muncie 2004), although, as will be discussed later, there may be some modest indications, since 2003/4, of more 'joined-up' governmental thinking in this area.

Within the UK, the age of criminal responsibility is set at 10 years in England, Northern Ireland and Wales and at eight years in Scotland. Thus very young people in all these nations can become caught up in the criminal justice system. Interestingly, these ages of criminal responsibility are lower than in other western countries in the European Union (House of Lords and House of Commons Joint Committee on Human Rights 2003), where, it has been argued, more humane and enlightened approaches are taken towards children who transgress (see, for example, Franklin and Petley 1996; Smith 2003; Muncie 2004). Having a very low age of criminal responsibility, however, does not necessarily mean that children in trouble will inevitably be treated differentially from children who come to the notice of professionals for other more directly welfare-related reasons, as will be seen when Scotland's situation is discussed later in the chapter. Nevertheless, in general, the age at which children are perceived to be criminally responsible has a significant impact on how they are dealt with if they behave in ways which are constructed as criminal. In particular, they risk being subject to responses that have been generated to deal with adults convicted of similar offences and which may, therefore, have negative, unintended consequences, including the infringement of their human rights (House of Lords and House of Commons Joint Committee on Human Rights 2003).

Certainly the 'dual status' of children and young people who have sexually abused, especially those over the age of criminal responsibility, who are usually in need of care *and* control, appears to have presented dilemmas for those formulating policy and other responses, resulting in ongoing contradictions and tensions in policy and guidance, legal provisions and organisational arrangements, which front-line professionals and their agencies have had to manage since the 'emergence' of the issue in the early 1990s. This is not to say that front line practitioners and managers in public organisations do not have some room for manoeuvre or discretion in interpreting policy and law, processes that have been analysed by various commentators over time (from Lipsky 1980 to Evans and Harris 2004). Indeed, the history of the development of services for children and young people who have sexually abused others or who display sexually harmful behaviours is the history of certain committed individuals and agencies at the local level working to create coherent, child-centred and effective systems of response to children and young people who have sexually abused others, despite continuing changes in philosophy, a lack of clear direction at government department levels and limited resources. Nevertheless, these factors have resulted in chronically patchy and inconsistent service provision across the UK (Masson 1997/8; Hackett *et al.* 2003).

International conventions and associated legislation

All four nations within the UK are subject to the provisions of *The UN Convention on the Rights of the Child*, which was approved by the UN Assembly in November 1989 and to which the UK became a signatory in January 1992. In this context 'child means every human being below the age of 18 years, unless under the law applicable to the child, majority is attained earlier' (Article 1 of the Convention). Space precludes a detailed discussion of the

Convention (the full text can be accessed at http://www.unicef.org/crc/fulltext.htm) but its articles cover a range of children's rights, requiring signatory states to take all appropriate measures to ensure that those rights are upheld and that 'in all actions concerning children, whether undertaken by public or private social welfare institutions, courts of law, administrative authorities or legislative bodies, the best interests of the child shall be a primary consideration' (Article 3).

In relation to issues of sexual abuse of and by children, Articles 19 and 37 are particularly pertinent. Article 19 requires states to take all necessary steps to prevent and protect children from child abuse and neglect, including sexual abuse, and Article 37 covers the rights of children in relation to criminal justice systems. In particular, it is stated that imprisonment of children should be used only as a last resort and that where this occurs, children must, unless there are exceptional circumstances, be detained separately from adult offenders, must have access to their families and must have prompt access to legal and other assistance.

The Convention's provisions, contained in these and other articles, set baseline standards against which all policy, legislation and services for children and young people who have sexually abused others or who are exhibiting sexually harmful behaviours should be measured. The UK Government, as a signatory to the Convention, has to provide the UN Committee on the Rights of the Child with a report every five years on how far it is meeting its obligations to the Convention, the most recent being its 1999 report (UK Periodic Report 1999), subsequently updated (UK Update Report, undated). The UN Committee then publishes its own report, commenting on each state's analysis of its record. Significantly, the UN Committee's 2002 report on the UK's 1999 report (United Nations Committee on the Rights of the Child 2002), whilst praising various of the UK Government's intentions and initiatives in respect of, for example, education, child poverty and child welfare generally, was also highly critical of the UK's record in other respects. Thus, in relation to the treatment of children in the youth justice system and in the secure estate and the prison service, in particular, the Committee expressed serious concern about:

- the UK's low ages of criminal responsibility which, it recommended, should be raised 'considerably';
- the removal of *doli incapax* (the rebuttal presumption that children aged 10–13 years are incapable of criminal intent) as part of the implementation of the Crime and Disorder Act 1998 (Section 34) in England and Wales;
- the high and increasing numbers of children in custody, at earlier ages for lesser offences, and for longer custodial sentences imposed as a result of new court powers to make detention and training orders;
- inadequate rehabilitative opportunities in young offender institutions, with high rates of re-offending for young people emerging from custodial sentences;
- rates of suicide and self-harm amongst juveniles in detention;
- levels of physical assault and physical restraint used against children in detention;
- the inadequacy of educational provision for children in detention, particularly for those with special educational needs (who, it is estimated comprise up to 50 per cent of all young people in custody), coupled with no statutory right to education;
- the routine use of adult prisons as 'overflow' accommodation for juveniles, both male and female.

In the case of children and young people who are dealt with by the criminal justice system because of allegations of sexual abuse, the above observations are of considerable relevance.

Indeed, findings from the UK survey conducted by Hackett *et al.* (2003) provide evidence that practitioners and managers share many of the above concerns, particularly those pertaining to the secure estate, although the findings also provide evidence of localised provision and services for such children and young people, which work effectively, meeting young people's needs, their best interests and their rights.

Unless the issues highlighted by the UN Committee and echoed elsewhere (House of Lords and House of Commons Joint Committee on Human Rights 2002; NACRO 2003a and b; Howard League for Penal Reform 2004; BASW 2005) are addressed, it is possible that, at some point in the future, action may be brought by a child or young person (or by someone on her or his behalf) under the Human Rights Act 1998, which has been in force since 2 October 2000 and which brings the rights of the European Convention on Human Rights, another piece of international provision, into domestic law. The Human Rights Act 1998 (HRA 1998) has implications for many aspects of child and family law, education and youth justice provision and the child's right to protection from abuse. In the adjudication of cases under the HRA 1998, courts are able to refer to principles set out in the UN Convention on the Rights of the Child, where the European Convention itself is less specific in its provisions. Government and local service providers would do well, therefore, to adhere to these international standards in their care and control of children and young people who have sexually abused others or who are exhibiting sexually harmful behaviours.

Relevant legislation and semi-statutory guidance in the UK

England and Wales

For the most part, the position on services for children and young people in Wales is broadly the same as in England, and the provisions in these two nations are therefore discussed together here. However, it must be acknowledged that, following implementation of the Government of Wales Act 1998, Wales has its own National Assembly, operating within the framework of primary legislation enacted by the UK parliament but with substantial scope for the enactment of secondary legislation distinctive to Wales. It is also worth noting that, ahead of England, a Minister for Children in Wales was appointed in 1997, followed, in 2001, by the appointment of a Children's Commissioner in Wales with wide ranging powers to promote the wishes, views and rights of children.

Notwithstanding these differences, in both England and Wales practitioners and managers in front line services for children and young people who sexually abuse others or who are exhibiting sexually harmful behaviours have to attend to legislation, policy and guidance relating to three areas: child welfare and protection; youth justice and sexual offending. Only a relatively brief discussion of each of these areas is possible here, focusing on aspects pertinent to the service user group under discussion.

Child welfare and protection

In relation to child welfare and protection a central piece of legislation is the Children Act 1989, which came into force in November 1991. Two principles are enshrined in the Act – firstly, that in making decisions about children, the welfare of the child is the paramount consideration and that, wherever possible, interventions should focus on prevention and voluntary work with parents and others, in order to support children and families in the community. Compulsory measures, in the form of court orders, should only be pursued if the child's best interests require such intervention.

The Act covers many aspects of public and private childcare law but Sections 17 and 47 and schedule 2 of the Act are particularly relevant in respect of allegations of sexual abuse or harm by children or young people. Section 17 places a wide duty on local authorities to safeguard and promote the welfare of children within their area who are in need; and so far as is consistent with that duty, to promote the upbringing of such children by their families, by providing a range and level of services appropriate to those children's needs. In paragraph 7 of Schedule 2 of the Act it is also stated that local authorities are required to take reasonable steps designed to reduce the need to bring care or criminal proceedings in respect of children within its area, to take reasonable steps to encourage children within its area not to commit criminal offences and to avoid the need for children within their area to be placed in secure accommodation.

In relation to issues of child abuse and child protection, Section 47 states that where a local authority are informed that a child who lives, or is found in their area, is the subject of an emergency order; or is in police protection; or where the local authority have reasonable cause to suspect that a child who lives, or is found, in their area is suffering, or is likely to suffer, significant harm, then the authority have to arrange for such enquiries as they consider necessary to enable them to decide whether they should take any action to safeguard or promote the child's welfare. Emergency measures within the Act, available in cases where child abuse or neglect is suspected, include Child Assessment Orders and Emergency Protection Orders. Where longer-term legal measures are needed the local authority can apply to the courts for a range of supervision and care orders.

As will be evident, it would be perfectly possible to deal with all potential or actual instances of sexual abuse by children and young people within the provisions of the Children Act 1989, either to prevent such abuse or to respond to it when it is alleged. Indeed, an early version of semi-statutory guidance on how agencies should co-operate to promote the welfare of and safeguard children, *Working Together under the Children Act 1989* (Department of Health 1991b), recommended precisely this course of action. However, what this guidance failed to address was the fact that children over the age of criminal responsibility were also subject to the provisions of the youth justice system. A subsequent version of *Working Together* (Department of Health 1999) does address this fact to some extent, as will be discussed once youth justice provisions have been outlined.

However, to conclude on the Children Act 1989, a few years after its implementation, increasing concerns were being expressed about local authorities neglecting their duties in respect of children in need and family support, most of their resources being tied up in investigations of allegations of abuse. Following the publication of *Messages from Research* (Department of Health 1995) and the subsequent refocusing debate in the late 1990s, the third edition of *Working Together* (Department of Health 1999) and its associated *Framework for the Assessment of Children in Need and their Families* (Department of Health 2000) have sought to introduce a re-balancing within child welfare work. Instead of devoting too many resources to 'heavy-end' investigations of allegations of abuse under section 47, most of which result in no further action and which leave families, who may be in need under section 17, traumatised and still without services, agencies are now required to focus their efforts on supporting children in need and their families through the provision of flexible and non-stigmatising services. This is all laudable but it can be argued that, in this re-balancing act, notions of risk and harm have rather dropped off the agenda, particularly as evidenced in the *Framework for the Assessment of Children in Need and their Families* (Department of

Health 2000), notions which do have relevance to the assessment of children and young people with sexually harmful or abusive behaviours.

Youth justice

Quite separately from developments in the child welfare and protection system, there has also been a sea change in responses to youth crime, which are having their own impacts on the development of services for children and young people who have sexually abused. At the beginning of the 1990s, the approach to youth crime was generally diversionary in emphasis, promoting decriminalisation, diversion from court process and community sentences. However, the Audit Commission's 1998 Report *Misspent Youth '98: The Challenge for Youth Justice* and the publication of the government White Paper *No More Excuses* (Home Office 1997) led directly to the passing of the Crime and Disorder Act 1998, a piece of legislation that has heralded a much tougher, retributive and punishment oriented approach to youth offending. Fawcett *et al.* (2004) have identified the main aim of youth justice measures within the Act as being the prevention of offending, thus attempting to remove the perceived conflict between promoting the welfare of the child or young person and taking firm action to deal with his or her offending behaviour. Measures include the faster processing of offenders, greater use of secure accommodation and tagging for persistent offenders, reprimands and final warnings in place of cautions, a series of new orders (reparation orders; anti-social behaviour orders; curfew orders; child safety orders; parenting orders) and action plans. A further piece of youth justice legislation, the Youth Justice and Criminal Evidence Act 1999, also introduced a sentence of referral to a youth offender panel, for all young offenders between the ages of 10 and 17 who plead guilty and are convicted for the first time by the courts. Building on ideas of restorative justice, the panels, which include lay members, expect offenders to make reparation to their victims or the wider community, and are attempting to develop more constructive and flexible ways of working with the young people referred to them.

As part of the provisions of the Crime and Disorder Act 1998, multi-agency youth offending teams (YOTs) have been set up in local areas, teams which, amongst their various duties, have been given the lead responsibility for juvenile sex offenders. An offence-specific focus is inevitably central to the work of these teams, in marked contrast to the more holistic, needs-led approach now in place within child welfare and protection services generally (Department of Health 1999; Department of Health 2000). Section 41 of the Crime and Disorder Act 1998 also led to the establishment of a national Youth Justice Board (YJB). This body has the remit to advise the Home Secretary on the operation of the youth justice system; establish national standards; maintain a rolling programme of inspections; approve local youth justice annual plans; initiate training; identify and disseminate good practice; and act as the commissioning and purchasing agent for the juvenile secure estate.

One of the YJB's first tasks was to develop and disseminate a series of general and offence-specific *ASSET* documents, including core assessment profiles, risk of serious harm and self-assessment documents (Youth Justice Board 2000). It is expected that all YOT staff, at the point of initial assessment of a young person and at re-assessment, should complete these forms. The importance of the assessment process was subsequently emphasised in the publication of the YJB's *Key Elements of Effective Practice – Young People who Sexually Abuse* (Youth Justice Board 2004b). In addition, the *Key Elements* publication has useful messages about the need for varying intensity in intervention approaches, based on an assessment of the risk posed to others and to the young person himself and about the kinds of intervention that may be appropriate, including focusing on offending behaviour and criminal thinking and factors; risk reduction and relapse prevention; family issues; victim issues, including proximity; the young person's own history of abuse (where this has happened); mental health, educational and accommodation needs and social skills and relationship deficits. The YJB has also funded six development projects specifically working with young people who have sexually abused, including the AIM project in Greater Manchester, whose work is described in Chapter 3 of this book.

Not withstanding the more fundamental criticisms of the general direction of youth justice policy and its current outcomes, which have already been discussed, at the local level there would appear to be aspects of the present arrangements that can be used effectively to address the needs of children and young people who have committed sexual offences. It is encouraging, for example, that the YJB has produced the *Key Elements* guidance and an associated Reader (Youth Justice Board 2004c), which emphasise the importance of working with the young person's problematic behaviour, as well as their wider needs, in keeping with current thinking about this work. Some of the orders within the provisions of recent legislation, such as reparation, parenting and referral orders, can also be usefully employed to 'encourage' the co-operation of young people and their families in the work that is required.

However, it is clear that at least some YOTs have a way to go before the ideal of best practice indicated above will be achieved. Thus, for example, a joint inspection exercise of YOTs (HM Inspectorate of Probation 2004), whilst noting considerable progress in a number of areas, such as organisational development and engagement with children and young people and their parents or carers, also reported on, for example, a lack of appropriately qualified and experienced staff in some teams, wide variation in the importance placed on preventative work, too many instances of 'mediocre' ASSET completion, poor identification of risk of harm, a lack of attention to religious and ethnic differences within the service user population and variable amounts of work with victims. Also commented on were safeguarding issues and links with social services, an aspect of child welfare/youth justice co-ordination, which is now considered.

Co-ordinating child welfare and youth justice systems

As will have become evident, in the cases of children and young people over the age of 10 alleged to have sexually abused someone, those agencies most closely associated with the child welfare and protection system, such as social services departments, have been having to make links and collaborate with relatively newly established organisations, YOTs, in a context where changed priorities in relation to youth crime have still to be fully implemented at the local level. Paragraphs 6.31–6.37, about abuse by other children and young people, in *Working Together* (Department of Health 1999) acknowledge the need for agencies across child welfare and criminal justice systems to collaborate in the development of appropriate systems of response. In summary, this guidance states that child welfare agencies and YOTs must together address the task of putting an operational framework in place so that cases of children and young people who have sexually abused can be assessed and managed effectively. Thus, child welfare and criminal justice agencies must consult each other in advance of making any decisions about any criminal process proposed, about whether the young person should be the subject of a child protection conference, and about the plan of action required to address the young person's welfare and abusive behaviour. In addition, the issue of child protection registration is clarified, child protection conferencing and registration only being considered in the case of young abusers who are also victims of abuse, this being an issue about which there had been uncertainty (Masson 1997/8).

Evidence from Hackett *et al.* (2003) suggests that the extent to which this guidance has been implemented at the local level is very variable. Over half of the services surveyed expressed concern that the continuing divide between child welfare services and systems for dealing with youth crime worked against the development and maintenance of effective ways of dealing with children and young people who have both 'care' and 'control' needs. There was still a significant minority of geographical areas where detailed guidance about how agencies and professionals should work together at a local level to manage cases of sexual abuse involving children and young people had not yet been developed. Moreover, even where local areas had developed such guidance, it was found by the researchers to be variable in volume, content and quality, with a small number of such documents making statements that were positively misleading about, for example, the likelihood of recidivism in this group of young people, statements probably derived from the equally misleading paragraph 6.32 in *Working Together* (Department of Health 1999). Respondents to the survey were, themselves, often expressing disquiet about the usefulness of their local guidance and clearly wanted a steer on how to improve its effectiveness.

There was also considerable evidence that the management of individual cases varied a great deal within and across local areas, for reasons unconnected with the particular features of the case, but often related to whether the agency to which initial referral was made was in the child welfare/protection or youth justice system. For example, respondents to the survey reported often being very unclear about when a child protection case conference as opposed to another form of multi-agency meeting was held in a particular case – 'a random event' one respondent commented. From the perspective of children and young people and their families and carers, this general inconsistency of response is, at best, perplexing and, at worst, unjust. One young person may end up with a sexual offences conviction (with all the implications this entails, which will be discussed below), whereas another, in similar circumstances, might be responded to entirely within the child welfare/protection system. Where a specialist service existed in a local area, which took a lead or co-ordinating role in the management of cases, this appeared to make a positive impact on practice, but many areas did not have the benefit of such a service.

In their report on joint inspections of YOTs, HM Inspectorate of Probation (2004) expressed surprise at the apparent lack of communication and joint working between YOTs and social services department. The report comments:

> Many of the children and young people seen by YOT staff were in need of protection and safeguarding . . . Whilst we saw some good examples of working together, liaison with social services occurred in only 61% of cases.
>
> (p. 26)

Given that children and young people with sexually harmful or abusive behaviours often have a variety of developmental, relationship and familial problems, then in many cases they require care and protection, as well as interventions designed to change their behaviours, which would seem to indicate the need for such joint working.[1]

Sexual offending and Multi-Agency Public Protection Arrangements (MAPPAs)

As if work to establish services for children and young people who have sexually abused was not complicated enough, given the changes in the last decade in child welfare/protection and youth justice described above, practitioners and managers also have to bear in mind developments in policy and legislation in respect of sexual offending generally. Following professional concerns, media hype and public outrage about adult sex offenders in general, and paedophiles in particular, the Sex Offender Act was passed in 1997, followed by the implementation of the Sexual Offences Act 2003, the purpose of which was to strengthen and modernise the law on sexual offences. The provisions of these pieces of legislation impact on all sex offenders, including young people over 10 years of age who are convicted of a sexual offence. These include the requirement that convicted sex offenders, who are given Schedule 1 status, must register their whereabouts with the police. Anecdotal evidence suggests that in the drafting of the Sex Offender Act 1997 scant consideration was given to younger convicted sex offenders and that, only at a late stage, were changes made to reduce, for example, required registration periods for such young offenders. Nevertheless, there are on-going concerns about the appropriateness of the provisions of the Sex Offender Act 1997 being applied to young sex offenders, concerns which were not addressed in the drawing up of the later Sexual Offences Act 2003. For example, in the survey conducted by Hackett *et al.* (2003), 78 per cent (n=87) of respondents from the 111 YOTs and 71 per cent (n=53) of the other services surveyed expressed disquiet about the position of young sexual abusers vis à vis this adult-focused legislation and the National Organisation for the Treatment of Abusers (NOTA) has also commented:

> There is considerable concern that a number of adolescents are unnecessarily and inappropriately subjected to requirements such as sex offender registration, custodial sentencing and involvement in intensive long-term therapeutic programmes with the result that they become increasingly isolated, defensive and stigmatised.
> (NOTA National Committee on Adolescents Who Sexually Harm 2003)[2]

In addition, the Criminal Justice and Court Services Act (2000), subsequently refined by the Criminal Justice Act 2003, has required that local multi-agency public protection arrangements (MAPPAs) are established, where local agencies together draw up plans to ensure close monitoring of registered sex offenders and other categories of offenders in their area. This is another forum, to which Area Child Protection Committees, YOTs and other local services must contribute and to which young convicted sex offenders are subject (Home Office 2003a).

More change and more to come

Policy, legislative and organisational developments in child welfare and protection, youth justice and sexual offending have all demanded significant responses from agencies and organisations in England and Wales who are charged with responsibility for work with children and young people who have sexually abused others or who are exhibiting sexually harmful behaviours. Aside from the findings of the survey by Hackett *et al.* (2003), other recent publications have served to highlight continuing problems with the quality of current systems of response to children and young people who have sexually abused, and have made recommendations as regards the future development of services. These include *Childhood Lost* (The Bridge Child Care Development Service 2001), a Serious Case Review of the case of DM, an 18-year-old with a history of sexual offending who had just left residential care when he attacked and murdered an 11-year-old boy in 1998 and *I think I might need some more help with this problem* (Lovell 2002), an NSPCC report and recommendations on responding to children and young people who have sexually abused.

In addition, however, other significant developments and organisational changes have also been taking place since 1999/2000 that have further implications for services for children and young people who have sexually abused. Various government initiatives have, for example, been introduced since New Labour came to power in 1997, as part of its *Quality Protects* and children as investment/social inclusion agendas (Fawcett *et al.* 2004), including Sure Start schemes for the early years age group, and the Connexions Services for 13–19-year-olds. Primary Care Trusts in health areas have been set up and new legislation has been passed, such as the Children Leaving Care Act 2000 and the Care Standards Act 2000. More recently, as part of the 2002 government Spending Review, piloting of Children's Trusts has been funded. All these initiatives increase the potential number of agencies and organisational arrangements which must be included in the network aimed at safeguarding and promoting the welfare of children and young people, including those sexually abused or sexually abusing, and the complexity of the work involved. In many local areas, indeed, one gets the impression of practitioners and managers feeling quite overwhelmed by the implications of these major organisational changes and by the mass of new policy documentation and legal requirements which descend upon them from central government departments.

Most recently, partly in response to the publication of Lord Laming's highly critical inquiry report into the state of systems for the safeguarding of children in need and at risk of harm, following the death of Victoria Climbié (Laming 2003), the government responded, in 2003, with its Green Paper *Every Child Matters* (DfES 2003). This paper proposed taking forward a broad range of strategies to improve services for vulnerable children and young people, some of which have been outlined above. At much the same time responsibility for children's services was transferred from the Department of Health to the Department for Education and Skills (DfES) and a first Minister for Children appointed. Subsequently, in March 2004, the government published its response to the Green Paper consultation entitled *Every Child Matters: Next Steps* (DfES 2004a) and a new Children Bill (now the Children Act 2004). The principal provisions of the Act are designed to encourage improved partnership and clearer accountability by placing a new duty on agencies and other local providers to co-operate to improve the well-being of children and young people so that all work to common outcomes; tightening the focus on child protection through a duty on key agencies to safeguard children and promote their welfare through new Local Safeguarding Children Boards (replacing Area Child Protection Committees); introducing a new national database ISA (Information Assessment Sharing) containing basic information about children; ensuring clearer accountability through the appointment of local Directors of Children's Services and lead Council Members for Children's Services; encouraging the further development of Children's Trusts, bringing together health, education and social care agencies; creating an integrated inspections service; taking on new powers to intervene in failing children's services and appointing a Children's commissioner for England (albeit with fewer powers than those enjoyed by equivalent post holders in other nations in the UK). In July 2005 a draft fourth edition of *Working Together to Safeguard Children* and a draft *Local Safeguarding Children Board Regulations* were published for public consultation until the end of October 2005 (available at http://www.dfes.gov.uk/consultations).

All these developments are requiring local areas to re-position themselves in line with government expectations, possibly putting at risk the relatively fragile arrangements already in existence, particularly in relation to children and young people who have sexually abused others or exhibiting sexually harmful behaviours. Some (see, for example, BASW 2004; Home Office 2004a) have expressed regret that the opportunity to introduce more integrated policies and services for children and young people in need and in trouble was missed when *Every Child Matters* (DfES 2003) was published separately from the 'companion' report *Youth Justice, the Next Steps* (Home Office 2003b), although *Every Child Matters: Change for Children in the Criminal Justice System* (Home Office 2004b) does attempt to demonstrate how the Children Act 2004 forms a basis of a long-term programme of change to which agencies within the criminal justice system will be making a positive contribution. Similarly the *Youth Green Paper, Youth Matters* (published in July 2005 for public consultation until the end of October 2005 and available at http://www.dfes.gov.uk/publications/youth/) envisages a much more integrated approach to the needs of all youth, including those with serious problems.

Even though similar messages about prevention and early intervention are evident in all these documents it is clear, however, that current government thinking about tackling youth crime will continue along the same largely retributive and punishment oriented lines as before and that youth justice services will remain under the direction of the Home Office. Indeed in July 2004, a five-year plan was unveiled in parliament which includes strengthened provisions to curb unruly young offenders (Travis 2004) through, for example, increased use of tagging, fixed penalties, antisocial behaviour orders and custody. It is clear that, for the foreseeable future, those in England and Wales working with children and young people who have sexually abused others will have to continue to negotiate systems for their management which are driven by very different policy, legislative and organisational imperatives.

Northern Ireland

As in England and Wales, child welfare and protection and youth justice functions in Northern Ireland are separately organised, leading to similar sorts of problems as those already discussed. Much of the underlying policy towards children in need, at risk or in trouble is also very similar, although Northern Ireland's services are organised somewhat differently. Social services responsibilities and activities are part of larger Health and Social Services (HSS) Boards and Trusts and HHS Boards have the lead responsibility for the establishment and effective functioning of Area Child Protection Committees. Since 2003 the Youth Justice Agency, an executive agency within the Northern Ireland Office, has been established, charged with delivering community services for young people involved in crime or at risk of becoming involved in crime; youth conferencing within a restorative justice approach under the Justice (Northern Ireland) Act 2002, and custodial services, via a secure Juvenile Justice Centre.

The Children (NI) Order 1995 reformed and consolidated for Northern Ireland most of the public and private law relating to children, along the lines of the Children Act 1989 in England and Wales and paragraphs 6.26–6.38 on working together in cases of sexual abuse by children in *Co-operating to Safeguard Children* (Department of Health, Social Services and Public Safety 2003) contain very similar messages to those in the equivalent document in England and Wales (Department of Health 1999). However, *Co-operating to Safeguard Children* is an improvement on the guidance in England, Wales and Scotland in that paragraphs 6.26–6.38 are written specifically to address instances of sexual abuse, as opposed to other forms of abuse, such as bullying, which may well require a different response. In contrast, the guidance documents in the other UK nations do not make such distinctions clear, with potentially confusing consequences (Hackett *et al.* 2003).

Scotland

In Scotland which, since the implementation of the Scotland Act 1998 has had its own Parliament, there appears to have been, until relatively recently, a more integrated system of response to children in trouble and children in need of care or protection than in England and Wales. The Scottish system is supported by the Scottish Office, which co-ordinates children's issues across various policy areas, and legislation in the form of the Children (Scotland) Act 1995 and the Local Government in Scotland Act 2003.

A central feature of the Scottish legal system has been that children over the age of criminal responsibility who commit offences have been regarded as being in need of care in the same way as children who are the victims of abuse or in need for other welfare-related reasons. Thus, apart from those prosecuted for the most serious offences, such as rape or murder, all young offenders under the age of 16 have been processed via Scotland's unique Children's Hearing system, rather than through the criminal justice system. Even serious young offenders who are prosecuted in court may have their cases remitted to the Children's Hearing for disposal or the court may seek advice from the Children's Hearing.

The Children's Hearing system came into being in 1971, following the implementation of the Social Work (Scotland) Act 1968 and in response to the recommendations of the Kilbrandon Committee (Kilbrandon Report, 1964). Cases are referred to the Reporter who then has a duty to investigate and decide whether no further action is required, or whether the child should be referred to the local social work department for informal support or whether to arrange for a Children's Hearing, a lay tribunal composed of three members, because it is felt the child is in need of compulsory measures of supervision. The grounds on which a child may be brought before a Children's Hearing are set down in the Children (Scotland) Act 1995. In respect of young sex offenders, paragraphs 6.6–6.9 of the Scottish Office's inter-agency child protection guidance *Protecting Children: A Shared Responsibility* (Scottish Office 1998) outline the process for investigating, assessing and managing cases of abuse by a young person, a process which is very similar to that followed in England and Wales, although set in the context of Scotland's Children's Hearing system.

The Children's Hearing System looks set to stay, notwithstanding it is currently under review 'to ensure that it has the right set-up and adequate resources to ensure that it does the best possible job to protect children' (Scottish Executive 2004). However, in recent years, youth justice has also been an emerging concept in Scotland. In 1999 a review of youth crime was initiated, in response to concerns about persistent young offenders, which resulted in an Advisory Group Report *It's a Criminal Waste. Stop Crime Now* (Advisory Group on Youth Crime 2000) and a response by the Scottish Executive (Scottish Office 2000), which largely accepted the Advisory Group's various recommendations for increasing the extent and effectiveness of options currently available to Children's Hearings and the courts. Amongst various measures introduced or proposed in recent years, such as youth courts, anti-social behaviour orders and electronic tagging, local authorities have set up multi-agency youth justice teams, working with various groups of young people, varying in age from 8–16 years (Scottish Executive 2005). It seems that these and other changes to the current system are leading to the further development of separate systems for dealing with some young offenders, with the result that young people who have sexually abused others may find themselves in a similar position to those in the rest of the UK.

Conclusion

This chapter has sought to demonstrate the complex nature of day-to-day work with children and young people who have sexually abused others or who exhibit sexually harmful behaviours and to highlight various policy, legislative and organisational changes occurring since the early 1990s in the various nations of the UK, changes that have impacted and continue to impact on this field. The strengths in and possibilities offered by current arrangements in the UK have been highlighted, as well as problematic areas and more general issues of consistency in provision.

In England and Wales one of the relevant systems of response, the youth justice system, has been the subject of particular critical comment, not only domestically but also in the international arena, for its lack of attention to children's rights. *The UN Convention on the Rights of the Child* is, therefore, an important starting point for these nations (and indeed the other nations in the UK) when developing appropriate policies, procedures and services for vulnerable young people. Consulting with children and young people themselves, and their carers, about what they want and how they want to be dealt with is also important. Simon Hackett's chapter on empowering practice, later in this book, provides findings from one of the first surveys of user and carer perspectives.

When developing policy and inter-agency procedures, local areas across the UK must also attend to their respective national legislation and semi-statutory guidance, key aspects of which have been outlined in this chapter. Findings from the survey by Hackett *et al.* (2003) demonstrate that different areas are at varying stages of development in these respects. This is problematic, but it does mean that relatively undeveloped areas can draw on the experience and 'practice wisdom' of more established areas. In this respect, the next chapter, written by Tony Morrison and Julie Henniker, will be of particular interest, as it outlines how various authorities in the North West of England have worked together to develop consistent and effective management, assessment and intervention services for young sexual abusers.

However, complexity and change now seem to be facts of life in the development of appropriate services for this service user group, as in the rest of children and families' work. Thus, in England and Wales, even the most up-to-date local area arrangements will have to be reviewed and modified in the light of the implications of the Children Act 2004 and the expected revised guidance for inter-agency working – the 4th edition of *Working Together*. Similarly, service providers in Northern Ireland and Scotland will have to be ready to address the implications of the on-going developments within their own national boundaries.

Notes

1   Significantly, in this context, it took a court judgement by Munby, J. (R *v* Secretary of State for the Home Department, ex parte Howard League for Penal Reform [2002] EWHC 2497) to remind local authorities that they continue to have obligations to children held in custody. This has led, in England and Wales, to the Youth Justice Board agreeing to fund LA staff in young offenders' institutions (YOI) to undertake Children Act 1989 duties to safeguard and promote the welfare of children in the secure estate and make sure there are links between YOI and local authorities.

2   In the draft 4th edition of *Working Together,* which is referred to later in this chapter, there are some hopeful signs that the government may be heeding some of these messages. In Section 11 it is stated that the blanket term 'Schedule One Offender' is being dropped in favour of phrases which make clear those individuals out of the total offender population who present a 'risk or potential risk of harm to children'. It is also stated that 'practitioners should also consider that where a juvenile offender (aged under 18 years) offends against a child it is possible that there is little or no future risk of harm to other children, and the stigma of being identified as presenting a continued risk of harm to children is potentially damaging to the development of the juvenile offender' (paragraph 11.7).

3 Building a comprehensive inter-agency assessment and intervention system for young people who sexually harm

The AIM project

Tony Morrison and Julie Henniker

Introduction

This chapter describes the origins, development and evaluation over the past five years of the AIM (Assessment Intervention Moving on) project, based in Greater Manchester. The AIM project represents one of the largest whole system developments in the UK, covering social services departments, youth offending teams, the NSPCC, child and adolescent mental health teams, education services and the police across 10 local authority areas in a conurbation of some four million people. The chapter is written on behalf of, and in recognition of, the commitment of all those agencies and practitioners who have made the project work and who continue to shape its development.

Origins

The issue of children and young people who sexually harm first emerged in the early 1990s (National Children's Home 1992) and, from the outset, it was recognised that multi-agency responses were required (Department of Health 1991b). However, research findings in the mid 1990s (see, for example, Masson 1997/8) showed that the development of such responses was uncertain and geographically patchy. In 1998, Her Majesty's Inspectorate of Probation, in their report *Exercising Constant Vigilance . . . Thematic Inspection of the Work of the Probation Service with Sex Offenders* commented:

> The largest and most worrying gap in provision was for adolescent sex offenders, responsibility for whom did not lie solely or principally with the probation service . . . There appeared to be no coherent national strategic approach and in many areas no provision specifically designed to tackle their sexual offending.
>
> (HM Inspectorate of Probation 1998: 50)

Consequently, in 1998, in the absence of a national strategy, a multi-agency group of experienced managers in Greater Manchester, committed to developing this area of practice, established a steering group. As a first step, they commissioned the Greater Manchester Youth Justice Trust to undertake an audit of current working practices, assets and gaps in the management of young people who sexually harm across the key agencies and 10 Greater Manchester local authority areas. Despite the fact that the North West of England had been a site for a considerable amount of work in relation to the management of sex offending during the previous decade, the outcomes of this study painted a gloomy picture. Its main conclusions were that:

- Training for those working with young people who sexually abuse was insufficient;
- It was frequently left to 'interested' workers to undertake work with this service user group on their own initiative;
- There was a lack of access to relevant services;
- There was a lack of structure and co-ordination between the agencies;
- There was insufficient monitoring and no long-term follow up of outcomes;
- No specific equal opportunities or anti-discrimination policies for these young people existed across Greater Manchester.

In the light of these findings the steering group submitted an application for development funding to the newly established Youth Justice Board for England and Wales whose remit was to establish national standards and disseminate effective practice. As a result Greater Manchester was awarded pathway status in recognition of its commitment to innovative and effective multi-agency approaches to tackling youth crime. The award brought in additional monies which were used, with matched funding locally, to establish the AIM project for three years. This arrangement was replaced in 2002 with funding provided by the 10 Greater Manchester youth offending teams, 10 social services departments and the NSPCC, supplemented by additional income generated by the project through consultancy and training to other local authority areas across the UK. In addition, AIM became a registered charity.

The AIM project: purpose and key elements

The AIM project was formally established in January 2000 and the current co-ordinator, Julie Henniker, appointed. This appointment recognised that, for too long, managers and practitioners had been struggling, 'on top of' their day job, to develop services for children and young people who sexually harm. The co-ordinator is responsible for developing policies, procedures, inter-agency protocols and information sharing systems; co-ordinating a training programme; providing additional support mechanisms; trouble shooting when difficulties emerge; keeping the issues on agencies' agendas and feeding back progress to key stakeholders. As authorities outside Greater Manchester have sought to develop a local AIM service, they have also recognised that the role of the co-ordinator is critical and, that without a dedicated resource, it is difficult, if not impossible, to establish an effective inter-agency project such as AIM.

The overall purpose of the AIM project is to develop a consistent and effective inter-agency assessment and treatment response to children and young people who sexually harm. The key elements of the AIM programme comprise:

- inter-agency policies and procedures;
- local and regional interagency networking and service partnerships;
- a common and multi-disciplinary model for initial assessment;
- specific versions of the assessment framework for children under 10 years, young people with learning disabilities and for parents and carers;
- guidelines for schools;
- training for both practitioners and managers;
- awareness raising of issues around sexually harmful behaviour and dissemination of best practice;

- creation of AIM consultants in each local authority;
- local practice 'surgeries' to which workers can bring cases for discussion;
- practice frameworks and toolkits for comprehensive assessment and treatment work;
- external evaluation of both the process and outcomes of the AIM assessment tools.

From the outset the project established a clear vision and strategic partnership objectives that connected with individual agencies' legislative requirements and core business. It was important that agencies realised they were not being asked to take on something beyond the scope of their core business, but rather to address more effectively a child protection issue that complemented and enhanced their existing roles and duties. The AIM project provides an inter-agency framework designed to reduce the isolation and anxiety which are commonly felt in making decisions about this group of children and young people (National Children's Home 1992; Morrison 1999; Bankes 2002), and which can result in either over- or under-estimation of risk.

Alongside this, the AIM practice frameworks have sought to locate an understanding of the sexual problems of these young people and children within a developmental and holistic framework which draws on a wide and well-established knowledge base about troubled and troubling young people. A consistent key message is that young people who sexually harm have much more in common with other troubled young people than anxious practitioners and managers may assume. For instance, many of the pathways that lead to sexually problematic behaviour in young people involve developmental and family factors that have long been recognised as contributing to other forms of adolescent violence and delinquency. This message has helped to demystify the AIM project and reduce barriers of fear and anxiety for practitioners engaging in this work. Both the assessment tools and the training emphasise the degree to which practitioners' existing knowledge and skills can be effectively transferred to this specific area of work. Practice protocols stress that good practice in this area is rooted in knowledge of child development, child protection, attachment and cognitive behavioural principles.

The AIM project framework of response

The AIM project is not a service provider to which agencies can refer children and young people for assessment or treatment. Focusing responses around a specialist resource would not only fail to address the level of demand, but also result in unhelpful delays to service provision. The advantage of promoting the involvement of front line agencies and workers directly in the work with this service user group is earlier recognition, assessment and intervention, thus increasing the chances of prompt engagement with the child or young person and their family. This, in turn, is likely to result in a more holistic assessment, reduced denial and the increased possibility of achieving successful outcomes.

In order to build confidence and consistent responses in practitioners and their managers, the project developed and implemented a set of policies and procedures that have been endorsed by the 10 local authorities in Greater Manchester and included in their local child protection procedures. There are 10 steps involved in the initial assessment process:

1   The lead agency identifies the assessors, a consultant, a date for the completion of the initial assessment report and organises the subsequent multi-disciplinary meeting to discuss the report.

The assessors then:

2 Watch the video interview or read the victim statement(s);
3 Listen to the PACE interview or any account given by the young person regarding their sexually harmful behaviour;
4 Read existing agency files and collate information from professionals involved with the child, young person and their family;
5 Use the AIM assessment model (see below) to identify at this stage what is known/ unknown with reference to the four domains of assessment;
6 Plan the interview with the young person/parents/carers, aiming to fill in missing information and engage the interviewees in a process that prepares them for a helping service to be received;
7 Interview the young person;
8 Interview parents/carers;
9 Use the assessment framework to draw conclusions around concerns, strengths, needs, capacity to change and the degree of support parents/carers can provide;
10 Take the completed initial assessment report to a multi-disciplinary meeting hosted by the Child Protection Unit, where roles, tasks and resources are identified and agreed. and a review date, if appropriate.

(Henniker 2001)

The procedures seek to ensure that regardless of which agency or local authority identifies a child or young person with sexually harmful behaviour, the case will receive a standard multi-agency response. Protocols with the police for young people coming through the criminal justice system provide for an extended bail period of up to 28 working days to allow for an initial AIM assessment to be completed which will include a recommendation to the police regarding disposal. Figure 3.1 on p. 35 presents the AIM case management flow chart.

AIM initial assessment tools

In this section the core elements of the initial assessment models are presented. The early decision to prioritise the development of a common initial assessment model for adolescents reflected a number of concerns identified by agencies in local research. Henniker and Foster (2000) had identified that there had not been any form of assessment in over a quarter of the cases of young people charged with a sexual offence in Greater Manchester, and, in addition, almost half of all youth offending team workers believed the process and outcomes for these young people had been inadequate. In other words, prior to the AIM assessment frameworks, local practitioners held limited or no confidence in their existing assessment tools.

The AIM model was developed based on an adaptation of work by Gail Ryan (1999a) and sought to develop a continuum of responses ranging from early community based intervention with low concern cases to intensive work with the most high concern groups, often in out-of-home settings. The model is depicted in Figure 3.2 on p. 36 as a pyramid, with levels of responses linked to the mix of strengths, concerns, and complexity in each young person's situation.

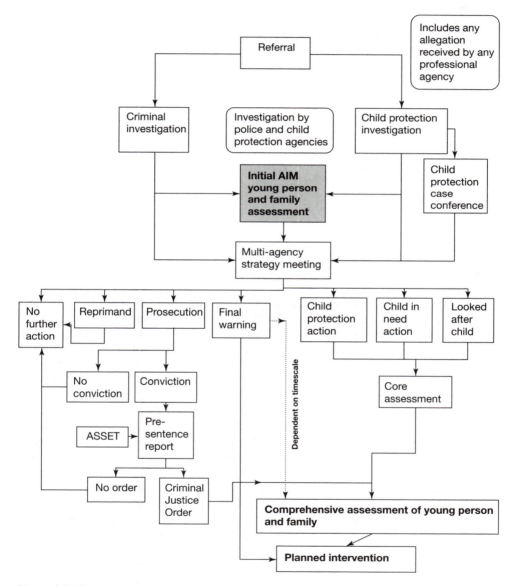

Figure 3.1 The AIM model process of intervention.

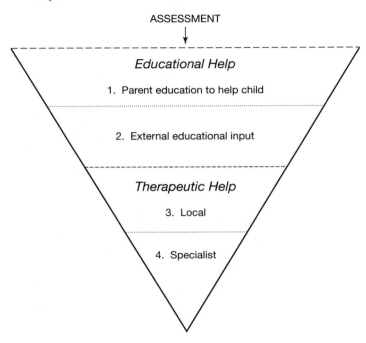

ASSESSMENT

Educational Help

1. Parent education to help child

2. External educational input

Therapeutic Help

3. Local

4. Specialist

Figure 3.2 Thresholds for services.

Source: Morrison, May 2001, adapted from Ryan 1999.

Level 1: Early presentation of non-aggressive sexually inappropriate behaviour in the context of concerned parents and a family with reasonable strengths. The intervention here is of an educational and supportive nature, in which practitioners help parents manage the emotional crisis and provide them with an information and counselling pack to work through with the child, focusing on issues of consent, empathy and boundaries. Such material is discussed in *Facing the Future: A Guide for Parents of Young People Who Have Sexually Abused* (Hackett 2001). One or two follow-up visits, by practitioners, would take place to check progress.

Level 2: Referral to a psycho-educational group for parents where there have been more concerning sexual behaviour problems and where there is a need to bolster parents' skills and commitment. There may also be a need for referral for brief, educational work with the young person on issues such as sex education, consent and the consequences of abusive behaviour. Other forms of intervention aimed at meeting needs that are non-offence/abuse specific might also be identified.

Level 3: Referral to a community-based treatment programme, involving the young person and his/her parents. A mixture of specialist and generalist staff might run such a programme.

Level 4: Referral to a specialist community/residential programme for the most complex and high-concern group where there are multiple problems and serious abusive behaviours.

As the model demonstrates, however, the entry point into any of the responses is effective assessment. The consequences of the absence of an effective and shared assessment model have been well documented (National Children's Home 1992; Henniker and Foster 2000; The Bridge Child Care Development Service 2001) and include inaccurate assessment of risk; failure to provide appropriate services; low-risk cases being referred for intensive and lengthy intervention programmes; neglect of wider family and social factors influencing offending behaviour; failure to engage parents; and inter-disciplinary conflicts and miscommunication. An effective initial assessment model ensures that cases enter the appropriate part of the system. This prevents the unnecessary clogging up of specialist resources with less complex cases, thereby freeing them up to deal with the more complex and high-concern cases.

It was decided *not* to pursue the search for an actuarial instrument designed purely to predict levels of future risk. As Sipe *et al.* (1998: 122) have observed: 'We cannot accurately predict future sexual offending behaviour of juveniles who participated in the non-violent sexual abuse of children.'

Prentky *et al.* (2000) have also concluded that it might be very difficult to design such a tool, given the complexity of factors influencing adolescent behaviours. These include developmental changes occurring during adolescence and the low base rates of sexual offending committed by adolescents, giving rise to small sample sizes from which actuarial predictions are difficult to make.

The decision not to pursue an actuarial instrument also reflects a growing professional consensus (Hackett *et al.* 2003) that the sexual behaviour problems of adolescents need to be understood within a developmental and ecological framework, in which their sexual difficulties are located within a wider context of family and community factors. Implicit in this approach is recognition that adolescents with sexual behaviour problems are not 'mini' adult sex offenders, and that they differ in a range of ways from their adult counterparts. Thus, in contrast to adult offenders, adolescents have lower rates of sexual recidivism (Alexander 1999); are unlikely to have established a fixed pattern of sexual thoughts and behaviours (Prentky *et al.* 2000); are subjected to greater influence and management by others, including parents and teachers, than most adults; and may have been or continue to be subject to some form of trauma or abuse themselves (Kobayashi *et al.* 1995; Spaccarelli *et al.* 1997). Acknowledging such differences is even more important when considering the assessment of children under 10 who display sexually inappropriate behaviours. Thus the AIM framework provides a developmental model that is holistic in approach and focuses not only on risks and concerns, but equally on needs, strengths and resiliencies.

The AIM assessment tools make deliberate use of the terms 'strengths' and 'concerns' rather than risks. Language is a powerful force that can shape professionals' responses. Thus the language of 'risk' which has, until recently, been the dominant discourse in this area of work, triggers responses which search for experts, certainties, diagnostic labels, categorisation, control and a focus on individual deficit behaviour. Once entrapped in the language of 'risk', responses can become one-dimensional, linear, failing to locate the young person's sexual problems in a wider family and systemic context. When 'risk' is the dominant language, practitioners find it hard to conclude anything other than the young person is a 'risk' and almost never that he/she is only low risk.

In contrast, the use of the terms 'strengths' and 'concerns' enables a more differentiated and multi-layered understanding to develop of the young person's behaviour *in context*. This encourages workers to accept that not all uncertainties can be eliminated and that risks need to be shared between agencies within a framework that emphasises understanding rather than categorisation, and developmental repair rather than risk management. Central to this is the engagement and involvement of family/carers. The AIM approach means paying equal attention to both concerns and strengths (Gilgun 1999).

The search for an appropriate assessment tool took into account the relative strengths and weaknesses of existing national assessment frameworks for young offenders, *ASSET* (Youth Justice Board 2000) and the *Framework for the Assessment of Children in Need and their Families* (Department of Health 2000). Whilst the ASSET framework was seen as helpful in assessing criminogenic factors, it was thought to be weak in assessing the family and developmental factors related to the development and maintenance of sexual offending. In contrast, the *Framework for the Assessment of Children in Need and their Families* (Department of Health 2000) whilst being seen as strong on needs assessment, was perceived as weak on identifying offence specific elements. The two frameworks also work to different timescales. Whilst 35 days are allowed for a core assessment under the DOH framework, the emphasis on speed and efficiency in processing young offenders within the criminal justice process was seen as limiting the degree to which young people and, just as importantly, their parents/carers could be engaged.

The AIM initial assessment, therefore, provides a structured, research-based, multi-disciplinary framework to guide the collation and analysis of relevant information, leading to co-ordinated management and therapeutic plans for young people which address their risky behaviours through a needs-led and strengths-based approach. Four initial AIM assessment frameworks have been developed:

- AIM Initial assessment of young people who sexually abuse others (Print *et al.* 2001);
- AIM Initial assessment of young people with learning difficulties who sexually abuse others (O'Callaghan 2002);
- AIM Initial assessment of children under 10 years with problematic sexual behaviour (Wilkinson and Carson 2003);
- AIM Initial assessment of the parents/carers of young people who sexually abuse others (Morrison and Wilkinson 2003).

Initial assessment framework for young people who sexually abuse others

From the outset the development of the AIM frameworks has included a high level of practitioner consultation. The shape of the initial assessment framework, which is described below, was influenced by practitioner feedback obtained during the early training pro-grammes. Interestingly, one of the external consultants, Professor Jane Gilgun, from the Twin Cities University in Minnesota, USA, commented in her review that this added considerably to the psychometric strengths of the final assessment tool (Gilgun 2003).

In order to build on practitioners' knowledge of existing assessment tools, ASSET (Youth Justice Board 2000) and the *Framework for the Assessment of Children in Need and their Families* (Department of Health 2000), it was decided to develop the core model around the three domains cited in the DOH framework but with an additional 'Offence Specific' domain. The resultant four domains provide a framework for information gathering as follows:

1.   **Offence Specific**
- Nature of index sexual offence/abuse;
- Young person's and family's attitude to victim;
- Amount and nature of offence planning;
- Use of threats, violence or aggression during commission of offence/abuse;
- Young person's offending and abusive behaviour history;

- Previous professional involvement with young person and family regarding offending/abusive behaviours;
- Motivation to engage with professionals.

2. Developmental
- Resilience factors;
- Health issues;
- Experiences of physical/sexual/emotional abuse or neglect;
- Witnessed domestic violence;
- Quality of the young person's early life experiences;
- History of behaviour problems;
- Sexual development and interests.

3. Family/Carers
- Level of functioning;
- Attitudes and beliefs;
- Sexual boundaries;
- Parental competence.

4. Environment
- Young person's access to vulnerable others;
- Opportunity for further offending;
- Community attitudes to young person and family;
- Wider supervisory and support network.

The concern and strength continuums

In line with the developmental basis of the model, two continuums are used as a way of analysing the information gathered above: a concern continuum and a strength continuum, each of which ranges from high, medium to low markers. These are presented in the appendix to this chapter.

For each marker, research and clinical indicators are listed, against which the assessor can identify relevant information from the case with regards to the young person, his abusive behaviour, his family and environment. The starred items in each continuum are those for which there is empirical support. Using the continuums comprises the first stage in analysing the information gathered in relation to degrees of concern and positive factors, as a basis for initial decision-making.

The second stage of analysis involves use of the Outcome Matrix (see Figure 3.3 below) to come to an overall judgement, based on the information collated along the two axes of strengths and concerns, and identify what further help or intervention may be required. The outcome matrix enables workers across agencies to come to a shared view of the case. By itself, however, this is not sufficient for development of a case plan.

The third and final stage of analysis is to identify from all the information gathered the five most important strengths, the five most important concerns and the five most important 'unknowns', using a single sheet *Analysis and Action Plan* framework. It is this final processing of the information that leads to the case plan.

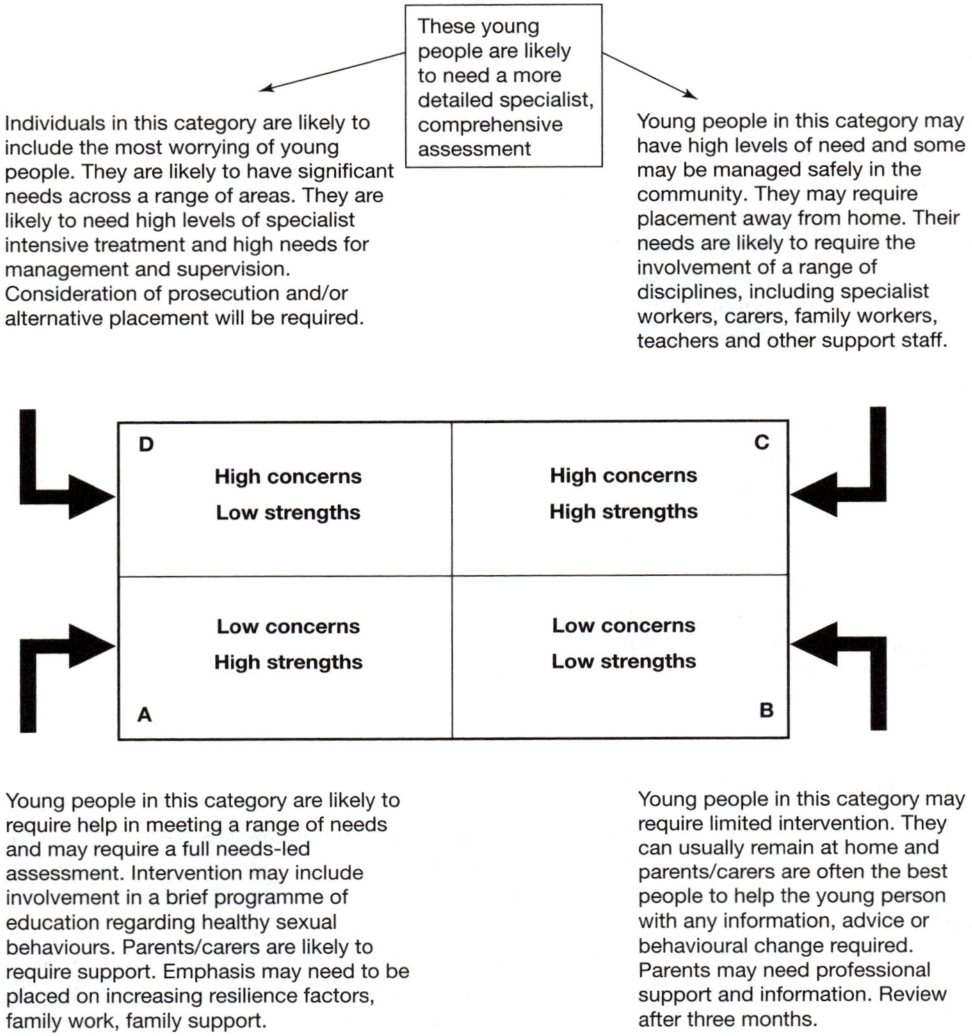

These young people are likely to need a more detailed specialist, comprehensive assessment

Individuals in this category are likely to include the most worrying of young people. They are likely to have significant needs across a range of areas. They are likely to need high levels of specialist intensive treatment and high needs for management and supervision. Consideration of prosecution and/or alternative placement will be required.

Young people in this category may have high levels of need and some may be managed safely in the community. They may require placement away from home. Their needs are likely to require the involvement of a range of disciplines, including specialist workers, carers, family workers, teachers and other support staff.

D High concerns Low strengths	High concerns High strengths C
Low concerns High strengths A	Low concerns Low strengths B

Young people in this category are likely to require help in meeting a range of needs and may require a full needs-led assessment. Intervention may include involvement in a brief programme of education regarding healthy sexual behaviours. Parents/carers are likely to require support. Emphasis may need to be placed on increasing resilience factors, family work, family support.

Young people in this category may require limited intervention. They can usually remain at home and parents/carers are often the best people to help the young person with any information, advice or behavioural change required. Parents may need professional support and information. Review after three months.

Figure 3.3 The AIM Outcome Matrix.

Four case examples around the Outcome Matrix

A. Low concerns, high strengths

Tom, aged 15, was left in charge of his step brother Ryan, aged 6, whilst their parents went shopping for an hour. Both boys were in Tom's bedroom. Tom was doing homework and Ryan was playing on the computer. Tom explained that he opened the zip of his pants and began to play with his penis. A short time later he felt 'tempted' and walked over to Ryan who remained focused on his computer game, until Tom moved closer and touched Ryan's bottom with his penis. At this point Ryan turn round and Tom realised what he was doing was wrong. Tom stopped, panicked and ran out of the bedroom. Later that day Tom's parents found him distressed and crying in the bathroom. Tom said 'I've hurt Ryan' and was able to tell them what he had done. His parents were shocked and went to see how Ryan was, and to check whether this had ever happened before. They were concerned to understand why Tom behaved like this, and to ensure that this did not happen again. They also reassured Ryan that it was not his fault.

B. Low concerns, low strengths

Sally aged 11 years was sexually abused by her mother's partner. Her mother did not believe Sally's disclosure and disowned her because she was causing 'trouble'. Sally went to live with her maternal aunt. Soon after she was found playing a 'mummy and daddy' game in which she got her 8-year-old cousin Peter to touch her genitalia on top of her clothes. Her aunt felt that she could no longer care for Sally and she was placed in residential care in a different local authority. Sally had to change school and lost touch with her friends and teachers. Thus although Sally's sexual behaviour was rated as low concern, she was also rated low strengths in terms of the care and attachment disruptions she was suffering.

C. High concerns, high strengths

Adam is 15 years old and attending mainstream school but has mild learning difficulties. He has lived in a foster placement for the last three years and during that time his behaviour and achievements have improved significantly. He plans to attend the local college when he leaves school.

Josh is the 3-year-old grandson of Adam's foster carers. He visits his grandparents regularly and appeared to have developed a very good relationship with Adam, often seeking him out to play games. After a recent visit to his grandparents Josh was unusually quiet and withdrawn and he went on to disclose to his parents that Adam had forced him on two occasions to 'suck his willie'.

Adam admitted his behaviour and said he wants help to stop. His foster carers whilst shocked and disappointed have stated that they wish Adam to continue to live with them.

D. High concerns, low strengths

Sam, aged 16 years, had presented with problematic behaviour since early childhood, for which he has received on-going monitoring and input from the Child and Adolescent Health Service. At the age of 7 he reported sexual abuse by a stranger and at 9 his name was placed on the 'child protection' register as a result of harsh punishment to the point of physical abuse from his mother, who consistently found him difficult to manage. From the age of 12 years he has attended a residential school for children with social and emotional behavioural difficulties.

Over the last 18 months Sam has committed a series of sexual offences which appear to have increased in frequency and severity over time. He is charged with indecent assault and common assault having attacked a 15-year-old girl in a local park. Despite clear evidence, Sam is unable to take responsibility for his actions. Sam's mother also struggles to accept that he has committed these offences but has clearly stated that he cannot return home as she has younger children.

Initial assessment frameworks for young people with a learning disability and for children under 10 years

These other initial assessment frameworks follow a similar format but have been adapted to look at particular features when undertaking an initial assessment on a young person with a learning disability (O'Callaghan 2002) or children under 10 years who are exhibiting sexual behaviour problems (Wilkinson and Carson 2003).

Initial parent/carer assessment framework

As part of the holistic approach, the engagement and assessment of parents or carers are seen as integral to the AIM framework, and their importance cannot be overstated. Failure to engage parents/carers has significant negative consequences at every point along the case management process. The development of the parent assessment framework was based on Smith's work on the assessment of the non-abusing carer's capacity to protect (Smith 1994: 184–5). This was adapted to consider 12 factors of particular importance at the initial assessment stage (see Table 3.1 below). For each factor a continuum of four possible responses is offered varying between the most positive to the most problematic. This *parent/carer + matrix* also allows the worker to rate each parent separately.

Table 3.1 AIM initial parent/carer assessment table

FACTOR	*Rating level: 4*	*Rating: 3*	*Rating: 2*	*Rating: 1*
Position on disclosure	Believed victim	Ambivalent	Minimises	Denial
Attitude to victim	Empathy	Confusion	Anger	Rejection
In cases of sibling abuse	Prioritises needs of the victim	Unable due to distress to prioritise victim's needs	Ambivalent	Unwilling to prioritise needs of victim
Feelings to own child as abuser	Accepts child but not sexual abusive behaviour	Conflicted and confused	Angry	Collusive
Role in disclosure	Brought concerns to light	No knowledge	Delayed the disclosure	Blocked/hid disclosure
Position on responsibility	Abuser responsible	Abuser and victim both responsible	External factors to blame	Victim blamed
Co-operation with agencies	Alerted agencies	Sought other help	Complies with agencies	Refuses
Wish for external help	Yes for both child and parents	Only for child not parents	Unsure	Denies need
Parents have established home safety rules	Yes or parents recognise the abuser cannot live at home	Unclear or only after agencies suggested	Unrealistic or punitive rules	Deny the need for home rules
Parents able to ensure rules followed	Yes parents show ability to set boundaries and monitor child	Unclear: needs to be seen over time	Unlikely due to parent's lack of consistency or authority	No
Concern with future risk	Is concerned	Lack details about offences	Only at intellectual level	Denies there is a risk
Capacity for change demonstrated in initial interview	Parents open to new information and responsive to any needs to change	Parents confused and over-whelmed by their feelings	Parents ambivalent re: concerns and their protective role	Parents rigid, resistant or chaotic

The findings from the initial parent assessment are then linked to the main Strengths and Concerns continuums. This might result in a change to the Outcome Matrix (Figure 3.3) if, for instance, the interview with parents highlights either considerable strengths or the opposite. The assessment protocol for the parents stresses the importance of practitioners providing parents/carers with an opportunity at the start of the assessment session to process some of the emotional distress that will have arisen from the 'discovery' of their child's sexually problematic behaviour. Interestingly, this period of free narrative often generates very significant information about the parents' attitudes to both the 'offender' and the 'victim'.

Using the AIM initial assessment framework

Several points need to be made about the context and use of the AIM initial assessment tools. First, the framework is *not* an investigative tool and is not designed to establish the guilt or otherwise of a young person. It is to be used only *after* it has been established by the professionals that a young person has sexually abused another person or is displaying sexually problematic behaviour. In some cases, especially with younger children, there may not be a victim but the child is displaying sexually problematic behaviour. For young people who are subject to criminal proceedings and a pre-sentence report is requested, the AIM assessment model will be used as the basis of that report. Second, the initial assessment process is designed to be used by co-workers from different agencies, typically bringing together youth justice and child protection workers, although other multi-disciplinary permutations can and have been used. An example might be where one worker is from a child and adolescent mental health agency whilst the other is from a child protection or youth justice background.

Third, the outcome of the AIM initial assessment is that a report is prepared for a multi-agency planning meeting attended by the young person and his parents or carers, as well as other professionals involved with the young person, including the police. Unless the offence is so serious that the police automatically proceed to a charge, the AIM report includes a recommendation to the police about what course of criminal justice action might be most appropriate. However, the planning meeting will also formulate a management and treatment plan and consider what other needs the young person may have, in addition to his sexual behaviour problems.

Finally, the initial assessment tools are designed to identify where young people or children are in terms of the continuum of concern demonstrated by the Outcome Matrix, presented as Figure 3.3 earlier in the chapter. Cases identified as 'high concern' are likely to require further in-depth assessment in order to:

- understand the young person's pathways and problematic behaviours;
- recognise elements of risk and the required levels of care and management;
- identify targets for change and levels of motivation to change;
- formulate intervention plans;
- provide a baseline against which progress can be measured.

For families, comprehensive assessment follows a four-strand model looking at:

- Family perceptions of the problem (covered by initial assessment);
- Family functioning, using Bentovim and Bingley-Miller's model (2001);

- Family history;
- Motivation and capacity to change.

To support practitioners with comprehensive assessment and therapeutic work, AIM has, therefore, produced three further resources within a comprehensive assessment and intervention guide (Morrison *et al.* 2005):

- Comprehensive assessment and treatment manual for young people who sexually abuse others (Print *et al.* 2005);
- Comprehensive assessment and treatment guide for the families of young people who sexually abuse others (Morrison and Wilkinson 2005);
- Comprehensive assessment and intervention guide for children under 10 years with problematic sexual behaviour and their families (Wilkinson 2005).

Alongside this, four multi-agency group treatment programmes are being developed across Greater Manchester.

Evaluation of the AIM project

Two levels of evaluation of the AIM project have been undertaken:

- Early evaluation of the initial training programme and practitioners' responses to the AIM initial assessment and procedures (Myers 2002);
- Evaluation of the AIM initial assessment model and its effectiveness

(Beech and Griffin 2003)

The early evaluation (Myers 2002) identified that the development of inter-agency procedures was seen as a foundation to the rest of the project:

> The project has demonstrated that it is possible to achieve agreement between disparate agencies on a major policy issue through local initiative.

(p. 19)

The content of the initial multi-agency training was welcomed by those who were new to the field, whilst more experienced practitioners reported that the training consolidated and enhanced their understanding of the issues. Follow-up interviews demonstrated that practitioners had incorporated the training into their practice and, importantly, that it had assisted their confidence by demystifying this area of work.

The evaluation of the AIM initial assessment model (Beech and Griffin 2003) concluded that the tool was largely functioning well in terms of highlighting concerns and strengths. A detailed analysis of the first 75 young people to be subject to an AIM initial assessment concluded that:

- 72 per cent of practitioners across Greater Manchester had followed all 10 steps of the process and an increased number of initial assessments had been undertaken each year;
- When the first 75 cases were followed in terms of outcomes, the AIM initial assessment tool correctly identified the six high-concern/low-strength cases. These were the six cases in which there were further concerns about the young people's sexual or violent behaviour;

- the psychometric properties of the AIM initial assessment tool were as good as other tools in use;
- the AIM initial assessment tool was providing a valuable framework for multi-disciplinary collaboration and planning;
- 81 per cent of recommendations following assessments were known to have been acted upon fully or to some extent;
- AIM training in the model(s) was rated as 'excellent' by 80 per cent of 350 participants.

Future developments

The project has recently negotiated a further three years' funding until March 2008. This will allow both continued maintenance of the existing AIM programme in Greater Manchester and alongside that, the development of new services.

In terms of expanding the work with young people who abuse, it is planned to develop:

- a revised AIM initial assessment model (in the light of the evaluation of Beech and Griffin 2003). It is planned to test the revised assessment model against a sample of both retrospective and current cases before it is disseminated;
- guidelines for residential establishments;
- protocols for the assessment of young females. This is as a result of exploratory research conducted across Greater Manchester by AIM, in partnership with the Lucy Faithfull Foundation, into the incidence, range and impacts of sexual abuse committed by young females (Ashfield *et al.* 2004b);
- intervention and treatment models for young people with learning difficulties;
- a customised initial assessment model for use in relation to Black and Asian young people. This follows the findings of a small-scale research project, undertaken by AIM in partnership with the NSPCC (Mir and Okotie 2002), which surveyed young people, their families and professionals about whether existing models of practice in work with young people who sexually harm were adequately meeting the needs of those from Black and Asian cultures. The research identified cultural factors that amplify the impact of sexually abusive behaviour when committed by young people from these communities.
- A *Setting up AIM Services* handbook and training programme for agencies outside Greater Manchester.

Finally, and perhaps most important of all, the next phase of the AIM programme will see a widened focus to look at the needs of victims. Although the project has always had a strong child protection focus, thus far no direct services have been provided for victims. However, we know that the number of victims is almost double the number of young people who have sexually harmed. In addition, in a recent study (Griffin 2003), out of the 72 young people who sexually harmed, one third were found to have witnessed domestic violence, 25 per cent had experienced physical and emotional abuse, 20 per cent had experienced neglect and 12 per cent had been the victim of sexual abuse.

This planned development will be rooted in current work undertaken by partner agencies and will build on current service provision to enhance further the existing skills of practitioners in these agencies. It will develop an assessment tool to gauge the appropriateness of a restorative approach using family group meetings within both child welfare and criminal justice arenas. This proposal would envisage an integrated model of assessment and intervention in respect of victim, abuser and their families, with initial concentration on cases of sibling abuse and intra-familial abuse, given that Griffin (2003) found that 79 per cent of the sample of 72 adolescents knew their victim. It will focus on families and extended families who wish to find ways of continuing to have contact.

This proposal will require the development of new policies and procedures, to establish a framework of response that integrates work with victims, offenders and their families. These will include assessment tools, therapeutic intervention tools/manuals; training programmes; consultation and advice services and evaluation.

So what does it take to improve practice? Lessons from the AIM project

It is the case that many organisational changes fail badly with unintended and damaging consequences.

(Hamlin *et al.* 2000: 17)

The AIM project has been instrumental in changing practice and inter-disciplinary collaboration for a client population with whom practitioners have traditionally felt isolated, anxious, unprepared and unsupported. Moreover these changes have occurred in a conurbation of four million people across the Greater Manchester area, comprising 10 local authorities, 10 youth justice services, a regional police force and a major voluntary agency, the NSPCC, in addition to co-operation from health and education authorities. Given the unrelenting pressures and pace of external change that all the constituent services have been under over the past six years, what has been achieved through the AIM project is all the more surprising. It suggests that despite this pressurised context, a level of shared commitment, professional consensus and practical leadership were achieved that overcame the potential barriers and pitfalls that might have derailed our efforts. In this final section we reflect on some of the key lessons, or traveller tips, learnt about what it took to change practice using the AIM project approach.

Travellers' tips

1. The journey is as important as the destination
Careful attention to the manner in which we worked with each other and managed a large and highly diverse group was crucial. The quality of working relationships between the steering group members and the positive and inclusive style of the co-ordinator were key factors in engaging staff and agencies alike.

2. Establish a core and highly committed driver group
Although members of the AIM steering group were not chief officers, they were experienced and committed operational managers who each had strong and credible links to strategic managers in their agencies. This ensured that the steering group was close enough to practice to know what would work, and to understand the necessary ingredients for a high-quality service, as well as what practitioners needed. At the same time, the group had good access to senior managers, which allowed decisions to be made and resources to be identified without undue dislocation to the process.

3. Appoint a change-agent: role of co-ordinator
It was essential to have a co-ordinator with a dedicated role to act as a focal point for the innovation process and to take on the role of change agent. The dedication of the core group needed translating into actions, which were beyond the scope of the full-time jobs of the steering group members.

4. Engage with front line staff

We sought to approach staff on the basis that they were crucial and that they would tell us whether policies, protocols and services were useful, appropriate and workable. Attention to local fora for practitioners to bring cases and the development and support of the local AIM consultants were also crucial.

5. Integrate new policies and practices within existing bodies of values, knowledge and good practice

A key message from the outset was that there was much more in common between young people who sexually abuse and other troubled/troubling young people than there was difference. This helped to demystify the work and reduce barriers of fear and anxiety about engaging in the work. Practice protocols stressed that good practice was rooted in knowledge of child development, attachment and cognitive behavioural principles. The strong holistic philosophy underpinning the AIM approach, for example, the use of the terms 'strengths and concerns' as core constructs, was also powerful in gaining practitioner support and enthusiasm. It seemed that for some practitioners this represented a rekindling of lost or submerged professional ideals.

6. Develop a common model of assessment

The importance of developing a common model of assessment across agencies cannot be too strongly emphasised. In the DM case (The Bridge Child Care Development Service 2001) the different models of assessment being used by the three agencies responsible for DM's care resulted in conflicting opinions about his level of risk. The AIM assessment model was the glue that enabled agencies to work together.

> Qualitative practitioner feedback generally proved the assessment model to be very valuable in both guiding practitioners and boosting their confidence. Practitioners felt the AIM model was user-friendly, practical and flexible – all factors that are essential to allow practitioner buy in.
>
> (Beech and Griffin 2003: 91)

The fact that AIM built on existing assessment frameworks, whilst extending and customising them to this client group, enabled practitioners to gain early confidence with the model.

7. Recognise the importance of a multi-disciplinary training programme

The literature on collaboration has consistently emphasised the role that multi-disciplinary training plays in winning hearts and minds, developing a common model and common language, and creating a mutual understanding of each other's roles. The combination of good training and the promotion of an acceptable common assessment tool to address an area of considerable anxiety to practitioners were powerful and enabling processes. The training programme also included teachers, foster carers and residential staff who, whilst not having responsibility for carrying out the assessment process directly, are crucial to identifying the problem, contributing to assessment and planning and to the care and supervision of the young person.

8. Engage and equip front line supervisors

Alongside the above, engaging with and equipping line managers to support and supervise staff within the AIM framework were equally crucial. Front-line managers are the cornerstone of the service delivery process. Policy and service innovation cannot happen without their 'buy-in'. They were provided with two-day training courses that combined learning how to use the AIM model themselves with training on supervision. A key element of this training was understanding the role of anxiety and learning how to use the Kolb reflective cycle (1988). As with practitioners, the key message was that good supervision practice is no different in this field, but that it needs to be combined with a working knowledge of the practice model their staff were using.

9. Use specialist resources strategically

Specialist resources should be used more to catalyse than to colonise. The Greater Manchester area had been a site of a number of smaller-scale practice innovations including NSPCC and G-MAP programmes. However, although some complex cases have been referred to these services for direct work, their main role, in collaboration with the AIM project, has been to act as a resource to the statutory agencies, providing much of the training, consultancy and writing the practice guides.

10. Plan evaluation from the outset

Last, but not least, evaluation was planned from the outset, which was, in part, a condition of funding. The initial feedback from the training evaluation reassured us that practitioners were enthused by the model. The external feedback, during the development of the assessment protocols, reassured us about the validity of the approach. The evaluation of the assessment model in action demonstrated that it successfully identified the small group of six high-risk young people who either re-offended, or who were the subject of on-going professional concerns.

Conclusion

This chapter has presented the origins, elements and evaluation of the AIM project in Greater Manchester, which has established an inter-agency framework for the assessment and management of young people who sexually harm others. The project has delivered and tested four initial assessment protocols and three guides to therapeutic intervention. The foundation has been the use of a holistic approach based on a strengths and concerns paradigm, and locating an understanding of sexually problematic behaviour within an ecological view of young people's development and socio-cultural context. Particular attention has been focused on the early engagement of parents and carers as supervisory and therapeutic allies. External evaluation of the AIM assessment tools has validated their accuracy both in identifying the 'high-risk' cases, as well as providing for a consistent inter-agency approach to the management of these young people.

However, the AIM programme has also been the story of large-scale practice innovation across an extensive inter-professional community. We end therefore with the voices of two practitioners discussing the AIM framework. One worker remarked that the AIM framework gave social workers the confidence and the tools to exercise professional judgement in anxiety provoking cases. The other recalled her first AIM assessment. It was a case with several factors that made her feel that this was a 'high-risk' situation. The AIM assessment emerged as confirming a case situation which included both high concerns and high strengths. When asked whether she felt comfortable with this outcome, the worker commented that analysing the information using the concerns and strengths matrix both reduced her anxiety, and increased her confidence as a worker. It had enabled her to move out of feelings, into thinking, analysis, professional judgement and action.

Appendix 3.1
Continuum of indicators of concerns

High concerns A
1. *Young person has previous convictions for sexual offences or evidence of previous sexual offending
2. *Formal diagnosis of Conduct Disorder or a history of interpersonal aggression
3. *Very poor social skills/ deficits in intimacy skills
4. *Use of violence or threats of violence during assault
5. *Self-reported sexual interest in children
6. *Young person blames victim
7. Persistently threatens to commit abusive acts
8. Has persistent aggressive/sadistic sexual thoughts about others
9. Has history of cruelty towards animals
10. Little concern about being caught
11. *High levels of trauma e.g. physical, emotional, sexual abuse, neglect or witnessing domestic violence
12. *High levels of family dysfunction/abusive or harsh child-rearing regime
13. *Evidence of detailed planning
14. *Early drop-out from treatment programme
15. *Highly compulsive/ impulsive behaviours

Medium concerns B
1. Young person has been suspected of previous sexual assaults
2. Early onset of severe behavioural problems
3. Young person diagnosed with ADHD
4. Cold callous attitude in commission of assault
5. Young person diagnosed with depression or other significant mental health problems
6. Young person has significant distorted thoughts about sexual behaviours
7. Obsessive/preoccupation with sexual thoughts/ pornography
8. Copes with negative emotions by use of sexual thoughts, behaviours or use of pornography/graffiti
9. Targets specific victims because of perceived vulnerability
10. *Pattern of discontinuity of care/poor attachments
11. Unsupervised access to potential victims
12. Young person regularly engaged in significant substance abuse

Medium low concerns C
1. Young person has poor capacity for empathy
2. Young person denies responsibility for assault
3. Has difficulties in coping with negative feelings
4. Has poor sexual boundaries
5. Parents express anger or no empathic concern towards victim
6. High level of parental/ carer together with family denial
7. Social group is predominantly pro-criminal
8. Family members include Schedule 1 offenders

Low concerns D
1. First known assault/one-off assault
2. Non-penetrative (including attempts) assault
3. No history of significant trauma or abuse
4. Demonstrates remorse/ empathy
5. Assault appears to be experimental or peer-influenced
6. No significant history of non-sexual assaults
7. Healthy peer relationships
8. No documented school problems
9. No history of behavioural/ emotional problems

Note: Those items marked with * are research informed indicators of risk. Those without such mark are based on a consensus of clinical judgments.

Appendix 3.2

Continuum of indicators of strengths

High strengths A

1. Young person has ability to reflect and understand consequences of offence behaviour
2. Young person is willing to engage in treatment to address abusive behaviour
3. Young person has positive plans/goals
4. Young person has positive talents and interests
5. Young person has good problem-solving and negotiation skills
6. Young person has at least one emotional confidant
7. Young person has positive relationships with school or employers
8. Young person has experienced consistent positive care
9. Parents demonstrate good protective attitudes and behaviours
10. Family has clear, positive boundaries in place
11. Family demonstrates good communications
12. Family demonstrates ability to positively process emotional issues
13. Family is positive about receiving help
14. Young person lives in supportive environment
15. Network of support and supervision available to young person

Medium strengths B

1. Young person has at least one parent/carer who supports and is able to supervise
2. Young person demonstrates remorse for offence (even if not accepting responsibility)
3. Parents/carers are healthy and there is no other family trauma or crisis
4. Parents demonstrate responsible attitudes and skills in family management
5. Parents/carers have no history of own abuse or abusive experiences are resolved
6. Family has positive social network
7. Community is neutral towards young person/ family

Low strengths (high need) C

1. Young person appears to not care what happens
2. Young person has poor communication skills
3. Young person has no support/is rejected by parents/carers
4. Young person has been excluded from school/ unemployed
5. Isolated family
6. Absence of supportive/ structured living environment
7. Parents/carers unable to supervise
8. Family is enmeshed in unhealthy social network
9. Family has high levels of stress
10. History of unresolved significant abuse in family
11. Family refuses to engage with professionals
12. Domestic violence in family
13. Community is hostile towards young person/ family

4 Understanding and managing sexual behaviour problems in school settings

Carol Carson

Introduction

As our knowledge about children and young people who have sexually harmful behaviours grows, as a result of research and clinical practice, guidance has been developed to aid practitioners in their understanding and management of young people with these behaviours. However, this has mainly been written for those engaged in social work, youth work or various kinds of clinical practice and there has been little written specifically for teaching staff who manage children and young people with sexually problematic behaviours within a school environment. In part, this has been due to a lack of research focused specifically on the extent of the problem in school settings and, in part, due to a lack of appreciation of the significance of schools in the system of agencies and organisations which make up a child or young person's network (National Children's Home 1992; Lovell 2002; Masson and Hackett 2003). These factors have had the effect of marginalising the role schools can play in managing and changing sexual behaviour problems and underestimating the very real difficulties school staff are often facing when dealing with pupils with such behaviours.

Practice experience indicates that dealing with children and young people with sexually harmful or abusive behaviours within school settings is a substantial problem. For example, an audit of enquiries to the Education Child Protection Service in Leeds in 1995, showed that one third of all calls for advice, from primary, secondary and special schools were concerns about sexual behaviours, and that half of all the calls from primary schools were about this issue (Carson, Leeds Education Department 1996). In the nine years since that audit my experience of training and consultancy work with education staff convinces me that many teaching staff are still searching for advice and support on this subject.

Teachers are a significant part of every child's network and they have to work with children and young people who display sexual behaviour problems in school, whether or not other agencies are involved. Good practice involves all members of a child or young person's network, including school staff, working together to provide consistent messages, support, and opportunities for the child or young person to develop pro-social behaviours. Indeed, if these efforts fail and exclusion from school results, this often only increases the difficulties of the child or young person and their family and can significantly affect their ability to change.

Teaching staff need information about normal childhood sexual development and about the wide range of sexually problematic and harmful behaviours, as well as guidance and support about how to deal with such behaviours in a school setting. Ideally such guidance should come centrally from Government via, for example, the Department for Education and Skills (DfES) in order to ensure a consistency of approach nationally (Lovell 2002; Masson and Hackett 2003). However, while the subject of children and young people who sexually abuse is referred to in *Safeguarding Children in Education* (DfES 2004c) there is little detailed guidance on how to understand and manage problematic sexual behaviours. The issue is not specifically addressed at all within *Every Child Matters: Change for Children in Schools* (DfES 2004b) but the five outcomes for children's well-being referred to in this publication, which are now been given legal backing within the Children Act 2004, are all useful platforms on which to base the development of responses to children and young people with sexual behaviour problems. These outcomes are that children should:

- Be healthy;
- Stay safe;
- Enjoy and achieve;
- Make a positive contribution;
- Achieve economic well-being.

Notwithstanding these potentially helpful developments, the current general lack of guidance and training in this area of work often leaves education staff feeling deskilled when it comes to dealing with sexually harmful behaviours. Lacking confidence, they may fear 'getting it wrong' and being criticised by others for under- or over-reactions, either internally within the school, or externally by parents or other agencies, particularly Social Services.

The AIM (Assessment, Identification and Moving On) project, based in the Greater Manchester area, emphasises the importance of all parts of the child's or young person's network receiving training and support to understand sexually harmful or abusive behaviours and to be part of a programme of work to help young people to take control of and change their behaviours. Recognising the invisibility of education staff within much inter-agency guidance, the project set about developing guidelines about understanding and managing sexually harmful behaviours in a school setting, specifically for education staff (Carson and AIM project 2002).

This chapter provides an introduction to the AIM guidelines and how they can be used to support practice in education settings, in the process covering three key questions that teaching staff typically raise:

> Identification of the level of concern – is the sexual behaviour healthy, problematic or harmful?

> If need for concern is agreed, how can the pupil be managed and supported in school and with whom should the teacher liaise?

> If the behaviour is of concern, how can other pupils be protected?

Identification issues

One of the main concerns of teachers is uncertainty about how to determine the level of seriousness of the behaviour they are worried about and therefore the level of risk posed by a particular pupil. The AIM project has therefore developed guidelines, divided into three sections dealing, respectively, with primary, secondary and special school pupils, in order to take into account differences in development and ability between primary and secondary school aged children and between children of average ability and those with a learning disability.

Each section contains a brief overview of current research findings and theorising about why a child or young person and those with learning disabilities may display sexually harmful behaviours (Cavanagh-Johnson and Gil 1993; The Bridge Child Care Development Service 2001; Print *et al.* 2002; O'Callaghan 2002) and of practice issues in education settings. A checklist is then provided for evaluating behaviours and hence the level of intervention required, within a continuum from healthy to harmful (the appendix to this chapter contains the primary school checklist as an example). Suggestions are also provided in each section about how schools can protect other pupils, and manage the sexually problematic or harmful behaviours both internally within the school environment and, externally, in conjunction with others in the inter-agency network around the child or young person.

Defining healthy, problematic and harmful behaviours

Healthy sexual behaviours (Cavanagh-Johnson 1999) are defined in the guidance as:

*   Being appropriate to the age/developmental stage of the pupil;
*   Possessing characteristics of mutuality, choice, exploration and possibly fun;
*   Evidencing no intent to cause harm;
*   Being in balance with other aspects of the pupil's life and development; and/or possibly
*   Being an ad hoc or one-off incident.

Problematic sexual behaviours are more difficult to define as they are less clear-cut than behaviours at either end of the continuum, that is, healthy or harmful (National Children's Home 1992). The behaviours may not be age-appropriate, or may be otherwise healthy behaviours taken to an extreme (for example, sexual preoccupation for a teenager, where his/her behaviour is out of balance with other aspects of their life). Alternately, the behaviours may be one-off events which are clearly not appropriate, but which are not repeated (for example, clumsy, naïve attempts at developing a relationship or behaviours such as inappropriate touching, but not extending to penetration). Problematic behaviour may also seem to be influenced by peer pressure rather than the individual's need to engage in the behaviour.

Harmful sexual behaviours are not appropriate to the age or developmental stage of the pupil and they often have aspects of threat, force, coercion, manipulation and/or secrecy about them. Harmful behaviours may appear compulsive, and the pupil's preoccupation with them may be disproportionate to other aspects of the pupil's life. The behaviours may well be frequent and persistent and it may not be easy to distract or dissuade the pupil from engaging in the behaviour.

When the behaviour is discovered or reported, the responses of the pupil and those they target are also important factors to take into account when evaluating seriousness and risk. In situations where healthy behaviours are in evidence, there may be some embarrassment about discovery, but the pupils involved are often comfortable, happy and open about the behaviours themselves. With problematic behaviours, if the pupil appears to respond to intervention and can take responsibility for the behaviour and demonstrate some remorse and empathy, even if they initially struggle with doing so, this would reduce the level of concern. The pupil targeted is likely to be uncomfortable about or irritated by the behaviour, rather than fearful or anxious and they are likely to be able to feel they can tell and seek help. When behaviours are harmful, however, the pupil at the centre of the concern may appear angry, dismissive, aggressive or distressed, blaming others, taking no responsibility and having no sense of empathy for the other pupil. The pupil targeted may well appear anxious, frightened and distressed and may well attempt to avoid the other pupil.

Other aspects which need to be considered are the relationship between the two pupils – would they normally socialise or are there any factors which suggest a power imbalance and that one young person is more in control than the other? In addition, in respect of the child or young person whose behaviour is of concern, are there any other behavioural problems, for example, difficulties coping with difficult emotions, conduct disorders? Finally, what is known about the family background which may be relevant?

Using the checklist

Each checklist requires that users evaluate their answers to eight aspects pertinent to the behaviours of concern. It is important that the sexual behaviour causing concern is checked against *all* of these aspects in order to generate a complete picture. Sometimes school staff may only have limited information and there may be some aspects about which there is little or insufficient information. If so, the checklist then acts as a prompt about the information that should be obtained. Any evaluation of behaviour without all relevant information available must be viewed as a temporary initial assessment, which should be reviewed and possibly revised once that missing information has been gathered.

When measured against the eight parts of the checklist, the behaviour of concern will either fall clearly within one part of the continuum or will possess elements of two parts, for example, both problematic and harmful elements. How the behaviour is evaluated depends on how many responses are in each part of the continuum. For example, five out of eight responses in the problematic end of the continuum and three in the healthy end would mean that the behaviour would fall in the lower to middle part of the problematic section of the continuum, as the healthy aspects would lower the concern:

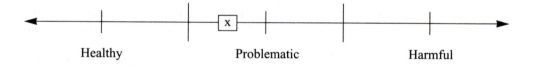

| Healthy | Problematic | Harmful |

Two case studies, based on the primary school checklist in the appendix, are given below as examples of how the checklists work.

Case Study One

Two 9-year-old girls are found in the cloakrooms, one has her pants down. This girl appears uncomfortable and anxious. It is known she is scared of the other girl and they would not normally socialise together. She tells the teacher who found them that the other girl had made her do it because she had wanted to see her 'rude bits'. The other girl denies doing anything and is angry that she is in trouble.

EVALUATION

Case Study One would be plotted as towards the high end of the harmful section of the continuum.

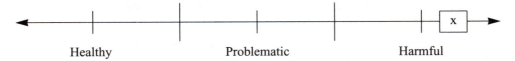

The factors influencing this evaluation are that the behaviour is planned, secretive and there are elements of threat and coercion. The child targeted seems fearful and anxious. The girls would not normally play together and there is a power imbalance in their relationship. The response of the other girl is angry and she takes no responsibility for the behaviour. Important unknowns are what the original intention of the more dominant girl was; whether there have been any previous incidents, how she has responded to any previous intervention and whether she is focused on sexual behaviours in a way that is disproportionate to other aspects of her life. Finding the answers to these may increase or moderate the level of concern.

Case Study Two

> Several 8-year-old girls have complained that a 10-year-old boy keeps touching them and grabbing them between the legs. This has happened in the corridor and in the playground. The girls say the way he touches them makes them feel uncomfortable. The boy initially denies he has touched them but then says it was just for fun. There are no further incidents after he has been spoken to. Other things known about the boy are that he is not particularly popular and is clumsy in his attempts to make friends.

EVALUATION

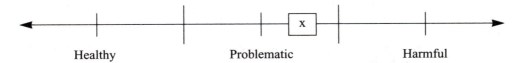

This boy's behaviour would be placed in the middle to top end of the problematic section as all the answers to the eight aspects fall within the problematic section. The factors influencing this evaluation are that the behaviour is not age-appropriate, mutual or exploratory; the girls involved feel uncomfortable and there is no ongoing relationship between the boy and the girls. It is also a recurrent behaviour. It is known that he has other difficulties in making relationships. Although initially denying the behaviour, he does then take some responsibility for it although he minimises what he has done. Ultimately he is responsive to the intervention as he does not repeat the behaviours.

At the end of the next section, some ideas are offered on what interventions may be needed in these two cases.

Investigation and management of sexual behaviour problems

There are a number of aspects involved in managing a pupil who has sexual behaviour problems or where there are concerns that this is the case. These are discussed in turn.

Observing and recording behaviours and communicating about them

One of the key areas which should be addressed is recording. Research by Farmer and Pollock (1998) and the *Childhood Lost* report (The Bridge Child Care Development Service 2001) have highlighted that, across agencies, recording of sexual behaviour problems is often not completed; or the information is vague or subsequently lost.

Accurate, detailed recording forms are essential. One currently being piloted by Carson and Education Leeds is based on the areas covered in the check lists. The expectation is that all concerns about sexual behaviour, no matter how apparently minor, are reported to a Designated Teacher for child protection (Department of Health 1999). These concerns can then be discussed to evaluate the level of possible risk and the level of intervention required. The reason for including even very minor incidents is to give an indication of their number over time and whether they are becoming more or less frequent.

In addition, a recording sheet listing dates of incidents and a brief outline of the behaviours involved should be kept so there is a running chronology of incidents. Both these tools can help the Designated Teacher to build up a picture of the behaviours, including their pattern, any possible triggers, their frequency, persistence and whether or not the level of risk is increasing or decreasing. The forms and recording sheet should both be kept on the child's file as any information on them should also be discussed with their parents or carers.

Working with parents or carers and other pupils

In the initial stages of evaluating concerns the local inter-agency child protection procedures, based on central government guidance *Working Together to Safeguard Children* (Department of Health 1999) should be used as a guide as to whether to talk with parents or Social Services first. In any event, the child's parents or carers will need to be spoken to and good practice would be to seek to develop plans along with them and their child in order to change the sexual behaviours.

Parents may initially be shocked, distressed or embarrassed by hearing about their child's sexual behaviour, therefore they should be offered support. However, if discussion with the parents increases the concerns then consideration should be given to discussing the family with Social Services.

Parents/carers of targeted children

The parents of any targeted child(ren) should also be made aware of the school's concerns and about the school's plans to manage the risks and meet the needs of all concerned, although personal information about the child whose behaviour is of concern and about his or her family must be kept confidential. Although the parents/carers of the targeted pupil(s) may initially be very emotional and angry, what they will mainly want is reassurance that action is being taken to protect their child(ren) from anything further happening. Although there may be demands for the removal of the other child, schools should not accede to this simply in order to assuage strong emotions. Most parents are reassured and do calm down if they feel that the school is taking the situation seriously and are taking practical steps to manage the risk and protect their child.

Pressure from other parents

Schools may also come under pressure from other parents who have become aware of the incident and are concerned about their own children. There have been several occasions when groups of parents have put immense pressure on the Head Teacher and Governors to remove a child or young person and have even directly threatened the child or young person and their family. These initial emotional reactions and responses must also be resisted and attempts made to reach a more informed perspective about the behaviour and the ability of the school to manage any risks and to protect other pupils. Although the current guidance on exclusions allows for Head Teachers to exclude on the grounds of sexual abuse or assault (DfES 2004c, Part 2, paragraph 12), it also states that 'Exclusion should not be imposed in the heat of the moment' (ibid., paragraph 17).

Parents and carers should be reassured that practical steps have been taken to minimise the risk and to strengthen messages about safety and protective behaviours through curriculum work, assemblies and pastoral care activities. The school should aim to work with parents to provide additional support for their children, by encouraging them to report any concerns they may have, no matter how low key they are. If parents are threatening the pupil at the centre of the concerns, school has a responsibility to take action to protect that child. In the worst-case scenario, if parents cannot be reasoned with, then banning them from the school premises and having them leave and collect children at the school boundaries may be necessary.

Threats from other pupils

Occasionally the threat may come from the other pupils, although this is most likely to occur in a secondary school setting. Again strategies for allowing pupils to express their concerns, dispelling some of the misinformation that they may have and offering reassurance that they will be protected should reduce their initial emotional reactions. If they continue to pose a threat, however, then they should be advised that their behaviour is unacceptable and that there will be negative consequences for them if they persist.

Moving pupils whose behaviour is of concern

In some extreme situations the Head Teacher may have to arrange for education off the premises for the pupil at the centre of the concern, for a short period of time until the emotional intensity of parental or pupil initial reactions has dissipated (ibid., paragraph 23). This may also be necessary if the pupil is expressing concern about their own safety or if the risk the child presents to others is high and cannot be immediately managed. However this situation should not be allowed to drift. The child or young person needs to be operating in as normal a way as possible and segregated schooling is unlikely to meet their educational and other developmental needs in the long term. When there have been threats or intimidation, returning the child or young person back to school after a period of time out may mean including protection of that pupil in the supervision and monitoring plan.

Working with other agencies

Some behaviours at the lower end of the continuum can be managed successfully by school alone, in conjunction with the pupil's parents/carers. For those in the problematic part of the continuum, however, consideration needs to be given to whether or not Social Services should be involved. For those behaviours deemed to be at the harmful end of the continuum, discussions with Social Services should always take place, following local inter-agency guidance based on *Working Together to Safeguard Children* (Department of Health 1999).

Where outside agencies are brought in, it is important to hold a strategy or planning meeting, in order to bring together relevant information from all those with knowledge of the child or young person, to develop a shared consensus on risks and needs and to negotiate and agree a plan for managing the child or young person, again within the guidance provided by *Working Together to Safeguard Children* (Department of Health 1999). This supports all parties working together and it enables the child or young person and their parents or carers to be aware that everyone is liaising with each other, which also reduces any opportunities for manipulation. Where there is no forum already established for such a meeting, then requests should be made to Social Services that one be convened. In the Greater Manchester area, where the AIM project is based, strategy meetings can be called, which are chaired by Child Protection Coordinators/Reviewing Officers. This has been a successful way of promoting good multi-agency practice, and provides a central point for the collection of data/statistics as well as consistency of practice.

As well as providing information about concerns, schools should also bring for discussion issues such as potential exclusions and the implications for work experience activities. Although the ultimate decision about exclusion rests with the Head Teacher, obtaining a multi-agency perspective can help to bring a more balanced appraisal of the understandable initial emotional responses of staff, parents and other pupils. With regard to work experience activities, consideration should be given to the suitability of a work placement (if, for example, there are children in the workplace or exposure to other possible risk situations) and about whether or not the work place supervisor should be made aware of what has happened.

Work with the individual pupil

The most effective way of changing behaviour is for everyone in the child's or young person's network to be giving consistent messages, setting clear boundaries and providing support so the child or young person is enabled to develop more positive strategies for coping with the feelings which are leading to the behaviours of concern. This joint approach requires clear communication and sharing of information between all the parties involved and clear planning and agreement about roles. Thus it is important to agree who the key worker is in relation to any individual programme of work with the child or young person and how can others support this programme. For example, if a youth offending team worker is undertaking a programme of work with an adolescent, there should be discussions about how the school can support that work, through sharing of relevant resources, complementary work in school, provision of a learning mentor and so on.

Supervision and monitoring

Supervision and monitoring are likely to be required to manage risk. Initially, the level of supervision may have to be high until a comprehensive assessment of risk and needs is carried out. Levels of supervision should always be under review, however, if only because high levels of supervision cannot usually be resourced on an ongoing basis. In addition, having to be in close proximity to staff at all times marks a pupil out as being different and may affect his or her ability to develop positive social skills and relationships. Importantly, too, such supervision takes the responsibility for controlling their behaviour away from the pupil when they should be working on dealing with their impulses to act in sexually problematic ways.

Individual work or pastoral programme: managing risks and meeting needs

The main objectives of any individual programme of work with a pupil about whom there are concerns is to reduce their need to engage in the behaviour, for the pupil to gain some internal control over their behaviour, and for him or her to begin to enjoy more normative developmental experiences. Whilst the focus rightly has to be on the level of risk posed by the pupil, it is important not to forget that these are also children and young people who are vulnerable and who have unmet needs. Indeed, meeting these needs may significantly alter their behaviour and reduce the risk they pose.

School staff have a major role to play not only in containing behaviours, but in beginning to address the needs of the child or young person through, for example, providing:

* emotional support and guidance;
* attachment opportunities and positive relationships;
* responses which boost self-esteem and develop resilience and positive behaviours;
* opportunities for the child or young person to communicate about and deal with difficult emotions and feelings;
* models of assertiveness and skills in problem solving and decision making;
* examples of ways of dealing with anger and anxiety management;
* education about healthy sexual behaviours.

All of the above work is appropriate to the school remit, and schools have the resources through curriculum and pastoral work to address these areas. School staff are also very skilled at dealing with difficult or challenging behaviours. In fact, teachers have a lot to offer colleagues in Social Services, Youth Offending Teams or Child and Adolescent Mental Health Teams, who may also be working with the child or young person. Teachers usually have a good understanding of the child or young person's learning style or ability level; they have access to excellent resources, such as the Excellence and Enjoyment: Social and Emotional Aspects of Learning (S.E.A.L.) curriculum materials (DfES 2005) and they can often reinforce learning, by repeating work in school or helping the child or young person practise new skills or strategies learned in their individual programme of work. Other ways of supporting pupils include allocating him or her a key worker in school such as a 'learning mentor' or, externally, a Connexions Personal Advisor, an Education Welfare Officer or a member of the local Behavioural and Educational Support Team (B.E.S.T.) (DfES 2004c).

Children with autism

Increasingly, teachers are asking about pupils on the autistic spectrum, who are also displaying sexual behaviour problems. It is not clear in some cases, whether the children's behaviour is linked to their autism or to their life experiences. Guidance on evaluating and managing these behaviours with autistic children is an area that needs further development and work is ongoing at present (Carson and Education Leeds 2005).

Returning to the case studies

So what might the intervention packages be for the young people described in the case studies?

In the case study involving the two girls, the dominant girl needs boundaries put on her behaviour and she needs to be made aware that her behaviour is unacceptable. A system of supervision, monitoring and recording should be set up immediately. Appropriate restrictions should also be placed on the girl's freedom of movement. For example, she should not be out of class alone or in the toilets or cloakrooms unless a member of staff is aware she is there. At break-times she should always be in sight of supervisors in the playground. A decision must be made about the timing of discussions with parents and about referral to Social Services. Local child protection procedures should be followed with regard to when the school should talk to her parents/carers. In the meantime, the girl who has been targeted needs to be given clear messages that she has a right to feel safe and that if she is ever made to feel uncomfortable or threatened again, she must tell someone.

In the case of the boy and the group of girls who have complained about his behaviour, the girls need to be reassured they were right to tell, that the school takes the incidents seriously and that they have a right to be safe. The boy needs a clear message that his behaviour is inappropriate and has a negative effect on others. He should be monitored and if the behaviour is repeated, closer supervision of his movements organised. Good recording systems are needed to gauge if his behaviours have stopped or are intermittent, or if they are increasing in frequency or seriousness. Individual work with the boy on emotional literacy, communication and relationship skills may also be important. His parents should be informed and a programme of work and consistent messages from home and school organised. A referral to Social Services at this point is probably not required.

Protecting other children

Those who are targeted may require individual help in their own right. They need to be asked how they feel about remaining in the same class or school, and about how they can be helped to feel safe. This does not mean giving them control over decision making, but their views (dependent on their age and understanding) should be taken into account. They may need help with generating strategies for dealing with future situations when they may feel uncomfortable or under pressure. Work with them on protective behaviours, life skills and assertiveness may be appropriate.

As well as thinking about how they might support individual pupils, schools also need to think about how they can prevent incidents happening; ensuring that the school is really a safe place to be and that all pupils are protected. Under the new guidance *Every Child Matters: Change for Children in Schools* (DfES 2004b) all schools should promote the rights of a child to stay safe, but how they put this into practice on a day-to-day basis is what actually determines how safe pupils actually feel. Several aspects need to be considered:

a   Attitudes and values: Staff are important role models for pupils. They can model positive, healthy interactions with others; conversely they can model behaviours which reinforce stereotypes about power and vulnerability or blur boundaries about acceptable language and interactions, for example, through sexual banter with teenagers. If these inappropriate attitudes and behaviours are present, they can reinforce distorted perceptions that some children and young people may have and make them feel their own behaviour is acceptable.

b   Policies: Sexually harmful or abusive behaviours do not require a stand-alone policy about their management. Guidance can be integrated into other policies already in school, for example, Behaviour, Discipline and Bullying Policies. This may only necessitate the insertion of a sentence or a paragraph which states that sexually harmful behaviour is unacceptable. For example, within the school's policy on bullying a single word could be added so the policy may read as 'Bullying is unacceptable, whether it is physical, *sexual,* psychological or verbal'. Including reference to sexual bullying in this way gives permission for staff and pupils to talk about the issue and to raise concerns if they have them.

       Similarly, child protection, equal opportunities, positive behaviour and pastoral care policies can be adapted to include concerns about sexually problematic behaviours. Thus, if the behaviour needs an internal school intervention, then useful guidance and strategies can be obtained from the positive behaviour and pastoral care policies. Also information and strategies drawn from the school's equal opportunities policy may be useful when addressing power imbalances, issues of vulnerability and resilience and distorted views, particularly about gender, which are often a significant factor in situations when sexually harmful or abusive behaviours happen.

c   School layout: Many incidents which happen in school happen in the toilets, corridors or other areas which are out of sight of adults. A useful exercise to undertake with pupils and staff is to plot these 'hotspots' or vulnerable areas around school and to work to reduce the chances of any abusive behaviour, physical or sexual, occurring at these sites.

d   Assemblies, circle time, year group and curriculum work: These can be used to promote themes about safety and protective skills, respect and responsibilities to others. It is important that these are promoted on an ongoing basis, even if there are no concerns, but they are particularly important if there are concerns about risk. They can be a way of heightening awareness of safety issues without drawing attention to an individual or breaking confidentiality.

Conclusion

School staff can feel deskilled and disempowered when faced with a pupil displaying sexually problematic or harmful behaviours. They can lack confidence in their ability to evaluate sexual behaviours which will cause them concern, fearing that their actions may be criticised by colleagues, parents and other agencies. Because of their duty to protect other pupils in their school they can also feel under immense pressure from parents to try to eliminate all risk, which can lead to unnecessary exclusions.

However, school staff are an essential part of the child or young person's network, both in identifying behaviours causing concern and, if supported and involved in planning, they can also provide time, support, resources and opportunities which can have a significant impact on work aimed at reducing sexual behaviour problems. It is hoped that this chapter provides useful assistance and support to the invaluable role school staff can play in this area of work.

Appendix 4.1

Checklist for evaluating sexual behaviours in primary school settings

	Healthy	Problematic	Harmful
1. Type of sexual behaviour	Age appropriate, mutual and exploratory	Not age appropriate or has some adult knowledge or language	Adult sexual activity, e.g. intercourse, oral sex etc.
2. Context of behaviour	Open, light hearted, spontaneous	No secrecy or force, but children involved seem uncomfortable	Behaviour is planned, secretive, there are elements of threat, force, coercion. The children targeted seem anxious, fearful, uncomfortable
3. Response of other children	Engaging freely, happy	Uncomfortable, unhappy with behaviour but not fearful or anxious If behaviour is directed at adults they feel uncomfortable	Uncomfortable, unhappy, fearful, anxious. Could be physically hurt. Could be trying to avoid the other child
4. Relationship between the children	Similar age and ability, would normally play together	Children would not normally play together or there may be some factors which suggest one child is more in control than the other	Children would not normally play together or there are clear power differences, e.g. due to age, size, status, ability, strength
5. Frequency of the behaviour	Behaviour is age appropriate, ad hoc and not the main focus for the child. The child is interested in other things	Some inappropriate sexual behaviour for age, however the child also has interest in other things, behaviour is intermittent	Frequent incidents and child seems focused on the behaviour. It is disproportionate to other aspects of their life. They seem to seek comfort/reassurance or control from the behaviour

6. Persistence of the behaviour	Behaviour is age appropriate, ad hoc and not the main focus for the child. The child is interested in other things	Behaviour is recurring and there are some difficulties in distracting and redirecting behaviour. Child however is responsive to some intervention	Child cannot be distracted from the behaviour easily and returns to the behaviour
			Focus on the behaviour is disproportionate to other aspects of their life
			It appears to be the main way they seek comfort/attention and control
7. Child's emotional response	Happy, embarrassed, able to take responsibility for their behaviour and its effects on others (dependent on their age and understanding)	Child unresponsive, ashamed, struggles to take responsibility for their behaviour or to show empathy	Child angry, fearful, aggressive, distressed or conversely passive, lacking in understanding why anyone would be worried
			Cannot take responsibility for their behaviour, nor shows any empathy to others
8. Background information	Nothing known of concern	Little known about the family or there are some concerns about the family. There are concerns about other difficult behaviours	Patterns of discontinuity of care/poor attachments
			High levels of trauma, e.g. physical, emotional, sexual, neglect, domestic violence
			Other behavioural problems or conduct disorder

From 'Guidelines for Identifying and Managing Sexually Problematic/Abusive Behaviour in Schools and Nurseries' (Carson and AIM Project 2002)

Part 2

Assessment and planning

5 Assessment issues in relation to young people who have sexually abusive behaviour

Hilary Grant

Introduction

This chapter covers several important issues in planning and conducting a clinical assessment of a young person who has sexually abusive behaviour. The chapter begins with a consideration of the purpose of such assessments and identifies different sources of information collection. Process issues, including assessing the young person's level of motivation and the need to work within a child protection context, are outlined. There is then a discussion of the basic structure, components and content of such an assessment. Subsequently, issues of risk assessment and amenability for treatment are addressed before, finally, consideration is given to formulating information from the assessment, writing a report and developing a plan for treatment.

Although the focus of this chapter is on young people have been found guilty of a sexual offence, many of the principles and much of the content of the assessment process described will have applicability to assessment of children and young people who have not been through the youth justice or criminal justice system.

Purpose of assessment

The purpose of any clinical assessment is to identify healthcare needs, to decide on suitability for treatment and to evaluate treatment efficacy. The assessment process, in addition to this, should evaluate risk and attempt to predict recidivism, recommending appropriate placements and necessary restrictions where indicated (for further discussion of these aspects see Chapters 6 and 7). It is also important to assess a young person's motivation to engage in the assessment process and to accept any proposed treatment.

As earlier chapters have indicated, a significant proportion of sexual aggression and abuse is perpetrated by children and young people and a small minority of these young people are at risk of continuing their abusive behaviour into adulthood. This highlights the need for the recognition and assessment of young people with sexually abusive behaviour and, where high risk of recidivism is indicated, early intervention to prevent any escalation of the problem (Vizard *et al.* 1996; Hackett *et al.* 2003). However, although there may be some similarities in the factors which underpin the behaviour of adults and adolescents who perpetrate sexual abuse, it is also vitally important to address the particular developmental issues facing the adolescent perpetrator of sexual abuse and the implications of these issues on assessment and treatment.

Source material for assessment

It is essential to gather as much background information as possible from available sources before assessment begins. In practice, many workers may not have immediate access to all necessary information; however, a complete assessment is not possible in the absence of key accounts about the nature of the index sexual offence and any prior offence history. The list of the possible sources of information may differ in each case but a general list of essential sources is given in Table 5.1.

The assessment process

The clinical assessment of juvenile abusers requires the same comprehensive evaluation as is required for other children and adolescents. O'Reilly (2001) has suggested several key characteristics of a good clinical assessment of young people. The assessment team should strive to create a non-collusive, collaborative relationship with the young person and his family, with the aim of building a holistic understanding of the young person's life and therapeutic needs. Marshall *et al.* (1999) have identified a number of features that clinicians should adopt in assessment that are linked with positive outcome, illustrated in Table 5.2.

Assessment of young people with sexually abusive behaviour requires considerable skills, as minimisations, evasion and denial frequently arise. Strong counter-transference can be evoked in the clinician, who must remain aware of such a possibility and seek supervision to address such processes (see also Chapter 17).

Motivation for assessment

Several models to assess a young person's motivation level for entering the assessment process (and treatment) have been suggested. These include motivational interviewing principles (Miller and Rollnick 1991) and Prochaska and Di'Clemente's Transtheoretical Model of Motivation (Prochaska and Di'Clemente 1983, 1986). However, Abel *et al.* (1984) describe their own approach to the assessment of motivation of adult sexual offenders as follows: 'Our own criterion for motivation is whether the patient walks into the treatment room.' It is suggested that such a minimalist approach to motivation should similarly be adopted with young people who have been sexually abusive, as it is important to recognise the ambivalent feelings that young people will inevitably have about assessment and treatment.

Young people and their families can present at various points along a continuum from complete denial to acknowledgement of sexually abusive behaviour. It is an important

Table 5.1 Source material for assessment

- Victim statement
- Police interviews
- Criminal records
- Education reports
- Previous psychological and psychiatric reports
- Collateral interviews, partners, parents etc.
- Behavioural observations
- Psychometric assessments
- Structured interviews
- Information from Social Services, Youth Offending Teams and Health

Table 5.2 Therapist features identified by Marshall *et al.* (1999) as reliably linked to a positive intervention outcome

- Empathic
- Non-collusive
- Respectful
- Appropriately self-disclosing
- Warm and friendly
- Appropriate use of humour
- Sincere and genuine
- Communicates clearly
- Rewarding and encouraging
- Encourage active participation
- Directive and reflective
- Encourage pro-social attitudes
- Confident
- Asks open-ended questions
- Interested
- Deals with frustration and difficulties
- Non-confrontational
- Spends appropriate time on issues

part of the assessment process to ascertain where each individual lies on this continuum. Recognition of where a young person is, with regard to their readiness for change, influences how to approach him or her during the course of the assessment and how to engage the young person within the therapeutic process.

Child protection issues in assessment

All assessment and treatment of young people who abuse other children should be undertaken within a child protection context (Department of Health 1999). It is important, therefore, to establish at the time of referral whether child protection procedures have been initiated; whether the alleged perpetrator is still living in a situation where other young people may be at risk; what steps have been taken to reduce the likelihood of further abuse and whether Social Services and other relevant agencies are aware of the referral. Often young people who sexually abuse are subject to both child welfare and youth justice provisions and the interviewer needs to remain aware of these agencies' responsibilities and roles with respect to the young person. An agreed approach to the assessment may need to be negotiated between the health, child welfare and youth justice practitioners or agencies involved. Similarly, shared protocols may need to be developed. All of these issues are addressed in greater detail elsewhere in this book.

Structure and content of assessment

A carefully planned and structured approach to assessment is crucial. Ideally, assessments should incorporate a multi-disciplinary and multi-agency process, as well as interviews with parents or carers or guardians and family. The assessment work should be spread across a number of sessions, with an opportunity to arrange individual and family interviews as and when felt appropriate. Vizard *et al.* (1996) suggest three overall stages to the assessment process:

1   Clarification and rapport building;
2   Mapping the abuse: the fantasies, strategies and behaviour;
3   The future: placement, treatment and personal change.

All stages of the assessment process should commence and finish with an opportunity for questions and feedback so that the young person and his or her carers feel listened to and the message is conveyed that their contributions are crucial to the success of the assessment.

It is important to begin by setting the scene for the assessment. The interviewer should explain in simple words the reason for the assessment and should identify the agency commissioning it. The limits of confidentiality should be clarified. Having given consideration to issues such as capacity, competence to consent and parental responsibility, appropriate consents should be sought from the young person and their carers.

It is always beneficial to spend time and effort in trying to build a positive rapport with the young person, who is often extremely anxious, angry or avoidant about the issues being discussed. The interviewer may start by acknowledging the difficulty the young person will probably have in discussing such issues. It is important to try and allay their anxieties by clearly stating that the role of the interviewer, in exploring the sexual abuse, is to try and find a way to help the young abuser, rather than to find fault and be judgemental. It may be helpful to explain to the young person that the interviewer has previous experience of completing similar assessments and that there is nothing to be embarrassed about. The interviewer should be aware of their body language and responses in order to ensure that these do not provide unintended negative feedback.

Graham *et al.* (1997) suggest undertaking a detailed developmental history at this information-gathering stage of the assessment as this provides for a less threatening beginning. Knowledge of the young person's developmental trajectory also assists in identifying the context of potential aetiological factors (including predisposing, precipitating and maintaining factors) pertinent to the young person's sexually abusive behaviour. This should be complemented by an assessment of family background, functioning, attitudes, resources and ability or capacity to provide support to the young person (see also Chapter 3).

Thereafter, assessment should focus on an exploration of the young person's sexual knowledge, the sources of this knowledge and their sexual experiences and behaviour, including their experience of any sexually abusive behaviour. It is essential to conduct the interview in age-appropriate language. The interviewer can start by establishing the meaning of basic sexual terms and what words the young person uses for them. A glossary of terms can be identified including terms for different sexual anatomical structures and processes. (If a younger child or a learning disabled child is being assessed, drawings, play with model figures and dolls, for example, can be useful to facilitate communication.) Becker (1988b) suggests that asking questions in a neutral fashion such as 'when was the first time you were touched in a sexual way?' can allow for disclosure of normative and non-normative experiences.

The objective of the next stage of the assessment process is to gain a detailed understanding of the specifics of the young person's sexually abusive behaviour. It may be important to re-emphasise to the young person that the purpose is not for the interviewer to be judgemental or critical of the young person, but to build up a shared understanding of the sexually abusive behaviour so as to identify possible strategies to reduce such behaviour in the future. It is useful to establish how many offences the young person has committed and to discuss in detail the most recent one. Details about typical and non-typical offences should be obtained. Factors to consider include antecedents, details of the abusive behaviour itself and the

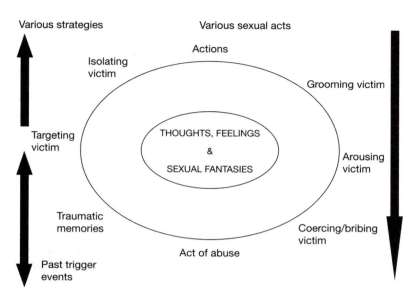

Various strategies   Various sexual acts

Figure 5.1 Integrated abuse cycle: actions and thoughts.

consequences of that behaviour. The interviewer should elicit the thoughts, feelings, attitudes and behaviour of the young person in relation to each of these factors.

A useful technique may include a pictorial representation of the young person's behaviour such as 'The Integrated Abuse Cycle' which is provided in Figure 5.1. This was developed (by Vizard *et al.* 1996) from earlier work with adult sex offenders (Mezey *et al.* 1990) and juvenile abusers (Lane 1978).

Developmental issues

Special attention needs to be given to developmental issues when assessing young sexual offenders, particularly so when assessing young people with a learning disability or cognitive impairment. Adolescents are different from adults in many significant ways. Their experience of life is more limited. They are often less socially, emotionally and physically mature. Their cognitive and emotional capacities and personality are not fully developed. Assessment of such young people should include determining their emotional, cognitive, intellectual and physical maturity and identifying the nature and extent of any delay or disability. It is important that the assessment is carried out in a way that is matched to the developmental or cognitive profile of the young person. Thus it is essential to establish the extent of the young person's understanding and knowledge with regard to sexual behaviour and the norms and limits of such behaviour. The pace of the assessment may also have to be varied according to the young person's needs. It may be necessary to seek a formal assessment of level of intellectual functioning in order to obtain a clearer view as to how to implement assessment and treatment.

A further problem to bear in mind is the possibility of suggestibility of young people, including young people with a learning disability. It is important to be sure the young person understands what is being asked of him or her and it may be necessary to ask the young person to repeat back to the interviewer in their own words what has been asked or said.

Medical and psychiatric history

It is also important to obtain a comprehensive medical and psychiatric history with specific attention to sexually transmitted diseases, human immunodeficiency virus infections, psychopathology and psychiatric co-morbidity. Juvenile sexual abusers can present with considerable psychiatric co-morbidity and often have a range of behavioural, emotional and developmental problems (Lewis *et al.* 1979; Kavoussi *et al.* 1988; Becker *et al.* 1991; Shaw *et al.* 1993, 1996; Shaw 1999). Psychiatric diagnoses of conduct disorder (45–80 per cent), mood disorders (35–50 per cent), anxiety disorders (30–50 per cent), substance abuse (20–30 per cent) and ADHD (10–20 per cent) occur as well as evidence of personality disorder and severe personality traits. It is also crucial to assess the risk of self-harm and suicidality. An understanding of presenting psychopathology is an essential component of treatment planning.

Use of psychometric tests

There are no specific empirical measures or psychometric tests that can identify, diagnose or classify sexual abusers. Many professionals in the field now strongly recommend a combined assessment approach, making use of existing assessment tools, to generate a structured or semi-structured clinical interview.

Psychological tests are often used adjunctively as part of an overall assessment. The most commonly used psychological measures are the MMPI, WISC-III, or WAIS; Rorschach; Thematic Apperception Test; Bender Gestalt; and Draw-a-Person. Neuropsychological testing and psycho-educational assessment may also be required when querying the presence of a specific learning disability.

The following tests have been used with adolescent sex offenders:

- *Multiphasic Sex Inventory* (Nichols and Molinder 1984): The measure is a 300-item, true–false test with 14 clinical and validity scales, which provide measures regarding sexually offensive behaviour, sexual deviations, sexual dysfunction, sexual knowledge and sexual attitudes. However, there is a lack of published data on the reliability and the validity of this instrument in the adolescent population (Becker and Hunter 1997).
- *Adolescent Cognitions Scale*: This is a 32-item, forced-choice inventory for juvenile sex offenders. Hunter *et al.* (1991), however, found it to have only marginal reliability and to fail to discriminate between sexual and non-sexual abusers.
- *Child Sexual Behaviour Inventory*: This inventory uses parent report of sexual behaviour in children aged 2 to 12 years and provides information on a number of domains including sexual anxiety, sexual interests, sexual knowledge, sexual intrusiveness, gender-role behaviour and boundary problems (Friedrich 1997). It is, of course, limited by its reliance on parent report.

Phallometric assessment

In this procedure penile erectile response to different sexual stimuli is measured by means of a flexible band placed round the subject's penis, which is connected to a polygraph, and which records the expansion and contraction of the penis in response to such images or stimuli. This procedure is, however, being used with great caution with juveniles because of the lack of empirical studies validating its use, problems of obtaining informed consent, and a reluctance to expose children and adolescents to further sexual stimulation through the portrayal of deviant sexual activities (Saunders and Awad 1988).

Risk assessment

There is considerable debate concerning the best approach to addressing risk assessment in adolescent sex offenders. Difficulties limiting the accuracy of risk assessment are the low rates of recidivism, the relative infrequency of sexual offending, the fact that offences do not come to the attention of relevant agencies and the fact that often there is inadequate or insufficient information on which to base judgements. Although there are a number of risk prediction checklists or guidelines available, there is little or no available empirical data regarding their validity (Calder *et al*. 1997; Epps 1997; Bremer 1998).

With these caveats in mind, a comprehensive risk assessment should include assessment based on multiple sources of information. The three main approaches to risk assessment are unstructured clinical judgement; structured professional judgement and actuarial measures. Unstructured clinical judgement has the advantage of allowing inclusion of many different potential risk factors. However, this form of risk assessment is known to have a poor level of accuracy and 'on average is slightly better than chance' (Hanson and Bussière 1998).

Structured professional judgement provides for a systematic and structured approach to risk assessment, although it continues to rely on clinical judgement. Given the fact that there is a list of risk factors that have been identified by research as being significantly associated with an increased risk of future sexual violence (see Chapter 15), there should be an increase in accuracy over unstructured clinical assessment.

Actuarial instruments have the advantage of high inter-rater reliability, the ability to test predictive validity and are usually easier to administer and score. Hanson (2000) points out, however, that such instruments cannot possibly include all possible risk factors. Such instruments also often rely heavily on historical factors and other 'static' risk factors, rather than identifying dynamic risk factors which are usually more amenable to treatment. There are a number of actuarial scales available, including the J-SOAP – Juvenile Sex Offender Assessment Protocol (Prentky *et al*. 2000), ERASOR – Estimate of Risk of Adolescent Sexual Offence Recidivism (Worling and Curwen 2001), and MASA – Multidimensional Assessment of Sex and Aggression (Knight *et al*. 1994).

Any risk assessment judgement will be dependent on the contribution of risk factors rather than simply on the number of risk factors identified. It is also important to discriminate between those factors that are static and dynamic. Those factors that contribute strongly to increased risk and are dynamic can be a target for intervention, and protective factors may be enhanced in order to reduce future risk of sexual offending.

Risk assessment of young people must also be considered within a developmental context as some factors that may constitute a risk during one stage of development may not represent the same risk at another developmental stage. In addition, the factors that may predict the onset of sexual violence may not necessarily be the same factors as those that predict the continuation of the future risk of sexual violence.

Issues around communicating judgements of risk are a further important consideration. It is vitally important to communicate the limits of such judgements. Thus, guidelines adapted from Boer *et al*. (1997) and Worling and Curwen (2001) would suggest that the worker should:

1   Inform agencies regarding the scientific limitations of risk prediction;
2   Note that estimates of risk are time-limited;
3   Justify risk estimates by referring to the presence or absence of specific high-risk factors;
4   Make their risk prediction as specific as possible;

5   List potential exacerbating factors; and
6   List potential protective factors or strategies that could be utilised to reduce risk.

Amenability to treatment

Factors that may indicate unsuitability for treatment, or need for placement in a more restrictive environment, include: persistent denial of a sexual offence; lack of remorse and lack of victim empathy; a well-established pattern of frequent and diverse acts of sexual violence and a number of previous arrests for sexual offences; the number of victims; degree of psychopathology; the failure of previous treatment; the degree of compulsivity and sexual arousal; and a documented history of violent and sadistic behaviour (Hunter and Figueredo 1999; Rasmussen 1999).

Factors indicating suitability for treatment include: some acceptance of personal responsibility for the sexually abusive behaviour and acknowledgement of its seriousness; evidence of motivation to change sexually abusive behaviour; willingness to participate in treatment; and cognitive ability to cope with or participate in a treatment programme offered.

The features of a comprehensive assessment

The American Psychiatric Association Task Force (APA Task Force 1999) has outlined the contents of what they regard as a comprehensive assessment (Table 5.3) which can act as a useful checklist for workers when completing an assessment.

At the conclusion of the assessment it is important to provide feedback to the young person and carers and allow for questions or further clarification. This will assist in future treatment or intervention planning.

Formulation

At the conclusion of the assessment process the clinician should prepare a formulation of the case. The formulation should include a description of possible predisposing, precipitating, maintaining and protective factors (see also Chapter 8). When formulating a case it is important to recognise that sexual behaviour is shaped by many factors and these factors are unique in each case. These factors include environment, family and interpersonal relationships, social learning, personal experiences and biological influences.

Report writing

The contents of the report should broadly include the following:

- Nature and purpose of report
- Reason for referral
- Family history
- Developmental and personal history
- Educational history
- Past medical and past psychiatric history
- Medication
- History of drug and alcohol use
- Previous forensic history

- Psychosocial development and sexual history
- Description of sexually abusive behaviour
- Results of psychometric assessment
- Mental state examination
- Risk assessment and management
- Formulation
- Comment on amenability to treatment or prognosis
- Recommendations regarding treatment
- Recommendations regarding placement
- Recommendations with regard to risk management.

The author of the report should be clear regarding the purpose of the report and its likely audience. Issues with respect to consent, confidentiality, information sharing and the sharing of information on a 'need to know' basis need to be considered. Reports may be written to

Table 5.3 APA Task Force recommendations for the main factors that should be included in an assessment of a young person with sexually abusive behaviour

- Victim statements to police, Social Services, mental health professionals, etc.
- Background information including family history, educational history, medical history, psychosocial history and developmental history
- Interpersonal relationship history
- Sexual history including deviant sexual interests and the emergence of sexually aggressive behaviour over time
- Reported use of deviant sexual fantasies and interests
- The intensity of sexual arousal during the time surrounding each offence
- The dynamic and process of victim selection
- Use of coercion, force, violence and weapons
- Behavioural warning signs
- Identifiable triggers leading to inappropriate sexual behaviours
- Thinking errors such as cognitive distortions or irrational beliefs
- The spectrum of injury to the victim from the violation of trust, creation of fear to physical injury
- Sadistic elements to the sexually abusive behaviour
- Ritualistic and obsessive characteristics of the sexually abusive behaviour
- Deviant non-sexual interests
- History of assaultative behaviour
- Issues related to separation and loss
- Antisocial characteristics
- Psychiatric diagnosis including disruptive behaviour disorders, affective disorders, developmental disorders, personality disorders, post-traumatic stress disorder, substance abuse disorder, and organic mental disorder
- Ability to accept responsibility
- Degree of denial and minimisation
- Understanding wrongfulness
- Concern for injury to victim
- Quality of social, assertive and empathic skills
- Family's response (from denial, minimisation, support, to ability to intervene appropriately)
- Exposure to pornography
- History of sexual, physical and/or emotional victimisation
- Ability to control deviant sexual interest
- Knowledge and expression of appropriate sexual interests
- School performance and educational level
- Mental state examination

advise other professionals, and to advise and inform other agencies including Social Services, Youth Offending Teams, Mental Health Services and the courts. In the case of reports for the court, recommendations with regard to fitness to stand trial, fitness to plead or attend court and recommendations with respect to sentencing may need to be addressed. The author may also need to comment on the presence or absence of a mental disorder prior to, or at the time of, the index offence and on psychological factors relating to the offence and the presence of any possible mitigating factors.

The report should be written bearing in mind that referrers, carers, young people and/or courts may read the content. Good practice suggests that the young person and their parents or carers should be taken through the content of the report by someone trained to explain the contents and to deal with their responses to that information (Vizard *et al.* 1996).

With regard to recommendations about the treatment of the young person's sexually abusive behaviour, there is an increasing recognition that it is much more than simply a disorder of sexual arousal (Becker 1988b; Hackett *et al.* 2003). Borduin *et al.* (1990) recommend a combined or integrated multi-modal treatment programme tailored to the individual's needs. New treatment approaches are being developed but treatment outcome studies are rare. The predominant treatment processes include behavioural interventions, relapse prevention, psychosocial therapies and psychopharmacological approaches (Becker 1988b, 1994; Schwartz 1992; Becker and Hunter 1993; Boer *et al.* 1997; Shaw *et al.* 1999). It is crucial that any conduct or mental disorder is treated appropriately.

Conclusion

A good assessment takes time, but it is time well spent. Expediting this process can result in important information being missed, with serious consequences for both clinical and risk management. This chapter has summarised the elements which are necessary for an adequate assessment of young individuals who have sexually abusive behaviour. Special attention has been given to developmental aspects, forensic considerations and issues related to child protection. Management and treatment planning have been described briefly, including some strategies for improving the young person's motivation to involve themselves in the process of assessment and treatment. The role of the clinician undertaking such assessment cannot be overemphasised as they are the first point of contact of a possibly long therapeutic relationship. Every effort should be made to make this experience as positive and beneficial for the young sexual person and their family as possible, to facilitate future engagement.

Acknowledgement

The author wishes to acknowledge and express her gratitude for the assistance of Dr Sobia Khan in the preparation of this chapter.

6 Placement provision and placement decisions

Resources and processes[1]

Nick Bankes

Introduction

The reasons why children and young people sexually abuse are varied and complex. No single theory or approach to understanding and assessing such behaviour is sufficient, in itself, for informing case management decision making (Finkelhor 1986), each case needing to be viewed from an holistic perspective (Ryan 1999a). The author believes that adopting an integrative approach (drawing on cognitive-behavioural, systemic, developmental psychology and psychodynamic theories and principles) is the most effective approach in this area of work (see Chapter 17).

In the first part of the chapter resource issues pertinent to the placement of young sexual abusers will be outlined, drawing on the author's experience in this field. In the second part anonymised case examples are used to examine the processes whereby practitioners make placement decisions. and suggestions are made for ways in which some of the pitfalls inherent in these processes can be avoided. This is followed by a brief concluding section which reviews the main issues raised in the chapter.

Placement resources

In the original edition of this chapter in 1999 the absence of suitable placements was described as one of the most pressing needs for this client group. In 1998, in the United Kingdom, the picture was one of poor and patchy service provision (Masson 1995). Sadly, little has changed in the intervening period (Hackett *et al.* 2003). There is still a lack of placement facilities and an often uncoordinated and ad hoc response by professionals. Lovell (2002) observes that in the UK, 10 years after the NCH Report (National Children's Home 1992) into services for children and young people who sexually abuse, few of the report's recommendations had been put into practice resulting in 'an ad hoc system in which there is a lack of consistent response to these young people; agencies do not work together; and children and young people frequently do not receive appropriate treatment and support' (Lovell 2002: 41). A report cited by Araji (1997) documented that nearly 50 per cent of sexually aggressive children were not in a placement of choice but rather in the only available placement. It is clear that there is little spare capacity, with service systems having insufficient appropriate placements for those children and young people who should be accommodated because of their sexually inappropriate or abusive behaviour. Worryingly too, many young people are often allocated to resources without a formulation of their difficulties or a thorough understanding of what led to the abuse. Thus some young people are directed into expensive and scarce residential programmes without due attention being paid to their specific needs.

Where no alternative placement can be found the young person may have to be maintained within their current situation, although this can be far from satisfactory. Cover stories may also be used by professionals as part of their attempts to get a young person placed. In such cases the young person's presenting behaviour can either be minimised or ignored altogether, leaving carers or residential workers unprepared and uninformed in dealing with any potential risk. The recent 'DN' case (The Bridge Child Care Development Service 2001) demonstrates how professional minimisation, a lack of inter-agency communication and poor lines of accountability contributed to a young man failing to receive the treatment he needed with tragic results. This can be understood as an example of the 'Responsibility Avoidance Syndrome' operating at an inter-agency level (see Chapter 17). Conversely, some descriptions may be exaggerated, for example, labels such as 'sex offender' may be applied in order to heighten professional anxiety and obtain appropriate resources despite the dangers associated with the use of such negative labels.

A principle of the Children Act 1989 is that children and young people are best cared for in their own family, wherever possible, and this principle is equally applicable to young sexual abusers. There is an orthodoxy, however, that suggests that in all cases of intrafamilial abuse the perpetrator should be removed from the home (Ryan and Lane 1991). Such a stance, it is argued, can be too prescriptive and at times unworkable. Bengis and colleagues produced a comprehensive set of standards for young people in sex offence specific residential programmes. Standard 4 states that young people have the 'right to treatment in the least restrictive setting that maximises resident and community safety' (Bengis *et al.* 1999: 16). Temporary separation of the victim and the abuser may be necessary but professional approaches to families at the point of disclosure should be refocused to ensure a more differentiated response based on a thorough assessment. The AIM assessment model (Print *et al.* 2001), currently being used in the UK across the whole of the Greater Manchester area, provides an extremely effective and research-based method for undertaking an initial 'screening' assessment on children and young people who present with sexual behaviour problems (see also Chapter 3). The AIM assessment model enables practitioners to differentiate between children and young people and their families or carers about whom there are:

- *High concerns and low strengths:* where specialist residential treatment is indicated;
- *High concerns and high strengths:* where specialist community based treatment is indicated;
- *Low concerns and low strengths:* where non-specialist intervention is indicated;
- *Low concerns and high strengths:* where short-term non-specialist intervention is indicated.

When consideration is given to keeping a young person in their home setting, parents must be supported and educated more effectively than they often are currently. Professionals need to engage with and listen to parents or carers who may be experiencing significant split loyalties and be acutely upset. Intervention is required not only to help them understand and deal with their own difficult feelings but also to help them manage the young person in the household by creating appropriate boundaries to protect actual and potential victims.

Although many young people who sexually abuse can remain safely placed in their family home, a new environment may be required for some young people if there has been an adverse reaction from the family towards the abuser, or where problems within the family are so great that the changes they need to make in order to protect, supervise or contain cannot be made either in the short or long term (Bentovim 1991). In addition young people may be vulnerable themselves and may face retaliation from the family, community or placement.

Adam, a white, 15-year-old boy charged with sexual offences against neighbourhood children, needed to be moved from his foster home when he and his carers received threatening calls and were harassed by members of the community. He was subsequently moved to a residential unit but his offence behaviour again became known and he was ostracised and scapegoated by fellow residents. There being no other alternative accommodation available he was placed in bed and breakfast accommodation where the possibilities for monitoring his behaviour were dangerously minimised.

Similar incidents have been reported in the national media (see, for example, *The Guardian* 11 August 1998).

Our care system is one that is changing and evolving but perhaps not in line with increased research and knowledge about the nature of sexual abuse by children and young people. This was identified by the NCH report in 1992 and, although some progress has been made on the intervening years, particularly amongst specialist practitioners, Hackett *et al.*'s research (2003) shows that the messages from research are still not being taken on board, either at the national policy-making level or at the level of the local ACPC (now Local Safeguarding Children Board) and Youth Justice team. Over the last 15 years there has been a move towards the phasing-out of residential care for young people, with more emphasis placed on fostering provision. Utting (1997) argues, however, that residential provision does have its place, providing the necessary intensity of therapeutic support, as well as a role in containment, in some cases. This is inevitably an expensive option and one that local authorities are, therefore, often reluctant to fund. Moreover, there are only a few residential units in the United Kingdom, and none in Ireland, specialising in this area of work, which means that the involvement of the family in therapeutic work becomes difficult if the child or young person is in a unit which is geographically distant. Equally, there is a lack of specialist foster carers, in the United Kingdom and Ireland, who are able to look after this client group.

Where a young person has been accommodated, reunification is seen as an important goal. As far back as the early 1970s research has been providing evidence that it is much more difficult to rehabilitate children with their families after time has lapsed (Rowe and Lambert 1973). But the very nature of work with young people who abuse often means that intervention is of a long-term nature. In addition, many young people have a history of repeated moves and breakdowns within the care system. A general review of young people accommodated in Surrey (Surrey Children's Services 1998) demonstrated that return-home rates within a year were low, at approximately 20 per cent. Short-term fostering becomes long-term and rehabilitation and integration back into the family of origin become a more difficult task. These problems are exacerbated when the young person is known or alleged to have perpetrated sexual abuse.

Bengis (1986) promoted the idea of developing a 'continuum of care', a notion that received further support in the British context through the publication and recommendations of the NCH Report (National Children's Home 1992). Such a continuum of care suggests that service provision needs to be sensitive to the range of young people who abuse and the risks they pose: from less restrictive, less intensive environments for those deemed to be low-risk, to secure accommodation and custody in some cases where there is a need for greater community protection. Within this range of provision should be included community-based options such as the young person living at home, in the extended family, in foster care or in supported lodgings schemes where there is some degree of monitoring and supervision. Decisions about which is the most appropriate placement should be made in the light of an assessment of risk, as well as an assessment of the young person's therapeutic needs and motivation for treatment. Additionally it should be borne in mind that the placement chosen should comprise the least restrictive environment available commensurate with these factors.

Risk has become a key criterion for determining resources (Morrison 1998) and decisions about which is the most suitable placement are often closely linked to the degree of risk that the young person presents in his own home or in the community. However, risk is difficult to determine and our approaches and models have not been empirically tested. Deciding on the risk which a young person may pose within the community can be daunting and it is easy to overreact. Decisions may not be made in a thoughtful and rational way. For example, studies by Doughty and Schneider (1987), Maynard and Wiederman (1997) and Harnett (1997) demonstrate that practitioners often rate the dangerousness of their client as higher than it actually is. In general, these studies report that professionals hold more negative attitudes to sexual offenders than non-sexual offenders, with sympathy reserved for victims and not perpetrators. Risks also need to be managed appropriately over time. As work progresses with a young person the 'perceived' risk may rise rapidly (and cause panic) as more information becomes available. In fact the actual risk may have significantly decreased because the young person's behaviour is better understood and can be monitored more effectively. Further guidelines are needed and use made of the lists of risk factors that might influence placement and therapeutic treatment decisions which have been provided by several authors (Wenet and Clarke 1986; Ross and Loss 1987; Perry and Orchard 1992; Hoghughi *et al.* 1997; Worling and Curwen 2001; Print *et al.* 2002).

Providing the right type of accommodation is very important in terms of avoiding relapse. Preventing re-offending often starts with the external constraints and careful monitoring that can be provided by the environment in which the young person lives and by the people who care for him. However, as work progresses with the young person this external control should give way to internal controls, insight and a real change in behaviour and thus a change of placement which enables the young person to exercise these internal controls may be appropriate.

> *'Jack' was a 16-year-old who admitted sexually abusing 3-year-old son of his foster carers. He acknowledged having sexual fantasies about young boys. He was placed in a residential children's home and attended a specialist therapeutic facility. After a period of weekly therapy he had developed sufficient internal controls to enable him to be safely placed back with the foster carers.*

It has been identified that a significant proportion of all sexual abuse is perpetrated within the environment in which the young person lives (Manocha and Mezey 1998). Powerful dilemmas are therefore raised about whether it is deemed necessary to remove the young person for a period of time and, if so, what alternative resources are available. A survey of referrals to ACT, a specialist treatment resource in Surrey, indicated that many young people did remain at home but without recourse to a risk assessment to establish the extent to which the young person's presence might place others at continued risk. For others, their sexually abusive behaviour facilitated removal to general residential care where there were children who were particularly vulnerable because abuse had already become an integral part of their history. Whilst there was a great deal of skill and commitment from staff in the residential sector, they appeared to be inadequately prepared and trained to deal with the type of behaviour the young person might exhibit. This often resulted in placement breakdown and the move of the young person to a more contained and specialist setting. Many carers and accommodation providers encountered in the survey described a heightened sense of anxiety when managing this client group. What is required in these situations is a commitment from agencies to train and support residential staff and foster carers so they are clear about the focus of their work and to provide effective, complementary educational and therapeutic services. The author's experience in the Republic of Ireland has found that the picture mirrors the findings of the Surrey survey.

For a small proportion of young people, their level of dangerousness is such that a more specialist residential environment is the only realistic option. These placements are costly. For other young people who are particularly difficult to place, specialist community options can be created where a single young person is staffed around the clock by a team of residential workers. This is a short-term solution as it can be seen as isolating for the young person. Foster care is an under-utilised option, primarily because there is a lack of available carers without younger or developmentally less advanced children in placement. It may well be, however, that the family environment and parenting which such placements can offer have the potential to fulfil many of the needs of these young people. The author's experience in Ireland suggests that this is, potentially, the most effective care setting for those young people who cannot remain at home, if it can combine the benefits of foster care, as opposed to residential care, with the benefits of intensive specialised community-based therapeutic treatment such as is usually only available in a specialist residential facility.

Based on the concept of a 'continuum of care', a range of available services are recommended with increasing levels of supervision commensurate with the level of risk. In particular the following are advocated:

- Specialist foster care
- Specialist residential unit
- Supported lodgings scheme.

It is vital that there is sufficient capacity within the system to ensure that children can be matched to placements by need rather than by available resources. Whilst it is recognised that with limited resources a continuum of care may not be possible within a small geographical area this may be achieved by utilising and combining resources across county or local authority boundaries.

In summary, in working with children and young people who abuse, professionals have largely focused on the investigation and treatment phases of work, whilst the issue of accommodation has largely been ignored and constraints on budgets have led to constrictions in the resources available. As others have also recommended (Farmer and Pollock 1998), it is argued here that the range and flexibility of accommodation must be increased, together with improvements made in the quality of services offered, through training, support and consultation. Effective links between different agencies within the community are needed to develop services which are appropriate to the needs of service users, in the context of a strategic vision and over-arching policies which dovetail with national policy and provision, as discussed in Chapters 2 and 3 of this book.

Making decisions about placements: process issues

A key issue in making placement decisions is the decision-making process itself. Successful management of cases involving children and young people who sexually abuse relies on a coherent and consistent response from all agencies working with such cases. It involves exercising professional judgement and authority by people who have been allocated power over the lives of others. The appropriate use of such power and authority in cases of sexual abuse (where power has been abused) is crucial. However, the application of such principles of good practice is not always easy, and the decision-making process can be fraught with misunderstanding and confusion.

In looking at the interactional aspects of the decision-making process it is important to distinguish between content and process. In the decision-making process the *content* might be described as the issue of how and where a young person who sexually abuses is placed. John Burnham defines this process as: 'patterns of negotiation that develop gradually through trial and error' (Burnham 1986: 11).

Such patterns can be formulated explicitly according to agreed rules about such things as hierarchy, roles and responsibilities or lines of communication. However, other patterns also develop and emerge outside the awareness of the workers involved. This might mean that as professionals (with different agendas, attitudes and expectations) seek to negotiate a common belief system and a way to proceed, so covert relationships and communication processes develop which can cause the decision-making process to founder.

The capacity for the professional system to mirror the dysfunctional processes in the client family has been well-documented (Britton 1981; Berkowitz and Leff 1984; Dimmock and Dungworth 1985; Reder 1986; Furniss 1991). Reder suggests that 'this process appears most pronounced when the central family has problems with organization and authority' (Reder 1983: 24).

This is demonstrated in the case of Bertie where disarray in the judicial and care proceedings tended to reflect the disarray in Bertie's family. Bertie was a white child of 12 who had been systematically abused by an uncle from the age of 3. In addition, his behaviour towards other children was described by his teachers as sexualised and abusive. The family and uncle were investigated and Bertie was removed from his home. He was placed in the most immediately available children's home. Due to contested care proceedings Bertie was subjected to a variety of assessments without any coherent plan involving his family or his overall needs. Throughout the process, relationships and patterns of communication between professionals became increasingly problematic.

Alliances were formed between professionals who agreed on certain courses of action. Those who held alternative views felt excluded. Sensing this they then attempted to introduce their opinions and views in unhelpful ways. As coalitions were established, the open forum for sharing of ideas was replaced by more covert discussions. Roles and tasks overlapped and boundaries became diffuse as those working with different aspects of the case sought to apply their points of view and support the interest of those they felt they represented. The social worker holding the case coped with a variety of conflicting agendas and injunctions from associates by allying himself closely with Bertie and so losing the much needed opportunity for an overview of the whole case. The effect of such incoherence was that professionals became stuck with their own processes and were unable to formulate a clear plan for Bertie's future. A systemic paralysis set in.

A key feature highlighted by this example is that of escalating confusion. The more workers tried to deal with the case according to their own ideas and beliefs, the more problematic things became. Instead of taking the time and space to consider alternative solutions collectively, workers, operating from within their own belief systems, applied their own particular approaches more rigorously and thus the attempted solutions became the problem (Watzlawick *et al.* 1974).

In order to explore how such processes occur within the professional system it is important to look at the contexts that define and organise behaviour. One influencing context may be the client family with which the professional system is engaged. Equally, the belief systems of the workers' agencies and families will inform the way workers undertake their respective tasks and interact with professionals and clients.

The model of the Coordinated Management of Meaning (Burnham *et al.* 1999) provides a frame for looking at the way multiple levels of context are hierarchically organised and operate reflexively in loops of reciprocal influence. Each level of context is influenced by the one above (contextual force) and to a lesser degree asserts influence upwards on the above context (implicative force). One can see how contexts defined behaviour in this recursive way in the case of Bertie. A pervading atmosphere of alarm about the degree of the abuse Bertie had sustained, coupled with alarm about his own sexualised behaviour, instigated his summary removal from home and the institution of care proceedings. Bertie's family, working in accordance with their own rules about family closeness and loyalty, promptly contested the care proceedings and sought to maintain contact with Bertie. Isolated from his family and confused by events, Bertie looked for comfort and intimacy via behaviours deemed inappropriate. In the absence of any assessment that took into account the contextual influences on his behaviour, Bertie was labelled as high-risk, contact with his parents was seen as dangerous and they were refused access to him and so the atmosphere of alarm was perpetuated.

It could be argued that unless workers are aware of the dictates and rules, and the belief systems generated by the multiple contexts in which they operate, they are more likely to be subject to the unhelpful and largely unconscious processes that can arise in cases such as sexual abuse. The following discussion considers the aspects of three significant contexts which can unhelpfully organise the way in which professionals engage in decision making about young people who sexually abuse and in particular, explores the way in which these contexts can produce the rigid or entrenched positions among workers that militate against useful therapeutic manoeuvrability and successful professional collaboration (Menzies 1970; Bentovim 1992; Morrison 1998; Bankes 2002).

Community, media and society: the atmosphere of alarm that surrounds sexual abuse

Social and cultural attitudes to sexual abuse by young people provide a powerful overarching context within which professionals in this field address their work. In any case where risk to others is involved there is a requirement for social workers to assess that risk and act decisively, with some speed, to protect those who are vulnerable. This can be experienced by practitioners as pressure and in cases of sexual abuse this sense of pressure is compounded. Sexual abuse is a highly emotive subject. The notion of young people as sexually abusive can inspire fear, repugnance and alarm at a most primitive level (Olafson *et al.* 1993) and these attitudes are commonly presented and indeed almost encouraged by the media (Soothill 1997). The community does not want its children to be at risk or to be seen as a risk and the media will quickly denounce those guardians who fail to sanitise or to protect. Blanchard (1995) suggests that constant exposure to the media and public opinion may lead to a less than humanistic attitude in professionals. Media censure is a powerful organising force.

Workers in abuse cases often feel this pressure – not only to 'Do Something Quickly' but also to 'Get It Right'. Such imperatives can easily contradict each other. Workers making placement decisions require time and an atmosphere of calm in which to share and consider all the information available. In the absence of such a context they make decisions with the paralysing fear that they may be responding too quickly or not quickly enough.

Creating a space for the decision-making process is vital. Part of this involves raising awareness of the fact of sexual abuse by children and young people. Where there is little or no knowledge, there often tends to be an unrealistic fear. In the imagination of the uninformed and through the messages of the media, children are transformed very quickly from innocents to evil monsters (James and Jenks 1996). Indeed a quick word search in *The Guardian* and *The Times* newspapers reveals that the word 'evil' is used almost three times as often in the reporting of cases of abuse than all other subjects put together. Organising training events and liaison with community groups, associated professional bodies, carers, families and, at a management level, in agencies is the only way to help forestall the paralysing atmosphere of fear and alarm that can hinder the management of such cases.

The professional context: agencies' different belief system

Alarm and anxiety in the community about sexual abuse by young people raises questions of responsibility. Work with young people who sexually abuse usually involves a number of different agencies, as well as carers, and a sense of alarm can impact upon all of these groupings. Each agency involved in the work and in the decision-making process will have a different perspective on the case, a different set of responsibilities and different statutory or discretionary powers (Bentovim 1998). It is in this professional context that one recognises the tension that is inherent in the decision-making process between meeting the therapeutic needs of the young person and their family, ensuring the safety of those who are potentially vulnerable and responding to society's need to see that decisive and retributive action is taken. In cases of sexual abuse the opportunity for disagreement and difference of opinion between involved professionals is considerable. This is most evident in the area of risk. Workers can polarise in their views. One GP, who saw a young person and his family, dismissed the concerns that had been raised, saying that the young person's actions had been no more than sexual experimentation. The parents of the child who had been abused did not see it that way and neither did the social worker. In another case a boy who had sexually abused his younger siblings and was receiving therapy was hastily removed from a residential establishment because he had been discovered engaging in mutual masturbation with peer-aged boys.

It is possible that some of the difficulties that these cases provoked could have been avoided if a forum had been available in which ideas, anxieties and opinions could have been aired. Unfortunately case conferences are unlikely to provide such a forum, being content- rather than process-oriented (Bacon 1988). They are also likely to include parents and so may well be an inappropriate context in which workers and professional carers can explore their own anxieties and differences.

If workers feel vulnerable and isolated (often this can be a 'mirroring' of the dynamics of sexual abuse within the professional system) they are more likely to become entrenched in their views and seek the safety and certainty of a particular position (Morrison 1994). This might mean forming an allegiance with the client they represent and/or an antipathy towards someone else in the family (Preston-Shoot and Agass 1990; Reynolds-Mejia and Levitan 1990; Justice and Justice 1993; Mintzer 1996; Bankes 2002). Such partisan positions are unhelpful in terms of gaining the emotional distance required to make holistic and collaborative assessments.

A meeting of professionals should afford workers the opportunity to express their fears; to explore the pressures they feel; to consider the way their agencies' agendas might conflict with each other and also to explore the risk factors in the case, imagined, real or possible. It is only through this initial process of sharing information, expertise and feelings that collaborative decision making can be undertaken. This process is likely to be more effective if facilitated by an independent consultant with experience in this field.

Personal: the workers' own experiences of and responses to the subject matter

The third defining context is the personal one. There are a number of reasons why workers may choose to hold certain views or take a particular position on a case with which they are working. Such choices are not always informed by conscious, professional assessment. Again the subject matter is at the heart of this. Every individual working with cases of sexual abuse among young people will bring to that work their own sexual development, sexual knowledge learned in the context of family rules, their own understanding and interpretation of cultural rules and their own emotional reactions. A worker's emotional position on the subject of sexual abuse by children and young people will almost inevitably inform their assessments and practice. Unless workers are afforded the opportunity to explore and understand their own material on this subject there is a risk that it may continually intrude on their work in unhelpful ways.

Alan Carr uses Stephen Karpman's model of the Drama Triangle (Karpman 1968) to look at the way workers in such cases can take different roles with their clients in response to their own unresolved experiences within their family of origin or unresolved issues relating to their own sexuality. He points to the way these countertransference reactions can create therapeutic impasses in the working teams:

> When one member experiences a countertransference reaction, another member usually experiences a complementary countertransference reaction, for example if one worker begins to rescue a child, another will try to rescue the parents.
>
> (Carr 1989: 95)

Carr goes on to suggest that these countertransference reactions operate at an unconscious level and if not brought into conscious awareness:

> may influence, in a dramatic way, assessment and decision making about families where child abuse has occurred.
>
> (Ibid.: 94–5)

Carr also describes the process whereby splitting and polarisation in the professional network may often mirror the splitting and polarisation within the family. In the case of Bertie, referred to earlier in this chapter, discussions took place about how the social worker felt very hostile towards the young person's family. His attitude was not shared by his associates in the case and this became an issue. Professionals trying to decide whether the young person should return to live at home were stuck with their different views and it seemed impossible to take the discussion forward. The subsequent information that Bertie's social worker had been abused himself by his father threw some light on the suspicion with which he viewed

Bertie's father. It was a courageous decision for him to bring this experience into the professional discussion, and it proved to be helpful in opening up a dialogue between him and another professional who had held a completely different view on the matter.

It has already been noted that workers who feel embattled or victimised by their own work system may over-identify with a particular client in the case. This may occur when a worker has an experience of having been embattled within his or her own family or of being the family fixer: always having to sort things out (Malan 1979; Loughlin 1992). In one such case it became evident that the female workers dealing with the case were feeling overwhelmed by the material and unsupported by their male associates who were also involved in the case. This was a direct reflection of the dynamics in the client's family and it transpired that it was also the family experience of the women workers. Whilst one might argue that such gendered dynamics can occur in any kind of work, in cases involving sexual abuse by young people the distress levels that arise can create a much more heightened response which organises professionals accordingly (Morrison 1990; Kennel and Agresti 1995; Little and Hamby 1996; Bankes 2002).

Engagement and collaboration with the young person's family is fundamental to the decision-making process but can be severely hindered by the worker's personal reactions to the case. This can be demonstrated in the way professionals decide whether or not a young person remains at home. As was suggested earlier in this chapter, the decision may, of course, be made in the light of limited resources. However, it may also be informed by a worker's feelings about the client family. A worker who has difficulty with their emotional response to the abuse or to the client's family may wish to remove the child from that family in an attempt to provide himself, the worker, with some distance from the emotional unpleasant-ness and complexity of the case. This attempt to sanitise can be rationalised by emphasising the family's severely dysfunctional nature and the need to work individually with the young person. If the goodwill and co-operation of the client family are not enlisted then a process, as described in the Bertie case, can arise whereby the family's attempts to maintain family authority and family rules with their child are viewed by the professional system as manip-ulative and dangerous. Power sanctions are then invoked by the professionals and an escalating conflict occurs, leaving the young person further bewildered and confused about issues of power and authority.

It would be unrealistic to assume that professionals' personal responses to the abuse, to the family and to the young person can be avoided. They can, however, be acknowledged, explored and used appropriately. In one case where two workers found themselves struggling with a conflict of attitudes towards a young person's behaviour, they realised through dis-cussion that they were adopting the conflicting positions of the young person's parents. The female worker minimised his offence and like his mother wanted to rescue him. The male worker, taking the father's position, felt deeply alarmed by the offence and angry with the young man. Their different reactions had threatened to disrupt the possibility of any success-ful plans being made for the young person's placement. Once these processes had been acknowledged and discussed the workers were able to use the insights these reactions offered to help their client. They expressed their dilemma to him and together explored with him the way this dilemma worked in his family. It was the beginning of a therapeutic conversation. These processes are explored in greater depth in Chapter 17.

In order for workers to feel that they can expose and explore their own sensitivities and responses to sexual abuse in this way they must have confidence and trust in the support of fellow team members. Supervision which takes such material into account is imperative; however, work like this within a team should not simply take place around individual cases.

Team-building and consultation should be on-going and should incorporate inter-agency team development. There is also an argument for professionals in this sort of work to receive additional out-of-agency consultation or therapy as discussed in Chapter 17.

Conclusion

The preceding analysis highlights the dilemmas that face many helping professionals when dealing with the vexing issue of placing children and young people who sexually abuse. Professionals do not operate in a vacuum and the delivery of services to this client group is influenced by social, professional, personal, political and financial agendas. In the light of these pressures, professionals can lose objectivity and the fundamentals of good practice can all too often be compromised.

In the first part of this chapter the placement needs of this group of young people have been highlighted, ranging from staying at home to secure accommodation. Fostering, specialist residential provision, semi-supported lodgings and living within the extended family all fall within this continuum. Decisions about the most appropriate placement should be made in the light of a risk assessment. In order to provide appropriate accommodation for these young people, it has been suggested that, at both local and national levels, consideration of financial, political and professional constraints should be addressed and strategies and guidelines produced to assist practitioners in making appropriate placement decisions. Equally, combining resources between agencies and local authorities may well be a more cost-effective way of providing some of these resources.

All the resources in the world, however, will not necessarily result in appropriate placements. In the second part of this chapter the discussion has focussed on how the decision-making process itself is beset by various conscious and unconscious agendas at societal, agency and personal levels which can result in inappropriate decisions being made. It has been recommended that practitioners and managers should be courageous enough to acknowledge and explore these processes, ideally with the assistance of an experienced independent consultant.

With the ongoing outcry about the need for community protection, the fear of many professionals is that young sexual abusers will become labelled and stigmatised in the same manner as adult paedophiles, despite the fact that the intervention and management issues are very different. Social workers and other professionals act as intermediaries between young abusers and a society that wishes to condemn them. The dilemma is simultaneously to provide for the needs of the young person, whilst protecting any potential vulnerable victims of sexual abuse, within a context of limited resources.

Note

1   In the original edition of this book, this chapter was written by members of ACT, a Surrey Social Services multidisciplinary assessment, consultation and therapeutic service for children and young people who sexually abuse and their families or carers. An important part of ACT's function is to advise social workers on appropriate placements for young sexual abusers at the point of referral and investigation through to the termination phase of therapy. The current chapter has been revised by one of the original authors who was the founder and manager of ACT from 1995 to 2002. Since the beginning of 2003 the current author has developed a similar resource in Ireland and is currently a consultant to numerous residential establishments and specialist teams in the UK and Ireland.

7 Looking after young people who are at risk for sexually abusive behaviour

Kevin Epps

Setting the scene

The care and management of children and young people with a history of sexually abusive behaviour continues to be a neglected area in the literature on young abusers. Whilst considerable attention has been given to assessment, treatment, service development and research, scant attention has been given to the challenges inherent in providing day-to-day care to this group of young people. This is a significant oversight when it is the adults providing care and education who have most contact with the young person. These individuals, whether as parents, professional carers or educators, are best placed to prevent further incidents of abuse. Their high level of contact with the young person also enables them to have a significant influence on behaviour, attitudes and beliefs. In addition, adult carers are at risk for being victims themselves, not only from direct acts of abuse, sexual or physical, but also from the anxiety associated with caring for someone who may harm others.

This task is often made even more difficult in residential settings by the exclusion of 'frontline workers' from meetings where information pertaining to risk is exchanged. Often it is the most junior, inexperienced, members of staff who are left to care for the young person, yet they have least information at their disposal. A comprehensive risk assessment is of little use if those involved in its implementation are uncertain what is required of them to manage the identified risks. In the previous version of this chapter (Epps 1999), the author concluded that 'Future development in this area of work must emphasise the need for closer integration of services, especially between residential services and fostering schemes, and the need for external agencies to monitor and evaluate the response of young abusers as they move between care and treatment settings' (p. 85). Yet, time and time again, cases come to light where information is withheld from, or not passed on to, new carers, or where obvious risks are simply ignored by service managers. Consider the following case example (in which identifying details have been altered), who was referred to the author a few weeks prior to writing this chapter.

Case example of Andrew

Andrew, aged 13, was referred for the preparation of a court report in relation to several allegations of serious sexual assault against another child. One incident was witnessed by his foster carer, who alerted the police. Andrew admitted to the charges during the initial police interview, but concerns were raised by his solicitor about fitness to plead in view of his learning difficulties and low educational attainment. During the subsequent psychological assessment the following sequence of events came to light. In childhood Andrew had been subject to considerable emotional, physical and sexual abuse by various males associated with his family. He had also suffered severe physical neglect, often sleeping on bare floorboards and having nothing to eat for several days at a time. At the age of 10 he was placed in foster care. This placement came to an end after 18 months at the request of the foster carer, who felt she was neglecting her own family and grandchildren. Andrew was then placed in several short-term foster placements until a long-term out-of-area foster placement was identified, where he remained for about one year. This placement broke down when he was accused of sexually inappropriate behaviour toward a 5-year-old boy, involving a variety of sexual acts. This incident was subject to police investigation, and no further action was taken, although Andrew openly admitted to the alleged sexually inappropriate behaviour. These incidents were fully documented and known to social services. Nevertheless, he was moved to another foster placement in his home area, where he shared a bedroom with an 8-year-old boy who was subsequently abused. This placement occurred despite the protests of local police who complained that Andrew should not share a home, let alone a bedroom, with another child. Their concerns were ignored by the duty social worker, and subsequently by social services managers, who expressed the view that the foster carer was able to provide adequate supervision to prevent further abuse. Clearly, this proved not to be the case, partly because she had not been informed of Andrew's history of sexually abusive behaviour.

The tragedy of this case is that the offence was completely avoidable. There are also two victims: the younger boy, yet another victim of sexual assault, and Andrew, facing serious criminal charges, having been placed in a situation where he was unable to manage his sexual behaviour. Andrew was not a predatory sexual offender, seeking to abuse children. He did not fully understand why his actions were wrong, although he knew that he might get into trouble if he was caught. He was a boy of limited intellectual ability who was struggling with his own sexuality, with no friends of his own age, who himself had been sexually abused. Any risks he presented would easily have been managed in a placement where his contact with other children was constantly supervised, allowing further assessment, sex education and intervention work to be carried out in the fullness of time. It is impossible to know how often this scenario is repeated across Britain. Social services managers, under pressure to save money, may feel obliged to take unnecessary risks when placing children. Effective communication, the exchange of significant information, and the implementation of a proper risk assessment strategy, were all absent in the above case, at a time when they were so critical. Sexually abusive young people such as Andrew are not the ones who should be causing us too much anxiety: there are many others where the risks are much, much greater, and where the risks are incredibly difficult to manage, even in secure settings.

Balancing the needs of the abuser with risk management

This chapter explores the problems inherent in looking after young people who are known to have engaged in some form of sexually inappropriate or sexually abusive behaviour. If this chapter has one important message it is this: carers have a responsibility to manage identified risks to avoid further incidents of abuse (a child protection issue) whilst at the same time strive to meet the needs of the young abuser (a child care issue). Achieving this balance is difficult. Programmes of care that are unnecessarily restrictive, in an effort to keep risk to an absolute minimum, will fail to meet the young person's developmental needs. In the longer term, this could increase risk because the young person will fail to develop the necessary social and emotional skills to cope with adult life. Striving to identify and meet needs, and meeting those needs, whilst also managing risks, is critical in helping the young person to develop sufficient personal skills and resources to get their own emotional and physical needs met, without recourse to inappropriate, abusive behaviour. There is now evidence that this focus on the needs and psychological well-being of the young abuser in an effort to steer them towards a more adaptive, non-abusive lifestyle, is becoming more prevalent in intervention programmes for this group of young people (Masson and Hackett 2003). Addressing the needs of young abusers is particularly important because they are developmentally immature and are more likely to respond to efforts to shift them back on to a more appropriate developmental pathway before they reach adulthood.

Inevitably, helping the young person to learn news ways of thinking, feeling and behaving involves facing up to the risks, not avoiding them. The balancing task is made more difficult by the dynamic nature of the significant variables. Young people develop and change, leading to different needs at different points in time. There are important differences between the needs of a 12-year-old and those of a 16-year-old. Similarly, the living context will change. For those living at home, as part of a family, the family structure and composition will change. Siblings grow older, people leave home, babies are born into the family, and the pattern of visitors, such as nieces and nephews, will change, creating varying degrees of access to potential victims. Consequently, risk assessment and risk management must be construed as dynamic, fluid concepts (Sheldrick 1999; Steadman *et al.* 1993). One-off, static risk assessments are time-limited. A young person considered to be 'at high risk of re-offending' on a particular day may move to the category of 'low risk of re-offending' the following day, simply because he or she has moved to a new living context with no access to potential victims. The availability of relevant, reliable, information is essential. Where risks are known, they can be managed, providing there is motivation and resources to do so. It is more anxiety-provoking to manage situations where there appear to be significant risks but little or no information, or where information is in abundance, but is unreliable.

The process of managing risk requires planning, monitoring and evaluation, sometimes over a period of several years. In addition, in common with all other management tasks, it involves making decisions and ensuring that decisions are implemented. Where should the young abuser live? What degree of contact should the young person have with potential victims? What types of therapeutic intervention are most appropriate? Decision-making requires information, and it is the quality of this information, and the decisions and actions that flow from it, that are fundamental to the management of risk. The remainder of this chapter is devoted to setting-out a decision-making framework, beginning from the point at which abuse is first identified, and balancing the needs of the perpetrator with the need to prevent further abuse. Of course, the first step in preventing abuse must be to acknowledge and accept the possibility that there is risk of abuse, and to take action to prevent it. Whilst there is growing public awareness that children can be sexually abusive, this thought is rarely uppermost in the minds of adults caring for children and young people.

Immediate priorities when abuse is first identified

Risk and the need for child protection

Discovering that a child has behaved sexually inappropriately toward another person usually comes as a shock, particularly for the child's parents. The immediate reaction will vary, but often includes powerful emotional responses, including anger, shame, fear and bewilderment, depending to some extent on the nature of the relationship with the child. The parents of the perpetrator will usually have a significant emotional involvement and a vested interest in protecting the interests of the family from external interference and the shame of being identified as an 'abusive family'. These strong emotional responses often cloud judgement and decision-making. In some instances there may be denial that abuse has occurred, or avoidance in dealing with the issue in the hope that it was a 'one-off' and will never happen again. Child-care professionals, on the other hand, have a professional obligation to report abuse and to follow local child protection procedures setting out appropriate courses of action.

However, the professional focus of attention may soon shift to trying to understand the actions of the abusive child, and identifying suitable therapeutic intervention. This can sometimes occur at the expense of immediate risk management, in which the focus is on taking steps to prevent further abuse to protect other children, whilst ensuring that the young abuser is safely looked after. Some form of local risk assessment and risk management should begin immediately. Whilst it may take some time to obtain an 'expert' view from suitably qualified and experienced practitioners, the young person should not be left in the meantime in a position where further abuse can be perpetrated. The main priority must be to secure the safety of potential victims. At this stage information is required about the likely degree of contact between the perpetrator and the victim(s) of abuse and the extent to which this contact is controlled and supervised. It is also desirable to have information about likely contact between the abuser and other children and the extent to which these may be at risk from the abuser.

If the safety of potential victims cannot be guaranteed within the current living arrangements, the perpetrator may need to be removed to another setting where the risk is reduced. Making these types of decisions is difficult as reliable information is sometimes lacking. Decisions can then be made without consideration of the possible outcomes. For example, the perpetrator may be removed unnecessarily, or placed in a setting where other children may be put at risk. Alternatively, he may be placed in a situation where he is at risk from various types of abusive experience, perhaps in a poorly supervised setting with older, delinquent children. Effective risk management plans should aim to maximise the benefits, and be reviewed regularly to ensure that negative consequences are kept to a minimum.

Currently, there are insufficient resources to deal with sexually abusive children (Masson and Hackett 2003). Young people who continue to abuse because they are inadequately supervised often find themselves being moved from one child-care placement to another, creating more victims along the way. They may also lose confidence in adults and become even more socially isolated, possibly withdrawing even further into a world of sexual fantasy which, in turn, increases the risk of further abusive behaviour. The development of specialised, local, fostering resources, with high levels of supervision and awareness of the need to protect other children would help to overcome these problems, allowing further assessment to take place in a safe environment (Lee and Olender 1992). This type of fostering placement can provide time for further assessment and planning, thereby facilitating the development of longer-term plans for care and intervention.

Meeting the needs of the young abuser

Whilst in the first instance it is important to address child protection concerns, attention also needs to be given to meeting the needs of the young abuser. Although some disruption to daily life is inevitable, this should be kept to a minimum. Unfortunately, the reality is that the lack of specialised resources often leads to a considerable degree of disruption in care and education arrangements. Young abusers are sometimes placed a considerable distance from home, making family contact and school attendance difficult. Similarly, they may be placed in unsuitable care settings. In a study of 40 looked-after sexually abused and/or abusing young people placed in either foster or residential care, Farmer and Pollock (1999) found that more than two thirds were placed with little consideration given to how the young person would fit in with other young people in that setting. Alarmingly, in many cases no information about the young person's history of sexual abuse was given to the caregivers, as in the case of Andrew described earlier in this chapter.

Consideration needs to be given to the amount and type of family contact that is appropriate, especially if the victim of abuse is a member of the family unit as other children in the family could be at risk. Initially, all family visits may need to be supervised to ensure that there is no inappropriate verbal or physical behaviour between the young abuser and other children, and to make an assessment of parental and family interaction. Information is also required about parental attitudes to the disclosure of sexually abusive behaviour, especially significant if the victim is part of the family.

Abusers who continue to make threats against the victim of abuse, apportion blame to the victim, or attempt to convince family members that the victim is lying, should not have contact with the victim. Some abusers can be quite subtle in their efforts to intimidate children, using eye contact and body posture to induce anxiety. The amount and quality of contact by telephone also needs to be considered. To avoid the possibility of the abuser harassing the victim it may be necessary to control use of the telephone. In many residential units this is managed by adults dialling the number to make the connection, and then passing the telephone to the young person. In extreme cases, visits and telephone contact with the family can be temporarily stopped, using Section 34(6) of the Children Act 1989 (Department of Health 1991a). It is important not to underestimate the damage that can be done by abusers through verbal interactions over the telephone.

The provision of education can also cause difficulties. Whilst many abusive children continue to attend mainstream school, there are instances where the risks are unacceptable, requiring the abuser to move school or have some other form of educational provision. There is likely to be particular concern if the young person has perpetrated abuse within the school setting, or shown some other form of sexually inappropriate behaviour, such as exposing his genitals or masturbating in public. Alternatively, the view may be reached that the risk of abuse within school is very low: there may be no evidence of behavioural problems, sexual or otherwise, and the victim(s) of abuse may be many years younger than the school peer group. For example, unless there is evidence to the contrary, there is no reason to believe that a 15-year-old boy who has sexually abused a 5-year-old girl will present a sexual risk to his male teenage peer group at school. However, it may nevertheless be prudent to arrange for the boy to be escorted to and from school, and to ensure that he is under adult supervision when there is a possibility of contact with younger children.

Finding suitable educational provision for abusive children who are removed from school can be problematic. Home tuition can sometimes be arranged, although this is often time-limited, with a restricted curriculum. In the longer term, attendance at a special school can sometimes be arranged. However, this may not be appropriate for the minority of abusive children who are particularly persistent and predatory in their abuse, as many schools do not have adequate resources to offer effective continuous supervision. One particularly abusive adolescent boy seen by the author attended a special school for several years, during which time he managed to continue to abuse younger, vulnerable children, and engage peers in sexual activity. His stay at the school came to an end after he was found in the school toilets with his trousers round his ankles, anally raping another boy, whilst the adult providing 'constant' supervision waited outside with other children, unaware of what was taking place inside the toilet cubicle.

Longer-term goals: developing a framework for managing risk

Abusive behaviour occurs within a particular context, at a specific point in time. It involves a perpetrator and a victim who both possess specific characteristics. An informed view of the extent to which an abuser is at risk of committing further acts of sexual abuse requires information to be collected about each of these factors.

Abuser characteristics

Assessment of the young abuser is covered elsewhere in this volume. Attention here is given to information that is especially pertinent to the management of risk and the prevention of abuse. There is sometimes overwhelming evidence that other children are at risk and yet, for some reason, the evidence is not acted upon. For example, several years ago the author was instructed by a solicitor to undertake an assessment of a young boy ('Francis'), as part of care proceedings. One of the questions to be addressed in the assessment was the extent to which Francis was at risk of sexually abusing other children, in view of the fact that he had been sexually abused during childhood. There was no suggestion in the instructions that this boy had been abusive. However, on receiving the background documentation the question of whether there might be a risk became superfluous: Francis had been sexually abusing other children since the age of 5 and had continued abusing in every placement and school since that time. This information was well documented, yet other children had continued to be exposed to abuse and no effort had been made to address his abusive behaviour. Assessment revealed that some of the professionals involved in his care and education were unaware of the history of abusive behaviour, whilst others considered it to be a historical problem or had minimised its significance. Communication between the various professionals was patchy, and the situation had been allowed to drift for many years until care proceedings were initiated. No one had taken an overview of Francis' development and considered him as a 'whole person'. Consequently, each placement had managed the presenting problems with no historical perspective.

Although this case example is by no means exceptional, information about the young person and the extent of his abusive behaviour is often difficult to obtain, particularly where there has been no previous statutory involvement. Abuse can sometimes go undetected for many years, and not all abusers display behavioural or emotional problems that attract attention: there is no one 'type' of person, no single personality 'profile', associated with sexual offending. For example, in contrast to Francis is the case of 'David', a 15-year-old accused of anally raping two younger boys in a local park on several different occasions. These are obviously extremely serious offences which, if proven and convicted, would have resulted in a long custodial sentence. David vehemently denied the offences, and there was no obvious background information suggesting that he had a propensity for this type of violent sexual behaviour. He came from an intact family with no criminal or psychiatric history, and no previous contact with Social Services; had no recorded history of offending or behavioural problems; was a 'model' school pupil; belonged to several local clubs and charities; regularly helped his elderly grandmother, doing her chores and shopping on a Saturday; and presented in interview as anxious and apprehensive. He said he had a girl-friend, whom he had kissed, but denied having any sexual experiences, abusive or otherwise, and limited sexual knowledge. Psychometric assessment showed nothing unusual with respect to his intellectual ability, personality or emotional functioning. However, although David did not seem like the 'type of person' who might commit acts of sexual violence against children, the absence of overt behavioural, family and psychological problems did not make it safe to conclude that he could not have committed such acts. David was in fact subsequently convicted and sentenced, partly on the basis of incontrovertible forensic evidence that later came to light. Nevertheless, he maintained his denial throughout, and has never admitted to the offences.

The examples of Francis and David are, fortunately, extreme examples. Not all abusers are as persistent in their abuse as Francis, and most of those who do come to the attention of child-care professionals present with less resistance and denial, and more overt behavioural and emotional problems, than David. Nevertheless, these two examples serve to illustrate that abusive behaviour is not associated with any specific cluster of behavioural, family or personality variables. Some offenders, however, are clearly more risky than others, regardless of the situation: they possess personal characteristics that increase the risk of offending. In assessing risk it is especially important to gain a holistic picture of the way in which the young person functions emotionally, cognitively and behaviourally in a range of situations. Most risk assessment measures, such as the ERASOR (Worling and Curwen 2001), provide a structured approach to this task, with a view to enhancing clinical judgement. One factor that is particularly important when assessing and managing risk is the ability and motivation of the abusive young person to control, manage and modify his behaviour. Abusive children who are impulsive, overactive, restless, agitated, emotionally volatile and preoccupied with sexual fantasies and sexual activity are more unpredictable and difficult to supervise, and certainly provoke a great deal more anxiety in their carers.

Various factors can diminish or undermine the ability and motivation to stop abusing. These include: established, habitual patterns of abusive behaviour; preoccupation with deviant sexual fantasies, especially when reinforced by exposure to pornography; entrenched beliefs and attitudes which support abusive behaviour, particularly when the same views are held by other members of the child's family; psychiatric disorders, such as Attention Deficit Hyperactivity Disorder (ADHD), or chronic substance abuse, which can impair the learning of behavioural and cognitive self-control strategies; cognitive difficulties, such as impaired intellectual functioning, which may restrict the ability to plan behaviour and to consider behavioural outcomes; emotional difficulties, such as an impaired ability to see things from the perspective of others or to empathise with others; and social and relationship problems, for example, an inability to trust adults, or to form attachments, or to make friends with peers. Some of these problems, especially in the emotional and behavioural domains, are more likely in children with disrupted care and attachments in early childhood, especially if this is compounded by abuse, neglect and inadequate attention to socialisation. The need to tease out the relative contribution of different factors, especially the extent to which abusive patterns of thinking and behaviour are entrenched in the daily psychological functioning of the young person, reinforces the need for individualised problem-focused assessment.

Abuse behaviour

Specific details about sexual offending behaviour are frequently neglected during the process of managing and treating sexually abusive children. Information about the circumstances of the offence, and the behaviour of the abuser, is sometimes never collected. Alternatively, it is lost or buried in the case files. Sometimes, however, it is important to be reminded exactly what took place during the offence. For example, consider the case of two boys convicted of rape against a child. One of the boys stopped his sexual assault when the victim became obviously distressed and upset, whilst the other continued his assault and seemed to derive satisfaction from the victim's distress. Whilst both were convicted of the same offence, these differences in offence behaviour provide important clues about the psychological make-up of the offender and also contribute to the formulation of risk and, ultimately, treatment approaches. When reviewing risk management plans it is useful to be reminded what the abuser did and to reflect on the psychological characteristics that allowed the behaviour to occur. After all, what psychological mechanisms or processes allow a boy to ignore the obvious distress of his child victim when he is committing rape? Is there evidence in other areas of his behaviour that he continues to be callous and lacking in empathy? Collecting information about offences, especially victim characteristics (age, gender, relationship to offender, physical characteristics, emotional and social functioning); the types of abusive behaviour perpetrated against the victim ('grooming' behaviours, sexual behaviours, verbal and physical threats, use of force and violence); and situational factors (location of offence, time of day, social context) contributes enormously to the estimation of risk and the development of strategies to reduce risk. Based on the principle that past behaviour is the best predictor of future behaviour, it is sometimes possible to describe consistent features of offence behaviour and identify high-risk scenarios that should be avoided.

Context

The significance of understanding the reciprocal relationship that exists between an abusive young person and his immediate social environment (family home, foster placement, residential setting or school) has been alluded to earlier. Whatever the care context, there is an expectation that adults will be proactive in preventing abuse and create a safe environment in which children are protected from abuse. Regardless of the type of care environment particular attention must be given to observation and supervision of the young abuser. Observation is often construed as a passive exercise. However, in care settings it is very much an action-oriented task, requiring direct behavioural observation, recording (i.e. log books, notes, clinical records) and, where necessary, some form of appropriate action in response to specific behaviours. Adults responsible for observation and supervision need to know what is expected of them. Good practice requires the level of observation to be made explicit in care plans. These may range from simply knowing the location of the young person (e.g. upstairs in his bedroom) to being within arm's reach at all times. At any one point in the day it should be clear who is responsible for observation and supervision. Further, it may be necessary to make arrangements for occasions when the primary observer is unavailable, such as during meal breaks and toilet breaks. A management strategy adopted in one particular children's home, for example, was for the primary observer to hold a key in their hand as a reminder of their role. If for some reason this individual could not fulfil that role they were required to hand the key to a back-up member of staff, who would then assume the role of primary observer. This strategy prevented breakdown in continuous observation and gave the primary observer a clearly defined role.

Good observation and supervision also require the establishment and maintenance of appropriate behavioural boundaries. The setting of behavioural limits is a basic requirement of good child-care practice, helping to promote healthy psychological and social adjustment. Children who lack boundaries are more likely to feel anxious and insecure, and be exposed to inappropriate learning experiences. The backgrounds of sexually abusive young people who exhibit behavioural and conduct problems are often characterised by a failure to establish and maintain appropriate behavioural and relationship boundaries. Research indicates that these children are especially likely to create difficulties when entering residential or foster placements (Farmer 1998).

Family and foster care

Within a family-type context attention needs to be given to the quality of parental and family functioning and the impact of this on the level of adult supervision. Whilst the research literature on the families of young abusers is sparse, practitioners and families now have access to a range of useful books and resources aimed at the families of sexually abusive young people (e.g. Hackett 2001). Family units operating with little or no external support can find themselves vulnerable to various factors that undermine the quality of adult supervision. There may be illness, work commitments, or the need to devote attention to other children. These factors can detract from the task of providing adequate supervision, and can contribute to placement breakdown (see Sinclair *et al.* 2004). In addition, some adults have the additional burden of dealing with their own experiences of abuse and victimisation. Wilson (1998) suggests that the ability of some women to protect their children is diminished by the psychological consequences of their own victimisation within an abusive relationship. Women who have been victims of childhood sexual abuse, and who live in an abusive adult relationship, may be particularly vulnerable to feeling powerless to draw attention to abuse that is taking place. Psychological avoidance strategies often develop as a way of coping with intolerable thoughts and feelings. Consequently, subtle warning signs indicating that abuse is taking place may be missed or not acted on. For example, changes in the abused child's behaviour may be ignored or viewed in isolation, and thoughts about the possibility of abuse may be dismissed or pushed out of conscious thinking. In other instances, however, the decision not to intervene may be deliberate. Some women are physically threatened by their abusive partner, or feel that they have too much to lose if they take action. Wilson recommends that child protection issues should be considered within the broader context of domestic violence.

However, concern has also been expressed in the child abuse literature that too much responsibility has been placed on women to protect children from abuse (Edleson 1997; Wilson 1998). The role of non-abusive men in protecting children, in contrast, has received relatively scant attention (O'Hagan 1997; Roberts 1998). During child protection investigations the focus is usually on mothers, while fathers and other male carers are often overlooked. If such stereotypes remain unchallenged opportunities to increase safety for children are often lost.

Children's homes and secure units

Children living in children's homes are particularly vulnerable to sexual abuse. Farmer (1998) collected data on 250 looked-after children. Of these, 96 (38 per cent) either had a history of sexual abuse and/or were sexually abusive, whilst 50 per cent of the adolescent girls in the study had been sexually abused. A number of factors can either help or hinder effective management of abusive children in a residential setting. Particular attention needs to be given to the peer-group composition, with respect to age, gender and vulnerability. The extent to which other children in the same placement share similar characteristics to the abuser's victim(s) is an important consideration when placing an abusive child in a residential setting. Unless there is evidence to the contrary there is no reason, for example, why a female adolescent abuser who has targeted younger boys aged 7 and 8 years should necessarily present a risk to adolescent girls.

In placing an abusive young person it is important to consider recent behaviour and attitudes in addition to historical information. Information held on file may be out of date, failing to reflect current concerns. In contrast, historical information may lead the young person to be inappropriately 'labelled' as a risk, particularly where there is an absence of detail about the specific nature of the abuse or allegations. In the absence of this information all other children are sometimes considered to be at-risk, severely restricting the type of placement that is considered suitable. In other instances information about recent abusive behaviour is overlooked or minimised, illustrated earlier in this chapter by the case example of Andrew. Another example is the case of an adolescent boy placed in a children's home because of his delinquent behaviour. Here he was observed to sexually threaten and intimidate adolescent girls, and members of staff expressed concern about the risk of sexual assault. However, when he was later admitted to a mixed-sex secure unit because of his violent behaviour, information about his sexual threats was not included in the referral. He subsequently committed a sexual assault on a female peer, and it was only then that information about his previous sexual threats came to light. It is always important to look behind labels to examine the behaviour of the young person and to consider risk in light of current behaviour.

Within residential settings the concept of 'dynamic security' is useful. In recent years considerable attention has been given to the need for physical security in schools and children's homes, and the need for buildings to be designed in a way that facilitates supervision. However, it is equally important that staff have sufficient insight into peer-group dynamics to be able to detect early warning signs so that they can prevent abuse. In extreme cases specialised care arrangements are necessary to avoid the risk of abuse. For example, the young person may be looked after in isolation away from the peer group, with a dedicated staff team to provide constant care. Clearly, this is not a satisfactory long-term solution: apart from the obvious resource implications, social isolation can be a damaging experience, especially during childhood and adolescence. However, there may be no other option, especially if the child has a long history of sexual assaults against children and is persistent and determined in his attempts to continue to abuse.

It is advisable in residential settings to have written policies informing young people, and carers, about the limits of acceptable behaviour, especially the degree of permissible physical contact. For example, should children be allowed to hug each other? Are older children allowed to form intimate relationships and, if so, what degree of physical contact is allowed? Should staff engage children in 'rough-and-tumble' play? Clearly, policy and practice in these areas will be determined by a variety of factors, such as organisational ethos and philosophy, age of the children, developmental needs and degree of vulnerability.

There is always a risk that some abusers will exploit opportunities for physical contact to gain sexual arousal or to groom potential victims. What may appear to be harmless play in the swimming pool, for example, could act as a source of sexual arousal for a young abuser. In making decisions about physical contact it is important to consider the extent to which the young abuser is deliberately planning and manipulating situations to gain sexual arousal, and the extent to which he is able to talk about his sexual feelings and fantasies in various situations. Sexual abusers who are persistent in their attempts to conceal their sexual behaviour, and who encourage other children to share secrets, are more difficult to manage and likely to provoke anxiety in their carers.

Sexually abusive behaviour is less likely to occur in care settings that strive to develop an anti-oppressive culture, in which children are encouraged to be assertive, open and honest in their attitudes and relationships. Part of the role of carers is to help children learn the boundaries of acceptable, healthy relationships, and to give children the confidence to assert their own personal boundaries (see Gilbert 1988). In one of the few studies looking at the outcome of abuse-prevention education and training, boys who had received training perceived themselves as less likely to be abused (Dziuba-Leatherman and Finkelhor 1994). Through social-learning processes, such as modelling, the behaviour of adults also has a significant influence on child behaviour.

There is a need for carers to be especially mindful of potential 'hot-spots' where there is an increased risk of abuse. Hot-spots include times of the day when children are in close proximity, such as in the classroom, at bedtime or at meal-times. Abusive children have been known to sit next to younger, vulnerable children at meal-times and carry out abusive sexual acts under the table hidden from adult view. Other hot-spots arise at unstructured times of the day, when adult supervision may be lax. For example, in the evening when children are engaged in individual recreational activities, or during the night, when children may be able to gain unsupervised access to the bedroom of another child. It is important that carers are aware of the need for vigilance and effective supervision, and to accept that abusive acts can be carried out in a matter of seconds.

Within any child-care environment there is a risk that behavioural boundaries will gradually shift to the benefit of an abuser, with adults failing to recognise the long-term trend. For example, in a residential setting there may be a gradual increase in rough-and-tumble play between children, to which staff become accustomed. Boundary shifting can be a particular problem in residential settings, where the high level of daily contact between staff and children can make it difficult to maintain an objective view of the social environment. The use of external managers and consultants who are able to provide independent overview can help to overcome this problem.

Reducing risk by helping the young abuser to stop abusing

The focus of the present chapter has been on the prevention of sexual abuse through developing an understanding of the abuser and his abusive behaviour, and creating a safe care environment in which adult carers gain a better understanding of the young abuser's needs and the likely risks he presents. The onus has been on the adult carers taking preventative measures and, if necessary, exerting control over the young abuser. However, this is not a long-term solution to preventing abuse. The status quo cannot be maintained indefinitely: sexually abusive children grow into young adults, gaining more freedom and access to situations in which they may be at risk of abusing. Consequently, some attempt should be made to intervene directly with the young abuser to reduce their risk of perpetrating further acts of abuse.

Becker and Kaplan (1988) identified three developmental paths taken by young abusers, one of which is the 'dead-end' path, in which the abuser stops abusing of his own accord with no intervention. Unfortunately, the current level of knowledge is insufficient to allow us to distinguish with any degree of confidence those young abusers who will follow the dead-end path from those who will continue their abusive behaviour, perhaps into adulthood. However, it is possible to identify young abusers who are more likely to present a higher degree of risk (Christodoulides *et al.* 2005). Although research in this field is limited, there is an obligation to use the knowledge that is available to direct therapeutic intervention resources to those young people considered most at risk of abusing. Young abusers who have experienced profoundly damaging and disrupting childhood trauma, who are persistent in their abuse, and preoccupied with sexually abusive behaviour, seem to be at particular risk.

The role of therapeutic intervention

Managing risk is less anxiety provoking when the abusive young person is fully engaged in a programme of therapeutic work, particularly when this work is underpinned by openness, honesty and trust. Practitioners in this field of work know only too well that most assessments leave many questions unanswered and provide inadequate opportunity to establish trust and confidence. Information is often lacking, creating uncertainty about potential risks. Insight into the psychological world of the abusive young person is best achieved through active engagement in a programme of intervention. This is illustrated by the findings on the proportion of young sex offenders who report a history of sexual abuse. Worling (1995) compared data on sexual abuse across different studies, with a combined total of 1,268 participants. The studies using pre-treatment data reported a mean abuse rate only of 22 per cent, compared to 52 per cent in the studies using post-treatment information. Worling notes that this finding 'corroborates the clinical experience of those who state that many adolescent sex offenders only acknowledge a sexual victimisation history after they have formed a trusting relationship with a therapist' (p. 610).

Recent years have seen an expansion in the number of treatment programmes for sexually abusive children. Most programmes use structured group-work and/or individual work, employing a variety of cognitive-behavioural interventions, although individual psychotherapy also has an important role to play. The benefits of formal intervention approaches are enhanced if the work is supported by those responsible for caring for the young person on a daily basis. The development of personal strengths that serve as protective factors (e.g. self-esteem, self-control) requires support and encouragement from carers and other significant adults, such as teachers and relatives. However, there is research indicating a chronic lack of confidence and skill in dealing with the problem of sexually abusive behaviour in some residential units, and the failure to link therapeutic work to the daily living context (Farmer 1998). Some of the possible reasons for this are outlined in a manual for *Residential Workers Caring for Young People Who Have Been Sexually Abused and Those Who Abuse Others*, prepared for the Scottish Office by The Centre for Residential Child Care (1995). The authors make the important point that the subject of sexual abuse arouses particular anxiety in care staff, leading to avoidance of the problem. This is not altogether surprising given the emotional impact of working with sexual offenders, and the lack of support and information that is often available to residential childcare staff and social workers (Ladwa and Sanders 1999; Green and Masson 2002). The manual identifies six factors to explain this reaction: (1) staff feel uncomfortable and awkward in responding to the sexually explicit and provocative behaviour displayed by some abused/abusive children; (2) it is difficult to listen to a child describing in detail the abuse he has experienced and/or inflicted; (3) staff feel vulnerable, often fearing that they may become the subject of allegations that they have sexually abused the child; (4) individual staff feel overwhelmed by the prospect of taking on responsibility for helping the child to stop abusing and providing a safe environment to prevent abuse, especially if unsupported by team members; (5) some staff may have themselves been the victims of sexual abuse, and find the experience of working with the victims or perpetrators of sexual abuse too distressing; and (6) staff feel anxious about the uncertainty and unpredictability associated with working with abused and abusive children, where new disclosures can be made at any time which need to be handled sensitively, according to policy and practice guidelines.

Despite these problems the authors of the Scottish Office report stress that staff in many children's homes already possess many of the skills required to undertake intervention work with sexually abused and abusive children, but that specialist training is required to develop confidence in this area of work and to facilitate productive collaboration with those providing formal treatment and therapy.

Arrangements for such collaborative working together must consider the boundaries of confidentiality and the need to establish effective systems for communication. Once established, the systems need to be sufficiently robust to deal with changes in care arrangements, such as a move to another placement. As noted earlier in this chapter, changes in context will result in changes in behaviour and possibly a change in risk. New carers require adequate information to prepare for the arrival of the young person, to ensure that the child can be safely looked after and that other children are protected. A sudden change in placement can result in a breakdown in communication, providing an opportunity for the abusive young person to gain the trust of his new carers and to engage in abusive behaviour.

Issues concerning confidentiality can sometimes prove especially difficult to resolve, especially where different agencies have different policies. Much of the anxiety is carried by those looking after the abusive child, who may be concerned that other agencies and professionals are not sharing information which has a bearing on risk, particularly those involved in intervention work. Consider, for example, an abusive young person who informs his therapist that he has strong and overwhelming sexual fantasies about another child with whom he has daily contact. From a child protection perspective, there is a professional obligation on the therapist to communicate this information to the child's carers to enable them to plan effectively for the protection of the potential victim of abuse. Indeed, if the information is not disclosed and the child abuser acts on his fantasies and abuses the other child, the therapist could be accused of negligence. Nevertheless, a minority of therapists continue to insist on complete client confidentiality, on the grounds that they need to foster a trusting relationship with the young person. Clearly, issues surrounding communication and confidentiality should be resolved before commencing therapeutic work. The Ohio Teaching-Family Association (OT-FA) (Lee and Olender 1992) insist that all children accepted on to their specialist fostering programme for sexually abusive children sign a waiver authorising the OT-FA to share information on a need-to-know basis. This type of written contract is useful whether working individually or within an organisational context as it avoids later confusion and turmoil about information sharing.

Ideally, information about treatment progress should be made available to carers so that they can make adjustments to the care and supervision of the young person. There may be times, for example, when there is a need for closer supervision, or a change in the amount of contact with certain family members. However, a significant proportion of young abusers actively resist treatment, or lack the ability or motivation to change their behaviour. Some will continue to present a serious risk to other children with little prospect of change. Even the most basic interventions, such as educational approaches, require the young person to pay attention and listen, and most interventions require a great deal more than this. Not all young abusers possess the motivation or personal qualities to participate in the kinds of intervention programmes that are considered desirable. Although some young abusers are relieved to have an opportunity to talk about their experiences and feel secure in the knowledge that they are receiving help, others refuse to participate in individual or group work. Alternatively, some begin the work but are soon overwhelmed by anxiety, perhaps finding therapeutic work particularly threatening. This can result in 'acting-out' behaviours, such as aggression, which disrupt therapeutic progress. Therapeutic progress may also be slow in learning-disabled children, particularly if the treatment programme is not modified according to the degree of learning impairment (Clare 1993). Young people with extreme attention and concentration difficulties, and oppositional defiant behaviour, can also be very difficult to engage in meaningful work, creating frustration in carers and professionals about the lack of progress in reducing risk.

Where therapeutic efforts fail to produce changes in attitude and behaviour, and young abusers remain motivated to abuse, the role of adult carers in promoting change is particularly important. Various behavioural techniques can be used to encourage personal change. For example, behaviour modification programmes alter the environment around the individual abuser with a view to encouraging and rewarding desirable behaviours and attitudes. In residential child-care settings members of staff have significant control over situational influences on behaviour, making this type of intervention particularly useful (Cullen and Seddon 1981; Milan 1987). Rewards for achieving specific behavioural targets may take the form of staff approval, access to desired activities, or points or tokens which can be used to gain access to activities or to purchase material goods. Behavioural contracts may also be used, whereby the individual agrees to behave in certain ways and receives rewards for doing so (DeRisi and Butz 1975). For example, a child may be contracted to attend twice-weekly individual or group treatment sessions for which he will be rewarded. Once a regular pattern of attendance is achieved, the reward system is gradually withdrawn.

Sexually abusive young people who are resistant to therapeutic intervention can sometimes be persuaded to adopt simple relapse-prevention techniques. Borrowed from behavioural medicine (Marlatt and Gordon 1985), relapse prevention aims to prepare people to anticipate and cope with high-risk situations that may precipitate a relapse, and is now an important component of many sex offender programmes (Pithers 1990; Marshall *et al.* 1992). There are several advantages to using the relapse-prevention model to work with poorly motivated sexually abusive young people. This model emphasises the 'here-and-now', requiring little in the way of introspective analysis; has a clear focus on avoiding further offending and the associated negative consequences for the offender, which may include prosecution, removal from home, and being locked up; and provides clear, concrete strategies for avoiding high-risk situations.

Monitoring, evaluating and reviewing risk

In addition to the task of constantly monitoring and reviewing treatment progress, it is also important to take a longer-term view: where will the young person be living in a few months' time? How will it be possible to demonstrate that there has been a reduction in risk? Most risk assessment tools distinguish between 'dynamic' and 'static' variables, on the basis that some factors indicative of risk can never change (e.g. number of victims). In evaluating progress, therefore, the emphasis is on the extent to which there has been a shift in relevant dynamic variables (e.g. reduction in deviant sexual fantasies). In settings where the young person is open to prolonged periods of observation, such as residential or educational settings, it may be possible for carers to identify and monitor the frequency of 'clinically relevant behaviours' (CRBs). These are behaviours that, in any one case, are considered to be central to the risk of re-offending, and therefore warrant particularly close monitoring and evaluation. In the case of a young person who is particularly sexually disinhibited, for example, the CRBs may be the frequency with which he engages in various observable sexual acts in a public setting. To assess the effectiveness of treatment on these CRBs requires detailed observations to be conducted pre-treatment ('baseline data') and post-treatment. A substantial reduction in the CRBs can be used as evidence of change, perhaps justifying a move to a less restrictive environment, or a return home. Different types of CRBs will be required for different children. It is often sensible to focus attention on no more than two or three significant behaviours simply because observation and recording becomes unreliable if too many behaviours are targeted. In assessing response to intervention, change in these critical CRBs carries more weight than change in other, less critical, variables. External agencies can sometimes be used as consultants to review and monitor progress, and to audit treatment and management programmes. Part of the consultancy role is to ensure that CRBs have been specified and to provide an independent, objective assessment of the extent to which risk has probably been reduced.

Conclusions

This chapter has identified a number of areas that need to be considered if sexually abusive children and young people are to be prevented from abusing, both in the short term and in the longer term. Acknowledgment and awareness that a young person is at risk of perpetrating abuse places an onus on adult carers to develop preventative strategies. The aim must be to create a safe environment in which needs of the young person are met whilst simultaneously protecting potential victims. Further, the care and management arrangements must be responsive over time to changes in risk and to the developmental needs of the young abuser. There is still a need for greater integration of child-care agencies and services and better information-sharing to minimise risk. Tracking young people over time as they move between different agencies, particularly in the transition between child and adult services, around 16 to 18 years, remains a particular concern. Sexually abusive young people who have been prevented from perpetrating further acts of abuse through careful and considerate care, management and treatment often begin to flounder when services around them are withdrawn on account of their age. Finding suitable adult provision is often difficult, particularly for complex or high-risk young people, and this is perhaps an area that warrants further attention through service mapping and longitudinal outcome studies.

8 Towards a resilience-based intervention model for young people with harmful sexual behaviours

Simon Hackett

Introduction

Resilience currently constitutes one of the most important and challenging concepts in developmental psychology (Von Eye and Schuster 2000). As such, resilience theory provides an important, but as yet neglected, framework for the adolescent sexual aggression field. This chapter seeks to take some of the main ideas arising from resilience research and apply them to work with young people who have sexually abused.

The emergence of resilience studies will be described first and resilience concepts defined. Protective factors and mechanisms which contribute to resilient outcomes in children and young people are then outlined and suggestions made for the promotion of resilience-based interventions at individual, familial and environmental levels. Various ideas are then offered about the possible steps to be taken at programme level for moving towards a resilience-based approach. Finally the ideas presented in this chapter are illustrated through the use of a real, but anonymised case example before, in the conclusion, key points relevant to adopting a resilience-based model of assessment and intervention planning for young people who have sexually abused are summarised.

From deficit and risk to positive adaptation and competence: a paradigm shift for the adolescent sexual aggression field

Over the course of the twentieth century and since, much was learnt about the factors that can inhibit the achievement of healthy developmental outcomes in children and young people. Such knowledge about *problems*, *psychopathology* and *risk factors* has comprised the cornerstone upon which our child protection and mental health systems have been built. At the same time, there has been relatively little explicit emphasis, at least until recently, on the processes which sustain the functioning of individuals in situations of adversity and risk.

The concept of resilience first emerged from studies of children living with parents with schizophrenia (Anthony 1974). Subsequent studies have broadened their focus on to a wide range of multiple, interacting adversities, such as other forms of parental mental ill health (Hammen 2003), socioeconomic status (Garmezy 1991) and poverty (Luthar 1999; Cauce *et al.* 2003), child maltreatment (Cicchetti and Rogosch 1997; Bolger and Patterson 2003) and family adversity (Fergusson and Lynskey 1996). Despite their very differing areas of investigation, studies such as these have demonstrated time and time again that a proportion of children and young people who are exposed to high levels of trauma, abuse, loss and risk nonetheless continue to defy the odds and demonstrate surprisingly positive outcomes at different developmental stages. The major focus of resilience researchers has, therefore, been to search for, and identify, the protective forces which differentiate these 'resilient' children from others in similar circumstances who appear to fare badly. Consequently, resilience researchers:

> have expanded our understanding of human development from explanations of positive development under normative conditions to better-than-expected development under adverse conditions.
>
> (Roosa 2000: 567)

As such, advocates of resilience have sought to shift the longstanding emphasis on deficits or risks on to a framework which encompasses strengths, attributes and competences.

This paradigm shift also represents a significant challenge for the adolescent sexual aggression field, which, in my view, remains focused on deficits and dominated by an over-arching risk reduction framework. Much work done with young people is designed to describe and understand the nature of their abusive behaviours, to identify how they developed and the degree to which they are accompanied by maladaptive cognitions and other problematic attributes. These are, of course, very important considerations. Many young people who sexually abuse have experienced multiple adversities in their lives and many of them have been propelled on to highly problematic developmental pathways. It is very evident that many have not demonstrated good developmental outcomes in the face of their problems. However, if we can understand why it is that some young people, who have the same range of adverse life experiences, do not go on to perpetrate abuse, or why some young people who have sexually abused show particularly good responses to intervention, then we can seek to apply these same factors and processes to other young people for whom the prognosis may appear poor. The difference between a 'risk reduction' and a 'resilience development' assessment framework is summarised in Table 8.1.

Ultimately, as can be seen in Table 8.1, both approaches share the same goal. However, their respective emphases differ in several important respects. Whilst risk reduction sees

Table 8.1 Resilience versus orthodox assessment approach

	Traditional	*Resilience-based*
Focus	To prevent further abuse	To prevent further abuse
Orientation	Abuse-focused, diagnosis and classification	Identification of factors to enhance strengths and competences
Approach	Individual young person seen as the problem or in pathological terms. Expert-led	Collaboration, focus on environmental influences underpinning and supporting abusive behaviours
Methods	Standardised protocols, risk assessment tools, psychometric testing	Conversation, emphasis on young person's understanding of behaviours and their meaning, including environmental influences
Result	Report produced containing deficit diagnosis and recommendations. Report is shared with family. Report is written by 'experts'	Report identifies key strengths and competences. Young person and family are central in the process of selecting goals and actively contribute to the report

the removal or avoidance of factors implicated in the development of abusive behaviour as the key concern, resilience development emphasises the building of skills and capacities that facilitate successful negotiation of high-risk environments. It is clearly important in the sexual aggression field that we take account of both of these dimensions in our work. In other words, whilst we should be paying specific attention to young people's sexually abusive behaviours, if this is all we do, then the outcomes of our interventions are likely to be limited. This is not at all surprising. If the causes of sexual abuse in adolescents are multifactorial, it follows that the things that reduce the likelihood of its reoccurrence are going to be multi-dimensional too (Vance 2002). With its emphasis on the building of skills, competence and external support, a resilience-based intervention approach shares many of the goals of a systemic and multi modal approach, such as Multi Systemic Therapy (Borduin *et al.* 1990).

How can resilience be defined?

Before going on to describe some of the factors which have been demonstrated as significant in influencing resilience in children and young people, it is important to more precisely define and qualify the term 'resilience'. Olsson *et al.* (2003) describe it as:

> A dynamic process involving an interaction between risk and protective processes, internal and external to the individual, that act to modify the effects of an adverse life event.

> (p. 2)

Several important points emerge from this definition. First, resilience is a dynamic process rather than a static character trait possessed by some young people but not by others. Whilst some children may be genetically or constitutionally better able than others to cope with, or bounce back from, adversity (Rutter 1999), a large part of what we talk of as resilience is actually socially driven and related to the quality of the environment in which a young person is placed, as well as the nature of supports and the broader external life opportunities available. Therefore resilience related to social influence may be particularly important for practitioners to target.

Second, the term resilience does not simply describe children whose life conditions are good, who are doing well and meeting their developmental targets. These are not children showing resilient outcomes. When we talk about resilience in adolescents, we are explicitly linking the co-existence of adversity or risk and better than expected developmental outcomes. In this regard, 'better than expected' does not mean the best possible outcome for any child, but signifies that the individual in question is exceeding the expectations given his or her life circumstances. For example, a young man with cognitive impairment may show educational resilience by achieving a range of basic school qualifications. Whilst other non-disabled children might be seen to be 'failing' educationally if they were to achieve only at this level, the achievement of these qualifications may represent a significant protective influence for this young man through the sense of real achievement they convey, with the knock-on effect of enhancing his level of self esteem considerably.

Third, resilience is more usefully viewed as a modification of the effects of adverse life events, rather than a total avoidance of problems. Whilst early definitions of resilience talked about 'invulnerable' children (e.g. Anthony 1974) we know that no child is immune from overwhelmingly high levels of stress and risk. Resilience relates to a young person's *relative* resistance to psychosocial risk factors. For example, in relation to the case example of the young man offered later in this chapter, such was the catalogue of disastrous and interlinking risk factors that the young man had been subjected to in his earlier life, it was of little surprise that he had committed a series of sexual assaults in his teenage years. Yet, this same young man evidenced an amazing capacity to respond positively to the environment in which he was placed following his conviction and to use this as the springboard for positive developmental growth. Thus, we can conclude that resilience does not describe an invulnerability to stress, but rather an ability to recover from negative events (Garmezy 1991).

What influences resilience in young people?

Despite some of the complexity in conceptualising resilience and a great deal of variance in definitions used across studies, a large number of protective factors have consistently been identified as contributing to resilient outcomes in children and young people in situations of adversity. Early studies focused particularly on the individual characteristics of 'resilient children' (Masten and Garmezy 1985; Garmezy 1985). For instance, Garmezy (1983) identified the following characteristics of school-aged children who demonstrated successful outcomes despite exposure to high levels of poverty:

- Positive peer and adult interactions;
- Low degrees of defensiveness and aggressiveness and high degrees of cooperation, participation, and emotional stability (as rated by their teachers);
- A positive sense of self;
- A sense of personal power rather than powerlessness; and
- An internal locus of control.

However, more recently, studies have sought to delineate the main groups of factors involved (Luthar *et al.* 2000), as well as the core protective mechanisms which underlie these various factors (Rutter 1999). Thus, resilience promoting factors have commonly been seen to operate at three distinct levels; within the individual child or young person; within the family context; and within the broader context of communities or society (Garmezy 1991) as depicted in Figure 8.1.

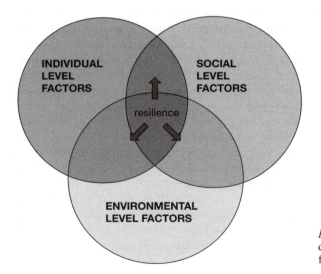

Figure 8.1 Three interlinking domains of resilience-enhancing factors.

As can be seen in Figure 8.1, resilience emerges as a consequence of the interaction between factors across all three of these domains. The implication for resilience-based practice is that we need to be enhancing a young person's overall adaptive capacity by bolstering and enhancing resources at each of these levels. Just as research has demonstrated that the impact of exposure to risk is cumulative (Rutter 1999), so protective processes are likely to work in a similarly cumulative way. Therefore, whilst single protective factors are unlikely to exert much of a protective benefit for a young person overwhelmed by risk factors, a pattern of relatively small protective factors may create a positive chain reaction in the life of a young person which helps him to get back on track developmentally.

Enhancing resilience at an individual level

According to Olsson *et al.* (2003: 5), the major empirically established protective mechanisms at the individual level are as follows:

- *Constitutional resilience* (i.e. through positive temperament, robust neurology);
- *Sociability* (including responsiveness to others, pro-social attitudes and attachment to others);
- *Intelligence* (through academic planning and decision-making abilities);
- *Communication skills* (through developed language and advanced reading); and
- *Personal attributes* (including tolerance for negative affect, self-efficacy, self-esteem, foundational sense of self, internal locus of control, sense of humour, hopefulness, strategies to deal with stress, enduring set of values, balanced perspective on experience, malleable and flexible, fortitude, conviction, tenacity, and resolve).

As can be seen from this list, key to enhancing resilience at an individual level is developing a young person's coping skills and resources, as well as problem-solving abilities. Often this is done, if at all, with young people who have sexually abused in the context of one-to-one treatment. However, young people learn these kind of critical, adaptive skills not so much through teaching but through experience. This necessarily means opening up opportunities in a young person's life to develop, test and maintain these skills. There is, of course, a dilemma here. Shielding a young person too much or 'over-protection' is likely to do little to enhance these abilities. At the same time, at the other end of the continuum, too much exposure to risk too soon would be equally counter-productive. However, improving a young person's self-esteem by facilitating a sense of connectedness (in other words, feeling satisfaction from being connected to valued people, places or things), providing a sense of alternative positive models (that young people who have abused can use to make sense of their world), communicating a sense of uniqueness (that they matter as an individual) and enhancing a sense of power (feeling that they can be successful in their lives) are key individual level goals.

Enhancing resilience at a family/social level

Olsson *et al.* (2003: 5) suggest that the key social level resource that supports resilience development in young people is the presence of supportive families, specifically through the mobilisation of the following factors:

- Parental warmth, encouragement, assistance;
- Cohesion and care within the family;

- Close relationship with a caring adult;
- Belief in the child;
- Non-blaming approach to the child;
- Marital support; and
- The presence of a talent or hobby valued by others.

At a family level, then, the importance of positive parent–child relationships is a particular theme. Despite the developing influence on adolescents of their peer group, family remains the primary influence. This is also the case for many young people who have sexually abused, despite the fact that many have experienced problematic or disrupted family relationships. Mobilising family-level resilience requires us to support parents in the immensely challenging process of parenting their children post abuse, to maintain (or sometimes develop for the first time) parental warmth and to equip them to offer practical assistance for their children. Teaching parents how to use positive strategies to manage their children without resorting to harsh disciplinary practices, developing parents' skills in monitoring and providing supervision, and extending the level of parents' involvement with their children are all key resilience goals at this level.

Enhancing resilience at an environmental level

At an environmental level, both school and the broader environment emerge as vital protective factors for young people. Olsson *et al.* (2003: 5) suggest the following core factors and mechanisms:

- *Socio-economic status* (through material resources);
- *School experiences* (including the presence of supportive peers, positive teacher influences and the achievement of academic/non academic success); and
- *Supportive communities* (including acceptance of the individual's distress, a non-punitive approach to the person concerned, resources to assist, and an overall belief in the values of a society).

It is well established that school can be a safe environment which can provide young people with a buffer against family adversity, as well as representing a place in which young people can develop individual level protective factors. Paying attention to young people's broader social environment and connecting them with safe opportunities to develop supportive relationships, to encourage their talents, enhance participation and develop relationships in an affirming, non-punitive context are key tasks within resilience-based practice at an environmental level, especially as, for many young people who have sexually abused, the wider community, and community members' responses to their abuse, represent a real threat.

Four key protective processes

It may well be that a few key resilience-enhancing processes or 'mechanisms' underpin the wide variety of resilience factors that have been identified above. Rutter (1987) suggests that there are four major protective processes that foster resilience:

1   Reducing negative outcomes by altering the risk or child's exposure to the risk;
2   Reducing negative chain reaction following risk exposure;

3   Establishing and maintaining self-esteem and self-efficacy; and
4   Opening up opportunities.

These four key protective processes set a clear agenda for resilience-based intervention with young people who have sexually abused. For example, how can we reduce the likelihood, following the identification of a young man's abusive behaviours, that he will be catapulted into a situation of further psychosocial adversity, such as exclusion from educational settings or repeated inappropriate placements, which would see his longer-term potential to forge appropriate relationships and relationships impaired? What opportunities are there to assist in the process of repairing and rebuilding a young man's self-esteem and to increase his ability to exert an appropriate level of influence on his own life? How can we safely offer opportunities for social and emotional growth whilst effectively protecting other people in the young person's environment?

There are clearly many opportunities potentially available to practitioners to exert positive influence on these four key processes. Table 8.2 provides a checklist of key questions which workers can use to assist in resilience-based intervention planning.

What should programmes do to promote resilience?

The preceding elements of this chapter have provided suggestions about how responses to young people may be oriented towards resilience-enhancing models of practice. In many cases, it will be the commitment and approach of individual workers which provide the backbone for such approaches with young people. However, there are also many structural opportunities for programmes or services to contribute to this process at individual, familial and environmental levels. Here are a few simple ideas about what programmes can practically do to add protective factors across the three key resilience levels.

At an *individual* level, programmes can ensure that they *celebrate successes* with young people by implementing a system of rewards or acknowledgement. *Fostering a sense of hope* in young people by sharing (anonymised) success stories of young people who have completed the programme previously can be especially helpful to young people in the early stages of intervention when they are often feeling hopeless about their future. Posters or booklets offering such stories can be a powerful vehicle. *Listening to young people and valuing their opinions* about the programme and building formal opportunities for young people to provide such feedback can help young people to see that they can positively shape their environments and that their views matter. *Meaningful participatory evaluation* is important in enhancing young people's sense of belonging and can be a springboard for attempting to influence other broader systems in the young person's life. Is it possible for your programme to use focus groups of young people to influence the further development of the service? Would it be possible for you to develop peer support and mentoring schemes for young people? Overall, it is vital that programmes *give appropriate choices and control to young people,* at whatever level is possible, as often as is possible.

At a *social or familial* level, programmes should ensure that they are *available for parents*; with the emphasis on actively listening to families' experiences. *Parent-mentoring schemes and support groups* are not widespread currently, but the evidence suggests that these are amongst the services most valued by parents in helping them to feel supported and in challenging isolation (Hackett *et al.* 2002). Given the centrality of parenting relationships in enhancing resilience for young people, *enabling access to parenting courses* is a key family-level factor. Simply *being sensitive to parents' own needs*, for example, relating to their own

Table 8.2 Some key questions to focus resilience-led practice and decision making with young
people who have sexually abused

Supportive adult relationships:	• What is positive in this young person's life? How could these factors be enhanced and promoted?
	• Who likes and values this young person? How can attachments be maintained and strengthened?
	• Who exercises a positive influence in the young person's life (e.g. at home, in school or in the wider community)?
	• Is there an adult in the family whom the young person trusts and can seek out for support? If not, how can this be built?
	• Is there an adult outside the family whom the young person trusts and can seek out for support? If not, how can this be built?
	• What is the nature of the relationships that the young person has with any professionals involved? If there is a key professional who has a particularly strong and positive relationship, how can this person's role and influence be developed?
Building peer relationships:	• How well does the young person relate to peers of his or her own age?
	• What opportunities are there for the development of appropriate and supportive peer relationships?
	• How can the young person's sense of self-esteem be enhanced through the experience of supportive peers?
Encouraging talents and school success:	• What hobbies and interests does the young person have both within and outside of the school environment? How can they be encouraged and developed?
	• How can the young person be reconnected to interests that have been displaced or interrupted since the abusive behaviour?
	• How is the young person progressing – socially and academically – in school?
	• Has the school been informed of the young person's abusive behaviour and home situation, so that support can be offered?
	• How has the school's knowledge of the young person been used in the assessment of the young person's behaviour, as well as in the identification of wider developmental issues, adversities and strengths?
	• What opportunities are there in school for the child to demonstrate success? How are these planned for?
Building family resilience:	• To what extent do the primary caregivers have people they can turn to? Is there a safe person they can confide in about their child's sexually abusive behaviour?
	• Have caregivers had a chance to articulate their worries and views as part of the formulation of a plan to address the abusive behaviours?
	• To what extent do caregivers have unmet emotional needs themselves? How can they be supported to get these needs met in their own right?
	• How can caregivers' parenting skills and resources be enhanced?
	• Do caregivers have interests and activities outside of the family?
	• What opportunities are there to encourage supportive and safe discussion between caregivers and young people about the abusive behaviour and other family issues?
Encouraging planning and participation:	• What opportunities are there for the young person (and family) to be centre-stage in the planning process?
	• What opportunities can be provided for the young person to have a say in what happens to him/her?
	• What goals, ambitions and aspirations does the young person have?
	• How can the young person (and family) be encouraged to meet these goals?
	• What tastes of success (however small) can we provide for this young person?

unresolved victimisation histories, also helps to convey to parents that they are important in their own right, rather than merely as an adjunct to their child's treatment. *Giving feedback to parents and carers* about progress being made by young people and conveying positive messages, even if these represent only small steps in the right direction, can be immensely confirming and sustaining for families. As with young people, *conveying optimism* about the future, even if the present is full of difficulties, can fuel a sense of purpose and optimism. Finally, it is often not enough for families who are in great distress and turmoil following the discovery of the abuse, for programmes simply to offer a passive 'take it or leave it' approach. The message from parents is that professionals must keep involving families at every opportunity (Hackett and Masson 2005). Programmes should ensure that they go out to the family home and see the challenges for family members in their home environment. Even if a programme's direct contact with families is limited, it is usually possible to send them regular letters or speak to parents on the phone.

At an *environmental* level, programmes should be committed to *supporting young people's participation in education*. In one instance this involved a key worker spending time in school and actively recruiting a 'circle of friends' (Newton and Wilson 2003) to help maintain the young person who was in danger of being excluded from the school. Employing an outreach worker whose dedicated role it is to go out into young people's schools, get young people networked in the care system or connect young people with community or sport and leisure groups, for example, may be a better choice for a programme than employing just another therapist to work within the confines of the project building.

A case example of a young man demonstrating resilient outcomes

Unravelling and understanding the stories of children who demonstrate good outcomes in the face of adversity can provide real life examples of resilience in action and can inspire practitioners to find resilience-enhancing ways of helping other children on similar developmental journeys. The following case example describes how one young person was supported following his abusive behaviour. The name and other identifying features of the young person have been changed to protect his identity, but in every other respect the details reflect the actual case.

> Gordon was a 17-year-old young man with a mild to moderate level of cognitive impairment, who had previously attended a special school for children with learning difficulties. From the age of 15, Gordon perpetrated a series of sexual assaults on young adult women in his local community. Typically he would approach his victims without warning in the street, grab their breasts and genitals over their clothes and run off. After a series of six reported assaults over a two-year period, he was apprehended and subsequently convicted.
>
> Gordon's family background was one of considerable disadvantage, neglect and abuse. He was the third youngest of four brothers and two sisters in an overcrowded and materially deprived family home. Although Gordon later recalled very good memories of his time at his special school, it was located some considerable distance from his neighbourhood, which meant that he was socially isolated and had few, if any, peer friendships outside of school. Both his parents had both cognitive impairment and mental health problems. His father was a Schedule One Offender having been convicted of underage sexual intercourse when he was 18. The family environment was violent and highly sexualised. Gordon was the child in the family who was singled out for particularly harsh treatment and scapegoating by his parents. Gordon recalled that as far back as he could remember, he was engaged with his siblings in sexually inappropriate and intrusive sexual behaviours. He also reported being sexually abused in his teenage years by a male cousin, as well as by his mother.

Having been identified for his sexually abusive behaviours, Gordon was initially placed in a remand setting in a Young Offenders' Institution, but on conviction (and through the considerable effort of a psychiatrist who had assessed Gordon in the custodial setting and deemed it to be highly unsuitable for him) Gordon was placed in a secure, community-based setting for adults with learning disabilities. The placement, though it came about largely by chance, proved to be a decisive developmental turning point for Gordon and offered an environment in which he thrived. Because of its secure nature, Gordon felt protected from the highly negative influence of his immediate family who were not allowed contact with him. This gave Gordon an opportunity for a 'fresh start' and he quickly built a series of meaningful relationships with staff members and other residents in the unit.

Quite by chance, Gordon was both the youngest and the most cognitively able resident in the unit. He was a popular resident who injected humour and energy into the group. Other residents trusted Gordon and some, valuing his ability to communicate and negotiate with staff, would go to Gordon to ask him to help them when they had a problem. Staff in the unit began to reciprocate by asking Gordon to negotiate and advocate between other residents in times of dispute. For perhaps the first time in his life, Gordon was fulfilling a valued role and one where he could positively exert an influence to improve not only his own but also the other residents' environment. His self-esteem grew. As he expressed an interest in cooking, he was allowed to help staff out in the kitchen. In particular, he developed a supportive relationship with the unit cook. Cooking for other residents also provided Gordon with an opportunity to be creative and have a clear purpose for his time in the unit. He was increasingly encouraged to develop his skills and to contribute his own ideas for menus and so on.

Staff members were increasingly struck by the degree to which Gordon recalled happy memories from his schooling. Indeed, he was immensely proud of a number of certificates of achievement he still possessed from his time at school and he would frequently show staff the few photos he had of his school class and of himself on school trips. They organised for a personal tutor to visit the unit to work with Gordon to achieve further qualifications. This involved significant effort and determination on Gordon's part and, in turn, gave him a sense of achievement, pride and self-belief.

Finally, Gordon had his first experience of a successful romantic relationship whilst in the unit. This was with a woman who was a fellow resident and who was some ten years older than Gordon. Their relationship was short-lived as the resident in question moved out of the unit some two weeks later (a planned move) and the relationship involved no more than the couple sitting together holding hands whilst watching TV in the unit. However, this brief and relatively transient taste of success in a relationship appeared to be a remarkably significant experience for Gordon. Maybe for the first time in his life he knew that someone had found him attractive, felt comfortable around him, wanted to be with him and reciprocated his own feelings. Though short-lived, this experience gave Gordon a sense that he would be able to succeed in relationships in the future and that his whole life need not be defined by abusive sexuality.

Case examples of resilience in children and young people, like that of Gordon, bear witness to the extraordinary potential of children to recover from significant difficulties if the prevailing circumstances in their environment support them in so doing. As can be seen in this case, these processes often come about as much by chance as by design or professional intent. Despite the presence of a catalogue of empirically supported psychosocial risk factors and significant adverse experiences in his life, Gordon provided perhaps the clearest example of resilience that I have encountered in the course of my work in the sexual aggression field. The factors that made a difference to Gordon were not, in themselves, complex or long-term. Providing appropriate opportunities in a safe environment and paying attention to Gordon as an individual, nurturing his talents and encouraging his achievements, gave him a sense of purpose and confidence which paved the way for more focused work with him on his sexually abusive behaviours. Without this broader structure of support, it is unlikely that this work would have been meaningful or productive.

Summary and conclusions

This chapter has sought to demonstrate the relevance of the concept of resilience in relation to work with young people who have sexually abused others. Several key points emerge about the nature of resilience and resilience-based interventions in respect of practice in this field.

First, resilience is a process, not a personality trait that some young people have and others not. As such, we should seek to influence this process in the course of our work by enhancing protective factors in young people's lives. Careful assessment of young people's vulnerabilities and adversities, as well as strengths and competences, is required in order to identify the most effective ways of mobilising resilience in individual cases. Multiple interacting protective factors at individual, family and environmental levels are likely to exert much more of a protective influence than simply focusing on one factor or one dimension of a young person's life. Positive growth can be influenced by the application of a wide pattern of protective factors.

Second, resilience is not a strange or esoteric process. It typically arises from the operation of common human adaptational systems, and is not a product of some rare or extraordinary process. These systems 'stem from a long history of biological and cultural evolution that has equipped humans with powerful tools for adaptive functioning' (Masten and Powell 2003: 15). As Masten (2001) says, resilience is *ordinary magic*. Young people who have sexually abused may have demonstrated non-resilient outcomes in their lives to date, but this does not mean that they are unable to respond if the circumstances are right. The case example of Gordon evidences the importance of being alert to the opportunities in young people's everyday lives to influence their developmental trajectories in a positive and practical way.

Third, and perhaps most significantly, resilience provides an optimistic framework for intervention. We cannot undo the fact that a young person has abused, nor take away from their victimisation histories where they exist. At the same time, as Gilligan suggests, it is all too easy to become distracted or seduced by the big questions (such as risk assessment tools or relapse prevention plans) and lose sight of 'crucial details of what can sustain the positive development of *this* child *today*' (Gilligan 2000: 45). Paying attention to the details of how we engage with young people to help foster their talents, competences and relationships and helping them take appropriate control over the lives are the vital elements that 'may foster in a child the vital sense of *belonging*, of *mattering*, of *counting*' (ibid.: 45). Such an emphasis is neither a luxury nor an incidental sideshow to the real work of cognitive behavioural offence specific treatment. It is the very heart of resilience-enhancing practice. Indeed, I would suggest that none of the ideas discussed in this chapter is incompatible with a more orthodox programme of cognitive behavioural offence specific intervention.

In conclusion, resilience-based interventions represent, in my view, an important paradigm shift in the adolescent field. Building resilience concepts into our intervention frameworks is not about pretending that everything is OK in a young person's life, nor is it about simply focusing on strengths and ignoring difficulties or failing to address the risk that young people present. That would be unethical and dangerous. But as Luthar and Zelazo (2003: 513) suggest:

[T]he advantage of this explicit focus on positives is that it can impel scientists to adopt fresh mind sets, leading them to consider strengths among groups usually thought of in terms of problems or failures.

Young people with sexually abusive behaviours are a very powerful example of one such group.

9 Young people who sexually abuse

The role of the new technologies

Ethel Quayle and Max Taylor

Introduction

This chapter will review the sparse literature related to young people who engage in sexually abusive behaviours through new technologies, and suggest ways of conceptualising the problems that such children and adolescents pose as being, in part, a product of a particular context. This is a difficult challenge – even the most recent texts on children and young people with harmful sexual behaviours make little or no reference to the Internet (e.g. Hackett 2004; O'Reilly *et al.* 2004; Calder 2005) or even to pornography. In the first edition of the current book, Will (1999) in his chapter on assessment issues, suggested that when examining the sources of sexual knowledge, it would be necessary to ask:

> Has the young person read pornographic books or magazines or watched pornographic videos? (A minority will have done so, often having illicitly watched videos owned by their fathers.)
>
> (p. 93)

However, such are the changes in technology that it would appear that in a very short space of time, the Internet has brought easy access to 'materials that portray and endorse the full range of sexual activities, from the consensual to the coercive, from the enriching to the degrading' (Barak and Fisher 2002: 268). More recently, Cavanagh-Johnson and Doonan (2005) have provided a useful assessment approach to children with sexual behaviour problems that included an examination of the role of pornography and Internet use.

Before trying to untangle the conflicting and limited information about this topic, it is important to try and understand how many children engage with these media, and what it is they do. DeBell and Chapman (2003) reported on computer and Internet use by children and adolescents between the ages of 5 and 17 in the United States during 2001. They found that 90 per cent of their sample used computers (47 million persons), and 59 per cent (31 millions) used the Internet. Use began at an early age, with 25 per cent of 5-year-olds using the Internet, rising to 50 per cent by 9 years and 78 per cent by 15 to 17 years of age. Whilst there were no gender differences in overall computer or Internet use, girls were more likely to use e-mail, and boys to use these media for games, shopping and finding information about news, weather or sports. Home was the most common location for Internet access. Another study examined Internet usage among Australian children (NetRatings Australia 2005) and found that most children in their sample (n=502) had accessed the Internet within the previous three years. Boys and younger children were more likely to access the Internet for entertainment (games, websites, music), while girls and older children were more likely to use it as a communication resource.

In the UK, Madell and Muncer (2004) have suggested that Internet use appears to have plateaued, with about 42 per cent of homes having access. However, they noted that there is evidence that a disproportionate number of non-users appear to be over the age of 50, and that the young are most likely to go online eventually. In a collaborative study between Ireland, Denmark, Sweden, Iceland and Norway (SAFT 2003) it was found that 80 per cent of Irish children had access to the Internet at home, although only 12 per cent said that they used it everyday, compared to 46 per cent of children in Sweden. A further UK study by Livingstone and Bober (2005) of 1,511 children and young people aged 9–19 indicated that school access to the Internet was almost universal (92 per cent).

These studies suggest widespread use of the Internet by young people, and also emphasise its remarkable qualities as an academic resource, a facilitator of communication and a source of inexpensive entertainment accessed from the safety of home, school or the library. However, NetRatings Australia (2005) also intimated a darker side to the Internet when they added that children in their study reported that the most common cause of accidental exposure to inappropriate websites was pop-up windows. Kanuga and Rosenfeld (2004) suggested that the World Wide Web makes it easier for an adolescent to stumble across sites with 'nefarious intention, such as sex-seeking chat rooms and pornographic websites, while searching for answers about sexual health' (p. 120).

Exposure to unwanted material

The physical, emotional and psychological changes that occur in adolescence prompt young people to have many questions about their bodies, relationships and health that are often personal, sensitive and embarrassing (Suzuki and Calzo 2004). One new source for such information, the Internet, brings with it accessibility, interactivity and anonymity. However, it is these very factors that increase the likelihood of exposure to violent or sexual material. In the SAFT (2003) study, almost one in five children had been invited to a face-to-face meeting with a stranger, and 34 per cent had viewed a violent website, either accidentally or on purpose. Other authors have highlighted the accidental exposure of young people to unwanted sexual material on the Internet (Finkelhor *et al.* 2000; Mitchell *et al.* 2003). These studies acknowledged the fact that existing research examining the effects of exposure to unwanted sexual material had been entirely based on college students or other adults, and that none had concerned children, particularly those younger than 14 years. They also emphasised that the research had been about voluntary or anticipated exposure, rather than accidental exposure, concluding that:

> The harm-to-children issue is really about whether exposure to sexual materials causes psychological, moral, or developmental harm to children as a result of the viewing, and this is an eminently empirical issue on which virtually no research has been done.
>
> (Mitchell *et al.* 2003: 334)

Mitchell *et al.* (2003) indicated that one in four of children who regularly used the Internet encountered unwanted sexual pictures, with only 8 per cent of the sample admitting to going to X-rated sites on purpose (which the authors concluded was likely to be an underestimate). The majority of children who were exposed to material regarded such exposure as not particularly distressing. However, the authors emphasised that such exposure, particularly unwanted exposure, may affect attitudes about sex, the Internet, and young people's sense of safety and community. Livingstone and Bober's (2005) study also indicated high levels of exposure to online pornography, with 57 per cent having come into contact with it. Most of this material was viewed unintentionally, through a pop-up advert, when searching for something else or through junk mail. Again, 54 per cent of these children claimed not to have been upset by it, but a significant minority did not like it. Cameron *et al.* (in press) used a web-based focus group methodology to examine forty young people's exposure to sexually oriented websites (SOWs) and sexually explicit websites (SEWs). Within this sample, there was a subgroup of boys who described intentional exposure to SEWs, citing curiosity and arousal as reasons for visiting these websites. As with Mitchell *et al.*'s (2003) study, while participants suggested that exposure to SEWs had no negative impact on them, the authors concluded that this may be either because their perceptions were affected by liberal attitudes or because they were developmentally unable to judge the effect of the content.

Potential problems related to exposure

So what are the problems that adults may see in relation to adolescents, sexual material and the new technologies? One concern is that accessing pictures and text with a sexual content may impact in an adverse way on current or future sexual and emotional development. A further concern is that looking at online deviant sexual material may act as a catalyst to engage in a sexually problematic way with another child or children. We might equally be concerned that finding material on the Internet leaves the young person open to sexual exploitation by others, particularly adults. However, a further 'harm-to-others' scenario relates to children and adolescents victimising other young people through accessing images of child abuse (also referred to as 'child pornography') through the new technologies, or through making sexual solicitations to others (Taylor and Quayle 2004). One additional area for concern relates to sexually abusive behaviours that may be construed as 'self-victimising' or 'self-harming'. Longo (2004) has argued that online sexual behaviour is one such area.

The media, pornography, young people and sexual abuse

On the Internet it is possible to find material to suit all interests and proclivities (Taylor and Quayle 2003), either through purposeful or accidental exposure. Until the advent of the Internet, material that would have been considered illegal was difficult to access. However, the changing context of the media as a vehicle for sexual materials has become increasingly important. MacKinnon (1995) had suggested that:

> Like a Trojan horse, each new communication technology – the printing press, the camera, the moving picture, the tape recorder, the telephone, the television, the video recorder, the VCR, cable and, now, the computer – has brought pornography with it. Pornography has proliferated with each new tool, democratising what had been a more elite possession and obsession, spreading the sexual abuse required for its making and promoted through its use . . . As pornography saturates social life, it also becomes more visible and legitimate, hence less visible as pornography . . . Pornography in cyberspace is pornography in society – just broader, deeper, worse and more of it.
>
> (p. 1959)

To date, there is little written about the use of pornography by young people who sexually abuse (Epps and Fisher 2004). Alexy (2003) re-examined a data set of 160 sexually reactive children and adolescents and described the characteristics of those who used pornography and those who did not. Several significant positive associations were found between pornography use and psychiatric symptoms, non-sexual criminal, antisocial and delinquent behaviours, and sexually aggressive behaviours. However, the data used came from the 1990s and pre-dated the use of the Internet to access pornographies. Earlier research by Kaufman *et al.* (1998) had compared the use of pornography in adult and adolescent offenders and reported that with adults it had a narrower focus. These authors suggested that being interested in pornography represents a normative, developmental experience for a large number of adolescents and a significant source of information about sexuality. However, Malamuth (1993) emphasised the importance of the content of the material, in that if the portrayal of sex was intertwined with violence, hatred, coercion and humiliation of women, then the individual could have the experience of being aroused to such material, with the result that those who already have a sense of being attracted to sexual aggression are most likely to be influenced by such material. Malamuth (2000) further contended that associations between pornography consumption and aggressiveness toward women could be explained by a circular relationship between high coercive tendencies and an interest in certain content in pornography, whereby aggressive men are drawn to the images in pornography that reinforce and therefore increase the likelihood of their control, impersonal and hostile association to sexuality. What may be of particular importance in relation to this is the emphasis placed by Malamuth on the fact that pornographic stimuli are part of a larger corpus of media images, and that the role of media stimuli cannot be appreciated in isolation from other variables.

The role and the influence of the media on children and adolescents have largely been examined in the context of violent content (e.g. Browne and Hamilton-Giachritsis 2005). These authors took a public health perspective to violence and suggested the need to consider the effects of violent imagery on the child within the broader context of child welfare, families and communities:

> Hence in addition to the habits and behaviour of the child or adolescent viewer, the behaviour of parents in monitoring the use of televisions and computers and knowingly or unknowingly allowing access to violent imagery should be considered. Furthermore, the role of communities and societies in providing standards, guidelines and education to families also needs assessment.
>
> (p. 702)

This raises an important issue with regard to locus of responsibility, and one that we will return to in the context of sexually problematic behaviours. Browne and Hamilton-Giachritsis (2005) also emphasised that with the advent of the Internet, many of the images that had traditionally been a cause of concern to parents, professionals and policy makers were now freely accessible on websites. Further challenges to our understanding of the influence of the media on normal child and adolescent development have come from Strasburger (2004), who has raised the issue as to whether the media mirrors an increasingly violent and sexually oriented society, or whether it actually causes change in behaviour. He has suggested that:

> The sheer volume of pornography on the Net, the arcane diversity of it (e.g. bestiality, rape and bondage) and the ease of access to it – within seconds – makes Internet pornography a force to be reckoned with.
>
> (p. 85)

However, the claims that pornography and related sexual media can influence sexual violence, sexual attitudes, moral values and sexual activity of children and young people (Greenfield 2004a) is more difficult to substantiate. Studies such as that of Emerick and Dutton (1993) had suggested that with high-risk adolescents, 80 per cent acknowledged the use of pornography for stimulation, and the number of female child victims was said to have increased progressively with the severity of the pornography used as a stimulus for masturbation. Similarly, in a sample of 485 'juvenile offenders', 31.6 per cent reported using pornography (Zolondek *et al.* 2001). Ford and Linney (1995) compared juvenile rapists, non-sexual violent juvenile offenders and juvenile child molesters and found that exposure to pornographic material differed among the groups, with sexual abusers having more exposure. However, other research (Sheridan *et al.* 1998) showed no differences in pornography use (magazines, films and sex lines) between youths who engaged in sexually abusive behaviour and those who did not. There is similarly conflicting evidence from research with adult sex offenders (Langevin and Curnoe 2004; Seto and Eke 2005).

More recently, social learning theory has been re-examined as 'an etiological proposition for sexually abusive male adolescents' (Burton and Meezan 2005). These authors suggested that:

> Pornography may be another medium for learning sexually abusive behaviour, and may help explain why some youth who are sexually aggressive do not have a sexual victimisation history.
>
> (p. 74)

The nature of the pornography to which the person is exposed (explicit or violent) may increase its salience, as well as the person who introduced the pornography, the verbalisations that accompanied it and the use of pornography as stimulation for masturbation. Burton and Meezon (2005) have argued that orgasm reinforces cognitive rehearsals of sexual behaviours or aggression generated from memories of sexual victimisation. Masturbatory fantasies, which are stimulated by pornography, then lead to cognitive distortions about sex, possible sexual partners, or potential partners for sexually aggressive behaviours. However, Gruber and Grube (2000) have argued that sexual activity might not be learned by observation and modelling in the same way as aggression, 'It is not clear, then, if the conceptual models employed in understanding aggression in the media will or should work equally well in understanding their sexual content' (Ward 2003: 372).

If it is difficult to establish a causal relationship between sexually violent or abuse media and the commission of contact offences, what additional things do we need to be concerned about? Zillmann (2000) has suggested that prolonged exposure to pornography leads to a skewed perception of normal sexual activity and it is argued that a diminished level of trust in intimate partners, loss of hope of sexual exclusivity with a given partner, and normalisation of promiscuous lifestyles are among the changes that have been observed in young adults who have been regularly exposed to pornography. Equally, Finkelhor *et al.* (2000), have suggested that from a social-scientific view, while it is impossible to evaluate the effect of exposure to sexual material on young people, media can affect attitudes, engender fears, and model behaviours (both pro and antisocial). Clearly such exposure is not only related to the Internet and in a review of the empirical research related to the role of entertainment media in the sexual socialisation of youth, Ward (2003) concluded that there was evidence that frequent and involved exposure to sexually oriented genres such as soap operas and music videos was associated with a greater acceptance of stereotypical and casual attitudes about sex, with higher expectations about the prevalence of sexual activity and of certain sexual outcomes, and, even occasionally, with greater levels of sexual experience. Greenfield (2004a) has also suggested that there is sufficient evidence to conclude that pornography and related sexual media can influence sexual violence, sexual attitudes, moral values and sexual activity in children and youth.

Conflicting perspectives

However, what appears challenging is that while concern is expressed amongst adults about the effect of sexually related Internet material on children and young people, young people themselves do not necessarily share this concern. Ebersole (2000) studied how students aged 10–21 years, in 10 public schools in a western US state, viewed the Internet and their attitudes towards it. The research demonstrated that commercial sites were visited much more frequently than other sites and that, while students reported their purpose for using the World Wide Web as 'research and learning' 52 per cent of the time, a sample of the sites examined revealed that only 27 per cent were actually suitable for that purpose. Those rated 'unsuitable for academic research' were visited by students twice as often as those rated 'suitable'. In the SAFT (2003) study, 42 per cent of Irish children who visited pornographic websites found them either 'cool' or 'funny'. In a slightly different context, Wolak *et al.* (2003) found that young people who formed close, online relationships, largely with people significantly older than themselves and who would have been described as 'adults', often did not see this as problematic, and were not victims of deception.

What framework then can we use to judge young people's sexual activities in relation to the new technologies? Hackett (2004) has suggested that young people commit a wide variety of sexually abusive acts that are beyond normative, developmental parameters and that, as a group, they are very heterogeneous. It has also been emphasised that when evaluating the sexual behaviours of adolescents, it is critical to avoid dichotomous thinking, and instead view them on a continuum from healthy to problematic (Longo *et al.* 2002). These authors have also emphasised that it is important to assess the function that the sexual behaviour serves for the particular young person, stressing that:

> . . . an important indicator of sexual health for teenagers is the degree to which the sexual behaviour is in the service of developmentally appropriate sexual needs as opposed to primarily nonsexual needs.
>
> (p. 92)

For example, exploring personal identity through sexuality, surfing the Web, participating in chat rooms and engaging in Internet sex may be ways of trying on multiple identities to see which fit. Equally, the function of sexual engagement with the Internet many relate to managing negative feelings. Longo *et al.* (2002) have argued that sexual behaviour and pleasure is a powerful way to feel better in the moment, and that this may result in the compulsive use of pornography and masturbation. As with adults, Internet pornographies may offer the perfect vehicle for the avoidance of negative emotional states (Quayle and Taylor 2002; Middleton *et al.* 2005; Quayle *et al.* 2006). In a similar way, Internet sexual behaviour can offer a way of developing age-appropriate social skills, but it brings with it a risk of exposure to distorted sexual stimuli, as well as exploitation by adults who offer desperately needed acceptance, attention and escape from isolation and invisibility.

Longo (2004) has suggested that one particular concern is how to differentiate the use of the Internet for sexual purposes by young people with sexual behaviour problems from the same use by a population of normal functioning adolescents who have no involvement with the legal system. In some ways this raises difficult questions about what constitutes 'normative sexual behaviour' in relation to the Internet. Cooper and Griffin-Shelley (2002) have argued that since its inception the Internet has been, 'inextricably associated with sexuality in a synergistic dance, each fuelling and ultimately contributing to the transformation of the other' (p. 4). Earlier research had estimated that 20 per cent of Internet users engaged in some form of online sexual behaviour, with sexual pursuits counting for almost 70 per cent of the time that was spent online (Sprenger 1999). One of the biggest challenges in the United States over the past 25 years has been the widespread acceptance of sexually explicit material such as pornography (CBS News 2004). Adult entertainment is a $12 billion business in the US (CNBC 2004), and employs over 12,000 people in California alone. However, what is important about the Internet in relation to sexuality is that it is not simply another vehicle for a supply of related goods but a medium in which people actively engage, both changing and being changed by the interaction.

Greenfield (2004b) examined this in the context of a teen chat room and concluded that:

> ... the sexuality expressed in this chat room was public rather than private; it was limited to strangers; and it had nothing to do with relationships. It was very explicit and focused on physical acts rather than emotional meaning.
>
> (p. 755)

She felt that the content of the chat room provided evidence of disinhibition in three areas: sexuality, aggression and race relations, which could impact on early sexual priming and provide a model for racism, negative attitudes towards women and homophobia. Of relevance is her conclusion that while some teenagers are unwitting, others are actively creating this culture and, 'constructing the Internet' (p. 757). To date, the focus has been on the problems of children being made the targets of commerce, ignoring the kinds of social and cultural worlds young people are creating online. However, children and adolescents are not simply the targets of adult Internet creations, but are active participants in creating their own cyber cultures.

Normality?

Is such sexual behaviour in children normal or not? If we take as our standard of normality the frequency of any activity within a given population, then there are some intimations that this is 'more normal' than we have previously believed. It may be that Greenfield's (2004a) alarm at the evidence of online sexualised behaviour in an Internet teen chat room is part and parcel of our ambivalent attitudes towards sexuality in children. Heiman *et al.* (1998) have drawn our attention to the fact that western society continues to view children as innocent and pure, lacking any sexual desires, thoughts or interests. While such beliefs are embedded in our culture, there is a discrepancy within a society which openly displays eroticism and yet exhibits great reluctance in discussing private sexual practices. Horner (2004) concluded that:

> Children are repeatedly exposed to sexual images in our erotic society, for example on television and in the movies, yet parents are reluctant to discuss sex with their children

because of beliefs that children lack sexuality and because they hesitate to discuss sexual practices in general.

(p. 58)

Is there not a risk in decontextualising young people's sexual behaviour in relation to the new technologies? What the Internet brings with it is a plethora of sexualised material and chat, which a large part of the adult population engages with. Should we be so surprised that children and adolescents also form part of this market place, availing of and moulding the medium to meet their own needs? Unlike any other arena, the majority of young Internet users can venture into areas that they would otherwise be denied access to, sampling the heady delights of sexual materials and relationships, and all the while sitting at home. Excitement, risk and even danger can be engaged with through an environment that remains largely unpoliced, and which leaves the majority of parents feeling unskilled, unknowledgeable and maybe with a false sense of security that at least their child is at home, visibly safe, rather than out on the streets. For the majority of parents, their children's online behaviour remains invisible.

A further example of this was provided by Greenfield (2004b) in the context of peer-to-peer file-sharing networks. These are a leaderless network of computer users that is not hosted by any website and are the places that most young people go to download music. They are, however, also a perfect vehicle for uploading and downloading pornography, which for some children results again in accidental exposure. On peer-to-peer file-sharing networks, files are not just passively consumed, advertently or inadvertently, by young people. Young people seek them out and make them available to others.

Victimisation

To date, the evidence that relates to adolescent online behaviour and the victimisation of children has been largely anecdotal and drawn from case material provided by practitioners (e.g. Longo 2004). Finkelhor *et al.* (2000) analysed telephone interview data from a large sample (1,501) of young Internet users about their experiences online. Their findings indicated that one in five children who regularly used the Internet experienced a sexual solicitation or an approach over the year examined. One in 33 received an aggressive sexual solicitation, which included being asked to meet offline, telephone calls or things sent through the post. One in four had unwanted exposure to sexual images, and one in 17 were threatened or harassed. Approximately one quarter of the children who reported these incidents were distressed by them. What is critical to our discussion relates to who was engaging in these sexually abusive behaviours. As with most Internet data, there are always difficulties establishing who exactly is who in the online world, as most of the communicants remain anonymous to each other (as there are many fewer face-to-face validity checks). Online it is possible to change age, gender ethnic group and so on, and for at least some people such deception is important in maintaining a persona (Quayle and Taylor 2001). With this qualification in mind, the data from Finkelhor *et al.*'s (2000) survey indicated that juveniles made up 48 per cent of the overall solicitations, and 48 per cent of the aggressive solicitations (27 per cent were of an unknown age). In relation to this they concluded, 'not all of the sexual solicitors on the Internet fit the media stereotype of an older, male predator. Many are young and some are women.' Many of the sexual solicitations appeared to be propositions for 'cybersex', and in almost half of the incidents the young person did not tell anyone about the episode. In this sample, 25 per cent received exposure to unwanted sexual materials and, in the main, this occurred while the young person was surfing or searching the Internet, or when opening emails or links in emails and instant messages. The unwanted sexual materials included images of naked people (94 per cent), people having sex (38 per cent) and violence (8 per cent). For ethical reasons, it was not possible to establish how much of the material involved child abuse images.

In 2004, Carr published a research report examining cases investigated by the Department of Internal Affairs Censorship Compliance Unit (CCU) in New Zealand. The results of this study were subsequently updated later that year by Wilson and Andrews (2004), using the same methodology, and including an additional 79 offenders. Their results indicated that of the 184 people in the study, only one was female, and 89 per cent were classified as New Zealand Europeans. The largest single group of offenders, which remained the same as in Carr's (2004) study, consisted of people aged between 15 and 19 years. Those under 20 years comprised a quarter of all offenders, although the age of the offender at the time of detection ranged from 14–67 years. The largest occupational group was students (32.4 per cent), followed by those whose career was in information technology (19.5 per cent).

These two New Zealand reports provided the first systematic analysis of seized materials. They caused considerable concern because they identified a high number of young people engaged in the collection of illegal images and this was substantiated in the second data set. The results were somewhat different from those reported by Wolak *et al.* (2005) in the US in a study called N-JOV (National Juvenile Online Victimisation Study) where only 3 per cent were younger than 18. What also emerged from these analyses is that the online offending activities of young people, in relation to abuse images of children, are similar to those reported in adults (Quayle 2004). There are four broad classes of offending: downloading (which may include the commission of a contact offence); trading; production; and Internet seduction. These are clearly not mutually exclusive categories, but all revolve around engagement with the Internet and the possession of abuse images. Downloading and saving child abuse images are invariably purposeful activity. Downloading can be conceptualised as a largely socially isolated way of collecting images, usually from websites or from newsgroups. Although it may involve searching for material, such passive collecting is unlikely to include substantial social engagement with others, but may still result in the justification of collecting abuse images because of the evidence that there are large numbers of other people similarly engaged. Downloading may also be accompanied by the commission of contact offences and these may be in response to what is seen online, either through imitation or through permission giving.

Carr's (2004) data analysis of the New Zealand sample revealed other interesting findings about the young people in the study:

> . . . while the collection of material portraying the exploitation of children, young people or both, for sexual purposes was common across all of the age/occupation categories, those individuals identified as school students were much more likely to trade and/or possess images of teenagers and/or older children than any other group of individuals. They were also most likely to select material showing children and young people with others of their age. Indeed, even when they chose images pertaining to other categories of the Act, school students tended to select materials portraying youth aged under 17 years. As such, it appears that their interest was within the realms of 'age appropriateness'.

However, it should be noted that all of the school students were found to trade and/or possess images of children and young people engaged in explicit sexual activity, including images of children aged between 2 and 7 years, giving cause for concern about their activities. Also of concern was that school children were also proportionately more likely to trade and/or possess images of children and young people that suggested or implied incest. Nonetheless, Carr (2004) felt that the data did provide clues as to the motivation for initially accessing this material and offered support for, 'the concept of a sexually curious group of adolescents'.

In support of this, the results of the New Zealand study also indicated that offenders identified as secondary school students were more likely than the others to collect large numbers of images that were well indexed. They were also more frequently associated with the collection of images of older children and teenagers, portrayed with other children, and were much less likely to collect images of adult rape or the torture of adults or children. Carr (2004) concluded that:

> What is worrying is that their Internet based exploration has led them to subject matter involving largely deviant activities at a time when they are most likely to be influenced by the message it conveys.

As anticipated, such young people were likely to be living at home and as such did not demonstrate in the same way as some of the older people in the sample the detrimental effect that collecting problematic Internet material can have on people's lives.

Mobile phone technology and self-harm

The focus in this chapter has been largely on the Internet in relation to children and young people who sexually abuse, but other emerging new technologies also seem to be problematic. To date, much of the relevant interest in mobile phone technology has focused on its use by adults to victimise children. Madell and Muncer (2004) examined the changing pattern of usage of mobile phones by young people over the last ten years, noting that in January 1999, 27 per cent of UK householders owned and used a mobile phone, which by November 2002 had risen to 69 per cent. The evidence would suggest that mobile phone ownership may be higher among children aged 11–16 than among adults, with 76 per cent of children having their own phone (Child-Wise Monitor 2002). Madell and Muncer (2004) surveyed 1,340 secondary school children from the Teesside area of the UK. Of these 86 per cent owned a mobile phone (89.7 per cent females and 82.3 per cent males). In this study, mobile phone use was restricted to voice calls and text, but there is evidence that increasingly mobile phones can also act as other forms of communication. Livingstone and Bober (2005), however, have argued this is now diversifying, and in their study 38 per cent of the young people had a mobile phone, 17 per cent a digital television and 8 per cent a games console, all with access to the Internet. Ishi (2004) examined Internet use via mobile phone in Japan which has the highest diffusion rate of the mobile Internet in the world and many Japanese carriers provide a variety of mobile Internet services. One conclusion from this is that the mobile Internet may develop in a diverse manner throughout the world, depending on local culture and customs. It may also be the case that within cultures there are differences in mobile phone use that relate largely to age. For many young people, the mobile phone is both a vital means of communication and a way of relating to, and participating in, an extended social world.

More recently mobile phone use has been associated not so much with the victimisation of children, but with behaviour by children that is self-harming. As yet, there are no academic or professional publications related to this, and the following account is based on press reports and unpublished single case studies. In January 2004, the Gardaí (Irish Police) launched an investigation into the circulation of a pornographic image of a schoolgirl by hundreds of secondary school students using camera phones in Cork, Limerick and Kerry (*Irish Examiner* 2004). The image circulated showed a teenage girl, partly clothed in school uniform, in a 'sexually compromising position'. The image had been in circulation for some weeks before it was brought to the attention of an adult who thought that he recognised the school uniform. A similar case was reported in the UK press in March 2005, only related to the Internet. Two girls, in separate incidents, took indecent photographs of themselves in their homes without realising how widely they could be circulated on the Internet (*TES Cymru* 2005). The first case involved a 14-year-old girl who took naked pictures of herself using a digital camera, which she downloaded on to her computer and sent via an instant messaging service. The second case involved a 13-year-old girl who sent photographs of herself in underwear, with handcuffs and a whip, via a web cam to an Internet site. This set of photographs were widely accessed by other pupils and led to a fight in the school grounds. The child's parents were very distressed by the event as they thought she was using the computer to do her homework. Both of the girls described their actions as either a dare, or fun. In a similar incident, the *Daily Mail* (2005) reported that police and social services were called in after six Suffolk schoolgirls took topless photographs of each other and posted them on the Internet. The 15-year-olds posted the pictures on a website they had set up and one of the girls was arrested on suspicion of taking indecent photographs of a child.

A further report (BBC News 2005), involved both mobile phones and the Internet. It related to an adolescent boy in India who recorded a sexual act between himself and a 16-year-old schoolgirl on his mobile phone. The pictures were then circulated across India and abroad. The clip, which lasted two minutes 37 seconds was copied on to video CDs and sold. Subsequently the head of an auction website was arrested after the sale of CDs appeared on the Internet showing the sexual activity between the two students. The person who had attempted to sell the clip on the auction site was himself a student, and the consequences for all concerned appeared to be catastrophic, particularly as in India shows of public intimacy, even holding hands, are largely frowned upon.

One context for these reports is the volume of sexually related material confronting children and young people, both solicited and not, in relation to the new technologies:

> It's online, on cable, on cell phone cameras, in chat rooms, in instant messages from freaks who go online and trawl kids' Web journals, on cam-to-cam Web hookups, on TV screens at parties where kids walk past it if it were wallpaper, in lectures about abstinence in Sunday school and in health class, in movies, in hip-hop lyrics like the one blaring from the loudspeaker as they lined up for pizza and burritos.
>
> (*Daily Herald* April 2005)

This same report quoted a 16-year-old boy saying 'Pornography is just part of the culture now. It's almost like it's not even, like, porn.' The suggestion is that the way that we think about 'normative' sex has expanded so considerably, that outside of legal definitions, pornography no longer exists. We have become desensitised to the advertisements for sexually enhancing drugs and sexually explicit pictures that arrive in a regular basis in our e-mail boxes (and those of many young people). They are an irritation because they clog up our mailbox, but their content hardly registers.

As discussed throughout this chapter, there is little empirical research that enables us to establish harm to selves or others in relation to young people's sexual behaviour and the new technologies. Paradoxically, teenagers currently have the lowest pregnancy, birth and abortion rates for decades. A study by the US Center for Disease Control and Prevention (2002) concluded that the vast majority of adolescents are virgins at the age of 15, and that number has increased since 1995. Further research in the US (Jones *et al.* 2001; Jones and Finkelhor 2003; Finkelhor and Jones 2004) has also suggested a decrease of 39 per cent in the overall number of sexual abuse cases in the last decade. It is not possible from this data to estimate whether there has also been a change in the number of young people engaging in sexually abusive behaviours. The statistics provided by the Home Office for 2003/4 for England and Wales (Home Office 2004) indicated that approximately one in five offenders found guilty at all courts, or cautioned for a sexual offence, were under 18 years of age. The scale of sexual offending as a proportion of all convictions and cautions in England and Wales has been relatively stable over the last decade in the UK, 'suggesting that adolescent sexual offending constitutes a significant minority of all sexual abuse coming to the attention of the criminal justice system' (Hackett 2004: 8). However, Hoghughi *et al.* (1997) have suggested that only between 10 and 15 per cent of all known sexually abusive adolescents are officially dealt with or reported for further legal intervention. It is unclear what the figures might be in relation to Internet abuse images, although as with adult offenders, it is much easier to secure a conviction in such cases because of the presence of evidential material.

Conclusion

This chapter inevitably raises more questions than it provides answers to. Clearly there is evidence of sexually abusive behaviours by children and adolescents that both come to the notice of the legal system (Wilson and Andrews 2004), as well as those that do not (Finkelhor *et al.* 2000). At this stage it is impossible to quantify the extent of such behaviours, but their topography is similar to that seen in adult offenders in relation to child abuse images and sexual solicitations, and also includes self-harm behaviours. The limited data available would suggest that such behaviours have multiple functions (Longo 2004), but that they also have characteristics suggesting sexual curiosity and risk taking (Carr 2004). The context for such sexually abusive behaviours is a medium that is saturated with sexually explicit material, which includes not only consensual sexual activity, but sexual acts such as rape, torture, scatology and sado-masochism, as well as non-sexual material that is sexualised (birth pictures, crash site victims, dead bodies and so on).

The Internet offers young people access to this world which is essentially private and is underpinned by what Cooper and Griffin-Shelley (2002) have called the 'triple A engine' – access, affordability and anonymity. The majority of young people now have access to the new technologies (both Internet and mobile phone), and while there is still a large divide between countries, the gap is slowly closing. However, there is still a substantial divide between the familiarity, knowledge and comfort that young people experience in relation to these technologies and that experienced by most adults. Several of the studies reviewed suggest that children prefer this world to be private, and even when things happen online or through their mobile phones that may be construed as sexually problematic, they keep this largely to themselves. The majority of young people in Livingstone and Bober's (2005) study did not want restrictions placed on their Internet use and 63 per cent of their sample had taken some action to hide their online activities from their parents. Equally, in this study, parents appeared to underestimate children's negative experiences, with only 7 per cent being aware that their children had received sexual solicitations.

The United Nations Convention on the Rights of the Child, which was ratified in 1990, states under Article 17 that:

> Parties recognise the important function performed by the mass media and shall ensure that the child has access to information and material from a diversity of national and international sources, especially those aimed at the promotion of his or her social, spiritual and moral well-being and physical and mental health.

Arising from this it recommends encouragement of 'the development of appropriate guidelines for the protection of the child from information and material injurious to his or her well-being'. While much of the information available to children and young people through the new technologies would be seen as promoting well-being, there is a substantial amount that clearly falls short of these recommendations. Thus, a bizarre situation appears to have arisen where children are potentially exposed to an unlimited range of materials (largely free) in a medium that is unpoliced and has no national or geographical boundaries. In this context they can not only explore ways of being that would be otherwise denied them, but can also engage in abusive and risk-taking activities that will largely go undetected. This is not to claim that children are unwitting victims of the new technologies, but that they are people who have agency and are part of the direction that such technologies take in the future. It would appear that what has happened with the Internet and mobile phones has taken us unawares, and has developed at a pace that we have failed to keep up with. We feel uncomfortable and worried that children may be exposed to problematic material or communication media, but we are equally reluctant to engage with the problem in a way that might reduce freedom of speech, or more importantly, the opportunity to create wealth. We might conclude that rather than criminalising such activities in relation to the new technologies we should see them as a child protection issue, both for the victims in child abuse images but also for those victimised by a largely unregulated environment.

Part 3

Interventions

10 Individual psychotherapy for young sexual abusers of other children

Eileen Vizard and Judith Usiskin

Introduction

This chapter is based on the work of the Young Abusers Project, which was established in 1992 to provide an out-patient assessment and treatment service for children and young people who sexually abuse other children. The Project is part of Islington Primary Care Trust and is supported by the NSPCC.

Literature review

A literature review in relation to the psychoanalytic aspects of young sexual abusers is inevitably brief given the present dearth of writing on the subject. By contrast there is discussion about the origins and meaning of adult sexually abusive behaviours, albeit that this is described in the early literature in rather old-fashioned and pejorative terms such as 'deviance', 'perversions', or 'aberrations' (see, for example, Freud 1905; Glasser 1979). More recently concepts relating to child abuse and trauma have introduced a more up-to-date psychoanalytical understanding of the inner worlds of child abuse victims (Miller 1984; Scharff and Scharff 1994); offenders with learning difficulties (Sinason 1997a); and abusing families (Bentovim 1992). However, little has yet been written about the inner world of the young sexual abuser since it is only relatively recently that there has been acknowledgment of the prevalence of the problem.

In discussing any abnormal pattern of sexual behaviour it is clearly necessary to describe the current norms for sexual behaviour, and yet one hundred years after Freud's papers on sexual aberrations and infantile sexuality (1905) there are few normative studies in relation to childhood sexuality. Indeed within the field of psychoanalysis even the concept of normal infantile sexuality without a traumatic basis has been questioned (Miller 1984).

Freud's own concept of normality in relation to adult sexuality was extremely conservative as might have been expected in Victorian times. He states that 'the normal sexual aim is regarded as being the union of the genitals in the act known as copulation', although he goes on to acknowledge that 'even in the most normal sexual process we may detect rudiments which, if they had developed, would have led to the deviations described as "perversions"' (Freud 1905: 149). However, Freud says little about the origins of sexually abusive behaviour in children, partly because he appears to have had certain difficulties himself in accepting the abusive nature of sexual contact between children and adults (Masson 1992) and partly because, as a clinician working with adult patients, he was not clear about the limits of sexual behaviour and experimentation in normal young children. Freud's final formulation that childhood 'sexuality' (that is, sexualised behaviour) was the result of attempts by the child to come to terms with Oedipal conflicts (that is, a wish to have sex with the parent of the opposite sex) remains highly unsatisfactory and limited. It ignores the sexualising role of an experience of child sexual abuse and there is no compelling evidence to suggest that normal children do want to have sex with their parents. Nevertheless, it is fair to say that Freud's work on sexuality points out the early origins of many adult sexual disturbances and the homeostatic function of perverse behaviour in maintaining a psychic equilibrium in a patient with the avoidance of serious emotional conflicts.

This is to some extent echoed by Glasser's view (1979) that the resistance to treatment of perverse sexual interests in adult life is connected with a fear of annihilation, known as the 'core complex' in which 'closeness and intimacy [are envisaged] as annihilating, or separateness and independence [are envisaged] as desolation-isolation' (p. 280). McDougall (1990) postulates a somewhat similar self-preservative solution to these early fears of disintegration by the adult sexual deviant when she states that 'perversions demonstrate that their creator is using sexual capacity to deal with deeper narcissistic dangers' (p. 179). However, even in this more recent writing there is little or no mention of the possible role of early trauma (abuse) in the origins of later deviance or abusing.

Limentani (1989) appeared to be struggling towards an integrated understanding of the origins of perverse behaviour which could relate both to a fear of psychic disintegration and also to early trauma when he stated that 'I suddenly felt that I was reaching the overriding conclusion that a perversion, after all, is not an illness but only a symptom' (p. 237). He goes on:

> This [symptom] forms the core of a syndrome which has its roots in disturbed object relations in early life, eventually surfacing as perverted acts. It should be noted that in general the original traumatic experience is subject to disavowal. The fantasies associated with the primary excitation [the traumatic experience] seldom reach consciousness but their derivatives [perversion/abusing] will be found in later life.
>
> (p. 238)

Stoller's *Perversion: The Erotic Form of Hatred* (1975) does openly acknowledge the key role of sadism and hostility towards the object or victim of the perversion without specifically naming child abuse as the hostile basis for paedophilia.

A more informed and reasonably up-to-date psychoanalytic text (Scharff and Scharff 1994) discusses the 'Traumatic Continuum' of child abuse within an overall object relational view of trauma. The authors are at pains to acknowledge the 'transmission of trauma to the next generation' (pp. 284–5) but there is no mention of the abused-to-abuser links which characterise much of the mainstream child abuse literature.

Clear links between childhood trauma and later sexualised disturbance in vulnerable children and adults with learning difficulties have been described from a psychoanalytical perspective (Sinason 1997a). In therapeutic work with abused children the need to use therapy as an emotional space in which the abusive experience can be 'forgotten', worked through via play, drawings and containment in therapy and then carefully 'remembered' with the help of interpretation from the therapist has been described (Alvarez 1990). A brief, focused psychoanalytical approach was taken within the Great Ormond Street research programme on young sexual abusers (Hodges *et al.* 1994) where extended psychotherapeutic assessments over twelve sessions with a therapist allowed conscious remembering and/or discussion of a boy's own abusing behaviour to open up the possibility of later therapy needing to address both abused and abusing experiences. The roots of sexual violence in children and adolescents have been explored in the light of more recent literature from the fields of traumatic stress, brain chemistry and emotion (Le Doux 1994; Perry 1994). The possibility is then discussed (Hawkes *et al.* 1997) that aspects of early sexualised behaviour which may have been induced by child sexual abuse can become imprinted on the brain chemistry hence leading to a persistent state of arousal in the young person which can then result in a tendency towards sexually abusive behaviour.

Clinical descriptions of psychotherapy with sexually abusive young people are now emerging in the literature (Hodges *et al.* 1994; Vizard 1997; Woods 1997). The therapeutic themes described include the sexualisation of violence, traumatic experiences resulting in psychic retreat; sexualisation of the therapeutic relationship, re-enactment of trauma, testing of the therapeutic boundaries; sexualised transferences; the implications for safe practice and working with issues of attachment and loss.

Important research looking at links between sexual victimisation and later abusing behaviour has been undertaken by the Great Ormond Street Team (Bentovim 1998), and has indicated that certain risk factors for later perpetration can be identified including experiences of physical abuse; witnessing of physical violence; discontinuity of care; and rejection by the family. These research findings are clearly relevant information for prospective therapists of such young sexual abusers and highlight the role of early trauma of all types in the genesis of abusive behaviour.

Truly evidence-based research in relation to analytic psychotherapy outcomes for children is hard to find and there are no known studies looking at long-term outcomes for such dynamic treatment with children who sexually abuse. Nevertheless, lessons can be learned from treatment outcome studies with non-sexually abusive but disturbed children referred to the Child and Adolescent Mental Health Service (CAMHS), since many of these children share demographic and dynamic features with abusive children.

A recent systematic review of psychoanalytic approaches in child and adolescent psycho-therapy (Kennedy 2004) has studied outcomes for analytic treatment with children from thirty clinically based studies, of which five were randomised controlled trials. The cohort were children with a range of emotional and behavioural problems presenting to various CAMHS settings in a London area but it is not clear how many, if any, of these children were presenting with sexually harmful behaviour. Findings from the review of treatment outcome (ibid.) were generally positive, and beneficial effects of treatment for children were shown on a broad range of outcome measures including social and educational adjustment, behav-iour, symptoms, relationships, family functioning as well as psychiatric and psychological disorder.

One study looking at children who had suffered extreme levels of sexual abuse (Trowell *et al.* 2002), found that, whilst gains were made with treatment, unsurprisingly perhaps, the cohort continued to present with residual difficulties after a relatively brief intervention of thirty individual sessions. The systematic review (Kennedy 2004) also showed that adverse effects were seen in children who were offered individual treatment only, in the absence of parallel parent/carer work, and in children who received insufficient dynamic therapy in childhood who were seen to be worse off in terms of their attachment security when com-pared with untreated children. However, a study with severely deprived children in residential care (Lush *et al.* 1991) not only showed that therapists may be able to predict therapeutic outcomes accurately, but that the vast majority of children seen in once-weekly treatment over a period of less than two years with parallel parent/carer work, improved considerably.

In relation to therapeutic group work with sexually abusive children and young people in the Young Abusers Project, a model of parallel parent/carer work has been described (Griffin *et al.* 1997). This model has operated on the basis that provision of a parallel service for the parent/carers will help to support the treatment process and will prevent potential for undermining the child's treatment. The need to ensure that there is an adequate, systemic child protection context for this parent/carer work is emphasised in this chapter, as well as for group work with children who sexually abuse (ibid.).

More recently, at the Young Abusers Project, the focus on working with parents and carers has been intensified. Our assessment package now includes an initial, in-depth interview with the young person's birth parent(s) or primary care giver. A detailed family history is taken and the material elicited from this interview is extremely helpful in supplementing the often scant and incomplete information contained in the child's file. In the event of new, hitherto undisclosed issues of abuse arising from the meeting, these will be reported to the relevant authorities. Interviewees are alerted to this fact from the outset. Such interviews, apart from fulfilling a useful function in terms of information gathering, also provide an opportunity for the carer to get to know some of the members of staff. This may alleviate some of the anxieties in respect of the young person's forthcoming assessment as well as harnessing support for future therapy, if indicated.

In conclusion, whilst the evidence base for psychodynamic treatment outcome with children showing sexually harmful behaviour is limited at present, certain themes do emerge from the literature that are relevant in relation to service provision. First, it appears that even severely deprived and disturbed children can benefit from psychodynamic therapy if it is provided at sufficient frequency, i.e. at least once per week, and for sufficient duration, i.e. at least two years of treatment. Second, the evidence shows that dynamic therapy with children who have complex needs will be more effective if it is delivered with parallel parent/carer work which will support the treatment process. Third, there is emerging evidence that too little therapy delivered to children with complex needs, and then stopped, may have more adverse effects on their capacity to form secure attachment relationships than having no therapy in the first place. Finally, there appears to be the suggestion that more intensive psychodynamic treatment of children with complex needs will show greater benefits on a number of outcome measures at long-term follow up (Kennedy 2004).

Hence, commissioners of child psychotherapy services for children with sexually harmful behaviour would do well to ensure that services purchased are evidence-based in terms of outcome measures, provide parallel services for parents/carers and are funded to continue, once weekly, for a minimum of two years.

Setting a safe child protection context for psychotherapy with dangerous children

The Young Abusers Project tries to provide a secure base for out-patient psychotherapy with a disturbed child population using the support and resources of a specialist multidisciplinary team in collaboration with referring agencies. Such a secure base is difficult to achieve since the behaviour of these dangerous but vulnerable children causes great professional anxiety and there is confusion about how best to meet their needs. Some of this confusion is reflected in uncertainty about how to describe these children and young people, with understandable concerns about labelling younger children as 'abusers', or 'offenders' when their presenting behaviours may be more akin to those of oversexualised child victims of abuse and apparently less comparable to the behaviours of older adolescent and adult abusers.

From a dynamic perspective, however, it appears that many colleagues are 'identified' with the victimised aspects of their young clients to such an extent that they may become relatively blind to the developing dangers posed to others by these sad, vulnerable but dangerous children. Such dynamics are part of everyday work with many child abuse cases but it becomes particularly important to clarify, name and resolve these dynamics in an open and cooperative manner with colleagues before psychotherapy is started, to avoid communication problems and the possible breakdown of therapy with resultant further emotional damage to the child or young person concerned. It follows that the clinical criteria for accepting a young sexual abuser into individual psychotherapy must take on board wider systemic issues including the creation of a safe child protection context, the pragmatics of funding, setting up and supporting treatment as well as the more subtle intra-psychic and dynamic issues involved in each case.

More specifically, certain key issues have emerged from the work of the Young Abusers Project, in relation to safe psychotherapeutic practice with this client group, issues which are now discussed.

The dangers of treating young abusers in isolation from colleagues

At the outset it is important to stress that, for several reasons, no individual from any discipline should undertake psychotherapy (of any type) with a young abuser on their own without a supportive, professional framework being in place. First, therapy with this client group involves child protection issues at every step of the process from assessment, during therapy, in holiday breaks and at termination of therapy. It needs to be remembered by prospective therapists of known or suspected young sexual abusers that 'acting out' with this type of client may well include further abuse of children who can be seriously damaged both physically and emotionally. Should re-offending occur during therapy or other past abusing emerge, the therapist needs to have a previously established, functioning and positively supportive professional network with whom to share concerns and any relevant information.

Therapists should remember that only local authority social workers and NSPCC social workers are authorised and expected to take child protection action when disclosures of abuse are made, either during therapy or at other times. The therapist cannot act alone to protect child victims on information given during therapy and, conversely, the therapist is not entitled to keep secret such child protection information which may have very serious consequences for prospective victims (Department of Health and Social Security 1988; GMC 1997). On a more positive note, adequate communication between the therapist and the wider professional network will usually pre-empt serious child protection issues, will greatly assist local management of the case and will, as a consequence, ensure the gratitude and continued support of colleagues in relation to therapy.

The second reason for not working alone with these cases is that there will be serious transference and counter-transference issues to be expected in relation to sexuality, sexual abuse, perversion and violence. Sexual overtures, both overt and covert, from such clients are commonplace and must be managed as a matter of course without panic or paralysis in the session. Although the likelihood of a rapacious assault is low in an appropriately assessed case, there is no doubt that some young sexual abusers do pose a serious risk of physical or sexual assault to professionals who may challenge their distorted belief systems. Clinical accounts (Woods 1997) of the persecuted, aggressive and sexualised behaviour of patients give a clear picture of some of the technical difficulties surrounding individual work with this client group. It is essential that a supportive systemic context exists around the therapist, not only to provide safe physical structures for the therapy and much needed emotional support for the therapist, but also to make clear to the patient that the therapist is in touch with colleagues and is not an isolated and vulnerable individual over whom he may gain power.

Linking external and internal realities: the key systemic role of the specialist social worker

Given the unusual forensic demands of out-patient work with this client group, it is important that there is one individual within the team who can maintain an awareness of all the external world complexities mentioned above and can link these to the main task of providing therapy for the inner world of the child concerned. In the Young Abusers Project, the NSPCC specialist social worker has a key role in arranging psychiatric, psychological and psychotherapeutic assessments, liaising constantly with local agencies on both practical and therapeutic issues and providing a conduit for relevant child protection information from the network to the therapist and vice versa. The specialist social worker is responsible (in consultation with other colleagues for reports and correspondence); for telephone liaison on cases, which is often extensive; for making, confirming and then checking local arrangements for the young person to be brought to therapy regularly, and for providing support and consultation to the carer or key worker with responsibility for the young person. Clinical experience suggests that it would be unwise to attempt to set up individual therapy with such a disturbed client group without this support and the cases seen in the Young Abusers Project make clear the pivotal role of the specialist social worker in discussing issues with foster carers, key workers, local clinicians and managers who are responsible for funding.

In relation to funding it is clearly essential that there is an undertaking at the outset from the funding agency to make a commitment to long-term treatment. Uncertainty about this issue is easily conveyed to the young person and the therapist, with the possibility that the patient may try to end the treatment destructively before the money runs out, thereby trying to take back at least some control over the situation.

The issue of open confidentiality in therapy with young sexual abusers

Traditionally, medical consultations, including interviews with psychiatrists, psychotherapists, psychoanalysts and counsellors, are contexts in which absolute confidentiality is usually expected. However, in recent years, the difficulties surrounding confidentiality in child abuse cases have been raised for debate and it has become clear that such cases cannot be seen within the traditional framework of confidentiality which might prevent the reporting of appropriate concerns about past or present child abuse. The issue still remains controversial, particularly with dynamically trained psychotherapists and analysts who may feel that the transference/counter-transference relationship will be irreparably damaged if the therapist is seen as a leaky 'container' with whom confidences cannot be entrusted. Such therapists may feel that child or adult clients experiencing or inflicting child abuse will not bring their disclosures of abuse or their most perverse fantasies or behaviours to the session if they know that the information will be passed to the local authority. The argument then goes that it is better to hear the disclosures, fantasies and behaviours and to work in confidence with the client to heal abuse sequelae or to stop abusing behaviour.

The other side of this argument, however, is that by maintaining confidentiality in abuse cases in therapy, the therapist is consciously or unconsciously colluding with the original dynamics of denial and secrecy which allowed the abuse to occur and that such collusion gives a message to the patient that the therapist is also untrustworthy and corrupt.

Furthermore there is a real possibility of abuse continuing throughout the course of therapy, a situation bound to be damaging to the victim if he or she is also attending regular therapy and returning home to be abused, perhaps frequently, before the next session. A clear message is then given, by not intervening, that all the grown-ups are in it together, as it were, and that no amount of meaningful drawings, comments or play by the child in therapy will be understood by the therapist as indicative of current abuse.

This is also true for abusers when their own disclosures of re-abusing a child or children are made in therapy. If no action is taken by the therapist to report the abuse or early attempts to target, isolate and groom other children, then the abuser will assume that the therapist does not really take the problem seriously and that, like in their contacts with previous authority figures, no consequences for their actions will follow. In other words it will be assumed that the abuser can do what he likes to the victim(s). In the mind of the abuser, it will seem that the wool can well and truly be pulled over the therapist's eyes and that the therapist can be 'groomed' (just like the victim[s]) into acquiescence and silence.

The need for safe practice by trained and supervised psychotherapists

Another consideration in relation to open confidentiality in work with juvenile sexual abusers relates to the need to protect the young person from an inept or possibly abusive therapist. It is important to stress that sexual, emotional and physical abuse of patients by therapists is a sad reality (Scharff and Scharff 1994) and that a traditional confidentiality model is the perfect context in which such abuse can occur. Furthermore, when the patient is an extremely vulnerable and sexually provocative young abuser who may project all of his most deviant, exciting and destructive impulses into the therapist and when the same young person may present as sexually aroused in the session, possibly making physical or verbal overtures towards the psychotherapist, then it becomes clear that much of this behaviour may be a re-enactment in the session of the problem of sexual arousal outside the session over which the young abuser has no control. A knowingly corrupt therapist may readily take advantage of such dynamics to sexually abuse the patient.

However, even the most experienced and responsible therapist may become caught up in the sexually charged atmosphere which pervades individual work with sex offenders and juvenile abusers. It is before this situation arises, when the therapist is overwhelmed by excited and omnipotent feelings about controlling the patient through his or her interpretations, that open communication and open confidentiality should be established. Such a transparent and non-ambiguous context should make it clear to the therapist, patient and professionals that no inappropriate secrets will be kept in this therapy and that the therapist and the professional network are safe and incorruptible, in contrast to the adults previously known to the patient. For these and other reasons, it is now good practice for professional work with the victims and perpetrators of sexual abuse to occur in a context of open confidentiality where all relevant information about known or suspected child abuse is shared.

Providing a safe clinical context and physical environment for young sexual abusers in therapy

Appropriate preparation of the young person by referring professionals for visits to the clinic is absolutely essential if therapy is to succeed. If the young person arrives for a psychiatric, psychological or psychotherapeutic assessment then he should have been fully prepared for the format and the length of the interview; where applicable, that assessment interviews will be videotaped (for child protection reasons) and that a consent form will need to be signed; whether the interview will be live supervised by other members of the team through the video system and that very specific enquiry will be made about the nature of the offences known or suspected to have been committed (Vizard *et al.* 1996). Carers should also be prepared in advance for the possibility of 'acting out', i.e. risk-taking behaviour by the young person before or after therapy sessions and there should be continued discussion with the young abuser about the mixed feelings which may be stirred up in the sessions.

The waiting area or waiting arrangements and the therapy rooms, toilets and refreshment areas in any clinic offering assessment and treatment for young sexual abusers of children are clearly important aspects which require careful thought and planning before children start to arrive at the clinic. First, arrangements need to be made to ensure that young sexual abusers are escorted to and from interviews and therapy rooms by their professional carers who need to be available for this task during the sessions. This is because the children and young people who are the subject of this book are both vulnerable to approaches from unscrupulous adults and also dangerous to other young children to whom they are sexually attracted. The clinical experience in the Young Abusers Project shows that certain boys in this client group will approach other young children in the toilets of clinics to which they are taken in the hope of targeting and isolating the child for sexual abuse.

More impulsive abusers may simply try to reach out and grab the clothing of another child to pull down their trousers, for instance, or they may expose themselves to other children causing great distress. Long absences in the toilet whilst the carer or therapist waits in the corridor may indicate anxiety or resistance to therapy but may also indicate masturbation to sexual images stirred up in assessment or therapy which the young person does not wish to disclose. Apart from risk to other children, the young sexual abuser may put himself at risk by making inappropriately friendly or sexualised comments to adults in or around the toilet.

A 13-year-old boy, Jimmy, who came for a psychotherapy assessment asked to visit the toilet. Since the boy's carer was engaged on the telephone, one of the Project's male workers accompanied Jimmy to the toilet and stood inside the door, facing away from the boy and waiting to take him back to the session. Whilst standing at the urinal Jimmy called over to the Project worker in a chatty way saying what a long, tiring journey he had today coming to the clinic and asking how the worker felt today? The boy had never met this worker before. Despite the worker making it clear that it was now time to leave the toilet, Jimmy continued to stand at the urinal, holding his penis, wanting to make animated conversation and quite unworried about talking so freely to a strange man.

Arrangements therefore need to be made to ensure that the children attending the clinic for help with sexual arousal to other children do not inadvertently mix with victim children and that such young sexual abusers are not allowed to wander unsupervised around clinics where there are also victimised children. When in place, such supervision arrangements are perfectly well understood (and appreciated at some level) by the young abusers who feel contained, as well as providing peace of mind for the accompanying carer, therapist and home-based professionals.

The assessment and therapy rooms should be comfortable and child or young person orientated with plenty of paper and drawing materials, traditional child psychotherapy assessment toys, a flip chart for drawing diagrams or writing messages, a box of tissues and some neutral pictures or decorations on the walls. The toy shop scenario with every known stuffed toy, doll, car and game, together with posters of sad, vulnerable children being exhorted to ring ChildLine or the NSPCC often seen in some children's homes or therapeutic institutions for victimised children would be wholly inappropriate for work with this client group of young sexual abusers. Many young abusers are turned on and excited by pictures of sad, vulnerable children and some clients of the Young Abusers Project (and adult sex offenders too) have been known to use ChildLine for heavy breathing phone calls in which their graphic sexual fantasies about the children in the posters are shared.

Care is therefore needed in furnishing and decorating the clinical rooms in which these abusing children are seen, although the psychotherapy setting (even for teenagers and certainly for learning disabled young people) should always include the drawing and basic play materials mentioned above. This is because the psychological processes of splitting, projection and denial which have, in a way, helped to keep the young person functioning at some level may be very challenged by a rigidly traditional psychoanalytic approach. 'Splitting' has been described as a process leading to 'feelings and relations (and later on, thought processes) being in fact cut off from one another' (Klein 1946: 6). Subsequently these 'split off' disavowed feelings may be 'projected' or pushed into another person (the victim or possibly the therapist) in such a way that the original owner of the unwanted feelings can more readily 'deny' their origins. Denial is a key mental mechanism in most sexual abusers, including young people, and there will be the strongest possible resistance by the abuser towards any discussion or verbal exchange which attempts to challenge this denial. Hence, the provision of drawing and play materials emphasises the importance of play (Alvarez and Phillips 1998), and gives a message that the therapist is sensitive to his resistance to open up and communicate and has provided additional methods for doing so where words are not needed.

In some cases children act out during their assessment. There may be many reasons for this behaviour; for instance, unwillingness to attend, often because of extreme anxiety, is common, though in some cases children are not adequately prepared by their carers. Examples of the kinds of destructive behaviour which have damaged clinic furnishings include:

- a boy who sat viciously and angrily digging chunks out of the wooden arm of a chair whilst discussing his abusive behaviour;
- another boy who sat silently getting red in the face with anger at interpretations and deliberately crushed his empty coke can with one hand after which he bit into the can leaving teeth marks;
- a boy who set fire to paper in the (group) therapy room and threw it out of the window on to cars in the car park below (this boy was subsequently convicted of an arson offence).

The level of persecutory anxiety in some young sexual abusers is so high that they may easily feel 'trapped' in a confined therapy room. It is usually sensible to arrange the seating such that the young person can, if absolutely necessary, make a quick exit without tripping over the therapist. However, developmental considerations may be important here since much younger sexualised children, for instance, may need encouragement to stay in the room and not to charge up and down the corridors.

An 8-year-old boy, Michael, resident in a children's home for severely disturbed children, was referred for an assessment of his psychotherapeutic needs. Michael refused to sit down in the room, threw the toys up in the air, and prevented the therapist from speaking by placing his hand over her mouth. Unable to acknowledge her comments relating to his extremely high level of anxiety, he attempted to climb out of the window. Eventually the therapist suggested opening the door to the therapy room and Michael managed to settle down long enough to look around him and verbalise his fear of finding monsters in the room. The door remained open for several more sessions until Michael's persecutory anxiety gradually diminished and he began to feel safe.

In some cases young sexual abusers may be brought for a risk assessment or an assessment for psychotherapy directly from secure accommodation or from a Youth Offender Institution either in handcuffs or accompanied by one or more prison officers. Arrangements will then need to be made for the young person to be seen by the assessment team whilst the prison officers keep him in view either through the video system or sitting next to him in the room. It does not follow that because a young person requires supervision and an escort of this sort that he is necessarily unsuitable for psychotherapy on release into the community. Obviously the exact nature of the offending, the degree of physical violence and the level of assessed dangerousness will be critical in determining suitability for outpatient treatment (see Chapter 7).

Recurrent themes in therapeutic work with young abusers

Fear of contamination

There is often a great fear in the minds of professionals and the public alike about any contact with sex offenders of whatever age. Serious over-reactions are reported in the press when vigilante groups get together to hound out sex offenders in the local community. However, less extreme reactions in otherwise balanced and well-educated professionals are still common and the fact is that very few professionals are interested in working therapeutically with this client group, whether child or adult perpetrators (Sinason 1997b).

When asked, colleagues will maintain that there are good reasons for not being able to take on the work such as a lack of resources, training or facilities. However, further enquiry usually reveals that there is considerable fear and resistance from colleagues about sitting in the room with young sexual abusers discussing their sex-offending behaviour. Male and female colleagues may fear sexual overtures and female colleagues may fear rape and/or physical attack whilst colleagues of both genders may fear the erotic counter-transference and sexual feelings stirred up in them by this work. In some cases psychotherapists who become consciously aware of these sexual feelings may then unconsciously convert these into feelings of parental concern, which, although less threatening, are equally inappropriate and disturbing to the therapist/patient relationship.

These reactions may not be expressed at a conscious level and colleagues may be unaware of their own behaviour in relation to the work. For instance, some colleagues may show an exaggerated fear or hesitation about entering the clinic premises or they may appear to be very shocked, angered or mesmerised by the information which they see emerging in the assessment session through the video system. Others may feel physically sick whilst watching assessment videos, whilst more vulnerable trainees may experience 'frozen' moments in the assessment interview when the reality of the type of client they are speaking to suddenly becomes clear. Some reactions to the work can be more idiosyncratic as in the case of the young, pregnant psychologist who watched assessment tapes calmly and with professional disinterest, but became very distressed, felt rather sick, held her stomach with both hands and could not share her feelings in the debrief session after watching a group of young sexual abusers discussing their fantasies about young children. Only subsequently could this young woman admit that it was the sight of 'all of them together somehow' which had made her feel sick and intensely protective towards her unborn child.

Such reactions are commonplace and are probably a perfectly normal reaction to working with unpleasant material which comes, confusingly, from a vulnerable but dangerous group of young clients. Supervision and support from senior colleagues and from other team members are essential to allow the person concerned to understand and deal with their feelings in a constructive manner. Difficulties arise if these reactions are noted in colleagues who are not part of the specialist team and who may be going back to an unsupported context after having brought the young person to the session. The need for supervision cannot be overemphasised for experienced and for novice practitioners alike and this is something for which preparations should be made before any therapy for the client is started (see also Chapters 16 and 17).

Trivialisation and minimising of abusing behaviour

It is not uncommon in work with adult sexual abusers to encounter trivialisation of the index offence not only by the offender but also by professionals involved in the case. The typical defence plea that this was a 'one-off' offence in a man of previously good character has been argued vigorously in criminal courts for many years. Such a defence is easier to pursue when the criminal laws of evidence do not allow for admission of evidence of earlier offending or of patterns of behaviour which suggest an interest in children. However, in the civil courts, where known or alleged sex offenders are dealt with in the context of Children Act 1989 proceedings, the whole evidential 'jigsaw of sexual abuse' (Hobbs and Wynne 1993) can be considered, including past histories and patterns of behaviour of both victim and alleged abuser. This wider evidential remit in the civil courts has allowed for a more systemic assessment of risk of significant harm to children based on the balance of probabilities. Having said this, trivialisation of abusive behaviour persists in all professions and at all levels.

> A 13-year-old adolescent boy, Roy, confessed to the police and to Social Services to the long-term sexual abuse of three of his younger sisters all under 11 years old. The young person, Roy, was seen in the Young Abusers Project for an assessment of risk and to look at the possibility of treatment. Roy's social worker and his team leader viewed the interview through the video system and again heard their client state quite casually and without embarrassment or remorse that he had been having regular sexual intercourse with all the sisters for three years since he was 10 years old. None of this was new information to the local authority but after the interview the Team Leader's response to the interviewers was that there had, after all, been no medical findings on any of the sisters so perhaps Roy was exaggerating or overstating the sexual contact which may have been occurring as a sort of mutual comforting experience between very deprived children? This Team Leader could see no problem for Roy in being returned home to live with his siblings as long as he, Roy, was in treatment and as long as his sisters were being watched closely by his parents.

Other examples include the use of trivialising language by professionals who may refer to abuse between older and younger children as 'inappropriate sexual relationships', 'sexual play' or 'experimentation' rather than recognising the components of coercion, bribery and abuse involved. The key issue which is often trivialised is the intent by the young person (whether conscious or unconscious) to abuse and to inflict pain on the other child (the victim).

At the root of this trivialisation is professional resistance to accepting that children can be cruel and sadistic to others and that this cruelty can be highly sexualised and compulsive. There appears to be a determination in some of us to perceive children and childhood as a passive, pure state of being in which children can only be the recipients of actions such as abuse and never the agents of actions such as abuse, particularly sexualised abuse. Sexual abuse of children by other children and young people is particularly likely to be dismissed or trivialised simply because children are not perceived as sexual beings and are not expected to have sexual feelings or show sexual behaviours until puberty. This denial of the premature sexualization of abusing children is exactly what most paedophiles would want and seems to play into society's collusion with the secret sexual exploitation of children.

Victim or abuser

> In the case of a learning-disabled girl victim of sexual assault by a group of four boys in a playground, the local authority refused to attend a professionals' meeting in relation to a pre-trial psychiatric assessment of one of the 11-year-old defendants, Shaun. The reason given for this refusal was that the local authority was acting on behalf of the girl as an alleged victim and that they could not be involved on behalf of Shaun since he was the alleged abuser and was facing a criminal trial. This situation was clearly unjust and wrongly denied Shaun his rights to services as a child in need in terms of the Children Act 1989. However, the local authority made it clear that it was either to be aligned with the child victim or with the boy defendant and that it simply could not hold in mind the needs of both vulnerable children.

A similar situation arises with young sexual abusers who are both victims of child abuse and also perpetrators against other children. Many professional colleagues can only envisage one view of the young sexual abuser, either as a sad, sexualised victim or as a dangerous young perpetrator. Either perception is usually inaccurate and incomplete, since both victim and abuser identities (Hodges *et al.* 1994) exist together with more healthy functioning identities within the mind of the abusing child.

In many ways this tendency to polarise views reflects society's impatience with complexity or with situations where there is no one simple unambiguous answer to a problem. Unfortunately, if psychotherapy with abusing children is to succeed, it is essential that the professionals supporting the process are able to bear in mind all aspects (however contradictory) of the young person's identity if there is to be any hope of future healing and integration.

'Acting out' by patients and professionals

Many patients in therapy will 'act out' with disturbed behaviours outside the therapy setting, often at weekends, over holiday periods or shortly before termination of the therapy. Such acting out seems to represent issues which have been too difficult to mention or too complex to resolve in the therapy sessions and, not infrequently, the acting out may be self-harming or risk taking and apparently intended to raise the therapist's anxiety levels. This often succeeds particularly if the acting-out behaviour involves targeting or abusing children whilst in psychotherapy. If the patient's provocative behaviour succeeds in raising the therapist's anxiety, then the therapist will need to be particularly careful that he or she does not fall into the trap of also acting out in response.

> A young boy, Troy, was seen once a week in psychotherapy and in his sessions played a game which involved him having been hurt in a car crash, writhing in pain on the floor and

getting the therapist to act as the doctor who had to physically examine him. Troy's need to be touched was paramount, and he continually created situations that might provoke physical contact.

Given the potential dangers of the erotic counter-transference mentioned above the therapist must be vigilant about professional standards including physical contact with the patient. It is often easy to feel very sorry indeed for certain young sexual abusers who are deprived and neglected and who may stir up strongly protective as well as disgusted feelings in professionals. Limentani (1989) has described the special features of transference and counter-transference in sexual deviations and makes it clear that psychotherapy sessions may be highly eroticised, the analyst may be dehumanised and treated as an object by the patient; the analyst may be forced into the role of a voyeur to the patient's repeated sexual fantasies and that very primitive, psychotic anxieties may be stirred up by treatment. Glasser (1979) has described the primitive anxieties stirred up by therapy with perverted individuals as follows: 'the patient conceives the state of oneness with the object he desires and fears as a passive merging with; being engulfed by it; getting into and being invaded by it' (p. 280). Limentani (1989) concludes that, 'The one-to-one situation, therefore, seems to play havoc with long standing defences' (p. 247) and this is clearly a warning to therapists considering work with 'perversions' including sexually abusive behaviour, to proceed with caution in terms of technique.

More up-to-date approaches to therapy with young sexual abusers have recently been described (Woods 1997) in which the potential dangers of the transference/counter-transference relationship are described and psychotherapeutic techniques appropriate for work with this client group are described within an overall child protection framework. Given the vulnerability to abuse of this group of children and young people, it is not, for instance, a good idea to start to give the patient friendly pats on the back or encouraging hand squeezes, let alone hugs, no matter how needy he may seem. Like many victims of abuse, the young sexual abuser may ascribe very different and erotically charged meanings to physical contact from the meaning ascribed by an ordinary child who may not even notice a pat on the back.

In relation to professional acting out, when funding is a key issue in arranging long-term psychotherapy, strange excuses can be found to avoid the commencement of therapy for a suitably assessed young person or to call a halt to current therapy.

> A 10-year-old abusing boy, Wayne, was progressing well in individual psychotherapy, was attached to his therapist and was starting to acknowledge his potential to abuse children without continued help. As a result, Wayne's sexualised and aggressive behaviour towards other children had greatly improved and he was far less of a management problem in foster care. The local authority's interpretation of this happy state of affairs was that since Wayne was better, he obviously did not need therapy any more and his sessions should therefore cease. The fact that Wayne had only been able to improve during therapy, that he had asked for his therapy to continue and that the therapist had predicted that there would be an adverse result from stopping the therapy was all to no avail since the local authority had decided that this particular boy had been given 'enough' therapy and that money would be better used on children who had so far been given no treatment.

There are complex psychoanalytical reasons why professionals may 'act out' in these ways in relation to work with young abusers. However, three common reasons include the professional being strongly identified with the abusive aspects of the young person; the professional being identified with the helpless victimised aspects of the client; and the professional having intense unresolved personal feelings about sexual abuse, possibly having been an abuser or victim themselves in childhood. Other examples of such acting out have included:

- letting the therapist know that the professional, perhaps the social worker or key worker, is leaving their job very soon, possibly, that very afternoon, and that the young person will not therefore be seeing them again;
- having agreed that therapy can start with the specialist project, the worker going ahead and arranging for more assessments in other projects and accepting a place for the young person in therapy to start two days before the agreed date in the specialist project;
- forgetting that a carefully planned and discussed first or last therapy session was to occur on such and such day and just not arriving with the young person; the professional bringing his or her own child along during the escorting of the young sex offender to his therapy session and being baffled and angry when the safety of their own child is queried; and
- acting out jealousy/rivalry with the therapist. This may include cancelling a therapy session in favour of an outing to a theme park, for instance.

Such attacks on the therapeutic process are not uncommon and cause a great deal of distress to young people who have managed to engage in treatment, often with many reservations.

Conclusions

Psychotherapy with young sexual abusers is an essential part of the recovery process for the abuser as well as being a vital part of child protection practice designed to protect victims. This chapter has described some of the relevant clinical issues and therapeutic dilemmas arising from this work which have been experienced in the Young Abusers Project. It is hoped that other colleagues will be encouraged to undertake therapy or to support others to undertake therapy with this client group to prevent further abusive behaviour and to enable the young people concerned to rebuild their lives.

Acknowledgements

All case vignettes have been altered to ensure confidentiality. We are very grateful to the NSPCC for their unstinting support of the Project's work over many years. Thanks are also due to the dedicated members of the Young Abusers Project Team who have contributed their considerable expertise and care to this therapeutic work. Particular thanks are due to Jane Dutton who has consulted to the team and helped us to make sense of the intense and distressing feelings arising from the work. Most importantly, thanks are due to the young people who are the subjects of this chapter and from whom we have learnt so much about trauma and recovery.

11 Working in groups with young men who have sexually abused others

David O'Callaghan, Jeremy Quayle and Bobbie Print

Introduction

Groupwork is widely reported in the literature to be an effective context for the treatment of adult sexual offenders (e.g. Beckett *et al.* 1994; Hanson *et al.* 2002; Friendship *et al.* 2003), and the number of groupwork programmes for adult sex offenders in the UK has increased during recent years (Proctor and Flaxington 1996). However, groupwork programmes for young people who have sexually abused have remained far less in evidence, being confined predominantly to specialist projects (HM Inspectorate of Probation 1998; Hackett *et al.* 2003), and the effectiveness of this approach to working with young people is relatively under-researched.

In a review of sex offender treatment programmes, Perkins *et al.* (1999) summarise the general, clinical advantages of groupwork over entirely individual approaches to treatment as:

- Groupwork involves interaction between individuals that can be utilised to facilitate change;
- Groupwork can reduce the likelihood of a therapist entering a collusive relationship with the client;
- Groupwork interactions can help offenders to become more open about abuse-related thoughts, feelings and behaviours, and by so doing, begin to address previously unresolved feelings of guilt, anger or anxiety;
- A safe and supportive group can provide an environment in which new skills and ways of thinking can be learned, practised and developed;
- Groupwork can provide therapists with valuable insights into participants' motivation to change, since participation in a group typically requires public acknowledgement that there are problems needing to be addressed.

This chapter explores the value of groupwork with young people who have sexually abused, and highlights some of the principles and approaches that appear to be the most effective. Also discussed is the importance of incorporating groupwork into an overall therapeutic response to young people. Finally, a groupwork programme developed by the authors is outlined, with examples of therapeutic exercises.

The benefits of groupwork for young people

Not all young people will benefit from inclusion in a groupwork programme (see pre-group assessment below), but there is a significant body of opinion that advocates groupwork for young people who sexually abuse as a particularly effective method of therapeutic intervention. This support arises from acknowledgement of adolescence as a key developmental stage, experience of groupwork with young people more generally, and theories relating specifically to sexually aggressive behaviours.

The developmental context

Most authors on groupwork with young people stress that particular developmental challenges of adolescence can be positively influenced and supported in appropriately led and focused groups (Carrell 1993; Evans 1998; Malekoff 2004). These challenges can be summarised as:

1   *Separation from family.* The striving for practical and emotional independence from parents/adults; increasing autonomy and greater intimacy with peers.
2   *Developing a consistent identity.* Young people's cultural, social and personal reference points may be highly volatile during adolescence. Group may provide another setting in which 'trying on' identities may occur.
3   *Developing a peer group identity.* Carrell (1993) suggests this is the 'hub of the developmental wheel for adolescents'. For those young people who are isolated from peers a group provides a valuable opportunity to begin this process.
4   *Forging a healthy sexual identity.* When working with young people whose sexual behaviour is problematic, it is essential to recognise that developing sexuality is a complex and important transitional stage in adolescent development.
5   *Development of a personal value system.* It is natural for adolescents to begin to question the values and beliefs of their parents and other strong influences. This is vital for many of the young people considered in this chapter, not only for personal growth, but also as part of progression to a non-abusive lifestyle.
6   *Preparing for the future.* Developing skills, career goals, and aspiring to more mature relationships.

Groupwork with troubled young people

As a therapeutic medium for children and young people, several advantages have been cited for groupwork techniques (Carrell 1993; Dwivedi 1993; Duboust and Knight 1995; Malekoff 2004). A summary of their findings include:

*   The group affords an environment in which young people who have difficulties in expressing emotions and experiences can learn from others, whilst developing competency in self-disclosure;
*   Groups can reduce a sense of isolation; particularly for young people whose problem has a degree of social stigma;
*   The group environment can become a safe place in which to explore difficult or anxiety-provoking issues;
*   Important interpersonal and social skills can be effectively learned and practised in a group setting;
*   Groups allow a range of experiential activities which actively engage children and young people, but are not practical within individual adult–child interactions;
*   Peer education and reinforcement are considered to be particularly effective with adolescents.

Groupwork with adolescent males who sexually abuse

Amongst practitioners there is a good deal of support for groupwork as a therapeutic approach when working with adolescents who have sexually abused. For example, Steen and Monnette (1989) state:

> Group therapy is unquestionably the modality of choice when working with adolescent sex offenders. It provides the offender with a safe milieu in which to explore his functioning, his sex offences, and his own victimisation with others who share similar experiences. Self-esteem is restored through group support and mirroring . . . Peer pressure breaks down denial and minimisation, and the techniques that will put him at low risk to re-offend are learned and practised.
>
> (p. 29)

What makes an effective groupwork programme?

Therapeutic interventions with sexually abusive young people are most often described as 'cognitive-behavioural' in approach (Richardson *et al.* 1997; Hackett *et al.* 2003). Such approaches suggest that therapeutic change is achieved through the employment of techniques that consider associations between thoughts, feelings and behaviours. For example, cognitive-behavioural theorists would argue that problem behaviours or emotions can be controlled or changed through work aimed at modifying dysfunctional thinking patterns, whilst dysfunctional thinking might be controlled or changed by practising new behaviours. The groupwork situation can provide a safe and supportive environment within which to learn and practise such new cognitive and behavioural skills. Malekoff (2004), for example, suggests cognitive-behavioural approaches do not preclude an understanding of effective group process. Similarly, Evans (1998) cautions therapists not to neglect the contribution other group members have to make, in order to avoid allowing them to become spectators in leader–member interaction. Attention to group process issues is therefore vital.

Few studies, however, have investigated adolescent participants' perceptions of the elements of groupwork that contribute to therapeutic change. Corder *et al.* (1981) found that adolescent group members emphasised the importance of being able to vent emotions in the group setting (catharsis), as did members of adult groups. However, adolescent group members' views on the value of insights generated via contemplation of historical experience differed from those of adults. Evans (1998) suggests that adolescents are so concerned with gaining distance from childhood and moving towards adulthood that reflection on early experiences feels uncomfortable or is of little interest.

Whilst analytically oriented groupwork theory identifies a number of features associated with therapeutic effectiveness, we would wish to highlight three key factors from our experience of running groups with young men who have sexually abused: clarity of purpose, group cohesion and emotional engagement.

Clarity of purpose

Malekoff (2004) proposes four aspects of group functioning to measure this:

• When the purpose of the group can be stated clearly and concisely by the workers and the group members;

- When the purpose has the same meaning for both the group members and workers;
- When the purpose is specific enough that both the client and worker will know when it has been achieved;
- When the purpose is specific enough to have direct implications for the group content.

Group cohesion

In a study of the association between therapeutic climate and the effectiveness of cognitive-behavioural treatments for adult sexual offenders, Beech and Hamilton-Giachritsis (2005) found a clear relationship between group members' perceptions of group cohesion and the extent to which facilitators encouraged freedom of action and the expression of emotion, and also reductions in pro-offending attitudes. Challenges in highly cohesive groups were carried out by group members in such a way that recipients felt supported rather than attacked, thus increasing the likelihood of them accepting what was being said.

Douglas (1995) reflects that it is difficult to isolate the factors which contribute to a sense of group cohesion, although the degree to which it is present tends to be instantly recognisable for members and leaders by its consequences for group functioning. Influencing factors include: a sense of common purpose; open communication; skilled leadership; and a positive view of group efficacy. As part of their evaluation of community-based groupwork programmes with adult sex offenders, the STEP study (Beckett *et al.* 1994) examined the therapeutic environment within which treatment was conducted, and identified particular elements which they considered characteristic of effective treatment:

- high levels of group cohesiveness, where all participants felt involved in the group;
- high levels of task orientation, placing emphasis upon practical tasks and decision making;
- clear structures and explicit rules;
- an atmosphere where members felt encouraged and respected as individuals and did not feel that they were viewed solely as 'sex offenders'.

Experiencing and expressing emotions within groups for adolescents

Garland (1992) identified five stages of 'collective competency' relevant to groups for young people in developing a genuine emotional content:

1   In the *pre-affiliation* stage young people explore their perceptions of other group members. The facilitators need to set boundaries, agendas and establish opportunities for developing trust.
2   As the distance between group members closes, *power and control* issues dominate, with a need to re-state purpose and boundaries.
3   Once the group has progressed through these challenges to meaning and authority, it can enter a more *intimate* stage, which is characterised by greater emotional depth and increased self-disclosure.
4   Successful and longer-term groups can develop a sense of identity, culture and values which survive membership and facilitator turn-over. New members progress through these personal stages of group integration more rapidly. Garland refers to the process as '*differentiation-cohesion*', thereby denoting how an individual can enter and participate in the group fully without threat to personal identity.

5   The final stage is *separation/termination*, which can relate either to the group as an entity or to an individual within the group.

Experienced groupworkers will recognise that these stages are not linear and that in long-standing, 'rolling' groups there can be regressive stages, either of individual group members or of the group as a whole (Clark and Erooga 1994).

Without some degree of emotional engagement, groups for young people can be a meaningless ritual, leading to distraction and loss of focus. For young males the sharing of emotionally significant events and supporting others may be a unique experience (Russell 1995), and will only occur if the group is considered a safe setting. Respect amongst group members is therefore a fundamental requirement for a group that aims to address abusive behaviour. Group mores must be established that take account of victims' experiences and promote respectful behaviour towards others in the group setting. Respect in this context refers to behaviours such as listening and not interrupting when others are speaking, avoiding pejorative statements, accepting that others will have different opinions on topics, tolerating individual differences in sexuality, culture and lifestyle, and maintaining confidentiality.

Differences between adult and adolescent treatment groups

The experiences of G-MAP practitioners who have facilitated both adolescent and adult treatment groups for sexual abusers suggest that there are important differences between these groups in terms of the therapeutic approaches that should be adopted, the contents of treatment programmes, and the situations in which programme participants find themselves and in which treatment is delivered.

Therapeutic approaches

Adopting a strongly confrontational approach when addressing issues such as denial or inappropriate behaviours and attitudes is even more likely to create resistance with adolescents than with adults, leading to arguing, interrupting, denying, ignoring or rejecting new ideas. These situations allow young people to express well-practised reasons for not changing, causing further entrenchment of such beliefs. It is best, therefore, to avoid such a confrontational approach.

Adult sex offender treatment programmes often place great emphasis on self-disclosure within the group setting, with other group members being encouraged to identify apparent gaps and denial in accounts of offending, as well as cognitive distortions such as minimisation and blaming. Whilst self-disclosure is not discouraged in our adolescent groups, we tend to expect this far less, and would not encourage other group members to challenge each other in relation to such disclosures. Group members are, however, strongly encouraged to self-disclose during individual treatment sessions that run concurrently with group sessions, and in most instances, we would not expect young people to join the groupwork programme until they have shown an ability to talk reasonably openly about their sexually abusive behaviour in these individual sessions.

A large body of literature highlights the importance of adopting an approach to addressing offending behaviour that is responsive to a person's individual learning style and capabilities (e.g. Gendreau and Andrews 1990; Bonta 1995). This 'responsivity principle' is particularly important when working with groups of adolescents, where having a good understanding of factors such as a group member's motivation level, cognitive ability, personality traits and maturity is essential to good treatment planning. Whilst these are clearly important considerations when working with adults, the scope for individual variability is far greater in adolescents, whose learning styles and personalities are still developing. In addition, the many developmental challenges of adolescence, such as separation from family, developing a consistent identity, and developing a peer group identity (see 'The developmental context' above) can profoundly affect motivation to change and participation in treatment.

These observations highlight the importance of adopting a more flexible approach to treatment – in terms of pace of delivery and the types and number of treatment methods adopted – than may be the case when working with adult groups, as well as the need for effective on-going monitoring and evaluation of factors that are likely to impact on a young person's ability to benefit from group participation. Practitioners should set realistic time-scales for the delivery of treatment components that make it possible to stay with components until it is felt they have been assimilated, or be able to revisit them at appropriate points in the future. The provision of individual treatment sessions to the young people on the G-MAP programme alongside groupwork sessions is another method by which flexibility and effective on-going monitoring and evaluation may be achieved.

Adult programmes often rely on the ability of group members to apply abstract concepts learnt in a group, to concrete situations outside the group. This capability, however, is often less developed in adolescents. Hence, responsive, adolescent programmes should engage young people in activities that are personally meaningful, and messages should be delivered in a style that makes sense to individual group members. This can mean employing a range of practical or physical activities that do not rely on formal educational methods requiring high levels of literacy and concentration.

Generally, we have found that the following principles can enhance the effectiveness of treatment with young people:

- Regularly revisit and reinforce messages;
- Check message retention by returning to topics, using spot checks, or applying the message to suggested scenarios;
- Use examples that are meaningful to young people and their everyday lives, using real places, people and situations;
- Brief carers on the use of any resources employed during treatment, and ensure they are familiar with key messages being delivered;
- Identify desirable versus negative behaviours, and promote clear labelling of behaviour by agreed language and self-talk.

Programme contents

The original G-MAP programme was more or less a version of the type of accredited programme typically delivered to adult sex offenders in UK Prison and Probation services, adapted for delivery to adolescents who have sexually harmed. Over the years, however, the programme has evolved in response to the clinical observations of practitioners about the effectiveness or appropriateness of the methods originally adopted, and in response to developments in the literature.

Many of the changes that have been made to the G-MAP programme are consistent with the less confrontational approach that is adopted, and the lower expectation for self-disclosure amongst group members discussed above. Other changes reflect views on treatment targets that may be considered less appropriate for adolescent sexual abusers than for adults, such as addressing victim empathy and methods like victim role-playing, 'hot-seating', the generation of detailed 'decision chains' (step-by step accounts of events and thinking leading up to an offence), and offence re-enactments.

The ability to feel empathy is something that takes time to develop, and people develop this capacity at different rates. Hence, it is difficult to determine what a 'normal' level of empathy is in a young person. What does seem predictable, however, is that empathy levels in adolescents are likely to be lower and more varied than for adults, and that consequently, victim empathy is unlikely to be a good predictor of adolescent sexual recidivism. Hence, whilst having victim empathy may be desirable, and attempts may be made to promote empathy, it should not be considered a key focus for treatment.

A similar argument can be made in relation to denial in adolescents. Infants and adolescents have an innate tendency not to accept responsibility for their misdemeanours – this can involve total denial; even in the face of overwhelming contradictory evidence, as well as cognitive distortions such as minimisation and blaming (e.g. so-and-so 'told me to do it'/'did it as well'). This can be considered an understandable self-protective strategy to avoid, for example, embarrassment, rejection by parents, carers or siblings, to protect self-esteem and self-image, to avoid punishment, or even to enable continuation of the behaviour. These undesirable consequences are likely to be more important to young people than adults. Denial at its different levels is, therefore, less likely to be directly accessible to treatment in adolescents than adults.

Rather than a 'risk–needs' model of treatment, that is, where the methods used are designed to address deficits in group members that are believed to be associated with a heightened risk of re-offending, a model traditionally adopted with adults, we use a more positive and optimistic approach to treatment. This is achieved by placing emphasis on positive goal attainment and the identification and development of 'resilience'/'protective' factors, alongside the diminution of deficits or problem behaviours (See 'Identifying therapeutic goals' below).

Situational factors

There are often important differences in the personal circumstances of adult and adolescent sexual abusers participating in groupwork programmes. For example, in contrast to many adult abusers, adolescent participants are less likely to have been convicted of a sexual offence, and are therefore more likely to be living with family, carers or in the community where their abuse was perpetrated. As a consequence of their legal status and corresponding living circumstances, many young people will have contact with the victims of their abuse, such as siblings or other family members, or even contact with individuals who have physically, emotionally or sexually abused them in the past. Such potential contact with victims or abusers is far less likely with adult group members. Whilst these situational factors can provide ready opportunities for young people to practise the risk-management and coping strategies they may learn through treatment – opportunities that are often not available to adult group members – they may also impact upon engagement with treatment, leaving the young person in an environment which contributed to or reinforced behaviours and thinking that led them to abuse in the past, and providing opportunities to relapse.

A further important difference between adult and adolescent groups relates to the extent to which information concerning performance, disclosures and other behaviour during treatment sessions is shared. When working with adult sex offenders a Probation Case Manager may be the only person with whom such information is routinely shared. However, a wider network of individuals are typically involved in the lives of young people who have sexually harmed, including: parents, foster carers, residential care workers, and social workers. Hence, establishing effective links and channels of communication between these different interested parties is very important, and can present many challenges that are not usually encountered when working with adults (see 'Groupwork as part of a therapeutic package' below).

Differences between groups for young people who have abused and other therapeutic groups

It has been shown that a number of features of therapeutic engagement with young people who have sexually abused others are distinct from traditional counselling relationships (Ryan 1996). In particular:

- It is likely that young people's participation in a therapeutic programme results from some form of external mandate. The mandate may be formalised through legal processes or may arise out of a family's wish for the young person to obtain help. Successful progress in work on abusive behaviours may be linked to increased community access and decisions about returning home or extending family contact. The implications of such mandates can often mean that a young person regards his involvement in a pro- gramme as involuntary and possibly coerced.
- The primary focus of concern is not the young person but previous or potential victims.
- There are limits to the level of confidentiality that can be offered in therapeutic work with young people who have abused others. It is important that information that could impact on the risk or safety of the young person and/or others is shared with those who 'need to know' in order to reduce risk and promote protection.
- The concept of a 'non-judgemental attitude' (Rogers 1951) must be applied differ- entially. It is important for the young people to receive clear statements (judgements) as to the unacceptable and harmful nature of their abusive behaviours.
- The therapeutic relationship cannot initially be based on mutual trust. A young person who has abused others has abused power, manipulated or coerced others, probably denied or minimised his behaviour and developed distorted cognitions regarding his behaviour and its impact. Hence, the level of trust offered to these young people must be firmly limited and increased only at a level commensurate to their demonstrable progress towards reduced risk through the therapeutic work.

The groupwork therapeutic relationship

In order to develop a positive and constructive therapeutic relationship within the constraints outlined above, it is important for group leaders to develop the motivation to change, set boundaries of confidentiality, show positive regard, promote a 'safe' group environment, model appropriate behaviours and identify individual therapeutic goals.

Developing the motivation to change

The motivation to change can vary considerably between group members, as well as within group members over time. Whilst some may be keen to address what they see as a problem, others may be quite ambivalent towards their behaviour, or even reluctant to participate in any form of intervention. Hence, it is very important that facilitators should develop skills to manage fluctuations in a young person's motivation to change.

Adolescents entering a programme often have low self-esteem, feel depressed, pessimistic, and/or may not yet fully accept that their sexually abusive behaviour is problematic. In order to enhance a desire for change, practitioners must assess, and when necessary, promote recognition of the negative consequences of past and continued abusive behaviour, both for the young people themselves and for the direct and indirect victims of this behaviour. Such work may of course impact adversely on a group member's mood and level of self-esteem. However, for young people to engage with the programme, and by so doing change their behaviours, they must experience their own issues on cognitive and emotional levels. This may involve 'reliving' traumas and retrieving unhappy memories. Groupworkers should be sensitive to this, being sure to demonstrate empathy, to give praise for openness and honesty, to acknowledge such engagement as an important step in taking responsibility for sexually abusive behaviour, and by ensuring that the group remains a safe place for group members to self-disclose.

Motivation for change may be further enhanced through the development and reinforcement of self-efficacy beliefs; that is, by reinforcing the optimistic belief that change is achievable using the knowledge and skills that group members are acquiring through programme participation.

Such motivational work requires a climate of respect within the group, together with regular and constructive feedback from group members and leaders. A young person who is helped to recognise his attainments and his potential to achieve further realistic targets will become more motivated to succeed than someone who feels they are being punished, disempowered or failing.

Setting boundaries of confidentiality

Group leaders should ensure that rules regarding confidentiality are clearly outlined at the beginning of participation in a group, and are regularly reviewed within the group. Each group member must fully understand the limits of confidentiality, that is, what information may be shared, in what circumstances, how information may be shared, and with whom. Whilst this may inhibit the disclosure of some information in some cases, it offers the young person an informed choice regarding disclosures and reduces the risk that he will view the professional sharing of such information as a breach of trust. Additionally, emphasis on responsibility rather than blame is important, not only within the group, but also with carers and external professionals in order to promote incentives for honesty and disclosure. For example, if a young man who is working well in a group discloses previously unknown abusive behaviour, it is important that others can be helped to see this as evidence of progress, and not simply indications of further concern and increased risk.

Showing positive regard

Group leaders should show positive regard to each group member, and ensure that his or her strengths and positive attributes are explicitly recognised and acknowledged. This is not to say that there should be any excusing, minimisation or collusion in relation to abusive acts perpetrated by a young person. It is important, however, to recognise that a set of behaviours does not define the person, and that group members are 'young people' who have abused, not 'abusers' who happen to be young people.

Promoting a 'safe' group environment

Group leaders should recognise that the nature of the experiences, thoughts and behaviours that it is expected group members will share in a group can give rise to particular difficulties. Young men who have abused others typically avoid any discussion of such issues outside of the therapeutic context. To promote openness, it is important for the group environment to be considered a safe place, where vulnerability and openness are not abused or misused. Whilst relevant group rules can contribute to the establishment of such a positive environment, it is the group leaders' modelling of sensitivity and respect that most profoundly sets the tone for group interactions.

Modelling appropriate behaviours

Group leaders have an important role to play in modelling desired behaviours. Such modelling not only includes the behaviour they demonstrate and the attitudes they express, but also the style of leadership they employ and the methods of control they exert. A confident, assertive group leader who adopts a relaxed approach to running a group is more likely to engender an atmosphere of security than someone who appears anxious, passive or rigid.

Effective modelling is also very important when challenging participants' denial or inappropriate behaviours and attitudes. As mentioned above, a strongly confrontational style is likely to create resistance in young people, many of whom will be at a rebellious stage of their development. Also, it is important to bear in mind the possible reasons for resistance. First, the individual may not feel able to change due to low self-esteem or lack of belief in his ability to change. Alternately, the young person may feel coerced into treatment, and may not therefore be ready to change. In certain instances, a confrontational style of challenging may serve to amplify pre-existing low levels of self-esteem and heighten feelings of shame. Skilled group leaders can model more sensitive and supportive methods of challenge, such as, in the case of a young person who gives a distorted account of a past behaviour, asking him/her to 'try to remember events more accurately' rather than accusing the young person of being untruthful. Miller and Rollnick (1991) have coined the term 'Rolling with resistance' to describe non-confrontational methods for dealing with resistance. Two useful methods they suggest are:

- *Simple reflection* – this simply involves acknowledging the young person's resistance in a reflective response (e.g. 'So you can't see why that behaviour might be risky?').
- *Amplified reflection* – this reflects the young person's resistance in an amplified form, whilst avoiding adopting a sarcastic tone (e.g. 'So you can't imagine any way in which that behaviour might be risky?').

Modelling of appropriate challenges in this way can encourage group members to challenge each other appropriately. This is important, as a challenge received from a peer can be more meaningful to a young person, and therefore more effective, than one made by a group leader.

Identifying therapeutic goals

Ward (for example, in Ward and Mann 2004) suggests that a therapeutic approach that emphasises positive goal attainment rather than the diminution of deficits or problem behaviours is more likely to elicit higher levels of motivation and engagement and hence success in clients. Ward provides a coherent theoretical outline of how treatment may be organised so that the individual may live a better life. The key elements of Ward's 'Good Lives model' are:

- The concept of primary goods – aspects of life (body, self and social) sought for their intrinsic value;
- Personal identity deriving from an individual's conception of how these primary goods may be attained;
- Human well-being, not risk management or relapse prevention, should drive therapeutic interventions;
- Individuals are contextually dependent and we should develop and adapt our intervention goals to the current or predicted environment in which an individual will function;
- Individualised treatment plans should be explicitly constructed in the form of a good lives conceptualisation (i.e. do not infer or add-on goods that workers consider should be included but the individual does not identify for themselves).

In essence, the adoption of such an approach suggests that intervention should focus on identifying realistic, achievable and meaningful life goals, together with the development of strengths, resources and assets that will assist in the attainment of these goals, while addressing any hurdles or obstacles (including abusive behaviours) to such progress.

Groupwork as part of a therapeutic package

Whilst groupwork approaches in working with young people who have sexually harmed are extremely valuable, such treatments should constitute only part of any therapeutic package. There is an increasing consensus that treatment interventions with young abusers need to be 'multi-systemic' (Cellini 1995; Bourke and Donohue 1996; Swenson *et al.* 1998; Curtis *et al.* 2004). Multisystemic Therapy (MST) seeks to intervene in the multiple systems affecting problem juvenile behaviour, including the young person, family and carer relations, school, peers and community.

   A number of well-controlled, randomised, outcome studies have compared MST with more traditional treatment approaches to addressing offending behaviour in juvenile offenders (e.g. Borduin *et al.* 1995; Schoenwald *et al.* 1996; Ogden and Halliday-Boykins 2004). These studies have shown greater reductions in recidivism using MST than standard programmes. For example, in a small sample, randomised study that compared the efficacy of MST and individual therapy (IT) in the outpatient treatment of adolescent sexual offenders, Borduin *et al.* (1990) found that participants who received MST were significantly less likely to have been re-arrested for sexual crimes than those who received IT, and that the frequency of sexual re-arrests was significantly lower amongst MST participants. Borduin *et al.* attributed the relative efficacy of MST to its emphasis on modifying behaviour and interpersonal relations within the young people's natural environment.

   Rich (1998) proposes a developmental framework in which the constellation of possible services is tailored to the needs of the young person and co-ordinated and cross-referenced, so that evaluation is based on the young person's overall global functioning. In order to support such an approach it is vital to establish a coherent case management strategy in which the young person and key individuals meet to review progress and ensure a consistency. This process is essential in determining whether young people are assimilating therapeutic messages and demonstrating behavioural change.

The role of carers, in terms of progress monitoring, the reinforcement of key messages, and in assisting the young person to identify areas of risk, is central to such a co-ordinated approach. Many of the young people who attend groups reside in care settings other than family homes, including children's homes that specialise in accommodating young people who have sexually harmed, general children's homes, foster homes, health provisions and probation hostels. Establishing good working relationships with carers, involving frequent contact and effective communication, is vital and can sometimes be as challenging as the direct work undertaken with a young person.

Even when a young person is not currently resident at home, family involvement can prove an invaluable motivator and source of support, supervision and information. An evaluation of the Dublin-based Northside Inter-Agency Project (Sheridan *et al.* 1998) found a correlation between positive treatment outcomes and the degree of familial support and participation in therapy. We have found the involvement of families to be an important factor, particularly when young people are able to share with them issues from the treatment context (Hackett *et al.* 1998). Families usually find it empowering to learn more of the nature of the work being undertaken, and respond to being approached as allies. Not all young people or their families, however, can function in such an open, positive or supportive way, and many will need help in doing so. As Bentovim (1998) emphasised in his work on family systemic approaches, many families need intensive concurrent therapy if they are to make changes to develop safe environments for victims or abusers.

An example of a groupwork programme

G-MAP has been running groups for young people who have sexually abused others for over 17 years. We have benefited from the involvement of a multi-disciplinary staff team in the programme, including child protection and youth justice workers, forensic psychiatry staff, residential social workers, forensic psychologists and an art therapist. Whilst the following outline of the processes, methods and programme content is offered as an example of current practice, it should be recognised that outcomes have not yet been thoroughly evaluated. The programme has changed considerably over the years, and it is anticipated that it will continue to evolve in accordance with advances in relevant theories, research, and clinical observations and opinion.

The programme described operates for young men aged 13–17 years who have sexually abused others. Potential group members are referred by professionals, and then involved in a process of assessment and individual treatment before being offered the opportunity to participate in the groupwork programme. Those who participate in groupwork have concurrent, individual sessions which complement and build upon work undertaken in the group.

The programme takes a largely cognitive-behavioural approach to understanding and treating sexually abusive behaviours. In forensic contexts, such approaches to treatment typically focus on addressing a range of potentially changeable factors that are associated with a heightened risk of re-offending (termed 'dynamic risk factors'). A number of cognitive-behavioural methods are employed in the programme, including:

- training in self-monitoring and self-analysis;
- self-instructional training;

- relapse-prevention training;
- training in problem-solving techniques;
- skills practices (role plays);
- graduated practice with feedback.

In addition to this 'risks–needs' approach, the programme also adopts an 'approach goal' paradigm in its model of change that has much in common with Ward's 'Good Lives Model' (see above).

The current approach was originally inspired by the work of Haaven and Coleman (2000), who developed the concept of 'New Me/Old Me' as a framework for working with intellectually disabled sexual offenders. This concept is used in a dynamic manner that acknowledges change to be an on-going process. It is suggested to group members that everyone has a New Life and an Old Life, and that although we may never attain everything we identify with our New Life, this should not prevent us from working towards it, and by so doing move away from our Old Lives. This approach seeks to address dynamic risk factors that are associated with Old Life thinking and behaviours, and to identify, reinforce or introduce strengths and positive life goals that are associated with an abuse-free, New Life.

Whilst Haaven and Coleman's New *Me* concept appears to focus principally on working towards changes within the individual, the use of the New *Life* concept allows for others, such as family and carers, to play a role in the change process, and allows a broader focus on the individual-in-context.

Pre-group assessment

There is always a risk when establishing a groupwork service that it will be seen as a panacea for all young people who have problems with their sexual behaviour. Groupwork is not, however, an appropriate method of intervention in all cases. For example, Craissati and McClurg (1997) found poor treatment outcomes associated with more severe offence patterns and childhood experiences of abuse. In such cases individual work has proved more effective in achieving change and progress, which may then allow the young person to benefit from inclusion in a groupwork programme at a later stage.

The value and potential benefits of inclusion in a groupwork programme must be assessed in each individual case. Such an assessment should not only identify the treatment objectives, but also consider the group's needs and how the individual may impact on the functioning of the group and its other members. For example, an individual who is exhibiting high levels of denial, hostility and manipulativeness may be a highly disruptive influence on the group. Additionally, the role of a groupwork programme within a network of responses should be identified, and potential problems in terms of boundaries, responsibilities and methods of communication should be examined.

Thus, when considering the value of inclusion in a groupwork programme, consideration should also be given to the suitability of groupwork for that individual, the role of groupwork in a comprehensive therapeutic package, and the suitability of the individual for the proposed or existing group.

The suitability of groupwork for the individual

A comprehensive assessment of the young person is normally required prior to consideration for group inclusion. The assessment not only provides a baseline for measuring and evaluating the young person's progress in group, but also allows an individual's specific therapeutic needs to be matched to the groupwork programme being considered. The comparison of individual need and groupwork provision, in most cases, is likely to identify areas of work that will need an additional service provision. It is important, therefore, to consider whether the gap between need and provision would be better addressed by alternative services. For example, a programme designed to work with young people of average ability may use techniques and methods that would be unsuitable for a young person with learning disabilities.

The role of groupwork in a comprehensive therapeutic package

As already indicated, groupwork, in most cases, is seen as only part of a required response to a young person and his family. It is important to identify how any additional needs are to be met and to establish very clear boundaries and effective methods of communication between the group leaders, the young person, those involved in other services or therapeutic work, the case manager and the carers. Without such considerations the potential for unrealistic expectations, dangerous misunderstandings and poor outcomes is greatly increased.

It should be made clear, for example, that the role of group leaders does not include making case management decisions. Whilst the information provided by them may influence such decisions, their therapeutic role should be clearly recognised as different from those responsible for case management. To minimise the possibility of such conflicts or confusions occurring, young people are only accepted for groupwork when:

- a comprehensive assessment of risks and needs has been completed;
- child protection issues have been addressed;
- a young person referred for intra-familial abuse is not living with his victim(s);
- a young person is not otherwise placed in a situation that promotes continuance of the inappropriate behaviours;
- professional case management responsibility remains with an external agency, such as social services, probation or the health authority.

Furthermore, in order to avoid confusion and to promote a positive and consistent comprehensive response to a young person and their family, it is important to ensure that clear and structured communication networks are established. This requires an effective feedback system with the active participation of all concerned. Groupworkers therefore provide:

- immediate telephone contact with professional case managers and/or carers in the event that significant concerns are raised by an individual in a group;
- regular written feedback on a young person's progress;
- periodic review meetings;
- responses to requests for feedback on significant behaviours, events and other relevant issues that may have been noted by others in the young person's network.

This feedback loop is a crucial part of making a young person's involvement in the groupwork programme relevant to their wider life experiences, and enhances the monitoring of progress and risk outside the therapeutic sessions. When considering the possibility of group membership for an individual, it is important therefore to determine the extent to which others in the young person's network are motivated and willing to engage in a systematic communication and feedback process.

The suitability of the individual for the proposed or existing group

This is frequently a difficult issue. It is often considered that those young people with a variety of problem behaviours are the individuals that would draw particular benefits from a supportive group that encourages and models appropriate behaviour. Whilst this may be true, it is necessary to balance the needs of the individual against the impact of their behaviour on the group and on the other group members.

Regrettably, such decisions regarding which young people are suitable for a group can lead to a service that excludes some of the most difficult and high-risk young people. Although a significant number of less problematic individuals may receive a more effective service, it is nonetheless important to ensure that alternative resources and responses are available to those not accepted into the groupwork programme.

In some instances it may be felt that a young person will not benefit from joining an existing group at a particular time, or will adversely affect the group if they were to join. Preparatory work, however, and/or factors such as anticipated changes in the make-up of a group, natural maturation or changes in living circumstances could mean that he could join at some point in the future.

Preparing young people for entry into group

Most young people will be anxious about joining a group. Many believe they will somehow be different from other group members or that they will not be accepted by the others. They may also have fears about the way the group will operate and what will be expected of them.

All young people have individual treatment sessions with specialist practitioners prior to being considered for group participation. In these sessions it is possible to assess readiness to participate, or to prepare young people in terms of factors such as motivation, attitude, and degree of anxiety over participation, as well as familiarity with basic concepts, terminology and treatment approaches that are employed in group sessions.

The model described operates as a rolling groupwork programme with entry and exit points at the ends of 'blocks' of work. It may not be appropriate, however, for some young people to join at the beginning of certain blocks. Decisions concerning the point at which a young person should join are made on a case-by-case basis, and are influenced by a number of factors, including: the focus of a forthcoming block (e.g. whether group members may be expected to consider personally sensitive materials before they are ready for this work), the nature and extent of any individual work already undertaken with a young person (i.e. whether sufficient preparatory work has been undertaken), and the make-up of the current group (e.g. ages and personalities of existing group members). For example, a young person who has been unwilling or unable to talk about their sexually abusive behaviour in anything more than a superficial manner during individual sessions may find joining the programme at the beginning of blocks which consider 'Steps to abuse' (Block 3) or 'Consequences of sexual abuse' (Block 5) too challenging, resulting in, for example, resistance, reduced self-esteem or low mood.

Young people who have particular anxieties over group participation are given the opportunity to attend 'taster' sessions before making any firm commitment to join the group. Feelings of anxiety can be reduced further by ensuring that two or more young people will join the group at any one time – in this way, a young person may derive a feeling of kinship and support from others who are sharing this new experience. Sessions in which new members join a group are largely dedicated to introducing the new and old members to one another through 'ice-breaker' exercises that involve group members sharing non-sensitive information about themselves and discussing experiences of being the group.

Contracting

Each young person entering a group, together with their case manager, parents and/or carers should have a clear understanding of what is to be offered to them, and what will be expected of them. It is useful to detail these expectations in the form of a written agreement. Such a document might outline in appropriate language:

- the programme aims;
- principles and commitment of the group leaders;
- issues and rules regarding confidentiality;
- rules regarding attendance;
- rules regarding behaviour in the group;
- rules regarding behaviour outside the group, including specific conditions, for example, regarding contact with victims or potential victims;
- timescales;
- personal goals – these are usually identified by the group leaders but can include issues identified by the young person or others;
- the methods for evaluating progress, including review meetings;
- the expectations of case managers, carers, parents and relevant others;
- contingency arrangements and consequences if the contract is breached by any of those involved.

Reviewing and monitoring progress

All young people who participate in the programme are asked to complete a battery of psychometric tests at the beginning, and again at the end of the programme. For 'mainstream' programme participants this battery includes measures of:

- self-esteem;
- impulsivity;
- empathic ability;
- anger management;
- coping styles;
- sexual knowledge;
- sexual interests;
- sexual deviance;
- responsibility taking;
- insight into sexual offending;
- motivation to participate in treatment for sexual offending.

The results of the initial psychometric assessment can serve to highlight concerns, inform a young person's treatment plan, and provide 'baseline' measures for assessing treatment outcome for the individual. Similarly, collating and comparing pre- and post-treatment psychometric data for a large sample of programme 'graduates' will ultimately provide insights into the overall effectiveness of our therapeutic approach.

In addition to psychometric testing, a comprehensive 'tick-box' form has been developed, and is employed at sixteen-week intervals to identify treatment needs and to assess treatment change in relation to six key areas:

- abuse-specific behaviour;
- family and personal history;
- sexuality;
- influences on participation;
- social functioning;
- non-sexual behavioural problems.

Each of these areas is broken down into a number of clearly defined therapeutic goals, as suggested by clinical experience and relevant literature. For example, therapeutic goals for addressing 'Abuse-specific behaviour' include:

- *Behaviour analysis*: The young person can provide an active account of their thoughts, feelings and behaviours regarding their abusive conduct.
- *Pathway into abuse*: Therapeutic workers have sufficient information to hypothesise key pathway elements; The young person can understand and apply the 'four-step' pathway model.
- *Sexual interests*: The young person is able to explore his sexual thoughts and interests with workers; young person can identify problematic thoughts and feelings; young person can identify appropriate, non-abusive sexual expression; young person can identify appropriate strategies to cope with unwanted sexual thoughts.
- *Consequences*: Young person is able to identify negative consequences of further abusive behaviours that are meaningful to him and appear to have a deterrent impact.

For each therapeutic goal, descriptors have been devised to assist practitioners in rating whether a young person's skills level is: *limited*, *developing* or *good*, and whether any skills are *demonstrable*. The tick-box form is completed by at least two practitioners who work with a young person, in collaboration with parents, carers or residential staff when applicable and appropriate.

The results of tick-box assessments are then summarised in easy-to-read, bar chart formats, in order to aid interpretation and to assist in the feeding back of progress to the young person and other interested parties. Verbal descriptions and justifications for ratings and treatment targets are provided in sixteen-week reports. Data from the tick-box assessments enable practitioners to review progress in a comprehensive and systematic manner, to generate or eliminate specific treatment targets, and to determine timescales for the completion of treatment. As with the psychometric assessments, collating tick-box data for a large sample of programme 'graduates' will, in time, afford insights into the overall effectiveness of our approach.

The groupwork curriculum

Young people referred for assessment and treatment are typically those who have been assessed as presenting a high risk of sexual re-offending. Consequently, the programme is relatively intensive, in terms of its duration (young people work with us for an average of 18 months to two years), the number of areas targeted for intervention, and the depth to which intervention topics may be explored. An adapted version of the programme, however, has been devised for use with young people who present a lower risk of sexual recidivism (O'Callaghan *et al.* 2004).

The G-MAP programme comprises eleven 'blocks' of work (see Table 11.1), and as mentioned earlier, is delivered in a 'rolling' fashion. Each block has specific objectives, and is designed to help group members address thoughts, feelings and behaviours associated with the maintenance of sexually abusive behaviour. As can be seen from Table 11.1, most blocks comprise six sessions. Group sessions run for one and a half hours, and are delivered at a rate of one per week, alongside weekly, individual, one-hour treatment sessions. In most cases, a young person will participate in additional sessions involving their carers, parents or other family members.

Occasional group sessions are led by members of the Geese Theatre Company, a specialist team of theatre practitioners who employ active dramatic techniques in rehabilitative and motivational work with offenders and young people within the criminal justice system. The focus of these sessions is consistent with the objectives of the block being delivered at that time. These practitioners also facilitate an annual 'block week', during which group members attend sessions each day, and work to create a short, rehabilitation-focused drama production, performed at the end of the week in front of an audience of the young people's programme workers, carers, parents, and other invited individuals.

During the first part of each groupwork session (approximately twenty minutes) group members are given the opportunity to report and discuss key events that have taken place in their lives since the previous session. The second part follows a set plan of work on topics identified within the overall programme.

The work undertaken in sessions is complemented by use of occasional homework assignments, and can require the involvement for monitoring and feedback purposes of carers, case managers and others involved in the young person's network. Free or unassigned weeks are included within each block to allow attention to additional points or matters raised during the blocks of work. These can include group process issues, additional time on a topic or on an individual in group or any other matter the group members and group leaders consider necessary and relevant. In this way, it is possible to give attention to issues raised without losing sight of the programme schedule and timetabling.

Each young person enters the programme with specific treatment targets and goals. These are reviewed at the end of each programme block, and at sixteen-week intervals when a

Table 11.1 The eleven blocks comprising the G-MAP groupwork programme

Block	Title	No. of Sessions
1	Beginning the group	3
2	Healthy sexuality	6
3	Steps to abuse	6
4	Old Life/New Life	6
5	Consequences of sexual abuse	6–8
6	Communication	6
7	Relationships	6
8	Staying safe	6–8
9	Assertiveness skills/anger management	6
10	Problem solving	4
11	Making choices for the future	4

formal progress report is produced. He will remain in the programme until such time as the programme workers, the young person, and those involved in the young person's network deem these goals to have been achieved. In rare instances, a young person may be required to leave the group if his level of motivation to participate or attitude during sessions results in him not benefiting from participation or adversely affecting the group.

Programme content

In this section the objectives for each block of the programme are presented, together with examples of the exercises that are used. These exercises are varied as the programme rolls through, so that an individual undertaking a block of work for a second or subsequent time is offered an opportunity to explore topics in a fresh, alternative way.

Block 1: Beginning the group

This block is only delivered at the commencement of a new group, although methods and exercises from this block are used in sessions when new members join an existing group. Through exercises, during which group members collaborate in drawing up guidelines for how the group should operate, are encouraged to share innocuous information about themselves, and discuss their expectations and concerns about joining the group, efforts are made to create a therapeutic environment in which group members feels safe and supported.

Objectives for this block:

* To establish a common understanding of the purpose of the group;
* To begin a process of self-disclosure;
* To establish a group consensus and commitment as to how the group will function and group members will interact.

Example Exercise 1

How this group will work together

Group members are asked to suggest rules that can be agreed upon to make the group a helpful and safe place in which they can work together. All suggestions are considered, although the group is encouraged towards concepts that relate to *group safety, co-operation, fairness, respect for others, supportive attitudes* and *honesty*. For example, suggestions concerning how group members should show if they disagree should give rise to a consensus that shouting, swearing and bullying will not be tolerated in the group. If 'respect for others' is suggested, then group leaders will try to elicit from the group what they understand by the term 'respect'. Key group rules that leaders prompt for include:

- Don't threaten others;
- No laughing at others;
- Listen to each other;
- Leave it in the group;
- No touching except when agreed by leaders (e.g. for handshakes and some activities);
- Try to be honest;

- Join in;
- Say when it's difficult.

Appropriate suggestions are listed on a flipchart, and the final list is copied and displayed in a prominent position during all group sessions. Group members are each given a typed copy of the group rules to place in their individual files.

Block 2: Healthy sexuality

Adolescence is a period during which there is a need to integrate physical sensations into an understanding of one's own and others' emotions, and simultaneously grasp societal rules and expectations. For many young people who sexually harm, factors such as family disruption, traumatic life events and under-developed social skills can serve to magnify the normal challenges faced during the onset of puberty. A limited ability to cope with these challenges and poor adjustment to changes in external and internal conditions during this period often appear to be associated with the onset of sexual behaviour problems. Hence, discussion of the major *physical, emotional* and *social* changes that typically take place during puberty and adolescence is important.

Many young people, perhaps as a result of their own abusive experiences, have a poor understanding of what constitutes abusive behaviour. Lack of learning or distorted thinking in relation to this issue may be a factor that has enabled a young person to perpetrate sexually abusive acts. It is useful, therefore, to consider the notion of abuse, in order to promote a clearer understanding of how a young person's own past behaviour, and perhaps the behaviour of others he has known, has been abusive.

The groupwork situation provides an opportunity for young people to share and challenge each other's views on sexuality and what constitutes sexually abusive behaviour, share their experiences of how key messages about sex were learned, and to discuss how to behave in a healthy sexual relationship. As Perkins *et al.* have noted (1999), such interactions can help group members to become more open about their abuse-related thoughts, feelings and behaviours, and by so doing, begin to address unresolved feelings of guilt, anger or anxiety.

Objectives for this block:

- To consider the influences on young people's developing sexuality;
- To explore unhelpful messages and attitudes;
- To clarify what is meant by 'healthy sexual behaviour' and 'sexually abusive behaviour';
- To establish guidelines for negotiating healthy sexual relationships.

Example Exercise 2

How young people learn about sex

Young people may learn about sex from many different sources. They not only receive factual information about sex, but also 'messages' about sex, in the form of representations and information that affect attitudes, beliefs and expectations concerning sex. The messages they receive about sex from these sources may be conflicting, confusing, distorted or inadequate. For example, sex education in school tends to focus on the biology of sexual reproduction, sexually transmitted diseases, contraception and monogamous relationships, with only limited acknowledgement of issues of sexual attraction, urges, arousal, sexuality in terms of gender preference and sexual promiscuity. On the other hand, messages young people receive from TV, videos and magazines may principally involve sexual attraction, urges and sexual relationships. Some young people may have had access to pornography in the form of magazines, videos or the internet, principally giving messages concerning sexual attraction, urges, arousal, sexual promiscuity and possibly sexual deviance. Making sense of these messages can be a great challenge for young people and, consequently, messages may have profound effects on a young person's thoughts, feelings, behaviour and attitudes concerning sex.

Group members are asked to identify the messages/information that are received from different sources, including: books/magazines, TV/videos, the internet, family, school and friends. This exercise is used as the prompt for a discussion on how individuals learn about sex from different sources, and how messages from different sources can differ, leading to confusion or distorted beliefs about sex.

Block 3: Steps to abuse

Many young people say that they do not know why they sexually offended, and often suggest that 'It just happened'. Clearly, this cannot be the case. In order to raise the young person's awareness of the offending process and to provide a framework within which to situate risk-management strategies, an adapted version of Finkelhor's (1984) *Four Preconditions Model* is introduced. This has been termed the 'Four Steps Model'.

Finkelhor (1984) proposed a model that attempts to explain the process by which sex offences are committed. The model suggests that four preconditions need to be met before abuse occurs:

1   The potential offender needs to have some motivation to abuse sexually;
2   The potential offender has to overcome internal inhibitions against acting on that motivation;
3   The potential offender has to overcome external factors that impede access to a victim;
4   The potential offender has to undermine or overcome the victim's possible resistance.

To make the model more accessible to young people, we have re-labelled the four preconditions as follows:

STEP 1: Wanting to;
STEP 2: Making excuses (to yourself);
STEP 3: Getting the chance;
STEP 4: Making the person go along.

The key aims in using this model are (1) to promote an understanding that sexual offending does not 'just happen' (that is, sexual offenders don't simply progress from having the motivation to abuse, to sexually abusing), and (2) raise awareness that there are several points in between 'want to' and 'making the person go along' at which it is possible to stop, employ self-management strategies, and 'turn back'. Specific use of the model as a framework for risk management is considered in Block 8 ('Staying safe').

A thorough consideration of such topics requires group members to acknowledge in each other's presence that they have problems needing to be addressed. Such disclosures and challenges from group members can raise an awareness of the motivations, cognitive distortions and strategies they may have employed to facilitate their sexually abusive behaviour. This can serve to enhance the motivation to change, provide practitioners with valuable insights into group members' pathways to abuse and how their risk may be managed in future.

Objectives for this block:

- To foster an understanding that different factors cause sexually abusive behaviour (causal factors) – it does not just happen;
- To explain Finkelhor's (1984) 'Four Steps (Four Preconditions) Model';
- To apply the Four Steps Model to examples of negative and abusive behaviours – both sexual and non-sexual;
- To apply the Four Steps Model to their own abusive behaviour.

Block 4: Old Life/New Life

The organising concept for the development of positive personal goals in the programme is that of Old Life/New Life. The concept of Old and New Lives assists in the identification of aspects of group members' current and previous (Old) lives that they wish to leave behind, as well as the identification of realistic, New Life goals, which may range from the broad and emotional to the specific and practical. In a supportive group environment, members can help each other to develop positive and realistic goals for the future, and to identify aspects of their past and present lives they may wish to leave behind or retain.

Objectives for this block:

- To encourage group members to identify aspects of their life which have been negative or have contributed to their abusive sexual behaviour;
- To encourage group members to identify positive features of their 'new life';
- To encourage group members to identify the personal changes that will assist them in working towards a 'new life';
- To encourage group members to identify who can help them work towards their 'new life' goals.

Block 5: Consequences of sexual abuse

During this block group members are encouraged to explore the negative consequences of sexually abusive behaviours for themselves and for others, with the aim that raising awareness of these consequences may have a deterrent effect.

Negative consequences can be a highly emotive topic for young people, particularly when considering the impact of their behaviour on victims and families. Expressing emotions in the presence of others may be a new experience for many group members. It is essential, therefore, that group members feel safe in the group and that a climate of trust and respect is maintained. In order for the group members to engage fully with exercises such as this, and by so doing, change their behaviour, they must experience their own issues on cognitive and emotional levels. This will often involve 'reliving' traumas and retrieving unhappy memories. It is important that group leaders demonstrate empathy, give praise for openness and honesty, and acknowledge that this is an important step for group members in taking responsibility for their sexually abusive behaviour.

Objectives for this block:

- To promote a clear understanding of the consequences to group members of future sexually abusive behaviour, and an ability to articulate this understanding;
- To promote a clear understanding of the impact of group members' sexually abusive behaviour upon those victimised;
- To promote a clear understanding of the impact group members' sexually abusive behaviour upon their families ('indirect victims').

Example Exercise 3

How abuse hurts people

The primary aim of this exercise is to provide group members with straightforward messages concerning the effects of sexual abuse on others, rather than to elicit or develop an empathic emotional response.

A sheet of flipchart paper is divided up into two columns, and the headings 'Powerful' and 'Powerless' are written above the columns. Group members are asked to consider a simple example of a non-sexual abusive experience, such as bullying in school.

Group members are encouraged to consider the effect this may have on the 'Powerless person'/victim (e.g. too scared to go to school, feel sad, feel they have may have done something to deserve it but don't know what). Next, they are asked to consider the effect this may have on the 'Powerful person'/perpetrator (e.g. a feeling of power, getting a tough image). Group members' responses are charted under the appropriate headings. This exercise is then using a range of sexual abuse scenarios.

Group members' responses are often concrete and simplistic. The concept of the abuser being in a position of power is sometimes difficult for young people to accept as true for themselves, as they may feel that the child, peer or adult they assaulted could have got away or stopped the abuse happening. Group members may be asked to consider, for example, the situation of a 14-year-old boy sexually abusing a 7-year-old girl who knows nothing about sex, and how this is similar to bullying. Typically, they are able to identify a number of similarities as well as differences, and in doing this, see how there is a clear power relationship in both.

Block 6: Communication

For many young people, social isolation and the inability to form, negotiate and maintain appropriate relationships can be factors that contributed to their sexually harmful behaviours. For such individuals, improved communication skills can be the key to beginning, maintaining and improving relationships. Also, better communication skills can help young people to stay safe; for example, by improving the ability and tendency to ask for help and support when confused, uncertain or when in a high-risk situation, and to disclose to others problematic feelings, thoughts or experiences. The group programme affords a safe environment in which members may practice communication skills and receive constructive feedback from group leaders and other group members.

Objectives for this block:

- To explore the various forms of communication people use;
- To identify what might be the more difficult things to communicate;
- To explore how good communication can help the young person to manage their risk of sexual re-offending;
- To consider what is helpful/unhelpful in communicating with others;
- To identify improvements in communication that would help the young person in work towards their New Life goals.

Block 7: Relationships

A lack of competence in relationships and experiences of unhealthy or abusive relationships can be factors that have contributed to a young person's sexually harmful behaviour. Hence, helping group members to identify what constitutes positive and negative relationships and to acquire skills that enable them to sustain appropriate relationships can be vital for young people who have sexually harmed. The group programme provides the opportunity for group members to learn from young people of a similar age that they are not alone in having experienced unhealthy or abusive relationships. This can be valuable in helping young people to come to terms with their own abusive experiences. The group also affords a safe, supportive environment in which relationship skills may be practised, and an opportunity to experience positive relationships characterised by respect and trust.

Objectives for this block:

- To consider different types of relationships;
- To identify the most important relationships in life;
- To consider where we learn about relationships;
- To identify what makes a relationship healthy or unhealthy;
- To identify the skills that help us to establish and sustain relationships.

Example Exercise 4

My social network

Group members are assisted in producing an 'eco-map' representation of themselves and those around them who can provide help and support. Each group member is provided with a large sheet of paper and coloured marker pens, and is asked to write his name in the centre of the sheet, to draw a picture of himself, or to produce some other representation of himself. Helpers/supporters are then added to the eco-map in a similar fashion. These can include those currently in the group member's support network (e.g. care workers, family members, friends, teachers), and realistic additions in the future. The proximity of representations of helpers/supporters to the young person should represent how close/attached they are to that individual(s). Alternatively, lines can be drawn between the young person and the helper/supporter to denote strength of relationship/attachment, for example, with a thick line indicating a strong relationship/attachment, and a thin one or dotted one a weak relationship/attachment. Group members are encouraged to use their imaginations in producing their eco-maps. For example, they may wish to represent men by one shape and women by another shape or use different colours to denote men and women, or may be encouraged to colour code or identify in some other way the type of support that helpers could give (e.g. emotional support, information, practical help, advice, etc.).

Block 8: Staying safe

This block is linked to Block 3 ('Steps to abuse'). In Block 3 group members will have begun to identify factors that may increase their risk of sexually harming in the future, and will have considered a conceptual framework (the 'Four Steps Model') within which risk-management strategies may be located. In this block, group members consider personal risky thoughts and situations in more detail, and learn and practise employing strategies that can help them to make use of any help and support available, and where appropriate to self-manage their risk. Interactions with others during this work can help group members to become more open and honest about their own abuse-related thoughts, feelings and behaviours. Also, young people who have had little practice in self-reflection may gain important insights into their own risk factors from listening to other group members' reflections.

Objectives for this block:

- To enable group members to identify factors that increase their risk of re-abusing/re-offending;
- To develop group members' risk-management/relapse-prevention skills;
- To promote group members' awareness of people who can provide help and support in managing risk.

Example Exercise 5

ACE

Group members are asked what they think the term 'risky situation' means. Group leaders elicit statements that are consistent with the idea that risky situations are simply any situations that increase the likelihood of something bad happening. The continuum line shown below is used to illustrate how the things people can be safe, very risky, or fall somewhere between these two extremes.

| Safe | Bit risky | Very risky |

◄──►

Examples of behaviours that are *safe* (located to the extreme left on the line), *a bit risky* (located around the middle of the line), and *very risky* (located to the extreme risky on the line) are used to illustrate this notion.

The ACE (Avoid – Control – Escape) model is then introduced and explained:

<u>ACE Model</u>

There are generally three ways to deal with risky situations. In some situations an individual may be able to choose the way to best deal with a risky situation, whilst in other situations the choice may be limited.

Avoid   can be used to think about something that may happen in the future, and to decide whether it might be safer to choose not to take part, go to, or join in with it.

Control   can be used when thinking about something that may happen, or is already happening. It is making the choice to take part, go to, or join in with something,

---

---

because it can be made safe (e.g. not being on your own with someone, having a time limit, having an 'escape' strategy if needed, etc.).

Escape   is knowing how to get out of a risky/problem situation in a safe manner when control is not possible.

Group leaders suggest examples of non-sexual risky/problem situations, and ask group members to identify the position on the risk continuum where they think each situation should be located, and to explain this decision. For those examples that are judged to be risky, group members are asked to generate examples of how they could make the situation safe using the ACE model.

When it is felt that group members have a good grasp of the ACE model, they progress to applying the model to more demanding examples of risky situations relating to sexually abusive behaviours. In each case they are asked to decide which (Avoid, Control or Escape) is the most helpful and appropriate strategy.

Block 9: Assertiveness skills/anger management

A number of empirical explorations of the role of anger in adult sexual offending have been reported. These studies suggest that whilst anger is often a precursor to sexual offending (e.g. Pithers *et al.* 1989), there does not, however, appear to be an association between trait anger and physical aggression in the commission of sex offences (Smallbone and Milne 2000).

Practitioners' understanding of the role of anger in adolescent sexual offending derives mostly from what is known from adult studies and clinical observation. Such observations suggest the importance of equipping young people who sexually harm with skills that can enable them to manage their angry thoughts and feelings in an appropriate manner, and in working with young people to identify any links that may exist between sexually harmful behaviour, sexual thoughts and anger. For some young people, however, the inability to manage feelings of anger appropriately may be associated with sexually harmful behaviour only *indirectly*. For example, poor anger control may affect a young person's ability to establish and maintain age-appropriate relationships, resulting in the young person seeking intimacy or attempting sexual acts with younger children or strangers. In many cases, however, there may be no identifiable link between anger and sexual offending. Indeed, consistent with studies of adult sex offenders (e.g. Holmes 1983; Barker and Morgan 1993), many of the young people with whom we work have a problem with over-passivity, a widely reported consequence of personal experiences of abuse or neglect. The group programme affords a safe environment in which members may learn and practice anger management and assertiveness skills and receive constructive feedback.

Objectives for this block:

- To understand the benefits of controlling feelings of anger;
- To be able to recognise the behavioural, thought and bodily changes associated with the build-up of aggression;
- To learn strategies for controlling the behavioural changes associated with anger;
- To learn strategies for controlling negative thoughts associated with anger;
- To learn strategies for controlling the bodily arousal levels associated with anger (e.g. relaxation techniques);
- To know the differences between passive, assertive and aggressive behaviour;

- To learn ways of expressing anger assertively;
- To practise assertiveness skills;
- To identify who can support the young person in acting assertively.

Block 10: Problem solving

Impulsivity and poor social problem-solving skills are factors that contribute to many young people's sexually harmful behaviour. In this block group members are introduced to a simple problem-solving framework in order to promote a less impulsive, systematic approach to solving social problems. Within the group environment young people have the opportunity to discuss the types of problems they have encountered or may encounter in the future, to consider how the problem-solving framework may be applied to these problems, and through group interactions, practise employing ideas and skills introduced in earlier sessions (e.g. communication, relationships and assertiveness skills) within this framework.

Objectives for this block:

- To identify elements that are common to problems that group members are likely to encounter at this stage in their life;
- To identify what problem solving strategies may be unhelpful;
- To learn and practise applying simple rules for effective problem solving;
- To consider the advantages of thinking before acting (not acting impulsively).

Block 11: Making choices for the future

Key messages from previous blocks are reviewed within this block, and group members are given the opportunity to discuss their experiences of participation. Since the programme is delivered in a 'rolling' fashion, where members join and leave the group at different points, newer members can have the opportunity to listen to the reflections of those who have been in the group for longer. It may be valuable, for example, for new members to hear from others how initial anxieties over participation are normal and can be overcome, and how they feel participation in the group has affected them. Group members can also offer feedback over changes they have observed in other members, and highlight what they consider to be the strengths and challenges that others will face in implementing change.

Objectives for this block:

- To integrate the key messages from the programme into simple and retainable concepts;
- To emphasise the need to maintain and continue making positive changes in working towards New Life goals;
- To identify key features of personal change that have already been made, that are to be maintained and expanded;
- To highlight indicators of a return to Old Life patterns.

Example Exercise 6

Making choices

The aim of this exercise is to encourage group members to consider the types of choices that may involve others, and to highlight how some choices may be SAFE and some RISKY.

Group leaders fasten four sheets of paper along a wall, showing the words 'PERMISSION', 'INFORMATION', 'ADVICE', and 'HELP'. Each group member is then provided with two cards: one showing the word 'RISKY', and one the word 'SAFE'. These are used as voting cards. Examples are provided of situations where it may be necessary to seek permission, information, advice or help before making a decision (e.g. choosing a holiday, choosing a car, etc.). Pre-prepared cards are then issued on which non-sexual situations requiring a decision are written (e.g. 'What am I going to wear today?', 'Shall I go to see that new film at the cinema?', 'Shall I buy that new CD player?' etc.). Each group member is then given one of these choice/decision cards, and asked to go and stand next to one of the signs on the wall. If a group member decides he does not need to go to any of the signs, he is making the choice ON HIS OWN. Once a group member has identified how he will make his choice, other group members are asked to vote on whether they consider this a RISKY or SAFE way of choosing. Group leaders then facilitate a discussion on why group members have voted either RISKY or SAFE. The cards are then re-distributed and the exercise is repeated.

Finally, the exercise is repeated using cards on which sexual situations requiring a decision are written; for example: 'Your name is Mike. You have previously got into trouble for sexually touching your young cousins. Should you go to the family Christmas party?' This exercise is repeated a number of times using the sexual choice/decision cards, giving group members the chance to have a turn with different situations.

Example Exercise 7

Some important things about my New Life

Group members are asked to practise interviewing each other on the theme of 'How others might notice I am working towards my New Life'. Group leaders suggest to group members that they might focus on the following:

- How I will treat others;
- Things I will remind myself of;
- Honesty;
- How I will cope;
- My family.

Each group member is given a turn at being both an interviewer and an interviewee.

Summary and conclusion

Whilst there is only limited empirical evidence for the effectiveness of groupwork as a methodology with adolescents who sexually abuse, there is widespread clinical consensus that therapeutic groups can provide a helpful forum for many troubled young people. Adolescents are at a complex and demanding developmental stage and often find it difficult to deal with issues of separation/independence, authority and emotional sharing. Groupwork can offer young people support, safety and opportunity to explore thoughts, feelings and behaviours together with the chance to develop and rehearse skills and coping strategies. Peer pressure and challenge are powerful influences that groups can utilise positively to influence change and a sense of group cohesion and achievement can enhance an individual's self-esteem and confidence.

These features of groupwork are of particular importance to young people who have experienced problems in their sexual behaviour. The thoughts, feelings and behaviours they need to examine are complex, intimate and often based on strongly held distorted thoughts, inappropriate coping strategies and powerfully gratifying behaviours. The support, challenge and modelling of openness provided by peers can be a most effective mechanism to help young people address these issues. Recognition by group members that they are not alone, are worthy of respect and have positive attributes that are valued by others can provide young people with a positive motivation to succeed. Additionally, seeing progress in others can also provide a potent message to the young person that change is possible and beneficial.

There are important differences between the ways in which treatment groups for adults and adolescents operate and some of the therapeutic approaches and techniques employed with adults may not be appropriate or effective with adolescents. Situational factors are likely to vary considerably between adult and adolescent group members. Practitioners must be mindful of these factors and how they may impact upon group members' motivation, level of engagement and treatment effectiveness, as well as how a multi-systemic programme is delivered.

There is growing support for treatment approaches that focus on the identification and attainment of positive life goals, the development of strengths, resources and assets that will assist in the attainment of these goals and militate against the harmful effects of risk factors, while addressing obstacles, deficits or problem behaviours.

To be effective, however, groupwork has to be managed in ways that promote aims and potential benefits. This requires considerable group leadership skills, planning, programming, reviewing and evaluation. The resource requirements to establish a useful group should not be underestimated. Group workers should be trained, supported and provided with sufficient time to plan, run and debrief group sessions. Groupwork with young people who have sexually abused others can raise intense feelings and challenges for group workers and good-quality supervision and consultancy should be available on a frequent and regular basis.

Groupwork, however well it is managed, is rarely a sufficient intervention for young people who have sexually abused. Individual and family work are likely to be additional essential components in any therapeutic programme. Similarly, a close and communicative network, involving professionals and carers, is important in order to extend support and monitor the changes that therapeutic intervention can bring about.

12 Similarities and differences in working with girls and boys who display sexually harmful behaviour

The journey continues

Jane Scott and Paula Telford

Introduction

> The weaker sex, to piety more prone.
>
> (William Alexander 1637)

Although work has continued to develop with children and young people who display sexually harmful behaviour, uncertainty and anxiety appear to remain around work with girls and particularly about the need, perhaps, to follow different intervention programmes with girls, as compared with those provided for work with males. A small-scale study undertaken in Greater Manchester by AIM and the Lucy Faithfull Foundation (Ashfield *et al.* 2004) found that professionals were less confident and had little experience of work with young females. The study highlighted that, whilst most workers had received training in work with adolescent boys, issues of work with girls had not usually been covered. It may be that this state of affairs reflects the ongoing impact of societal beliefs about female sexual behaviour. As Vick *et al.* (2002) comment:

> Societal beliefs about female and in particular young female, sexual behaviour and the covert nature of sexually abusive behaviour are more likely to have limited the advancement of research and treatment for this population.
>
> (p. 19)

The philosophy at Kaleidoscope, based on work with 22 girls and over 100 boys during the last 10 years, has continued to be that, whilst specific consideration needs to be given to the needs of young females, the differences between them and young males continue to be heavily outweighed by the similarities between the two groups. Considered in this chapter are the areas that have repeatedly proved to be central to understanding sexually harmful behaviour by young females and those aspects which appear to highlight differences with young males are identified.

The original version of this chapter which appeared in the first edition of this book (Blues *et al.* 1999) began with a quote from US author Toni Cavanagh-Johnson about the need for the development and widespread availability of specific interventions for girls and young women. This call will be explored further in this chapter in the light of our practice experience during the intervening six years since that chapter's publication. Many of the issues covered in the previous version of the chapter are still as relevant today: the centrality of victim experiences; the nature of the girls' sexually harmful/abusive behaviour, including use of force; and responsibility taking. However, other issues are also addressed, in particular, professionals' and societal responses to girls as compared with boys who sexually harm.

Since 1999 clinicians in this field have benefited from the Serious Case Review *Childhood Lost* (The Bridge Child Care Development Service 2001), which reflected on the learning in the case of DM, an 18-year-old, who abducted, sexually abused and murdered a much younger boy in the late 1990s. As well as sending other valuable messages, the review strongly recommended the need to take a holistic view of young people with sexually harmful behaviour – a recommendation equally applicable to girls and to boys who harm. The review also indicated those factors that might suggest a high degree of risk of continued offending, a topic which is fully discussed in Chapter 15 of this book. In the absence of specific research into high-risk factors for girls, we suggest here that these findings are likely to be applicable to girls. Finally, intended outcomes for both girls and boys are explored with reference to the Evaluation Indicator tools developed by Kaleidoscope.

A brief note about the terminology used in the chapter. Because our practice has ranged from work with children as young as 4 years old to young adults up to 18 years old, equally applicable terminology is hard to find. Using the term 'sexually harmful behaviour' is by no means intended to minimise the seriousness of some of the behaviours demonstrated – some of these young people are indeed 'offenders'.

Reflections on practice

We have already emphasised the importance of taking a holistic view of the young people involved in sexually harmful or abusive behaviour, a view which would take into account both their developmental needs and the risks they pose. What is also important to attend to, in relation to work with girls, are the often, polarised societal reactions to instances of sexual harm or abuse committed by young females. Each of these aspects will be discussed in turn.

Developmental issues and sexually harmful behaviour by young females

Robinson (2005) considers a number of specific developmental factors in relation to girls, factors that are also highlighted by other authors (Gilligan 1982; Gilligan *et al.* 1990; Jordan *et al.* 1991; Brown and Gilligan 1992; Miller and Stiver 1997). Development of identity for girls is largely relational, occurring through their relationships and connections with others. Girls demonstrate a need to fit in with peers and a need to meet with others' approval. This can result in their identities being weakly constructed especially since, unlike boys, their confidence tends to decrease as they get older. Boys, on the other hand, typically value autonomy, independence and achievement in developing their identities. It would be expected then that girls with sexually harmful behaviour will pay more attention to and seek the approval of others in relation to their behaviour. Blues *et al.* (1999), indeed, found one of the major differences between their male and female service users was exactly this concern for others' approval, which positively affected girls' ability to develop victim empathy. This continues to be the case in our experience.

> Krissy, 15 years of age when referred to Kaleidoscope, had encouraged two much younger foster children to indecently assault each other. She had a family history of emotional abuse and neglect as well as there being a strong suspicion that her mother had involved her in prostitution. It was also considered likely that Krissy had been sexually abused by some of her mother's clients. At the time of the referral, Krissy was being looked after in a small

children's home. The whole residential team supported Krissy in the work she subsequently undertook with Kaleidoscope. On the day Krissy had her first, informal visit to Kaleidoscope she went home and disclosed to her link worker that she had been and was being sexually abused by her maternal uncle who had a learning disability. A multi-agency investigation, however, concluded that he could not be charged, although the abuse was stopped.

From the outset of the therapeutic work, Krissy demonstrated a remarkable level of victim empathy. Although there was a clear agreement with Krissy that her sexually harmful behaviour would be addressed, we decided to begin the work around Krissy's needs and life experiences. All through this recovery work we helped her to make links to the possibility that her experiences contributed to her behaviour. The work was very Krissy-centred whilst following cognitive behavioural approaches. Krissy was able to make sense of her own behaviour using a child-friendly adaptation of the Lane and Zamora cycle (1978).

Once a trusting relationship had developed with her worker she was able to work through both her own victim experiences as well as addressing offence specific issues to a point where risks were considered much reduced; where she built on strategies to avoid the behaviour as well as using her own experiences to further enhance her level of victim empathy; where her self-esteem had improved and she had an abuse prevention plan supported by trusted adults and owned by all.

Societal reactions

Literature considering the respective sociocultural sexual 'scripts' for boys and girls points to females suffering greater societal pressure, with an expectation that female sexuality will be restrained and silenced (Fine 1988; Thompson 1990; Tolman 1991, 1994, 1999, 2001, 2002; Wolf 1997; Lamb 2001). It is not surprising then that there are also major difference in the attitudes of professionals to female and male adolescent sexual offenders. It has been Kaleidoscope's experience that when dealing with females being sexually harmful, professionals' attitudes often polarise at extreme positions, either overly punitive or minimising the behaviour and its impact.

Gillian was referred to Kaleidoscope when she was 17 years old. The request was for a risk assessment because of continuing concerns about the sexually harmful behaviour she had exhibited towards her younger sister, behaviour which had occurred seven years previously. No victim statements or detailed reports of this abuse were available at the time of referral. At the point when Gillian had been placed in the care of the local authority at 10 years of age, it had been known that she had witnessed significant domestic violence as well as emotional abuse and general instability. However, the decision to remove her from home had been based on the sister's allegations.

Gillian had subsequently lived in foster care before being placed in a series of family group homes. During this time she disclosed being sexually abused by other young people, including an adolescent female. Although, however, no further concerns had been raised about Gillian's own sexually harmful behaviour, she continued to be considered as a risk due to the 'serious sexual behaviours' from her early years.

At the time of the referral to our service the local authority was involved in care proceedings in relation to Gillian's younger siblings. Gillian had returned to her mother's care. Concerns at that stage related to the safety of the children due to domestic violence, emotional abuse and potential risk of sexual harm from both mother and her partner. It was Gillian, however, who remained the focus of their concern. Following lengthy discussion it was agreed that Gillian should access our service but that work must continue with the family as a whole.

Gillian engaged well with the therapeutic work and was able to look at life events and to consider where risks regarding her behaviour had started. She repeatedly stated that she had no memory of the allegations that had been made but she had a clear recollection of the period of time, recalling an older baby sitter sexually abusing her sister and her, both together and separately. Gillian was keen to understand more of that time but feared being likened to the babysitter.

Through person-centred work (Jung 1933) that allowed Gillian to go at her own pace, she was enabled to look, chronologically, at her own experiences and she disclosed that she had been abused by a number of adult men and, adolescent boys, as well as twice by adolescent girls.

Our experience backs up research findings that young people need an opportunity to address these experiences before they are able to fully explore harmful behaviours. Gillian used the work to explore issues of responsibility, not only for the sexually abusive experiences she had had but also other harmful experiences whilst living with her birth family. She made use of poetry and story telling to identify ongoing issues such as flashbacks, sexual identity and future hopes.

Gillian became increasingly concerned that she had no specific recollection of the behaviour alleged against her. Consequently, discussions took place with Gillian's social worker who agreed to go back through files and clarify the allegations. Through this he discovered that the allegations were inconclusive and that whilst clear with regard to the adolescent babysitter, Gillian's role had been far less serious. We were not able to rule out that no sexually harmful behaviour had taken place but it appeared that this was likely to have occurred by coercion or in the context of Gillian demonstrating sexually reactive behaviour.

What became increasingly apparent was that the incident when Gillian had been 9 years old had had huge consequences on her life. She had quickly become labelled in the local authority as a high risk and the focus of professional attention, despite significant concerns that were known about adults in the family. Despite these concerns, however, a direct service for Gillian had not been considered until over seven years later, when Gillian was considering becoming a mother herself. It was agreed that offence-specific work that focused heavily on those historic incidents was not required but that Gillian still needed the opportunity to consider the impact on her sister of the role she had played. Having worked through her own experiences Gillian was in a better position to consider events from her sister's perspective and to keep in balance her sister's needs as well as her own.

Through the social worker's knowledge of her sister's circumstances, Gillian was made aware of her sister's questions about their shared history and was keen to help. With our support, and in consultation with her sister's therapist, Gillian wrote a letter outlining her regrets and sense of responsibility but also putting events into some context which was helpful to both girls and allowed them to have a relationship again within safe boundaries.

It was of concern throughout that Gillian was seen as the main focus of any work under-taken despite the significant historic and ongoing concerns about other members of the family. During our involvement, no further work was undertaken with those adults and Gillian's ongoing negative relationship with and lack of support from her mother, in particular, impacted significantly on the progress she was able to make.

In contrast to Gillian's story was Mary's.

Mary was 11 years old when she was eventually referred for an assessment and subsequent control and change work service. Her sexually inappropriate and then sexually harmful behaviour had been known about since she was 5 years old, as had the fact that she had been sexually abused (although at that point there was no clear disclosure to support the medical evidence). Both Mary and her younger sister, Emily, had been subject to a child protection conference at the time and had been 'registered' under sexual abuse, but Mary was not considered as needing a service for her sexually harmful behaviour.

At the point Mary was approaching 9 years of age, her mother, Joanne, made constant referrals to the Social Services Department over a two-year period about Mary's behaviours towards her younger sister and younger children in the extended family and community. The services that Mary was receiving at that time were deemed inappropriate by her mother because they did not directly address this sexually harmful behaviour and, as therapy was given in Joanne's presence, this inhibited Mary. Joanne contacted Kaleidoscope directly during this period and, eventually, after almost three years of campaigning and advocacy, Mary was finally referred for, and received, a Kaleidoscope service. By this time, Mary's behaviour was not only of a chronic nature, but it also often involved acts of penetration, directed at a small number of much younger victims.

Our practice is to use trusted, supportive adults in children's lives as part of a partnership or team in the work. In Mary's case, her mother, maternal grandmother and maternal aunt were an extremely supportive network for Mary. She had been well prepared with helpful messages such as: 'We know you have a problem with your sexual behaviour; it's not ok and it hurts other people but we love you and we'll stand by you.' Without them the outcomes for Mary's work could have been very different. In addition the support of key people in Mary's school helped to manage risk and to 'hold her' during the work.

Mary engaged in the work, which was conducted largely within a cognitive behavioural therapy model, adapted for her age and situation. At the beginning, Mary found it easier to work through the medium of a hypothetical girl whom she called Shirley, who was the same age as Mary and who had done similar things. She used this story to let her worker know the hurts she had suffered and how they felt for her; to better understand the behaviour and when it was most likely to happen; to hear about 'exceptions' to the behaviour and the strategies she had in place to control the behaviour (which could then be built on). Mary was able to say, in time, that really she was Shirley and was able to identify the adults who would need to help her stay safe while with other children. She could share her feelings with adults and also discuss current sexual thoughts. Together Mary and all the adults in her 'Helping Team' made an abuse prevention plan and identified their roles within it. Key elements in engaging and progressing with Mary were an approach based in working in partnership and a relationship with her therapist that was child-centred and child-led, whilst also taking account of risk-management issues At the end of the work all concerned considered that risks were much reduced, Mary's emotional needs were better attended to and Mary had had the opportunity to recover from her own sexual abuse.

These two cases highlight the often polarised views of professionals in considering sexually harmful behaviour in girls. In Gillian's case she was thought to be the centre of risk in her family, despite little evidence about her but considerable evidence of abuse by some of the adults in the family. In Mary's case, her mother had to diligently highlight ongoing evidence of risk and advocate for an appropriate service.

In the paper cited above Ashfield *et al.* (2004) studied a group of female adolescent sexual offenders in looked-after situations. They were concerned with the lack of professionals' response to these girls' behaviour and, as Blues *et al.* (1999) had commented, identified a reluctance to appropriately label the behaviour. The increase in referrals to Kaleidoscope of girls of all ages in the last six years would, however, suggest a growing professional awareness of the need for service.

Theoretical frameworks

In many instances the theoretical frameworks cited in Blues *et al.* (1999) have stood the test of time. Information continues to be gathered, based on Ross and Loss's 21 assessment finding factors, albeit in an adapted, user-friendly format (Ross and Loss 1991). Information continues to be analysed with the use of Finkelhor's four preconditions (1984), though in keeping with a solution-focused approach with children and families, Brearley's risk assessment (Brearley 1982) is also used to identify and build on strengths as well as clarify risk. Recent research (Hackett *et al.* 2003) has helped to question a once widely held premise that children and young people with sexually harmful behaviour tend to grow into rather than out of their behaviour. Current research suggests this is not the case, but the need for greater sophistication in identifying those who have higher risk factors and who therefore might need a specialist service is regularly highlighted (see Chapter 15 in this book). Many specialist services have been assisted in refining prediction of risk by the AIM (Assessment Intervention and Moving On) Initial Assessment model. At first this was used by Kaleidoscope in consultation with potential referrers, to identify concerns and strengths in the young person and their situation, leading to recommendations for service and for risk management. Currently, local training is being provided so that referrers undertake that initial assessment and, through multi-agency decision-making, refer children to the most appropriate, albeit often scarce service(s). Using the AIM model with both girls and boys has highlighted no significant gender differences within our service.

Evaluation of interventions

Hackett *et al.* (2003) have highlighted the need for clearer evaluation of interventions.

Kaleidoscope has developed and evolved its own *Evaluation Indicator Tool*, exploring such factors as:

- General responsibility taking;
- Feelings;
- Gender views;
- Social skills/relationships;
- Being equal;
- Victim experience;
- Self-esteem;
- Family change;
- Sexual knowledge;
- Victim empathy.

This tool is used in planning and reviewing therapeutic work, both in supervision and with the young people themselves. Through the *Evaluation Indicators* more similarities than differences between girls and boys continue to be seen. However, the exceptions to this general finding are in relation to girls' relative 'ability to access and express feelings'; the developmental 'head-start' they have in relation to the development of 'victim empathy' and their higher reported levels of experiences of having been sexually abused themselves (see later). In considering these evaluation indicators we are also reminded that one protective factor for girls is their having had one or more positive relationships with an adult outside of the family (Levene *et al.* 2001). In our experience this has been equally important for boys.

The nature of the girls' sexually harmful behaviour (and accompanying features)

For some time it has been a matter of debate as to whether sexual abuse by females has as significant an impact on victims as abuse by males. Certainly during awareness-raising training in the early 1990s, professionals often assumed that girls' sexual behaviours were exploratory only and hence likely to have little impact. It is encouraging to be able to say that these perceptions are gradually changing to match the harsh reality. The girls in our sample have demonstrated a range of serious behaviours, including penetration with implements, digital penetration, touching, voyeurism and encouraging indecent assaults between other, much younger children, zoophilia and oral sex. Some of the girls have displayed a combination of these behaviours. Interestingly, since the implementation of the 2003 Sexual Offences Act, a greater number of these behaviours, such as oral sex, now constitute criminal penetrative offences. Seventy-five per cent of the girls used force, coercion and/or fear in their sexually harmful behaviour.

> Leanne, who was 15 when referred for assessment to Kaleidoscope, had been behaving in sexually inappropriate and harmful ways since she was 3. So concerning had been her behaviour, in fact, that she had been excluded from nursery, a rare occurrence in the early 1980s. She had continued to behave in increasingly harmful ways (which included behaviours towards animals) but had only received a service for her victim experiences. Eventually she and another girl, at her instigation, forcibly pinned down a similar-aged but much less able and less popular boy and indecently assaulted him. Workers had access to his written statement in which his traumatisation was clear. However, within days of peers verbally bullying the boy and telling him not to 'be a wimp' and 'how lucky he had been', he retracted his statement.

The outcome for this boy is not known, but it can be assumed it was not positive. Not only does this example highlight girls' potential for aggression but it also reinforces the importance of early, accurate referral, often overlooked in the case of girls.

A number of writers have suggested that female sexual abusers are likely to have been coerced by male perpetrators and to have sought opportunities through care-taking roles to harm children (Faller 1987; Mathews 1987; Wolfe 1987; Kaufman *et al.* 1995). Kaleidoscope's experience would still not bear this out. However in producing the figures below, we have erred on the side of caution, including in the 'coerced' figure those who *might* have been coerced – an overall figure of 25 per cent. Nearly 69 per cent of the girls had acted alone and only one girl, Leanne, had definitely acted with someone else, although Leanne had been the instigator. Only five of the girls had sexually harmed within their families (whether birth or corporate families). None had been baby-sitting at the time of the incidents, although two had probably had some care-taking role within their family.

Age of onset

It is acknowledged that both girls and boys are capable of behaving in sexually aggressive ways from approximately 6/7 years of age, if not younger (National Children Home 1992; Hackett *et al.* 2003). At Kaleidoscope the youngest child who has used our service was 4 years old. The age at which sexually harmful behaviour is deemed to be a cause for concern and referred for specialist intervention, however, has often been much later. Ryan and Lane (1997) and O'Callaghan and Print (1994) have reported that young people have been approximately 14–16 years of age when they were referred, although their histories have often revealed that their abusive behaviours had begun earlier than this, but without attracting concern.

In their 1999 chapter, Blues *et al.* questioned research that suggested that females were more likely to engage in sexually harmful behaviours at an older age than boys (Matthews *et al.* 1989; Mayer 1992; Elliot 1993). They found that the girls using their service had been between the ages of 6 and 14 years. Updated figures show that the girls attending Kaleidoscope since 1999 have continued to demonstrate an earlier onset of behaviours, although this has rarely meant referral at the first identification and assessment of concern, as in Gillian's case. Her story is very similar to that of other girls referred to the project and highlights the ongoing difficulties in early identification.

Own sexual abuse

It continues to be a consistent finding that girls who sexually abuse are much more likely to have experienced sexual abuse themselves. Matthews *et al.* (1997), for example, suggested that approximately 77 per cent of girls and women who sexually abuse are also sexual abuse victims. By contrast, Cavanagh-Johnson (1989) and O'Callaghan and Print (1994) suggested that 30 per cent and 50 per cent, respectively, of boys were themselves victims of sexual abuse. Of the girls attending Kaleidoscope, 93.75 per cent are known to have experienced sexual abuse.

Clearly it would be inappropriate to consider experiences of sexual abuse as a precondition to sexually abusing behaviour as only a few of the many tens of thousands of female victims of child abuse become perpetrators. Studies have, therefore, sought to identify the additional factors that may need to be considered in understanding this behaviour and, indeed, when considering treatment needs.

Vick *et al.* (2002) undertook a national survey of clinicians in North America regarding the assessment and treatment of female sexual offenders. In terms of the females' own experiences, they found that young female sexual offenders may have greater numbers of victimisers at a younger age and may have experienced more frequent victimisation. Kubik *et al.* (2002) made a comparable study of male and female offenders. They also found that females appeared to have more severe and pervasive abuse, including larger numbers of victimisations and larger numbers of (usually known) victimisers. Kubik *et al.* (2002) found that young women were more likely, due to these experiences, to experience post-traumatic stress disorders which, in turn, had implications for their treatment needs. Kaleidoscope has found that, of the girls that they have worked with, 37.5 per cent have had multiple experiences of abuse. The majority were harmed by people known to them, 75 per cent of the perpetrators being boys or men and 12.5 per cent being girls or women. A further 12.5 per cent were abused by both genders. Whilst the figures at Kaleidoscope are perhaps rather lower than expected experiences of multiple abuse, this may relate to the fact that we are a community-based project working with boys and girls at a younger age.

Emotional abuse

Emotional abuse continues to be a significant factor for the children and young people seen at Kaleidoscope. Girls' experience of abuse by distant, inaccessible parents, coupled with experiences of degradation, humiliation and 'put-downs' continue to be commonplace. When considering this issue in 1999, Blues *et al.* were beginning to note the significance of unstable attachments and found that this was a significant feature in girls' patterns of abusing behaviour. Our current figures show that 93.75 per cent of the girls attending Kaleidoscope have experienced emotional abuse, with a very similar percentage in the case of boys. Whilst we continue to assert that parents are not responsible for their child's sexually harmful behaviour, unless they have directly sexually abused them, their responsibility for their child's emotional climate is significant.

Physical abuse

Physical abuse also continues to be a significant feature for both boys and girls with whom the authors have worked. Current figures show that 62.5 per cent of the girls have experienced physical abuse. It is hardly surprising that, as in the case of domestic violence, this power-taking behaviour provides children with a model that, in the absence of other protective factors and experiences, can contribute to the development of sexually harmful behaviours.

The impact of domestic violence

Unless they are part of a longitudinal study, statistics are only a snapshot of a situation at a given time. With that proviso, we note that, at one point, 89 per cent of Kaleidoscope service users had witnessed or experienced domestic violence or abuse. Of the girls worked with to date, almost 63 per cent have been in families where there was domestic violence. We would argue that for both boys and girls this provides a highly dysfunctional model of behaviour based on an abuse of power. For a great many of these young people, boys and girls alike, their mothers' ability to provide protection and care in such circumstances was significantly impaired. In addition, 40 per cent of boys and 40 per cent of girls we have worked with have mothers who experienced mental ill health, some of this, no doubt, related to their experience of domestic abuse.

Attachment issues

Research increasingly highlights the significance of unstable attachments in the development of harmful behaviours. Crittendon and Claussen (2000), for example, have developed an understanding of the attachment styles that young people develop into adulthood based on early experiences. What is clear from Kaleidoscope service users is that very significant numbers have experienced attachment difficulties. However, there does not appear to be any significant difference between the numbers of boys and girls affected by a lack of attachment to a main caregiver (73 per cent for boys and 80 per cent for girls). In Ashfield *et al.*'s study (2004) the percentage of girls with 'attachment deficits' to mothers and others was 76 per cent. Where poor or anxious and disrupted attachments to mothers have been in evidence, these have usually to be understood within the context of many of those women experiencing domestic violence.

The importance of attachment issues for the children and young people we work with has meant that Kaleidoscope workers have undertaken further training and have strengthened the level of family and attachment repair work undertaken.

> One such piece of work was with Craig and his mother, Laura. Craig and his mother had had a very fragile attachment, which was, in all likelihood, contributed to by Laura having experienced extreme domestic abuse from Craig's father when Craig was an infant. When

she finally ended that relationship she had another baby, Alan, with whom she had a very different relationship. Craig experienced Alan as the favoured child and through a pathway of complex contributing factors, sexually abused his brother.

Once Craig had been assessed and undertaken a period of individual therapeutic work, work took place jointly with him and Laura to strive for a shared understanding of their histories. Together they recalled, in detail, the time line of their lives, filling in the gaps for each other of how life had been experienced. Laura was able to recall Craig as a child who cried all the time and, as he grew up, as someone who lacked confidence and who clung to her. She also shared her own experiences as a woman experiencing domestic violence, of feeling emotionally numb and not able to respond to Craig other than to meet his physical needs. Craig disclosed vivid memories of hiding from his father's violence and of the shame he had felt. It became increasingly apparent that what had happened in the years that followed was an increasing separation between this mother and her son. Laura had been managing her acrimonious separation from Craig's father and the practical difficulties that went with this, and Craig had felt increasingly isolated and unprotected by his mother.

Laura had since met and married a new partner but she was aware that life was still not good for Craig. He was able to share his experiences at school of feeling bullied by other children and, at home, of being the focus of name calling. Together they considered how to manage this differently.

With a greater sense of their shared history, Craig and his mother looked at existing and desired Parent Messages (Fahlberg 1991) and Laura was able to say how she wished things could have been different for Craig. This was an emotional and powerful stage in the work, which demonstrated the potential for repair of their relationship, based on the commitment on both their parts to change. With a greater shared understanding they were more able to discuss and make sense of Craig's sexually harmful behaviour towards his brother and to consider a way forward as a family.

Shortly after the joint work concluded, Craig disclosed that he had been and continued to be sexually abused by his birth father. Whilst this was devastating news for Laura she was in a stronger position to support Craig and their strengthened attachment was evident as they worked together to face up to the painful time that followed.

When considering therapeutic work in relation to attachment problems, it is striking how few girls have worked on these issues in joint work with their parents. Indeed a significant proportion of the girls worked with by Kaleidoscope have been looked after by local authorities and nearly 63 per cent have experienced a discontinuity of care This may well be an indication of the girls' more complex needs and harmful (family) experiences, as previously discussed, but this would also be in keeping with a pattern of later referral for girls.

Outcomes and responses

Along with many practitioners in this field of work we continue to consider parents, carers and trusted adults' responses to the young people to be a key factor in their ability to engage in therapeutic work. The engagement of this group of people, therefore, in supporting the work and giving appropriate messages to their children is crucial to the outcomes for children with sexually harmful behaviour. We have found that both the young people and parents/carers can show remarkable courage in addressing the issues whether this is in joint, individual or group work (Hackett *et al.* 2002).

All of the girls worked with have completed assessments, 56 per cent going on to complete change and control work. Based on this we have developed some tentative suggestions as to the factors contributing to drop-out rates. First are professionals' polarised views of girls' behaviour. Many continue to minimise the behaviour as less harmful, its taking place as part of normal care giving or girls being coerced to behave in this way. Despite some very serious and harmful behaviours none of the girls seen by Kaleidoscope, who were of the age of criminal responsibility, has been interviewed by the police, let alone charged. In contrast, there is a concentration of referrals for 10–12-year-old boys, many of whom have been convicted and are subject to legal sex offender registration requirements. At the opposite end of the continuum, as in the cases, of Louisa and Gillian there has been over-reaction and over-labelling.

In some cases a lack of clarity on the part of referrers (in the case of 56 per cent of the girls) about the services needed has led to referrals needing to be made to other services. Kaleidoscope has to take some responsibility for this in the past and we are now much clearer about the need for specialist services for both girls and boys. Further, over half of the girls referred had been to at least one other therapeutic service previously.

Conclusions

As discussed in this chapter, there continue to be more similarities in their presentation, circumstances and responses between females and males than differences. One important exception to this is the level of disclosed sexual abuse. The percentage of girls worked with who have been sexually abused and abused by multiple perpetrators is much higher than the percentage of boys who have disclosed similar experiences. Increased levels of post-traumatic stress disorder found by some researchers would suggest that greater attention should be given to past victimisation of girls (Vick *et al.* 2002), although, in the long run, this may well prove to be just as important an approach for boys. Many respondents in the Vick *et al.* study advocated using the same treatment approaches for girls and boys, particularly in relation to offence-specific work, although Vick *et al.* comment that 'it is unlikely that a single treatment modality is appropriate for every young girl with sexual behaviour problems' (p. 19). While there is a need for longitudinal research to consider the outcomes of various approaches for all these children and adolescents, a holistic and child-centred approach, delivered respectfully and empathically, is most likely, first of all, to be accepted by young people and families and carers and, second, to have more positive outcomes.

Although some positive changes in professionals' attitudes to the behaviour of girls who display sexually harmful behaviour have been noted, perceptions are still often at the extremes of a continuum, from denial and minimisation to over-reaction. This can result in an absolute lack of service, a delayed service or an inappropriately high level of service for girls. It follows, therefore, in these circumstances, that protection of the victims and potential victims of young female abusers, and services for victims, will also be negatively affected.

13 Stop and Think

Changing sexually aggressive behaviour in young children

Linda Butler and Colin Elliott

Introduction

This chapter will discuss a framework for working with children of 10 years and younger whose behaviour is sexually aggressive. It describes the use of a Stop and Think model, an inter-personal problem-solving approach based on cognitive-behavioural theories, which can be used with individual children or with groups. Strategies for simplifying complex, abstract concepts into concrete forms that can be understood and used by young children will be described and illustrated with brief case examples. Issues of particular relevance to this population will be discussed: the importance of working with the non-abusing carer; safety and protection issues; developmental aspects of the work; the dilemmas of working with children who are both victimisers of other children and victims themselves; and the importance of working within statutory and professional networks.

Examples will be provided throughout for illustration, based largely on work with a particular child, Billy, an 8-year-old boy, whose serious, sexually aggressive behaviour towards a number of smaller children extended back three years.

> Billy came from a chaotic background, where he had been rejected emotionally by his mother such that the local authority had accommodated him on several occasions. He had been physically and sexually abused by several of his mother's partners. His mother had not regarded his sexualised behaviour and sexual aggression at home as a reason to seek help. However, following referral to the Child and Adolescent Mental Health Service (CAMHS) for generally aggressive and disturbed behaviour, it was discovered that there had been numerous incidents of sexual aggression at home and in school over the previous three years. These had been minimised in school, largely on the basis of his having suffered rejection by his mother, with the work undertaken by the Social Services Department focusing on trying to improve their relationship.

To date, the Stop and Think programme has only been used with young boys, initially as a groupwork programme, and subsequently on an individual basis. For this reason, only boys will be referred to when describing the model and its practical implementation. Existing literature on children with sexual behaviour problems makes little reference to gender issues, with most practice examples referring to male children (see, for example, Cavanagh-Johnson and Doonan 2005). This is not to say, however, that the approach described in this chapter cannot be used with girls, rather that its efficacy in work with female children with sexual behaviour problems has yet to be explored.

Theoretical background

Sexual aggression can be a behavioural manifestation of early traumatic sexualisation (Finkelhor 1986). However, whilst many young children who become sexually aggressive have been sexually abused themselves, others have learned to behave in this way through exposure to pornography or developmentally inappropriate sexual materials or behaviour.

The cognitive-behavioural theoretical model of the development of psychological problems integrates learning theory, particularly the influence of conditioning, contingencies and models in the environment, with the impact of cognitive factors (Kendall and Braswell 1985). This model can be applied to explain the development and maintenance of sexually aggressive behaviour in young children through a mixture of classical conditioning (Pavlov 1927), operant conditioning (Skinner 1953), and vicarious learning or modelling (Bandura 1969). For example, particular stimuli or triggers can become associated with a particular response (in this case a sexually aggressive act) through classical conditioning, which may then be maintained through processes of positive and negative reinforcement.

Many sexually aggressive children come from violent backgrounds where aggression is the norm; their home environments are often chaotic, with few boundaries, and the children have developed few internal controls, tending to be generally impulsive and aggressive (Cavanagh-Johnson and Doonan 2005). Research shows that the model of self-control children develop is influenced by the models they observe (Bandura 1969). Some sexually aggressive children come from backgrounds where their emotional needs are not met and they have learned to meet their needs for comfort and nurture through sexuality. Those who have been abused may also have become confused between ordinary care-giving affection and sexuality, particularly if their abuser was an attachment figure (Cavanagh-Johnson and Doonan 2005).

Assessment

The Stop and Think work undertaken with young boys who are sexually aggressive has taken place in the context of a busy generic CAMHS team, rather than in a specialist unit dealing with abused and abusing children. Several boys were referred specifically for overtly sexually aggressive behaviour, and others because they displayed extreme sexualised behaviour or language, or disturbed behaviour, such as touching animals in sexual ways. When a detailed assessment was carried out, some of these children were found to have committed previously unidentified sexually aggressive acts towards children, or acts of sexual aggression that had been minimised or dismissed as normal sexual curiosity.

To distinguish between behaviour that is exploratory, sexualised or sexually aggressive requires careful assessment of the child and his or her environment (see Chapter 5). Ryan and Lane (1997) suggest that, in defining abuse of one child by another, factors of consent, equality and coercion become paramount and provide the basis to distinguish between behaviours that are sexually abusive and those reflecting normal curiosity and exploration. Behaviour described as abusive is normally described as calculated, power-based, or subtly coercive behaviour, typically involving elements of secrecy, and behaviours which, if the child had been of the age of criminal responsibility, would have been considered a sexual offence.

Assessment process

Assessment should involve gathering information from multiple sources (Kendall-Tacket *et al.* 1993) and it is as important to assess the child in the school setting as it is at home, given the frequency with which worrying behaviours are often displayed in that setting. Information should be obtained from all the significant people in the child's life including any social worker or other support workers involved.

Assessment interviews with carers

It is vital to help carers deal with feelings such as shock, distress, self-blame or disbelief, which they may be experiencing, in order that they can participate meaningfully in what will be a detailed, essentially ongoing and often upsetting assessment process. In order to achieve this, it is extremely useful to explain how sexually aggressive behaviour often develops, and give them some reassurance that effective help for their child is available.

Detailed assessment should cover such areas as:

* Precise details of the sexually aggressive acts;
* The responses of adults and other children to those acts;
* People's attributions regarding what has happened;
* Protective measures already taken or planned;
* Any other sexual behaviour problems;
* Family beliefs around sexuality.

This specific information should be considered in the context of the more general information gathered from a full developmental history of the child, a family history and an assessment of current family functioning and other potential stressors, such as domestic violence. Sexually aggressive children often display significant levels of inattention, impulsivity and over-activity and it is worth attempting to distinguish the extent to which any such behaviours pre-dated their sexually aggressive behaviour or any abuse they may have suffered themselves.

Time spent assessing these behaviours in some detail – with the aim of determining what intervention might be undertaken to address them specifically and at what stage in the worker's involvement with the child – will be time well spent. Any positive change in these areas not only benefits the child directly in everyday life but also maximises the potential impact of interventions for their sexual aggression, by facilitating their active engagement in and understanding of the sometimes difficult material that will be covered.

Assessment interviews with the child

It is important to remember that a young child coming to see professionals may be frightened that they are going to get an angry response because they are bad, or that they will be sent away, on the basis that the adults in the child's life have often already expressed anger or disgust regarding the incident(s) of sexual aggression that have occurred. The child needs to understand that they have come to a place where it is safe to talk about the things that they have done. However, it is also vital to state at the outset that, if it becomes apparent that someone is being hurt, including themselves, this information would be passed on to ensure safety.

The interviews should be conducted in a way that is appropriate to the child's level of development, using drawings, puppets, small figures and other materials that can be used to represent people and situations in a concrete way.

It is useful to explore with the child:

- Precise details of the sexually aggressive acts;
- Any history of other sexually aggressive thoughts or behaviours;
- Any strategies they used to involve and/or silence the other child/ren;
- Their understanding of the other child/ren's perspective;
- Their attributions regarding the events;
- Their motivation for future sexual aggression;
- Their understanding of the likely future consequences of their actions.

Interviews such as this are very difficult for young children and it is important to affirm with them how well they have done to talk about difficult and embarrassing matters in a way that has helped the professionals to understand what happened. Finally, many children have experienced great relief at having their sexually aggressive acts separated from them as a person. This can be achieved by explaining that, although they have got some things wrong and hurt another child, this does not make them a bad person (as they may have been told), but rather someone who needs to work hard to become a safer person.

Treatment issues

A number of issues should be considered carefully in relation to working with sexually aggressive children.

Safety and protection issues

Safety and protection issues must be addressed prior to beginning any work with sexually aggressive children, for their own protection as well as that of other children and the workers. Interventions with children who are sexually aggressive are usually complex and should involve work with the child, their non-abusing carer and the wider system. It is not appropriate to work with a young child who is not in a safe placement, or who does not have emotional and psychological support from a carer. If these protective factors are not in place, the priority should be on achieving a safe and supportive environment before treatment starts.

At the beginning of treatment, it is unlikely that the full extent of the child's inappropriate behaviour will be known, nor the degree of impulsivity involved. It is, therefore, most important to agree safety rules and establish some practical arrangements with those adults in regular contact with the child to ensure that he is not put in situations that increase his own or other children's vulnerability.

Ongoing close contact with carers, school staff and any sessional workers is vital throughout the treatment process, as there is a natural tendency for adults to become less worried and, therefore, less vigilant as treatment progresses, because someone else is seen to be working on the problem behaviour. At various points in the treatment programme, it may be necessary to share information to ensure the safety of other children: for example, if it becomes apparent that a strong stimulus to being sexually aggressive is present in a particular situation. Planning may be required initially to enable this situation to be avoided, or later in the treatment programme, to deal with the situation under close supervision.

It is often helpful to arrange for the child not to return to school immediately after a Stop and Think session because there is an increased risk, particularly at the beginning of the work, that memories will have been triggered which may increase the likelihood of the child behaving in sexually aggressive ways.

Working with non-abusing carers

It is crucial to involve the child's non-abusing carer(s) in treatment (Jones and Ramchandani 1999), so that the child is not expected to change in an unchanging environment: without their support and involvement, treatment is not likely to be unsuccessful (Vizard *et al.* 1995), just as for children generally (Wolfe *et al.* 1993). When working with sexually aggressive children, carers are critical in ensuring the safety of the child while treatment is being carried out. Furthermore, if carers are not involved, they can feel excluded and may consciously or unconsciously undermine treatment progress. Lastly, and possibly most importantly, carers can be our best resource to help the child practise their developing skills in real-life situations. It is, therefore, important to continue the engagement process begun during assessment by training carers to become co-workers in the work with the child. Maintaining this relationship is time-consuming but pays dividends as the work progresses.

A psycho-educational component is a critical part of the work with the carer. For many carers, this is their first experience of working with children who have been sexually aggressive towards other children and they are likely to have a range of responses to the child's behaviour. This can involve an initial rejection of the child, or a minimisation of events, or the projection of feelings of anger and blame towards the system – and individuals – who have identified the problems and who may continue to do so when the carer would prefer to forget what has taken place.

Many people prefer not to believe that young children can be sexually aggressive and carers seldom have much understanding as to how their child became sexually aggressive in the first place. If they understand the ways in which young children learn to behave generally, this general understanding can be used to explain how the child may have learned to be sexually aggressive. Accepting this explanation and understanding the processes by which such behaviours are learned and maintained typically helps carers to accept that the behaviour can be changed or 'unlearned' and to maintain this perspective when the process of change is slow. Carers can be encouraged to be alert to areas of possible risk in their environment, to establish appropriate boundaries and to avoid inadvertently putting the sexually aggressive child, or other children, at risk. Using knowledge of how behaviour is learned, maintained and changed, the carer can also be helped to develop, if necessary, behavioural management skills (Patterson 1982; Webster-Stratton 1990; Herbert 1991) to reduce sexual aggression and increase pro-social behaviour.

This educative work may be undertaken in a number of different ways: in sessions which involve the carer alone, or with the carer and child together; through regular network meetings that include the carer, the child's school teacher, social worker or sessional worker; or, if running a children's group, by having a carers' group running in parallel to the children's group. Whatever the format, it is extremely helpful to provide carers with simple handouts covering session material so that they can review the ideas as necessary in their own time.

Issues arising during treatment

When working with a child who is both a victim of sexual abuse and a victimiser of other children, the order in which issues are dealt with in treatment is less clear-cut than when working with adolescents or adults. It has been recommended when working with adolescents (O'Callaghan and Print 1994) and adults (Salter 1988) that treatment focuses on offending behaviour prior to addressing victimisation issues, to avoid the possibility that the abuser's own victimisation is used as an excuse for sexually abusing others. Experience of working with young children, however, shows that it is not always easy for them to separate out their own victimisation from their sexual aggression to others, as one is so often a re-enactment of the other. For this reason, work on their own abuse and on their sexual aggression often takes place interchangeably, with one aspect informing the other as the work progresses.

During the course of treatment, some sexually aggressive children disclose verbally for the first time that they have been sexually abused themselves. With others, where it is known that they have been abused themselves, it can become apparent that their sexually aggressive behaviour is a re-enactment of their own known victimisation. For children not known to have been abused, the suspicion may grow that they have been. On occasion it happens that, as the work progresses and the realisation dawns that what they have done to another child is wrong, the child begins to think that what has happened to them was also wrong. This complicates matters, as often the child will not want this information shared. The previously shared position around limited confidentiality is, therefore, helpful.

If a disclosure occurs during the course of treatment, then child protection procedures must be followed and relevant agencies informed to ensure the safety of the child and any other children who may be at risk. If legal proceedings follow the child protection investigation, it is important to confer with colleagues from the police and crown prosecution service regarding matters of evidence before continuing with treatment. Practice varies nationally regarding what is regarded as permissible in terms of treatment prior to the completion of any criminal proceedings. The views of the various agencies involved at this point in time may differ regarding the child's therapeutic needs versus the needs of the legal system and so this decision should not be taken in isolation. Throughout the decision-making process, the child's best interests should remain paramount and, whatever the decision reached, it is important that the child understands what is happening and why.

The Stop and Think programme

Introduction

Many of the treatment programmes that have been used with sexually aggressive children have been based on programmes designed for adults and so have not satisfactorily addressed developmental issues. Conversely, effective cognitive behavioural therapy (CBT) approaches with children, such as the intervention programmes for impulsive, attention-disordered children developed by Spivak and Shure (1974) and Kendall (1993) and Kendall *et al.* (1995) and Social Skills Training (Spence and Donovan 1998) or self-instructional approaches which can be used in developing empathy awareness (Freidberg and McClure 2002), were not specifically designed for use with children who were sexually aggressive. (Subsequent to the development of the Stop and Think programme, Jones and Ramchandani (1999) reviewed the research literature on child sexual abuse and concluded that short-term cognitive behaviour therapy had been found to be superior and more effective than other forms of treatment that had been researched with younger children showing sexually inappropriate behaviours.) CBT for children comprises various techniques that teach them cognitive mediational strategies to guide their behaviour and increase their adjustment (Durlak *et al.* 1991). It can be used effectively with quite young children provided that their cognitive-developmental level is taken into account and abstract concepts are translated into concrete terms that are accessible to the child (Ronen 1997). The younger the child, the more concrete must be the methods used. Braswell *et al.* (1985) argue that verbal methods of inducing cognitive change are weakest with younger children, and that demonstrations of self-efficacy produce the most change.

Our Stop and Think programme, therefore, combines concepts from the field of sexual abuse, adapted to be understandable and usable by young children, with CBT concepts and treatment techniques used with children who are generally impulsive and aggressive. The programme provides the child with opportunities to acquire skills that they lack and gives opportunities to practise in naturalistic settings. It was developed initially as a group work programme (Elliott and Butler 1994) and then subsequently modified so that it would also facilitate work with individual sexually aggressive children and their carers.

A major tension in this approach is that, while the material needs to be repeated many times for learning to be effective, the children often have a short attention span and get easily bored. This repetition, therefore, needs to be carried out in a variety of ways to sustain interest, using creative material that is age-appropriate and appealing. Consistent with the observation by Himelein and McElrath (1996) that, as well as the acquisition of problem-solving skills, the development of a sense of humour increases the resilience of abused children, and the reminder from Masson and Hackett (2003) that children who display sexually harmful behaviours are still children, we have developed a range of enjoyable, child-friendly games, quizzes, cartoons, mnemonics, situation cards and role-plays for teaching and practising problem-solving skills. By and large, children do display – and carers often express – their actual enjoyment of the programme format, as well their appreciation of the benefits it brings, despite the difficult nature of some of the areas covered.

Much of this material was subsequently used to develop 'The Stop and Think Game', essentially an attractive board game played with counters and dice, where the children proceed round the board and land on items that trigger specific activities. While the use of dice means that the precise selection and order of these activities is not pre-determined, the layout of the board and its components does allow us to organise beforehand the range, nature and specific content of the activities that are likely to come up, which we adjust session by session in relation to what is required for that particular stage of our overall intervention. The game certainly appears to make the work more interesting and fun for the children while at the same time providing for us a consistent, structured but still flexible framework for including the wide range of activities required for the work.

The Stop and Think model

The treatment programme is designed to help a child inhibit his impulsive behaviour and organise his thoughts and feelings in such a way as to engage in more appropriate behaviour and is based around the Stop and Think model, a problem-solving technique, which is organised into four steps:

Step 1: What's the problem?
This requires the child to inhibit his initial response and accurately identify the problem.

Step 2: What can I do?
Here, the child brainstorms possible solutions to the identified problem.

Step 3: What might happen?
Now the child needs to think consequentially in predicting, as best he can, possible outcomes for the different solutions he generated.

Step 4: Decide and do
This last step requires the child to pick a course of action, carry it out and then evaluate its effectiveness.

Effective use of this model requires a child to follow through the complete sequence of steps which, of course, will be impossible if they do not have the skills necessary to perform each individual stage. For this reason, before the integrated model is presented in this sequential format, the basic skills that underpin each step are covered with the child to ensure that they have been acquired.

Laying the foundation for the Stop and Think model

Throughout this initial stage, many varied activities are used to help the child acquire the necessary component skills, some of which are outlined below. In relation to Step 1, helping the child to go beyond initial, sometimes mistaken, perceptions to accurately identify the nature of a 'problem' may necessitate analysis of thoughts, feelings and behaviours for the child and any others involved in what may be a complex sequence of events. Initial work, therefore, focuses on developing the child's capacity to achieve these skills. Similarly, the child begins to address the requirements of Step 2 using activities in which he learns to generate ideas as to what he or someone else might do in particular situations. Step 3 involves predicting future outcomes for particular courses of action and so requires an understanding of increasingly complex issues in social interaction such as perspective-taking, reciprocity and cause and effect. Moving towards the presentation of the complete model involves progressively linking the preparatory work together in larger and more complex sequences, which specifically address the links between cognition, emotion and behaviour.

Think–Feel–Do

Experience has shown that sexually aggressive children often have particular difficulty understanding their own and other people's emotions and so this part of the programme involves considering emotions in a more detailed way. Extensive input is provided to help the child, first, to identify their own and other people's feelings and extend their emotional language; second, to identify associated thoughts and, finally, to link feelings, thoughts and behaviours in situational contexts. The importance of this work is derived from the central premise in CBT that cognitions, emotions and behaviours are highly interdependent and that an intervention that targets any one of these areas does affect the others (Deblinger and Heflin 1996).

Initial work involves using games, quizzes and cartoons to identify emotions and having the child practise 'spotting feelings' with their carer as a homework task. The child is then helped to detect and use verbal and non-verbal information to read other people's emotions more accurately. Using an emotion that they are familiar with, such as anger, children can be helped to identify the physical sensations that accompany their different feelings, which facilitates their understanding of their own feelings and their learning to handle them differently.

Because of the child's developmental stage, one way to make the experience of emotion more concrete is by drawing the child's body outline (life-size is usually fun) and helping them to map out the different parts of their body in which they experience various emotions, using colours or drawings.

> Billy's body map showed an angry fist coloured in red, a sad heart containing a drawing of someone he had lost from his life, and a tummy that felt wobbly when he was scared.

As the child learns to think about the times and places and people with whom they have experienced various emotions, the links between these emotions, cognitions and behaviours can be developed in increasing complexity by adding 'thought bubbles' to the map, in which the child can describe his thoughts in relation to the emotions he has mapped and the behaviours which may be associated with them.

This section of the work is completed by presenting the inter-relationship between cognitions, emotions, and behaviours in the form of a 'Think–Feel–Do' triangle, with a thought bubble representing 'Think', a heart representing 'Feel' and a hand representing 'Do', as illustrated in Figure 13.1. A child's thoughts, feelings and behaviours are written or drawn on the diagram, initially for general incidents and then later for specific incidents of sexually aggressive acts, thoughts or feelings.

Introducing the Stop and Think model

When the child is ready to move on to learning the Stop and Think model, the model is introduced formally to the child and their carer. As the content of the steps will be familiar from the preparatory work, what is being learned at this stage is essentially how the skills they have been practising fit together in the problem-solving sequence. The model is used initially to practise problem-solving with general everyday problems before tackling the more difficult problems of sexual aggression. As soon as possible, the child and the carer are encouraged to identify real-life problems to practise problem-solving in sessions and then at home and in school.

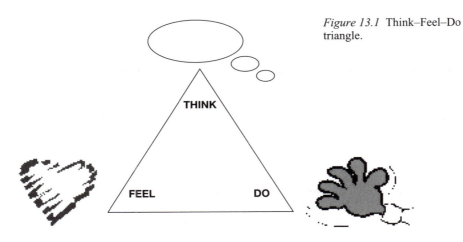

Figure 13.1 Think–Feel–Do triangle.

Billy interrupted his carer constantly. She found this extremely annoying, as she never got to finish a sentence; she felt as if he did not want to listen. When the model was used, Billy's responses were as follows:

Step 1: What's the problem?
His carer got angry with him because she thought he didn't want to hear what she had to say.

Step 2: What can I do?
Carry on interrupting; shut up; listen.

Step 3: What might happen?
If he continued interrupting, he would be sent to his room.
If he shut up or listened, his carer would not get angry; he might hear something interesting.

Step 4: Decide and do
He decided to try to interrupt less. This was practised initially in the session and then worked on as a homework task, with his carer, with the outcome reviewed in the next session.

Since habitual behaviour is difficult to change, Billy was not able to stop his interrupting immediately, simply by having gone through the four steps. In order to help him continue to make progress towards the final goal of not interrupting at all, the process was broken down into smaller, achievable goals. It was agreed with his carer that he would be rewarded initially for catching himself interrupting, then for attempting to inhibit his initial interrupting response, and then for interrupting less frequently, rather than for not interrupting at all; he was always congratulated for trying.

Throughout this stage of learning to apply the model, carers are encouraged to bring incidents that have occurred at home or school to be role-played within sessions.

Using the Stop and Think model with sexually aggressive behaviour

When the child is able to problem-solve general everyday problems using the Stop and Think model, albeit often still with help, the Stop and Think model is used to work on problem-solving the more complex issues connected to sexually aggressive behaviour. Again several issues are worth mentioning:

Language

Young children usually feel more comfortable using the names for body parts and acts that they are familiar with in their family and we go along with this (as long as there are no unhelpful abusive or pejorative connotations). If the Stop and Think work is taking place in a group setting, then it is useful, albeit sometimes more complicated, to agree terms for body parts and acts early on in the programme.

Sex education

Many sexually aggressive young children have been sexually abused themselves (Cantwell 1995), which means that they have had experiences of which young children are not normally aware. These experiences are often distressing and young children may not have the cognitive or emotional ability to deal with them. Often they have little or no knowledge of what would be considered 'normal' sexual behaviour. It is therefore helpful for the child to acquire some developmentally appropriate knowledge, perhaps using age-appropriate sex education material. Helping carers to establish appropriate sexual boundaries will also help the child not to signal vulnerability.

Practical work

To begin working on sexual aggression, it is helpful to return to an incident that was discussed during the assessment period. Often the child is reluctant to do this and may need motivating by being reminded that this is to give them the opportunity to apply their newly acquired knowledge to become safer. The child is reminded of the behavioural description of the incident and then facilitated in describing the sorts of feelings he was experiencing and his thoughts at the time.

> Billy had assaulted a 5-year-old girl in a playing field. The sequence of events described at assessment was that Billy threatened the girl with a knife if she did not comply, pinned her to the ground with one hand, pulled her knickers down with the other hand, and then squeezed her 'bottom' until she cried. He then stopped and let her go, issuing a warning not to tell or he'd get her again. When helped to look at the incident in a more complex way, he identified that, when he *did* the 'rude things' to the little girl, he *felt* 'scared and excited'; he *thought* 'why shouldn't I do this?' because he'd seen other older boys doing it to older girls and nothing bad had happened to them!

It can be helpful here to use a 'Think–Feel–Do' sheet to help the child make the connections between their thoughts, feelings and behaviours explicit in a concrete way that is developmentally appropriate.

> Billy was enabled to identify that he felt angry because he had been left out again. He thought 'Why does my little sister get all the love?'; he wanted to hurt his sister, or someone who reminded him of her. He felt scared in his tummy and excited in his 'willy', and he did some 'rude things' and hurt the little girl in the park.

Subsequently the same techniques can be used to look at the planning of the sexually aggressive act and identify the child's associated thoughts and feelings. For example, developing a sequence of drawings describing the process of the act may help the child begin to identify thoughts and feelings linked to sexually aggressive behaviours, again highlighting the links between thoughts, feelings and behaviours in a concrete way.

Returning to the material used to explain how different emotions are experienced in the body can help the child to understand the confusion of experiencing competing emotions, for example, the 'scared' feeling in his stomach at the same time as that 'excited' feeling in his penis. As a child becomes familiar with this process and begins to understand the connections, he may be able to identify that, for example, some of his feelings were angry and some of his thoughts were about hurting someone smaller or younger because he was hurting himself. Through this process, the triggers that stimulate a sexually aggressive response are gradually identified and made overt in a way that the child understands. Later in the programme, this 'Think–Feel–Do' approach can be used to develop victim empathy by looking at the impact of the child's behaviour on other people's thoughts, feelings and behaviours.

Being able to identify thoughts and feelings that are precursors to sexual aggression is an important foundation for learning to inhibit the initial response by 'Stopping' and then changing the behaviour, by 'Thinking' and 'Doing' something different. By moving through the range of emotions and gradually developing the ability to identify how each emotion is experienced physically as well as emotionally, the child develops the basis for making the important link between his feelings and thoughts and the behaviour that follows. This provides some basic material to use in the problem-solving module.

Precursors

Enabling the child to think about the emotional, cognitive or situational triggers that are precursors to his sexual aggression and to decide what alternative behaviours might be more appropriate holds out the possibility of learning to do something different. It also provides information about high-risk situations for the child that enables the adults to organise a more protected environment. This reduces the likelihood of setting the child up to fail by unwittingly placing them in situations that may trigger a sexually aggressive response.

The trigger may be:

- a cognition ('no one cares about me', 'people hurt me, so I'm going to hurt someone else');
- an image (of being hurt or hurting someone);
- an emotion (feeling sad, afraid, or lonely);
- a situation (being alone with a child who reminds them of a previous victim);
- a sensation (such as a smell, or a non-sexual touch that the child has eroticised).

Several triggers may occur simultaneously or at close intervals. Through the process of making the triggers overt, the child begins to see the connection between them and his sexually aggressive behaviour and is able to start working on alternative responses to the triggers.

> Once, when in the waiting room with his carer, Billy insisted on going to wait in the corridor outside the waiting room. He revealed later that this was because a small child had come in to the room who reminded him of his little sister he had abused from her babyhood. As he said, he 'Stopped to Think' and did something different, using one of his agreed coping strategies developed in earlier treatment sessions – namely, to get out of a situation where he became aware of a trigger to sexual aggression, and then talk to someone about it.

Impulsivity and consequential thinking

Children who are sexually aggressive tend to be impulsive, acting first and thinking later (although this does not mean that there is no degree of planning in some of their sexual aggression – some quite young children will select a victim who is less likely to tell and a situation in which they are less likely to be caught). Much impulsivity is learned behaviour, as the children often come from environments that are chaotic and sometimes violent, where they have observed family members behaving in impulsive and aggressive ways. For this reason, getting the child to 'Stop' is crucial, as it gives the child the space and opportunity to then think about possible consequences *before* acting. Once the initial impulsivity is inhibited, the child has an opportunity to use some of the cognitive-mediational skills they have developed to think consequentially. The Stop and Think problem-solving model is then used to look at the way the child responds to the various triggers and the consequences of these responses, initially for them (although this may include consequences for people that they care about). As the work progresses, the same process can be used to look at the consequences for the child victim.

> Billy's view of the consequences for himself were as follows. The little girl told her mum, who told the police; then he had to talk to social workers, his mum cried and shouted at him; there was a meeting about him and he thought he might have to go into a home. He felt sad because no one liked him anymore, he got into loads of trouble, he was grounded and he had to come here and talk about the rude things he did.

The Stop and Think model can now be used to look not only at what *did* happen, but what *might* have happened if he had 'Stopped to Think' at different stages in the process of being sexually aggressive towards the little girl.

Generalisation and maintenance

There is no point in teaching impulsive children theory only – they need to be given many opportunities to practise their new skills. While this happens increasingly often in sessions, it is obviously not sufficient for them to be able to 'Stop and Think' and behave differently just in treatment sessions. Given how difficult it is for young children to generalise any changes achieved in treatment sessions to the point of performance in everyday life, and to maintain any such changes over time, the continued support and involvement of the significant people involved in their network is crucial. This is why, in order to help children move on from using the model in treatment sessions to using it in naturalistic settings, time is taken to ensure that carers understand and are comfortable with the model themselves.

At the appropriate time it is, therefore, important to provide the child with opportunities to practise the Stop and Think approach in real-life, higher-risk situations, without placing him or other children at risk. This can be achieved by extensive preparation within sessions, including imaginal rehearsal, and then helping the child to 'Stop and Think' in those actual higher-risk situations, in the context of appropriate levels of supervision to ensure safety. The child can also be encouraged to 'Stop and Think' at specified times of the day, as well as in situations that spontaneously arise.

> Billy was playing in a 'ball pool' at a children's play area, under the careful supervision of his carer, when he noticed a little girl who appeared to be stuck in one of the climbing frames. He decided to help her down, and his initial thought was to lift her down by the bottom half of her body (which would have been in reality the most natural way to do it). However, Billy knew that he was not supposed to touch little girls' bottoms for a number of reasons, which included getting into trouble and little girls not liking it. He 'Stopped to Think' and tried to lift her down using her upper body, which turned out to be quite awkward! The girl's parent/ carer told him to leave her alone. Billy's carer saw what happened and was able to talk the event through with him later, congratulating him for stopping to think and not touching the girl's bottom, while being sympathetic with him because he had been told off when he was trying to be helpful.

As with more general problem-solving, it is important to continue to praise the child's attempts to inhibit their initial responses by 'Stopping to Think', rather than only rewarding complete successes. Children may not always get the process quite right but they need to be rewarded for trying. Awarding 'Stop and Think' certificates at specific points in treatment has proved to be an attractive reward for many children. In addition, their subsequent proud display of the certificate at home has obvious potential benefits as a stimulus for maintenance of change.

By this stage in treatment, much should be known about the child's precursors to being sexually aggressive, allowing for the identification of real high-risk situations that are likely to occur in the future. A simple form of relapse rehearsal can then be undertaken (Pithers *et al.* 1988b), problem-solving around those situations by helping the child to rehearse how they might deal with their precursor thoughts and feelings in ways that did not involve hurting another child.

It is therefore important, as the therapy progresses, to use the meetings with carers, teachers and social workers to remind them of the child's progress, discuss how they can continue to help the child practise the model, encourage vigilance regarding any areas of continuing risk and look at relapse prevention for when treatment is discontinued.

Victim empathy

Developing victim empathy is known to be an important factor in successful relapse prevention (Ryan 1999a) but it is also one of the most difficult aspects for young children to acquire. Aside from cognitive-developmental issues related to perspective taking, long-standing emotional issues often hinder the child's progress in this area. Many sexually aggressive children have attachment problems with caregivers, and they may find it difficult to understand the impact their behaviour has on others emotionally when their own emotional needs are unmet. It can also be difficult for young children to deal with the emotional impact of realising the pain that their victimisation of another child has caused, if their own experience of victimisation has not been addressed.

In practical terms, what often happens when working with young children is that aspects of victim empathy are introduced during the process of treating the sexual aggression (for example when the child is learning how to choose between different possible solutions to a problem) but then returned to specifically and in more detail towards the end of treatment. The child is encouraged to apply the Stop and Think model to the various incidents of sexual aggression that have already been worked on but with a much stronger emphasis on the victim's perspective. Sometimes it is helpful to use some of the emotional impact of the child's own experiences as a victim to help them achieve this.

Although desirable in terms of relapse prevention, it is not possible with some young children to achieve victim empathy because of their stage of cognitive or emotional development. In that case, the focus needs to be on helping the child to inhibit inappropriate behaviour by thinking about the consequences any future sexually aggressive behaviour will have on *them*.

Conclusions

With some severely damaged children, treatment to change sexually aggressive behaviour can involve seeing the child at least weekly for up to a year, as well as regular meetings with all those in the child's social network. In addition, 'top-ups' are likely to be required at various stages of the child's development, such as at key transition periods like moving schools, changes of placement or the onset of puberty. In terms of timing, it is extremely beneficial to begin working with the child before the onset of puberty if this is at all possible, before the inappropriate behaviours and distorted cognitions that the child displays are con-founded with the normal physical, emotional and cognitive changes of adolescence related to sexuality.

Since the work is emotionally demanding as well as intensive and long-term, two workers should ideally be involved (essential in groupwork), and preferably a male and female dyad, as they can model appropriate male–female relationships and work together to deal with gender issues that may arise. In this high-risk area of work, it is also important to ensure that clinical supervision and/or consultation is available (Watkins 1997; Morrison 2001b).

The literature on evaluated treatment programmes for dealing with sexual aggression is sparse. The Stop and Think programme addresses some key areas that research has shown to be helpful in changing behaviour in young children, both in general and specifically relating to sexual aggression. These include working closely with non-abusing carers and the child's social network (Wolfe *et al.* 1993; Vizard *et al.* 1995; Deblinger and Heflin 1996) to implement aspects of the treatment programme in the child's environment and helping the child decrease inappropriate behaviours and increase appropriate behaviours through the learning of new coping skills (Durlak *et al.* 1991; Kendall 1991; Ronen 1992). By working on the cognitive and emotional events that occur between triggers and behavioural responses, the programme helps the child develop self-regulation skills (Braswell 1991; Himelein and McElrath 1996) and move towards a more normative developmental pathway (Ryan 1999a).

14 Therapeutic work with families of young people who sexually abuse

Joan Cherry and Deirdre O'Shea

Introduction

This chapter begins with an exploration of the rationale for working with families when a young person has been reported for sexually abusive behaviour. Influential theoretical approaches are then outlined, positive indicators for family work are identified and a number of case examples are provided as illustration. Finally, various clinical issues are discussed.

The Northside Inter-Agency Project (NIAP) provides a community-based treatment programme for young people between the ages of 13 and 18 years who have sexually abused, and their parents/carers. A primary goal of NIAP is to prevent further sexual abuse by early intervention with the young people. Depending on their therapeutic needs the service provided to them may include a combination of individual, group and family therapy. Families attend the programme for an average of twelve to eighteen months.

Rationale for working with families

There are a number of reasons for working with the families of sexually abusive young people. These are outlined in this section, beginning with a discussion of the family as a resource.

The family as a resource

For most of us, the family is our initial learning environment and it is there that we first learn about relationships and ways of relating. Consequently, family members usually possess valuable information about the young person's development and the strategies they have developed for coping with their day-to-day life. Family beliefs about sex and sexuality, about men and women, family patterns in relation to emotional expression, including the expression of aggression and violence, and family coping styles and problem-solving strategies are also central in helping us to understand the young person. In the case of Peter, outlined later in this chapter, he appeared to deal with difficulties by avoidance and denial, which seemed to be a pattern of coping similar to that of his parents. Peter's parents, in particular his father, had a belief that it was not helpful to dwell on difficulties and that it was better to move on and forget about problems. This resulted in past problems not being acknowledged, in particular Peter's sense of hurt and injustice about decisions that had been made about his life by his parents which had been avoided and denied. Peter had adopted this as a coping style for dealing with his current difficulties but he was often left with unresolved and displaced anger, which appeared to be part of the difficulties leading to his sexual offending.

When a young person has committed a sexual offence, the family's response to the abusive behaviour directly impacts on the young person's motivation to face up to what they have done. Fear of the family's reaction, perhaps anger, rejection or even exclusion from home, can affect the young person's ability to take responsibility. When parents are able, or are enabled, to hear what their son or daughter has done and still support them, this gives permission for the young person to take responsibility and encourages them to address their behaviour. The family is thus central in encouraging and supporting the young person to participate in therapeutic work (Sheinberg and Fraenkel 2001). In the absence of any mandate for treatment, for example from a court, it is sometimes a family's determination alone that ensures that a young person engages in therapeutic work. Family members also play a central role in the network of protection through supervision and monitoring.

Finally, the family is a resource for the young person for the future. At times of stress and difficulty, young people should be able to turn to their family for support and so their involvement from the outset in relation to the work with the young person is essential to maintain their engagement and connection with the young person's situation, strengths and vulnerabilities.

Family difficulties

Families often report difficulties in parenting their teenager who has presented with challenging behaviour. These difficulties are best addressed in the family context and not in isolation, just with the young person. The Pro-Social Family Therapy Model (Blechman and Vryan 2000) was devised for work with young people and their families where the young people had got into difficulties with offending and anti-social behaviour, though not specifically sexual offending. However, it can be relevant in this area as many of the young people who have sexually abused also present with other difficulties. In this approach a number of sessions are offered to the young person, with their family, which specifically target difficulties at home, school and coping skills. The focus is on improving communication, charting behaviour, identifying a 'Good Day Plan' (expected behaviour) and developing an associated reward system. In the sessions there is an emphasis on rehearsal of communication skills. NIAP has also successfully incorporated into their treatment work the Parents Plus Programme, a comprehensive video-based parenting course for managing and solving discipline problems in children and young people (Parents Plus 2002).

There may, however, be family difficulties that are affecting the young person currently, or unresolved difficulties from the past, that impede the ability of the young person to make progress in treatment. Working with both the young person and the family provide opportunities for relationships to be repaired, both in relation to the impact of the sexually abusive behaviour and past difficulties.

Support and education for the family

There are direct benefits for parents in being involved in therapeutic work. It offers support at a time when families often feel most isolated. It helps them to explore and express their feelings about their child and their abusive behaviour, to develop their understanding of their son or daughter, to rebuild their relationship with him or her and to develop an understanding of what leads to abusive behaviour. It can also help them to regain confidence in their parenting. In a qualitative study of parents who had participated in the NIAP programme (Duane *et al.* 2002) parents' self-reported psychological adjustment, self-esteem and perceived social support improved over the course of treatment. Parents also reported an increase in their general well-being and ability to cope, an increase in parent–child communications and a decrease in parents' anger with their sons.

Intrafamilial abuse

In cases of intrafamilial abuse, account needs to be taken of complex relationships and loyalties. In situations of intrafamilial sibling abuse there can be complex loyalty binds for the parents – anger with the young person who has abused but also a wish to support them, concern for the child who has been abused and also concern about how to support them. This can be very complicated for parents – trying to support both children without either child feeling excluded or unsupported. Children can be very sensitive to the subtleties of how parents are responding to each. For the child who has been abused, there are also often mixed feelings towards the sibling who abused them. They may have had good experiences with them, as well as the abusive experiences and it can be difficult to reconcile these and make their own sense of why they were abused. For others there can be strong feelings of anger. For parents they may feel confused about whether and how to maintain a relationship with the young person who abused. Whether families live together, reunite or continue to live apart, individual family members remain part of the same family and it is helpful to look at what level of reparation of relationships is wanted by all family members and what is possible.

Influential theoretical approaches

There are two main areas of research and theory which inform our work – first, research and theory which have explored aspects of sexual abuse and offending by children and young people and their treatment. Second, theoretical ideas drawn from family therapy and family work are also influential in our particular approach to work with young people and their families. These two areas are discussed in turn.

Research and theory in relation to sexual abuse and offending by young people

Research into the development of sexual offending highlights the significance of family experiences. Barbaree *et al.* (1998) emphasise the significance of attachment problems in the subsequent development of sexually abusive behaviour. Difficult attachment experiences impact on a person's ability to form positive interpersonal relationships, to have their intimacy needs met in an appropriate way and to recognise and express emotions, all of which influence their sense of self. Ryan (1999b) also noted that parental loss, parental violence and substance abuse by parents are often significant factors in the development of sexually abusive behaviour in children and young people. Worling (1995) compared adolescent males who had sexually abused siblings with those who had abused non-sibling children. He found that those who had abused siblings reported more marital discord, parental rejection, physical discipline, negative family atmosphere and a general dissatisfaction with their family relationships.

Chaffin (2003) identified six risk and resiliency factors within the family that can influence the development of or prevent further offending: the quality of parental monitoring and supervision; levels of parental warmth, support, praise and comfort; parental approaches to discipline; parental support for the young person's education; the family's problem-solving style and the nature of parental modelling. All these factors are useful in assessing a family's strengths and are areas where intervention may promote more effective parental capacity.

A number of Irish studies have also highlighted the need to engage parents of young people who sexually abuse in treatment. Duane *et al.* (2002) found that, compared with parents from clinical and community control groups, more parents of young people who had sexually abused had personally experienced child abuse, reported more difficulties with general family functioning, family roles, affective responsiveness, affective involvement and behaviour control within the family and expressed lower levels of parental satisfaction. O'Reilly *et al.* (1998) found that the young people who had sexually abused but who failed to respond to treatment reported poorer levels of family functioning in the areas of role performance, affective responsiveness and affective involvement.

A number of authors have written about family work in this area, drawing on the factors outlined above. Thus the AIM (Assessment, Intervention and Management) Framework (Henniker *et al.* 2002) proposes a systemic assessment encompassing the young person who has sexually abused, their parents and the wider system. Morrison and Wilkinson (2005) have developed this further, as is discussed in Chapter 3. They have developed a comprehensive model for assessing families, which integrates the DOH *Framework for the Assessment of Children In Need and their Families* (2000) with findings drawn from literature on delinquency and on young people who have sexually abused. Hackett (2001) also discuss areas for assessment work with parents and suggests various assessment tools.

Multi-systemic treatment (MST) as proposed by Borduin *et al.* (1990) involves intervening therapeutically on a number of levels – with the young person, their family, and working to address difficulties in school and peer contexts through direct liaison with the school or through the young person and their parents. Borduin *et al.* (1990) found MST to be more effective than individual therapy alone, its efficacy being attributed to the emphasis on changing behaviours and interpersonal relations within the offender's natural environment.

Ideas from family therapy and other therapeutic schools

In our work with families we are influenced by ideas from the systemic field, narrative approaches, social constructionism, solution focused work and the feminist field. The most significant ideas in our work are outlined below. It should also be stressed that the NIAP programme emphasises a strengths-based approach: the families referred to us often fear being blamed and feel disempowered. It is our experience that respecting families' strengths and knowledge helps to promote engagement in the therapeutic work and increases motivation for change.

Systems theory

Key systemic ideas (Dallos and Draper 2001) that influence our work are:

• The significance of context: understanding young people in the context of the many systems of which they are a part – family, sibling, peer, school, cultural, legal, social context. In the previous edition of this book, Burnham *et al.* (1999) describe a model for understanding these different levels of context and how they impact on different levels of meaning. Behaviour can be best understood by exploring the context in which it arises as this facilitates developing an understanding of the meaning and function of the behaviour for the young person and the family.

- Each person in the system is both influenced by and influences others in a recursive cycle – in other words change in one part of the system can lead to change in another part of the system. This being the case, a strategic approach to work with the whole or parts of a family system can be taken, depending on the intervention goals selected, therapeutic leverage points and even family member availability.
- Identifying connections between beliefs, behaviour and relationships is important. There is a recursive relationship between beliefs, behaviour and relationships, so for example, understanding and looking for alternative beliefs can lead to changed behaviour and new ways of relating. Equally, if the focus is on behavioural change, this can also affect beliefs and relationships.
- Family life cycle stages are significant, particularly periods of transition, for example, to adolescence or young adulthood; the meaning of these transitions for the young person and their parents and how they are or are not managed.
- The importance of process as well as content in influencing family dynamics and functioning;

Ideas from narrative therapy

Narrative therapy (White, 1989, 1991, 2002; White and Epston 1990; Morgan 2000) discusses how problems can lead to totalising descriptions of people which can restrain change. In the case example below of John it was very helpful to look for stories about him outside of his abusive behaviour, for example stories based on what his friends would say about him, what they valued about his friendship, what they would say were some of his special qualities. This was a very useful conversation with John who seemed to find it helpful that he and others could see other aspects of his identity, which were more positive and hence empowering for him. This approach emphasises the importance of looking for alternative descriptions of the person and alternative narratives that may be obscured by their problems. Re-authoring techniques search for more empowering stories, for example, identifying times when the young person has faced up to responsibility, times when the young person has shown care for others. This alternative description encourages the young person to see that the sexual offending is not the totality of their identity. This more positive self-description leads to increased self-esteem and influences change as is illustrated in Richard's case, which is also described below. Other family members can be useful in helping young people to re-author their stories. It can also be important for the family to be able to re-author their own story – often they come for therapy with stories of shame and failure in their history. Re-authoring can help them to identify stories of pride and competency that can positively affect their sense of family identity and parents can be empowered through helping them to identify their parenting skills.

Social constructionism

Social constructionism (Speed 1991; McNamee and Gergen 1992; Burck and Daniel 1995; Burck and Speed 1995; Burr 1995) proposes that there is no truth to be discovered, but multiple ways of viewing and understanding – multiple perspectives. In therapy this involves drawing out different family members' beliefs and understandings, without seeing any one perspective as the truth. When we are talking with families about how they understand their sons'/daughters' offending, or other difficulties, such as problems with the expression of anger, this can be a useful way to develop new understandings. This incorporates the concept of both/and thinking rather than either/or. This involves exploring different descriptions and understandings without trying to identify a 'truth' or right answer, but looking for and valuing multiple descriptions that all hold validity. The power of dominant cultural knowledge, for example, in relation to gendered identity and sexuality, is important in terms of how it influences beliefs, behaviour and meaning. Slattery (2003) describes how beliefs about masculinity impact on young men's sense of identity and ways of being in a way that can be constraining and unhelpful. She discusses a young man who described himself as a different person in different places. This seemed to relate to his beliefs about masculinity and particularly the importance of 'toughness'. This in turn was influenced by relationships with other males and the context in which he lived. He believed that toughness was important in terms of gaining respect and protecting himself. It was very useful to explore his sense of identity in different contexts and his preferred way of being.

Solution-focused approaches

Solution-focused therapy is a strengths-based approach (de Shazer 1988; Selekman 1993; Berg 1994; George *et al.* 2001). It emphasises the importance of problem-free talk – looking for what is going well, what the client does well, identifying their strengths, skills and resources. This is important as it is empowering of people, builds confidence for change and identifies skills they can use in addressing problems. Another important focus is on identifying exceptions – times when a problem does not happen or happens less – what is the client doing then, what is happening in their life then. The use of goal setting – identifying concrete, measurable and achievable goals provides clarity about where the client wants to get to and it then becomes possible to identify steps toward these goals. Scaling is something we often use in therapeutic work. For example, we might ask someone 'On a scale of 0–10, with 0 being where there are no problems with anger and 10 being where anger is running your life where would you say you are? Where do you want to be?' In this way one can understand how clients perceive their difficulties and it is then possible to explore what would need to happen for them to move one point lower/higher. One can ask 'What would you be doing?'

Feminism

The systemic field has been criticised in the past for its emphasis on circularity (Cecchin 1987) without taking into account imbalances of power, particularly in the area of domestic violence and sexual abuse (McKinnon and Miller 1987; Goldner 1988, 1990). There has been concern that circularity and therapist neutrality can lead to victims feeling or, indeed, being blamed for contributing to their abusive experiences. In our work we are clear that the person who abused has responsibility for their abusive behaviour. A major goal of the work is helping the young person and their parents to recognise this responsibility, to understand what may have lead them to abuse and to recognise their choices about ways of behaving in the future. The programme also aims to address negative and abusive attitudes and beliefs about women, and explore attitudes and beliefs about men's ways of being. It is important to explore how these beliefs may facilitate and support abusive behaviour.

When is family work indicated?

All families referred for services could benefit from family work, at the very least to explore the impact of the abusive behaviour on family relationships. Limited resources often mean, however, that this is not possible and it can be helpful to have criteria for deciding in which situations family work is essential. These factors can be helpful in this process:

- What is the family life cycle stage for the young person, in particular, what is their level of dependence or separation with respect to their family of origin? As he or she grows older, it may be more appropriate to help the young person to develop healthy independence and separation, rather than work with him or her jointly with other family members.
- How significant are family difficulties and strengths in preventing or promoting a healthy lifestyle for the young person? Does family functioning have a direct bearing on the young person's propensity to offend or adopt dysfunctional coping?
- Do family difficulties directly affect the young person's ability to engage in the therapeutic work?
- How important is the family in supporting an offence-free lifestyle? Is the family a change agent in systemic terms?

It is also important to consider the timing of any family work. Should therapy begin with individual, group or family work? At what stage should other therapeutic approaches be considered? A thorough assessment of the young person and their family, via, for example, the AIM Framework (Henniker *et al.* 2002) should identify whether family work is indicated and guide the timing of this. For some young people the primary focus will be on addressing their offending and risk-taking behaviour in individual or group work. Similarly, family work may take different forms – work with the parents individually or in group, review meetings with the young person and his/her parents, or whole family sessions.

Case examples

In this section, four case examples are presented that illustrate our approach to work with young people and their families, cases that highlight different aspects of the theoretical ideas we have outlined earlier. These have been anonymised and some details changed in order to protect family confidentiality.

Family life cycle issues: Peter's case

Themes of autonomy and control and dependence versus independence are issues that all families negotiate as children reach adolescence and prepare to leave home. At this stage of the family life cycle (McGoldrick 1998) it is not unusual for there to be increased tension and conflict between parents and young people as the latter strive to assert their identity and take more control of their day-to-day lives (Haley 1980). Most families manage to readjust relationships to a new equilibrium while others get stuck at this stage and fail to move on. Reasons for this vary and, from the young person's perspective, may relate to a less secure attachment with parents (Marshall *et al.* 1993), which contributes to feelings of inadequacy and low self-esteem, poor peer relationships and social isolation. From the parental perspective, for those who have overly depended on children to meet their emotional needs and have failed to invest in adult relationships or interests, the 'empty nest syndrome' may lead to feelings of worthlessness, abandonment and a reluctance, either overtly or covertly, to allow young people to leave home. Marital breakdown at this time may also be a contributory factor for both parents and young people. The following case example illustrates the dilemmas faced by families and how sexually abusive behaviour can compound these difficulties.

Peter was 17 years of age and presented as a quiet, unassertive and emotionally lonely young man. Having dropped out of school early, Peter had few goals in his life, and lost one job after another as he failed to arrive for work or complete tasks adequately. His alcohol and drug use were also of concern. His parents were very active in finding employment and courses for him to attend. Peter's sense of failure and difficulty in facing up to problems resulted in him pretending to have employment, until his parents found out that this was not so. This happened on a number of occasions and resulted in his parents not trusting him and continually monitoring his whereabouts, leading to a difficult and often acrimonious relationship.

Peter exposed himself in a public place on a number of occasions. This usually occurred when he was unemployed but pretending otherwise to his parents. The police decided to caution him and he and his parents agreed that they would attend therapy. While committing these acts he identified feelings of self-loathing, anger and frustration but also a sense of control over others.

One of the main aims of family work was encouraging Peter to take increased responsibility for his day-to-day life while encouraging his parents to step back, at the same time as continuing to support him. The family had clearly got into a negative cycle in that the more efforts his parents made to enable him to lead a responsible life the more Peter failed in this endeavour. It was not easy for his parents to do less of what they had originally considered appropriate, particularly as they feared that he would re-offend. For Peter, as regards finding his own job, he worried that it would not meet his parents' expectations. Family sessions enabled communication about these issues to take place, while individual work focused on Peter's personal goals of increased responsibility, competence, independence and self-esteem.

Although there were setbacks, Peter improved in his ability to face up to his problems. His drug and alcohol use decreased, although his alcohol intake still affected his ability to get to work on time. His cognitive distortions in relation to being late for work were similar to those connected to his offending; for example, he would think, 'I will get away with it, I will just do it once, they won't mind.' The new thinking he identified to counteract this mindset was, 'If I am late for work it is the first step towards losing my job, I don't want to walk the streets again to look for another one.' Similarly, in relation to the offences he had committed, he recognised that his use of adult pornography was the first step towards him exposing himself in public.

Communication between Peter and his parents increased and improved. Obtaining a job through his own efforts increased Peter's self-esteem, desire to succeed and social network. His previous sense of hopelessness about his life changed to one of hope as he developed new interests and future plans. His parents' anxiety decreased and they felt able to go away on a holiday leaving Peter at home for the first time. This was a clear indication that the family had moved to the next stage of the family life cycle with his parents rediscovering life as a couple and Peter enjoying life as a young adult less dependent on his parents. It is our belief that failure to address issues in Peter's day-to-day life would have contributed to an increased risk of him possibly re-offending. Work with Peter and his family illustrates the more holistic developmental approach that is now recommended when working with young people who sexually abuse (Ryan 1999).

Re-unification/reparation of relationships: Ruth's case

Ruth aged 10 years disclosed that her older brother John (aged 17) had been sexually abusing her over the previous year. Following the initial investigation by child protection services John was asked to leave the family home. He initially lived with a paternal aunt and then moved to stay with friends. He continued to see his family on a regular basis.

Ruth was referred for individual therapy and then attended group work over a period of two years. John was seen for individual and group work to address his sexual offending. Both parents attended the parents' group at NIAP and were involved in reviews of Ruth's therapy. They supported Ruth in disclosing the abuse and were clear that John was responsible for the abuse and were keen for him to complete the therapeutic work required. Over time, as the work progressed, the parents, John and Ruth enquired about the possibility of John returning to live at home. It was therefore decided to undertake some family work to explore this possibility and to consider whether joint sessions with Ruth and John might be helpful.

Initially the work focused on strengthening the relationship between Ruth and her parents. Together they talked about their feelings about the abuse, their memories of John's behaviour when he had lived at home and their feelings about him having to leave home. Both parents and Ruth described times when John had been very controlling and bullying, particularly in relation to Ruth. Time was also spent talking about how they saw their future relationships with John. We explored how Ruth felt about John coming back home, and she spoke about the changes she had noticed in his behaviour, particularly that he was more respectful of her and her mother. She wanted him to be able to live at home again.

Jenkins *et al.* (2003) discuss the concept of forgiveness when sexual abuse has occurred. The authors look at different levels of forgiveness – relinquishment of feelings, pardoning and reconciliation. They explore this on two continuums – obligation (feeling obliged to forgive) and self-realisation (feeling freedom of choice about forgiveness). They discuss how a victim may let go of their feelings about the abuse but maintain their sense of outrage. Others may choose to 'pardon' but not want a continuing relationship. Others may chose to reconcile without pardoning and others may choose to do both. Therapy with Ruth helped her to explore her sense of obligation and to facilitate her to in making a decision that felt true to herself. She was very aware of her parents' sadness about the break-up of the family and felt some sadness about this herself. She had some positive memories of John and hopes about a different relationship. We explored her feelings about a meeting with John and her mother, what questions she may have, what she would like to happen at such a meeting.

The next stage of the family work involved meetings with John and his parents. We focused on exploring John's view of the therapeutic work he had undertaken and what changes he thought his parents and Ruth needed to see before a decision could be reached about him returning home. We also explored John's relationship with Ruth in the past, how he felt about her and his view about a future relationship with her. Whilst he accepted responsibility for the abuse, he felt frustrated about his lack of choice about being able to return home and was angry with Ruth as he believed that she had told her friends about the abuse and now it was known in the local area. Some sessions focused on his views about a meeting with Ruth and what questions he thought she might have and how he might respond to these.

At times John found the family therapy process difficult. When we used narrative therapy ideas to explore alternative narratives about John, he was able to engage more positively in the therapeutic work. He spoke about how other people saw him and described him, in particular his friends. He was able to talk about his concern about how his abusive behaviour could influence the way people see him. It seemed helpful that John knew that the therapist and team had heard more positive descriptions of him and were aware of his concern about the abuse dominating his identity.

Following this Ruth and John were seen by their individual therapists to prepare for a joint session. Ruth was asked who she would like to be present, what she would like to happen, how she could indicate if she was distressed or unhappy in the session or if she wanted it to end. Practical issues such as where she wanted herself and her parents to sit were discussed. Time was also spent looking at how she could manage her anxiety and what her parents and the therapist could do to support her. Preparation work with John included exploring his anxieties about attending the meeting, completing a letter of apology to Ruth and preparing responses to the questions she wanted him to consider.

The parents, Ruth and John attended for one session together. John's individual therapist attended to support him in apologising to Ruth. Ruth chose not to invite her individual therapist. In this session John apologised to Ruth and took responsibility for the abuse. At John's request his therapist read the letter of apology that he had written. Ruth was then offered a chance to respond and the parents also spoke about their feelings. The session then focused on identifying safety rules that need to be in place should a decision be made that John could return home. The parents, Ruth and John all spoke of a sense of relief following this session and a sense of moving on. Ruth spoke positively about the experience. She was particularly pleased that John had apologised and found it very helpful to hear his letter of apology.

A number of therapeutic and other issues were identified from this piece of work that may well apply to work with other families. First, the work involved two agencies – a therapeutic service for children who have been sexually abused and a service working with young people who have sexually abused. Shared and agreed protocols were, therefore, needed in relation to interagency working, liaison and communication. This involved an interagency meeting being convened, following the child protection investigation, where the therapeutic work required for both young people and the family was considered, and agreements were reached about what work each agency would be undertaking, including the appropriateness of joint work (e.g. with the parents or family work) and planning for regular liaison meetings. Second, it is important to stress that there were several stages in the therapeutic work before an apology session could be undertaken (Sheinberg and Fraenkel 2001). This is not work that can be rushed. Third, as discussed earlier, there can often be loyalty binds for parents which it is important to explore.

Attachment/unresolved issues: Richard's case

The following case study illustrates that the outcome for some young men we have worked with is not always as positive as with the case of Peter, for reasons that are partly family-related.

Richard, aged 16 years, attended a groupwork programme for three months. In reviewing his participation we questioned whether a therapeutic group, which requires an emotional engagement on behalf of the members, was a good idea for him. Richard presented as compliant and overtly co-operative; however he failed to engage at an emotional level. He was quiet and unresponsive, happy to let other members take centre stage. We felt that he sometimes went unnoticed in the group particularly if the therapist's time was taken up with more demanding young people.

Richard then attended individual therapy, one of the main aims being to establish a therapeutic relationship with him, within which he could improve his emotional understanding of himself and others. It was important for the therapist to be consistent and affirming even though Richard continued to be compliant and avoidant. For example, he attended for appointments but sometimes at the wrong time or on the wrong day. It was a tremendous personal struggle for Richard to open up and share with his therapist. He was distrustful of all adults, viewing them as negative and controlling. This was evident in his reluctance to disclose even the smallest piece of information about himself. He was never openly non-compliant but covertly would show what he was really feeling covertly. For example, if the therapist asked him to complete an exercise that he was reluctant to undertake, it could take him 40 minutes to write three lines.

Understanding something of his family background helped us to understand his current behaviour. From an early age Richard had felt controlled by his father and under pressure to achieve academically. He presented as a fearful and timid young boy whose distress was viewed by his parents as laziness and 'not caring'. Richards's solution had been to withdraw and become self-reliant. This enabled him to protect his sense of self from what he viewed as extreme and unhelpful control. However he avoided any negative emotions or memories in relation to this, insisting that his 'father cared too much'.

Richard acknowledged feelings of loneliness and isolation and expressed a desire for intimacy. His failure to achieve this was blamed on girls who, according to him, 'only wanted to be with the good-looking fellas'. He expressed continued helplessness about the possibility of being able to do anything about this.

Richard had sexually abused his 10-year-old sister, which involved fondling her genital area. He claimed that she knew how lonely he was and, in relation to the abuse, he saw himself as a victim also. Ward *et al.* (1997) put forward a link between the attachment styles people have and the characteristics of their sexually abusive behaviour. For those, like Richard, with a fearful, avoidant attachment style, they suggest the following aspects might be characteristic of the individual's attitudes and behaviour:

- Desires intimacy but experiences distrust and fears rejection;
- Blames others for their lack of intimacy;
- Keeps others at a distance;
- Avoidance of closeness has these individuals seeking impersonal contacts or impersonal sex;
- Unconcerned about victim's feelings, self-focused during offences;
- Uninhibited about using force, if necessary.

Apart from the last characteristic, Richard fitted the above profile almost identically. He denied any strong feelings of anger about his relationship with his father or about his failure to achieve intimacy with others. Indeed Richard presented as 'shut down' and appeared to try and regulate his emotions by ignoring or denying them. This was brought home strongly to the therapist in one session when Richard told her that he had watched some young men steal his moped, 'the one thing in my life that I care about'. However, he denied having any feelings of upset and anger about this, claiming he was a pacifist!

Richard acknowledged that he was very stuck in his life and his relationships. Individual and family work focused on how he could move forward and achieve autonomy while maintaining a relationship with his parents. He acknowledged his feelings of upset and anger with his parents but neither his father nor Richard could validate each other's experience. His mother, with whom he enjoyed a better relationship, tried to mediate between them both.

In individual work Richard mapped the different roads that he could follow in the future:

Road 1. Parents control Richard

- No free thoughts;
- No social life;
- Working all the time, in a job of their choice.

Road 2. Richard pushes parents away

- Not looking for permission;
- Not explaining;
- Not listening;
- No contact.

Road 3. Co-operation between Richard and his parents

- Planning a job/course of his choice;
- Feeling in control of himself and his life;
- Arguing less with his parents.

Work with Richard was very slow and he attended our therapy programme for over two years. He became more able to share his thoughts and feelings, found himself a job of his choosing, and began to socialise more often with his peers. His relationship with his father remained strained, however, and, more worryingly, his view of his ability to have a relationship with a girl remained unchanged when therapy ended.

Family communication: Ben's case

The M family was referred following the discovery that Ben (aged 12) had sexually abused his 7-year-old female neighbour on two occasions. Ben was the youngest of four siblings – two sisters and two brothers. Mr M had sexually abused one of his daughters approximately 13 years previously over a period of six months when she was 14 years old. This had been investigated by the child protection agencies following her disclosure to her mother. Mr M had served a prison sentence during which he had attended for treatment. His daughter had attended for individual therapy. Following his discharge from prison he had returned to live with the family. Child protection agencies had deemed Mrs M to be protective of her children and had closed the case.

At the time of referral of Ben there were a number of concerns about him and his family. First, given the sexual knowledge that Ben had at such a young age, could he too have been sexually abused by his father? Second, there were concerns about the level of secrecy in the family. His sisters were aware that he had abused his neighbour but Ben did not know that they knew. His brother was unaware of what had happened but had noticed changes in relationships with the neighbours with whom the family had previously enjoyed a close relationship. Neither Ben nor his brother was aware that their father had sexually abused his sister. The therapeutic team were concerned about how the original abuse had affected the family and family relationships. We questioned what therapeutic benefits could be gained from opening up communications within the family and what difficulties might arise? Third, there were associated concerns about family patterns of communication. It seemed that Ben tended to cope with difficulties by avoidance. In what way might this have contributed to the development of his offending and how might it reflect patterns of communication in the family?

Following the initial assessment Ben joined our group for young people who have sexually abused. Joint sessions were undertaken with Mr and Mrs M to explore some of the concerns raised above. From the outset it was clear that there were unresolved issues about Mr M's abuse of his daughter. Mrs M spoke of her anger with him about the abuse, her anger that he had received therapeutic intervention but that there had been less support available at that time for the family. She described how her anger had led to her withdrawing from her husband and excluding him from parenting, in order to ensure the children's protection. Mr M spoke about how he had noticed his wife's anger but had not understood that it was connected to the abuse. He described being less involved in parenting and choosing to step back from this role following the abuse, because he felt he was less entitled to be involved. Sessions focused on encouraging them to communicate with each other about these issues. Mrs M said that she had never spoken with her husband about how she felt. They talked about how their relationship had changed and their sadness about this. Sessions also explored how the abuse had impacted on their relationships with the children, what changes the children may have noticed in their relationship and parenting roles, and what sense they might have made of this.

We also explored with them the reasons for choosing not to share information about the abuse with other family members and how this might have affected them in relation to both the abuse by Ben and Mr M. They could see benefit in being open about Ben's abuse, that it could be positive for him to know that his family knew and still accepted and supported him. They could also see the benefits of giving the other children some context for understanding the changes in relationships and reducing their sense of exclusion from 'secrets'. However, Mrs M was reluctant to disclose the abuse by Mr M. She thought that this might not be of any benefit to the boys and was concerned about how her daughter, who was now an adult, might feel about this. We talked about how she could have a conversation with her daughter about this.

A key theme throughout was the pattern of communication in the family. This was addressed particularly in relation to Ben who, we noticed, tended to withdraw and not communicate about important matters. We explored what he might have learnt about communication in his family and particularly gender patterns around this. Mr and Mrs M were encouraged to discuss their views on men's and women's roles in relation to parenting, decision making and communication, looking at what they had learnt from their families of origin. We talked with them about what they wanted to teach their children about these issues. We also explored whether they had any concerns that Ben might have been abused. Mrs M was adamant that she had supervised the children closely and had talked with Ben about the possibility of abuse, although he had denied this had happened to him.

The next stage of work involved appointments with Ben and his parents, to improve family communication and encourage skills development in this area. The parents were able to tell Ben that his siblings were aware of his abusive behaviour. Two sessions were held with the whole family to discuss what Ben had done and people's reactions to this. Ben shared some of the work that he had done in NIAP. The family discussed ways of improving communication with each other. Discussion also took place about rules in relation to safety and supervision. All these sessions were productive. The daughter, however, was not open to sharing her own abusive experience with her siblings. Her father accepted that disclosure to the whole family might have some benefits and was willing for this to happen but Mrs M did not want any additional distress to be caused to her daughter. This raised a dilemma for the workers that we shared with Mr and Mrs M – on the one hand, the therapeutic benefits that could be gained and on the other hand, their daughter's right to confidentiality and the risk to her mental health if this information was shared without her consent. At the time of concluding work with the family, the parents felt they had to respect their daughter's position.

Clinical issues

Team work

Working with young people who have sexually abused and their families can be very complex and challenging. It is, therefore, important to consider what structures and supports need to be in place in order to facilitate staff to do this work. When undertaking family work we have found it particularly helpful to co-work or work as part of a family therapy team. Team members often have different perspectives and thoughts about families and bring different skills, and in this way co-working enriches the service that families receive. Staff can also find co-working supportive. Where possible, it may be helpful to have mixed gendered co-workers. This can be useful when exploring gendered beliefs in families, for example, about what it means to be male/female. It can be helpful to think about family members' different experiences of relating to men and women throughout their lives, both positive and negative, which may be influencing them in the therapy session. It may also be that co-workers can provide alternative experiences of relationships with men and women and can model different ways of relating, e.g. communication styles.

The reflecting team (Anderson 1987) involves the family therapy team having their mid session discussion in the presence of the family who are then invited to comment on what they have heard. This approach provides a more open, collaborative and empowering way of working with families although the approach requires training and practice by workers before undertaking it.

Supervision

Given the complexity of difficulties that families present with, regular supervision is a requirement both as a support to staff and to guide them in their work. Supervision facilitates workers to reflect on their own practice, beliefs and feelings, and how these may influence their work with a family and helps workers to develop ways of viewing the family, open avenues for other therapeutic work and identify when the system is mirroring the family. Morrison (2001) has proposed a framework for supervision and identifies four stages to the supervisory process – experience, reflection, conceptualising and action. This encourages staff to identify what issues arise from their work with a family, what may be triggered for the staff member and how these then influence their approach. Having time to prepare for sessions, reflect on the last session and consider possible areas to explore and address with the family are also essential when undertaking family work. External consultation for the team as whole can also help teams to reflect on team beliefs and practice, team ways of relating and how these affect the work.

Family context

Throughout our work we try to take account of the wider context in which families live, particularly taking account of the impact of race, culture, class, religion, gender, sexuality and ability. These multiple levels of context influence families' belief systems, patterns of interaction and relationships. They can be a significant influence on how families view abusive behaviour and what it means for a young person to face up to what they have done.

Creating a cultural genogram (Hardy and Laszloffy 1995) is a useful technique for exploring with families how culture, class, religion, gender and sexuality have been influential in their life. Whilst this is a useful approach, it is important that these different levels of context are borne in mind throughout the work with families, rather than separating them out as a separate topic/issue to be addressed. They are integral for families' identity and belief systems and should be an integral part of our way of working with and understanding families.

Impasses in family work

Finally, there can be times when we feel 'stuck' in our work with families. Flaskas's exploration of this (2002) can help workers to understand these difficulties and identify ways forward. She describes how impasses can be related to the family's (or individual member's) struggle with the issues that brought them to therapy and their struggle with change. Alternatively, impasses may be related to issues of therapeutic process and the extent to which the therapist's responsiveness is creating openings for change. Impasses can also be related to the therapist becoming fixed in their own ideas about the changes required, or becoming 'married' to a particular family member's view or becoming caught up in the interactional processes of the family. Flaskas also describes how an impasse can be related to the therapist's own usual patterns of relating that may not be the best fit for this family and about how the therapeutic relationship can begin to mirror the family relationships difficulties. These aspects further highlight the benefits of team working and regular supervision.

Conclusion

This chapter has illustrated that therapy strategies that are useful in family work generally are equally applicable when working with families where sexual abusive behaviour has occurred. Work may not focus solely on the abusive behaviours but also on other factors that may influence a young person's risks and resiliencies. Professionals have the skills to work with this client group and should not allow the issue of sexual abuse to deskill them. Family work forms part of an integrated approach and complements individual and group work. For effective therapy, attention also needs to be given to the wider professional system to ensure an integrated and co-ordinated response in managing complex situations.

A number of studies (Marshall *et al.* 1993, 1998) have identified the family factors that contribute to the development of sexually abusive behaviour. However, more studies are required to evaluate family work and its impact on a young person in terms of their progress in therapy and to identify the family therapy approaches that most effectively address these factors.

Finally, self-care is important and should, at a minimum, include adequate supervision and a team approach in working with families. 'Staff are the most precious resource available to the services in which they work. If they are not well managed, their motivation, knowledge, skills and emotional responsiveness will be under-utilised at best and lost at worst' (Morrison 2000).

15 Risk prediction, decision making and evaluation of adolescent sexual abusers

Richard Beckett

Introduction

Adolescent sexual abusers are a highly heterogeneous group and, compared with adult abusers, there is a paucity of research to guide risk prediction, decision making and evaluation. This chapter is divided into four sections. The first considers what is known about sexual and general recidivism in adolescents. It argues, on the basis of currently available research, that with adolescents the risk of both violent and general reoffending appears greater than the risk of sexual recidivism. Well-designed and standardised assessment measures are the central building blocks of effective evaluation. Because of this, section two provides a brief guide to some of the main considerations relevant to psychological test design particularly as they apply to the assessment of adolescent abusers. The third section provides a brief introduction to the Adolescent Sexual Abuser Project (ASAP), a multisite UK study designed to improve the understanding of dynamic risk factors in adolescent abusers. The final section provides information on the ASAP findings specifically with regard to general and victim empathy, and cognitive distortions.

Risk of reoffending

One of the main purposes of assessment is to identify adolescent offenders who are at high risk of recidivism. In assessing risk, we are interested in both short-term risk and in the likelihood that sexually abusive behaviour may persist through adolescence into adulthood. The question also arises as to whether the risk is of further sexual, violent or non-sexual offending and the relative likelihood that any of these might occur. Risk of violent offending is of interest and concern, not only because it creates victims but also because, with adult offenders, risk of sexual recidivism is increased in those individuals who have previous violent and non-sexual convictions (Thornton and Travers 1991; Hanson 2000).

There are a number of obvious benefits to being able to identify adolescent abusers at high risk of reoffending. First, where treatment resources are limited, it is important to concentrate resources on high risk adolescents with low risk individuals given less costly interventions. This strategy is in keeping with treatment efficacy literature (Andrews 1995) which shows that treatment and supervision is most effective when applied to higher-risk cases. Moreover, as seems likely, if the demand for monitoring, surveillance and notification of sexual offenders increases, then it is the high-risk individuals who should be the priority for such activity. Applying registration and long-term notification to low-risk adolescent sexual offenders is not only potentially costly, but risks stigmatising young people and increasing their vulnerability to ostracisation and vigilante attention. This not only goes against the current philosophy of youth justice, but high-level surveillance or public notification of low-risk abusers might increase their likelihood of sexual offending by alienating them, disrupting their peer relationships and restricting their social and employment opportunities.

Sexual recidivism in adolescents

Compared to the study of recidivism in adult sexual offenders where a number of developmental, historical and criminological characteristics have been identified as contributing to risk prediction (Quinsey *et al.* 1995; Hanson and Bussière 1996; Prentky *et al.* 1997), our knowledge of, and ability to predict, sexual recidivism in adolescents is still in its infancy. In one of the few studies in which untreated adolescent sexual offenders have been tracked into adulthood (Elliot 1994), 66 self-reported and largely undetected adolescent rapists were followed-up over an approximate 15-year period. During this time 22 per cent of subjects self-reported a further sexual offence, and 78 per cent a further non-sexual offence. The large majority of adolescent reconviction studies report following-up adolescents discharged from treatment programmes. Many of these suffer from the methodological problems that have previously impeded our understanding of adults' sexual recidivism. These include an over-reliance on sexual reconvictions as opposed to actual rates of reabuse; a lack of untreated and matched comparison groups; small sample sizes and short follow-up periods. Moreover, studies of adolescent sexual abusers often suffer from mixing adolescents who abuse children with those who assault peers or adult women. As a result, differences in reoffence rates which might be reasonably expected to exist between different sub-groups of adolescent abusers cannot be identified.

In Weinrott's (1996) review of adolescent sex offender recidivism he examined twenty-two treatment studies, the majority of which followed-up subjects for under five years. Subjects across studies ranged from adolescents who had committed relatively minor behaviours or offences (excessive masturbation, indecent exposure, voyeurism and 'immorality') through to serious sexual assaults. The treatment interventions ranged from prosecution in open court combined with 'sex hygiene guidance' and 'reorientation' (Doshay 1943), through to more familiar cognitive-behavioural interventions (e.g. Becker 1990; Scram *et al.* 1991; Milloy 1994).

Weinrott's review showed that relatively few adolescents were charged with subsequent sexual crimes, though the reasons for this were not possible to determine, and it should be borne in mind that no study used untreated control groups. Two-thirds reported sexual reoffence rates of under 10 per cent. Furthermore, where sexual and non-sexual reoffence rates were reported, adolescent sexual offenders were at least twice as likely to receive a non-sexual, as opposed to a further sexual conviction. For a five-to-ten year period following conviction, most boys who assaulted children did not appear to sexually reoffend. More tentatively, Weinrott also concluded that for adolescents whose only offence was sexual, further non-sexual convictions were uncommon and that, overall, adolescent sexual offenders were less likely than delinquents to generally reoffend.

With adult sexual offenders a previous history of antisocial behaviour contributes to the prediction of sexual recidivism and has consequently been incorporated into many risk prediction scales, e.g. Static-99 (Hanson and Thornton 1999). However, the role of antisocial behaviour in predicting adolescent sexual recidivism is less clear. Knight (1999) in a 25-year follow-up of adolescent rapists found that adolescent victimless crimes contributed to predicting later serious sexual crimes. However, Rassmussen (1999) in a five-year follow-up of adolescent sexual offenders found that sexual recidivism was not associated with prior non-sexual offences. In this regard further work needs to be undertaken to clarify the relationship between adolescent non-sexual convictions and sexual recidivism.

Unfortunately, because there are so few follow-up studies on adolescent sexual offenders there is no reliable guide to the relative sexual recidivism rates of adolescents who abuse males as opposed to females; whether extrafamilial as opposed to intrafamilial abusers have higher recidivism rates; nor indeed whether adolescents who sexually abuse multiple victims as opposed to single victims have higher rates of reconviction. There is, however, at least some evidence regarding short-term reoffending rates of treated adolescent rapists and child abusers. Hagan and Cho (1996) reported on a sample of 50 adolescent child abusers, and 50 adolescent rapists who were discharged from a juvenile correction facility, having undergone cognitive-behavioural and adjunctive therapies. At the two-year follow-up point, 10 per cent of the rapists and 8 per cent of the child abusers had been convicted of a further sexual offence. Neither this difference, the difference in non-sexual reoffending (child abusers 54 per cent versus rapists 38 per cent), nor the seriousness of new offences were significant. These findings remained largely the same at the eight-year follow-up point (Hagan *et al.* 2001); that is, there was no difference in the rates of sexual reoffending between child abusers and rapists.

Predicting the persistence of sexual offending into adulthood

As yet there are not enough prospective studies which might enable us to reliably identify those characteristics which predict which adolescent sexual offenders will continue their sexual offending into adulthood. We do, however, have information from retrospective studies of adult sexual offenders. Abel *et al.* (1986) reported on 561 adult sexual offenders and, through confidential interviews, found that 53.6 per cent of abusers reported the onset of at least one deviant sexual interest prior to the age of 18. This study has been used as evidence not only that adult sexual offending is preceded by early onset of sexual deviancy, but also that deviant sexual interest in adolescence predicts the emergence of sexually deviant behaviour in adulthood.

Caution, however, must be applied when interpreting this study. Most importantly, the study was retrospective and could give no indication as to what proportion of adolescents show deviant sexual interests but do not go on to be sexual offenders. Moreover, whilst these offenders reported deviant interests in adolescence, the authors did not claim that these men acted on those interests by committing sexual assaults. Because of the high profile of the Abel clinic an unrepresentative group of particularly deviant and persistent adult sexual offenders may have been recruited, a disproportionately large number of whom may have developed their deviant sexual interest in adolescence. Although similarly high levels of early onset of deviant sexual interest were found in the Laws (1986) adult sexual offender programme, this was not found to be the case when Marshall and Barbaree (1990) examined their own clinical files on men referred to their service.

In a sophisticated study Prentky and Knight (1993) conducted clinical interviews and examined file data on 131 adult rapists and child abusers and compared those who had committed their first sexual assault in either adulthood, adolescence or as a child. The authors found that all three groups had similarly high levels of deviant sexual fantasy and behaviour. As such this study did not support the hypothesis that those who begin sexual abusing in childhood or adolescence have higher levels of sexual pathology, including sexual deviant interest, than those who begin their sexual offending in adulthood.

Given these contradictory findings, the role of deviant sexual interest in adolescents as a predictor for adult sexual offending has yet to be resolved. The Prentky and Knight study did, however, identify a number of characteristics which were more often present in abusers who began their offending in adolescence as opposed to adulthood. Adolescents who continued to sexually abuse into adulthood were much more likely to have a history of impulsive, antisocial behaviour than those who first abused as adults. This was the case for both rapists and child abusers. Second, those who did not begin their offending until late adolescence or adulthood were found to be much more socially competent than individuals who began offending during adolescence. Again, this was true for both rapists, and particularly for child abusers.

These findings are consistent with the general literature of antisocial and criminal behaviour. Individuals who present with behavioural problems at school, and who show lifestyle impulsivity, delinquent and antisocial behaviour, who get into fights and are generally assaultative, are much more likely to develop chronic patterns of offending in adulthood (Farrington 1973; Hanson *et al.* 1984; Loeber 1990; Knight and Prentky 1993). The Knight and Prentky (1993) study also found that adults who had begun their sexual assaulting in adolescence as opposed to adulthood were more likely themselves to have been sexually abused as a child. Finally, child abusers who began assaulting during adolescence were found to be more often physically abused, whereas physical neglect was found in the backgrounds of rapists who began their offending in adolescence.

Persistence of delinquency into adult criminality

It is now recognised that there are two types of adolescent who show antisocial behaviour: those whose antisocial behaviour is temporary and limited to adolescence, and those whose antisocial behaviour starts in childhood as conduct disorder and persists through adolescence and into adulthood (Moffitt 1993). The concept of adolescent-limited delinquency is based on the recognition that offence rates in general peak by the age of 17 and then decline markedly as adulthood approaches (Blumstein *et al.* 1988). Whilst a majority of male teenagers engage in some form of delinquent behaviour during adolescence (Elliot *et al.* 1983) there is a small group of adolescents whose antisocial behaviour remains stable and persistent from childhood to adolescence, into adulthood. This group, approximately 5 per cent of males, are responsible for about half of all crimes committed (Farrington *et al.* 1986), and are regarded as 'life course persistent'.

Elkins *et al.* (1997) reported on five recent longitudinal studies on adolescents, and examined those characteristics which distinguished adolescent limited delinquents from those who persisted in behaviour into adulthood. The studies reviewed were longitudinal studies conducted in the UK, North America and New Zealand. The findings generally supported the predictions of Moffitt (1993) that adolescent-limited and life-course persistent antisocial behaviour have different aetiologies and histories. Delinquents who ceased their criminal behaviour as they entered adulthood were found, in many respects, to be similar to non-antisocial adolescents, although they did tend to be more impulsive and less conventional. In contrast, delinquents who become adult criminals were distinguished by low IQ, and poor school attainment.

Life-course persistent criminals were also found to have a range of personality difficulties. These included being more aggressive and hostile, impulsive and thrill-seeking in their orientation to life, and more responsive to frustration with negative emotions (angry and destructive behaviour). High levels of alcohol and drug abuse are also linked to persistent antisocial behaviour. Farrington and Hawkins (1991) found, for example, that heavy drinking at the age of 18 was a good predictor of persistence of antisocial behaviour into adulthood.

Furthermore, Elkins *et al.* (1997) found that lifetime persistent criminals were more likely to start drinking earlier, and to get intoxicated younger than either non-criminals or adult criminals who did not have a delinquent history. Blumstein and Cohen (1987) found that amongst criminal offenders who used drugs, frequency of crimes was six times as high during periods of heavy drug use.

The preceding section has discussed what is known about the prediction of sexual, violent and general offending. A number of themes emerge from this discussion. The first is that whilst research informs our prediction of sexual and non-sexual recidivism in adult offenders, and while there are factors known to increase the risk that delinquents will become adult criminals, we do not as yet have reliable information to guide the prediction of sexual recidivism in adolescent sexual abusers. Another theme to emerge is that the majority of factors currently used to predict sexual recidivism in adults have yet to be established as reliable sexual risk prediction factors with adolescents. Furthermore most of the current risk factors used with adult sex offenders are static (e.g. pattern of previous offending) and therefore either not open to treatment or highly resistant to treatment change (e.g. psychopathy). Importantly, even were such static factors found to be predictive of adolescent recidivism their utility with this group is limited. In the UK Adolescent Sexual Abuser Project (described later in this chapter) the average age at which 372 adolescent child abusers committed their assaults was 12.79 years, and for 77 peer (non-rape) sexual assaulters 14.8 years. The 67 incarcerated rapists in the study committed their index offence at the average of 16.76 years. At these ages there is little time for sexual or non-sexual criminal histories to accrue or, for example, to warrant a diagnosis of psychopathy, both of which contribute to the prediction of sexual recidivism in adults. Similarly where failure to establish long-term relationships is a risk factor for adult sex offenders, this factor could not be reasonably applied to juveniles of these ages.

Dynamic risk factors

Recent studies of general adult criminality have found that although static variables are important in predicting recidivism, dynamic variables such as socioaffective problems (e.g. anger and impulsivity) or pro-criminal thinking are increasingly emerging as powerful predictors of non-sexual recidivism (e.g. Gendreau *et al.* 1996). In the field of sexual abuse, Thornton (2002) has identified four domains into which dynamic risk factors for sexual offending can be categorised. These are Sexual Interests, Distorted Attitudes, Socioaffective Functioning and Self-Management. The first domain, Sexual Interests, refers to the direction and strength of sexual interests. With adult sexual offenders, particularly child abusers, deviant sexual arousal is one of the strongest predictions of recidivism (Quinsey *et al.* 1995; Hanson and Bussière 1996; Prentky *et al.* 1997). However, the relationship between deviant sexual arousal and sexual recidivism in adolescent abusers has yet to be clarified. Hunter *et al.* (1991), for example, found less correlation between adolescent sexual offenders' measured sexual arousal and their offence histories than has been reported in the literature of adult offenders. Consequently, they cautioned against interpreting adolescent sexual arousal patterns in the same way as one might interpret adult data.

The second domain, Distorted Attitudes, encapsulates beliefs and attitudes about victims and offending that justify sexually abusive behaviour. Pithers *et al.* (1988b) identified cognitive distortions as precursors to offending and Ward *et al.* (1995) also identified cognitive distortions in the positive-affect pathway to sexual offending. Distorted attitudes and beliefs are found more commonly in child abusers than comparison groups (e.g. Beckett *et al.* 1994;

Hanson and Scott 1995). There is also some, albeit more limited, evidence to link certain attitudinal distortions with rape (e.g. Malamuth and Brown 1994; Hanson and Scott 1995; Bunby 1996). The extent to which adolescent abusers exhibit cognitive distortions has not to date been systematically evaluated, although this chapter will provide some preliminary findings regarding cognitive distortions in adolescent child abusers.

The third domain, Socioaffective Functioning, refers to offenders relating to others and the emotions they feel in the context of interpersonal interactions. There is good evidence that certain aspects of socioaffective functioning are related to sexual offending. Pithers *et al.* (1988a) found negative affects such as anger, anxiety and depression as common offence precursors in both child abusers and rapists. Hanson and Harris (2000a) found that anger was reported as becoming more intense prior to reoffending. General inadequacy manifested as emotional loneliness, low self-esteem and under-assertiveness has been found to distinguish particularly high-risk child abusers from comparison groups (Beech 1998). Certain affective states seem to be more common in one type of abuser than another. For example, emotional over-identification with children (emotional congruence) is an affective state particularly reported by high-risk child abusers (Beech *et al.* 1999) but is not so relevant to rapists. Conversely, aggressive thinking as manifested in suspiciousness, grievance and angry ruminations appears more commonly a precursor to sexual assault of adults than child abuse. The type and extent of socioaffective problems in adolescent child abusers and rapists has not been as thoroughly explored. Where studies have been conducted findings have been mixed. For example, some investigators have found that adolescents who sexually assault children are socially isolated and have low self-esteem (e.g. Saunders *et al.* 1986; Carpenter *et al.* 1995) whereas others have not found significant differences between groups on these variables (e.g. Ford and Linney 1995; Worling 1995).

The fourth domain, Self-Management, refers to an individual's ability to achieve long-term goals through planning, problem solving and impulse regulation. Self-management deficits have been identified in a number of studies as precursors to adult offending. For example, Hanson and Harris (2000a) found that denial of the possibility of risk and engaging in behaviours which give access to victims are characteristics commonly exhibited by individuals as they move towards offending. With rapists, lifestyle impulsivity, in which offenders have chaotic lifestyles governed by poorly planned or impulsive searches for short-term and often antisocial goals, is a characteristic which predicted reoffending in adult rapists (Prentky and Knight 1991). As described in this chapter, there is a constellation of adolescent characteristics which are strongly associated with the development of delinquent behaviour and its persistence into adult criminality. However, even though one would expect self-management problems to be relevant to the development and persistence of adolescent sex offending, this area has not been the focus of systematic investigation.

The extent to which dynamic risk factors contribute to the prediction of adult and adolescent sexual recidivism has yet been determined. There are several reasons for this. First, large-scale reviews of adult sex offender recidivism (e.g. Furby *et al.* 1989; Hall 1995; Quinsey *et al.* 1995; Hanson and Bussière 1996) have not included many studies where dynamic risk factors had been measured or reported. Similarly, large-scale studies of treatment outcome (e.g. Hanson *et al.* 2002) do not for the most part examine the role of individual dynamic risk factors. One of the main reasons why dynamic factors have not been examined is because it is only relatively recently that adequate measures have started to be developed to measure (adult) dynamic variables. As a consequence it is only very recently that links are starting to be made between changes in dynamic variables brought about by treatment and subsequent reductions in recidivism. For example, following a series of studies designed to measure dynamic risk Beech (1998) developed a psychometric typology in which recidivist adult child sexual abusers were found to have a distinct cluster of dynamic risk characteristics. These include high levels of cognitive distortions, globalised victim empathy deficits and high levels of socioaffective problems. In a subsequent study, Beech *et al.* (2002) found that taking into account these dynamic risk factors significantly increased the accuracy of risk predictions that were achieved using static risk factors alone. Thornton (2002) similarly found that high levels of dynamic risk factors (e.g. cognitive distortions and socioaffective problems) distinguished recidivist adult child abusers from first-time offenders and that the inclusion of dynamic variables improved the prediction of recidivism.

With adolescent sexual abusers, however, the field is not as advanced and there have been few studies reporting on dynamic risk factors. Worling (2001) found that his antisocial/ impulsive type adolescent offender was more likely to be charged with violent, sexual or non-sexual offences when followed up for six years post-release. Knight (1999) followed up rapists for a twenty-five year period and found that pervasive anger was consistently the best predictor of both violent and serious sexual reoffending. Knight (2004) subsequently found some incarcerated adolescent sexual offenders to be high on a range of pervasive anger factors and proposed that the pervasive anger domain might predict the persistence of sexual offending into adulthood. In the field of social competence Kenny *et al.* (2001) found poor social skills significantly discriminated first-time and recidivist adolescent abusers. Knight (2004) failed, however, to find a relationship between social competence and persistence of juvenile sexual offending into adulthood, even though a previous study (Knight and Prentky 1993) study appeared to have found such a link.

In summary, while there has been progress in developing measures of dynamic risk factors in adult abusers, the equivalent work has largely yet to take place with adolescent abusers, Because of this adolescent sex offender treatment programmes have difficulty in measuring their immediate impact and refining treatment procedures.

Despite the above problems there are a known constellation of characteristics evident during childhood and adolescence which do predict the persistence of violent and non-violent criminality into adulthood. If we are concerned to identify adolescent sexual abusers at risk of persisting in general and violent antisocial behaviour, as well as sexual reoffending, we should give treatment priority to those individuals with risk factors as described above. These can be summarised as follows:

1   A history of frequent physical abuse (in adolescent child abusers) and for adolescent rapists, a history of childhood neglect;
2   Childhood Conduct Disorder as defined by verbal and physical assaults on peers at school and aggression against teachers, cruelty to animals and other people, severe destructiveness, fire setting, stealing, repeated lying, truancy and running away from home (ICD-10 Classification of Mental and Behavioural Disorders 1992);
3   In adolescence, antisocial behaviour, delinquency, vandalism, aggression and high impulsivity. High scores on the adolescent version of the Psychopathy Checklist (Forth *et al.* 1994);
4   For adolescent sexual offenders, low social competence as shown by poor social skills, assertiveness deficits, and isolation from peers.

Assessing adolescent abusers – developing assessment scales

In order to assess adolescent abusers properly, whether through direct behavioural observation or through self-report, valid and reliable measures must be developed. Good psychological tests have a number of psychometric properties, details of which can be found in many texts (e.g. Coolican 1996). Psychological measures must be valid, that is, genuinely measure what they purport to do, and also be reliable along a number of dimensions. These dimensions include having questionnaire items which inter-relate to focus on the central construct under investigation (internal consistency). They must also be stable over time (test–retest reliability), and where direct behaviour observations are made, independent observers should have a good level of agreement as to what is taking place (inter-rater reliability). With questionnaires, items should be constructed in such a way that the 'correct' answers are not transparently obvious since, if they are, the measure is vulnerable to faking. Where questionnaires are used to evaluate treatment progress, tests selected should give stable scores with untreated subjects, yet also be sensitive to change when such changes take place as a result of treatment intervention. Furthermore, although follow-up studies are required to determine this, changes in test scores should have predictive validity. That is, for example, improvement in victim empathy, or reduction in cognitive distortions should be associated with a reduced risk of sexual offending.

Socially desirable responding, giving answers which are incorrect but which cast the individual in the most favourable light, can also be a problem. This is especially the case with questionnaires investigating themes where, if true answers were given, the subject anticipates disapproval or fears embarrassment, for example antisocial or sexual behaviour. Consequently, tests should be chosen which have investigated vulnerability to faking and socially desirable responding. For this reason there is an advantage to routinely including scales to detect openness and bias to socially desirable responding.

As well as detecting faking and socially desirable responding we also need to know how open an adolescent is prepared to be about their sexual drives and interests. The less open a person is about their general sexual behaviour the less likely they are to disclose deviant thoughts and behaviour.

There are also a number of general issues which need to be taken into consideration when using questionnaires with adolescents. First, measures need to have age appropriate language. In this regard, during the piloting stage questionnaires can be discussed with young people to ensure the appropriateness of language used. This may be necessary, for example, when adapting measures developed in North America. When adapting adult measures for use with adolescents language may need to be simplified and, for example, double negative questions removed to avoid confusion. When using questionnaires focusing on sexual, especially abusive or deviant, behaviour care also needs to be taken to ensure that adolescents are not exposed to sexual ideas or practices which are beyond their realm of experience and which could be viewed as corrupting.

Psychological tests cannot be adequately interpreted without reference to control and comparison groups. The lack of comparative studies has been a major problem in the study of adolescent abusers to date. Standardising tests on normal adolescents provides a range of scores against which to compare adolescent abusers. Without information on normal adolescents it is not possible, for example, to determine whether particular cognitive distortions or lack of sexual knowledge are abnormal or typical for a particular adolescent age group. Standardising questionnaires on normal subjects not only enables judgement as to whether an adolescent is different from his peers, but also provides targets for treatment change. For example, when therapy is targeted on improving victim empathy, the goal set might be to improve an adolescent abuser's appreciation of victim harm to a standard found in the general non-offending adolescent population.

Because such considerable change takes place during the course of adolescence, it is important to standardise measures on a range of age groups, for example, 11–13, 14–16, 17–19. Standardising psychological tests on different age groups not only allows more accurate test interpretation but also enables adolescents who receive treatment over an extended period to be compared with the appropriate age groups, both before and after treatment. This helps ensure that changes, for example, in perspective taking or sexual knowledge, that take place as a result of treatment, can be distinguished from those which occur as part of a normal maturation process. Given that apprehended adolescent abusers tend to come from social classes 3–5, it is also important to ensure that when tests are standardised, that this is done on the appropriate social class groups. Finally it is also important to bear in mind that it is not appropriate to use North American norms when interpreting the test scores of British adolescents.

As well as standardising measures on normal adolescents, it is highly desirable to also standardise measures on other adolescent offenders. This can help distinguish those characteristics which are unique to adolescent abusers from those which are shared by general antisocial youth. Where adolescent sexual abusers are found to share characteristics with other high-risk adolescent offenders this improves risk prediction. For example, where adolescent abusers are found to share significant characteristics with violent delinquents (e.g. high levels of impulsivity and generalised aggression), this increases the likelihood that they are also at risk of violent offending.

Evaluating dynamic factors – the Adolescent Sexual Abuser Project (ASAP)

The Adolescent Sexual Abuser Project (ASAP) was established in an attempt to address some of the problems in previous research on adolescent abusers (Davis and Leitenberg 1987; Vizard *et al.* 1995; Weinrott 1996). These include the lack of valid and reliable measures of dynamic variables, lack of comparison groups, the over-reliance on small samples and the failure to separate adolescent abusers into meaningful subgroups. The ASAP is a multisite study which has assessed 516 adolescent males who had committed hands-on sexual assaults. These young people were referred from thirty-seven community, residential and juvenile prison treatment programmes across the UK and the Republic of Ireland.

Table 15.1 provides details of victims assaulted by the young people referred to the ASAP. Because of referral procedures the characteristics of the young people assessed did not necessarily reflect a representative sample of adolescent child abusers in the UK. More extrafamilial child abusers were assessed than would have been expected in a more representative sample. Similarly, rapists were over-represented in the sample of peer sexual aggressors. In total 372 adolescent child abusers were assessed of whom 50 per cent were extrafamilial and 35 per cent intrafamilial abusers. A further 15 per cent had crossed over between intrafamilial and extrafamilial abuse. The majority of intrafamilial victims were solely female (67 per cent) whereas only 44 per cent of extrafamilial victims were females alone. Crossover rates were similar in both the extra and intrafamilial samples. By the time of referral nearly half the adolescent child abusers (46 per cent) were known to have had two or more victims, with multiple victims being more commonly found in the extrafamilial sample (50 per cent). Peer sexual assaulters were divided into two groups. The rapist group comprised youth who had all committed or attempted to commit full vaginal or anal rape.

Table 15.1 Victim characteristics of those assaulted

| | Child abusers (n = 372) | | | Peer sexual assaulters (n = 134) | |
	% of total sample	Interfamilial %	Extra familial %	Rapists %	Indecent assaulters %
Female victims	55	67	44	92	68
Male victims	24	17	37	6	22
Male and female victims	21	16	19	2	10
Single victims	54	71	50	83	71
Two or more victims	46	29	50	17	29
Stranger victims	4	N/A	11	50	18
Acquaintance victims	30	N/A	89	49	71
Immediate family victims	32	66	N/A	1	5
Extended family victims	16	34	N/A	0	

Most of these youths were incarcerated in Young Offenders' Institutions. The Indecent Assault group comprised youths who had committed sexual assaults, excluding rape or attempted rape. Most of these youths were assessed in community settings. While most of the rapists had assaulted females (92 per cent) this was less the case for Indecent Assaulters (68 per cent). Rapists had mostly assaulted single (83 per cent) and stranger (50 per cent) victims whereas Indecent Assaulters were more likely to have multiple victims (29 per cent) and less likely to have assaulted total strangers (18 per cent). Whereas all the adolescent rapists were convicted or about to be criminally convicted offenders, this was less the case with Indecent Assaulters of whom 57 per cent were assessed having been or imminently about to be criminally convicted. With child abusers, only a minority (36 per cent) were assessed in the context of criminal proceedings. Most of the remaining child abusers were assessed in the context of child protection investigations where criminal proceedings were unlikely.

Table 15.2 provides details as to the age at which the young people started to sexually abuse compared with the age at which they were assessed. With child abusers, it is interesting to note that young people who had committed intra- and extrafamilial abuse had on average started this behaviour more than two years before the other types of child abuser began their assaults. It is also evident that with the exception of rapists, more than two years elapsed between the time of abuse onset and the point at which the young people were assessed. As

Table 15.2 Comparison of age at abuse onset with age at assessment

	N	Age at onset of abuse	Age at assessment
Child abusers total	372	12.79	15.42
Intrafamilial	179	12.99	15.35
Extrafamilial	126	13.45	15.67
Intra- and extrafamilial	51	10.67	14.69
Rapists	67	16.76	18.57
Peer indecent assaulters	77	14.80	16.03
Non-contact abusers	29	14.04	16.29

described above, 46 per cent of child abusers had two or more victims, and anecdotally it was sometimes found that it was only after a young person had assaulted their second victim that the behaviour was deemed serious enough to be referred for assessment. This helped to account for the considerable time that had elapsed in some child abuse cases between the time a first assault was committed and the eventual assessment.

Adolescents referred to the ASAP were systematically assessed on a range of psychometric tests, which had been standardised on various groups of normal, male adolescents and also on comparison groups of non-violent and violent delinquents. Psychometric tests were developed according to a range of criteria: to capture problems as identified in the literature on adolescent abusers, and to test theoretical models. For example, with rapists measures were selected to test developmental models of rape particularly as proposed by Malamuth *et al.* (1991, 1993) and Knight (1997). The scales developed included measures of socio-affective functioning (e.g. self-esteem, emotional loneliness and assertion), of distorted attitudes (cognitive distortions, victim empathy, rape prone attitudes) of self-management (impulsivity, drug and alcohol use), and validity scales designed to measure social desir-ability bias and openness about sexual drives and interests. Scales drawn from adult measures were adjusted and trialled on adolescents before standardisation. The majority of scales were tests on three age samples: 11–13, 14–17 and 18+. This enabled an investigation into the extent to which test scores varied with developing maturity and, where differences were found, it helped ensure that when assessing treatment its impact could be distinguished from developmental change. As part of an initiative across European countries, the ASAP scales have been translated into several European languages. This will enable comparisons to be made between youths of various European countries and form a framework within which treatment programmes from different European countries can compare the young people whom they assess and the extent to which their treatment programmes are effective in changing dynamic risk factors.

Measures used and findings from the adolescent sexual abuser project

The purpose of the following section is to provide details on the measures used to assess general empathy, victim empathy and child related cognitive distortions and the findings from the study.

General empathy

There appears to be broad agreement among researchers and practitioners that lack of empathy plays a significant role in the perpetration of sexual offences (Marshall *et al.* 1999). Consequently, victim empathy training is seen as a core component of many treatment programmes for adults (e.g. Freeman-Longo *et al.* 1996; Pithers 1999). It is probable that many adolescent programmes also see the enhancement of empathy for victims as a key treatment task. However, the extent to which adult and adolescent abusers have generalised (trait) empathy deficits is less clear. Studies of general empathy in adult child abusers have produced inconsistent results. For example, Chaplin *et al.* (1995) reported lower levels of empathy in incarcerated child abusers than in non-offenders, as did Marshall and Maric (1996). However, Hayashino *et al.* (1995) found no difference between incestuous offenders, intrafamilial child abusers, non-sexual offenders and normal subjects with regard to their general empathic abilities. Similarly, Marshall *et al.* (1993) found incarcerated child abusers not to be deficient in general empathy when compared with normal subjects. With adult rapists the findings have again been mixed. For example, Rice *et al.* (1994) reported lower levels of general empathy in convicted rapists than in non-sexual offenders. In several other studies, however, differences have not been found in general empathy between rapists and non-offenders (e.g. Langevin *et al.* 1988; Marshall and Maric 1996). Smallbone *et al.* (2003) found no association between trait empathy and sexual offending, though they did find an association between trait empathy and non-sexual offending.

To date, however, no studies have reported on whether adolescent sexual abusers have general empathy deficits. To investigate this the ASAP study used the Interpersonal Reactivity Index – IRI (Davis 1983) which was adjusted for use with adolescents. The IRI is one of the most common measures used to assess general empathy in adult abusers. It is a 28-item self-report measure composed of four seven-item subscales. These four subscales are designed to measure specific components of generic empathy. Two of these subscales, Perspective Taking and Fantasy measure cognitive aspects while the other two subscales, Empathic Concern and Emotional Distress, measure emotional aspects. The adolescent form of the IRI was found to have good internal reliability (Cronbach's alpha 0.89). The adult form of the IRI has satisfactory test–retest reliability though this has not yet been established in adolescent form.

Findings

Table 15.3 Mean scores for Interpersonal Reactivity Index

	N	Perspective taking	Empathic concern	Fantasy	Personal distress
Normal adolescents	105	13.93	17.63	13.57	10.24
Adolescent child abusers	311	12.87	16.71	13.72	11.95
Incarcerated rapists	70	14.70	17.76	13.71	10.41
Peer indecent assaulters	59	13.81	17.52	12.66	12.10

Taken overall, no significant differences were found between normal subjects, child abusers, incarcerated rapists and community indecent assaulters on the Perspective Taking, Empathic Concern or Fantasy scales on the IRI. The only significant difference found concerned the Personal Distress scale. Here adolescent child abusers were found to have significantly higher levels of Personal Distress than normal adolescents ($p > 0.05$) and incarcerated rapists ($p > 0.05$). No significant differences were found between child abusers and community indecent assaulters. These findings suggest that, for the most part, general empathy deficits are unlikely to make a significant contribution to explaining sexually assaultative behaviour committed by adolescents. Nonetheless, despite this general finding, there may be individual cases where general empathy deficits (e.g. general lack of empathic concern for others) may provide some insight into why a particular assault took place. Perhaps more importantly where such general empathy deficits are found, e.g. psychopathic, callous disregard for the feelings of others, this may be an important risk factor for further offending.

Victim empathy

Although not all adult offenders show general empathy deficits, there is strong evidence that they lack empathy particularly for their own victim (Stermac and Segal 1989; Beckett *et al.*

1994; Fernandez *et al.* 1999). A number of approaches can be used to assess victim empathy in young abusers. With younger children, teachers' ratings of children's empathy have been found to correlate highly with ratings of helpfulness, cooperativeness and caring (Roberts and Strayer 1994). Information gathered from others (teachers, friends and family) can also provide evidence of a young person's ability to form caring relationships and whether their behaviour (e.g. cruelty to animals, bullying or violence) suggests a lack of sympathy or compassion for others. Empathy and emotional responsiveness can also be assessed by observing and asking young people to report their reactions to reading material about sexual abuse and video tapes of victims talking. Writing 'victim apology' letters (e.g. Jenkins 1990; Beckett 1994a; Eldridge and Still 1995) or reading accounts of abuse from the victim's perspective are also means of examining an abuser's ability to accept victim harm and distress, and these can be used as baselines against which to measure therapeutic change. Written vignettes of adult and child interactions have also been used in a number of studies to assess victim empathy. Both Stermac and Segal (1998) and Beckett *et al.* (1994) found that vignettes in which a child showed few overt signs of resistance increased a child abuser's tendency to underestimate victim harm and distress. In a series of studies with both child abusers (e.g. Fernandez *et al.* 1999) and rapists (e.g. Fernandez and Marshall 2003) it was found that offenders showed the most marked empathy deficits towards their own victim as opposed to general victims of sexual assault or victims of other crimes or accidents.

The ASAP study used two Victim Empathy scales (VES) one of which was originally developed for use with adult child abusers (Beckett *et al.* 1994) and another similar scale which has been developed for use with adolescent and adult rapists (Beckett *et al.* in preparation). The adolescent child abuser VES is a twenty-eight item questionnaire with acceptable internal reliability (Cronbach's alpha 0.91) and test-retest reliability (0.89 over a twenty-five day period). Principal component analysis found four factors to this scale: Emotional Disturbance and Distress, Acceptance of (long-term) Harm, sexual contact with the abuser as Pleasant and Desired and whether victims felt Safe and In Control.

The adolescent rapist VES is a thirty-four item questionnaire (Cronbach's alpha 0.89). Both VESs can be administered in two ways. First, by asking the young person to 'think about what happened [sic] with [victim name or description]' and to answer the [victim empathy] questionnaire. The second form of administration can be used not only with abusers who admit their offences, but also with 'deniers' and for standardisation on normal adolescents. Here the young person is asked to read a brief vignette describing a sexual assault and 'to think about the girl/boy or woman in the story' and answer the questionnaire. Vignettes have been developed to depict intra- and extrafamilial assaults on both male and female victims as well as stranger and acquaintance rape.

Example 1
A 15-year-old youth was asked to baby-sit for a 9-year-old girl. He was alone in the house with her while her parents had gone for a night out. While he was with her, he exposed himself to her. He then undressed her and tried to have sex with her.

Example 2
A 15-year-old lad really fancied a girl that he had met a few times at his youth club. He asked her out and they went to the cinema together. After they kissed and cuddled, she let him touch her breasts. The next weekend they went to a party. While they were alone in an upstairs bedroom they were kissing and the boy asked her to have sex. She said she did not want to go that far. The boy was feeling very aroused so he locked the door, pulled off the girl's clothes and had sex with her.

Findings

Table 15.4 Victim empathy scales mean victim empathy error scores

	Pre-treatment child abusers	*Post-treatment child abusers*	*Pre-treatment peer sexual assaulters*	*Post-treatment peer assaulters*	*Normal adolescents*
Own victim	30.61	17.19	25.28	12.26	N/A
Child abuse vignettes	23.30	17.99	—	—	11.26
Acquaintance rape vignette	—	—	18.33	12.38	13.23
Stranger rape vignette	—	—	17.71	14.09	11.36

Table 15.4 provides a summary of some of the findings from this section of the study (Beckett *et al.* in preparation). Adolescents who had sexually abused children were found to have significantly poorer empathy for their own victim than when compared with post-treatment child abusers (p>0.01) and normal adolescents who had been assessed using child abuse vignettes (p>0.01). Before treatment 58 per cent of the adolescent child abusers were found to have poor empathy for their own victim as defined by having a VES error score more than one standard deviation above the treated norm. This compares with 37 per cent (N = 51) for adult child abusers who were found to have poor pre-treatment empathy for their own victims when assessed on the same victim empathy scale (Beckett *et al.* 1994).

When adolescent child abusers were given child abuse vignettes considerable variability was found in VES scores, to some extent reflecting the nature and severity of the child abuse depicted in the vignettes. As a consequence, while no overall significant differences in VES scores were found between adolescent child abusers and the comparison groups (post-treatment child abusers and normal adolescents) significant differences were found on some vignettes. For example, with the vignette describing a 15-year-old youth baby-sitting and trying to having sex with a 9-year-old girl, the mean score for normal adolescents was significantly lower (p>0.01) than found in adolescent abusers tested with the same vignette. Conversely significant differences were not found between adolescent child abusers and the comparison groups when they were presented with a vignette describing a 12-year-old boy touching his 6-year-old brother's private parts and exposing himself to his brother.

Both incarcerated adolescent rapists and adolescents who had committed acts of indecent assault were found to have significantly poorer empathy for their own victims than treated rapists (p>0.01) and normal adolescents who had been given rape vignettes (p>0.01). In this regard 34 per cent of the combined group of incarcerated rapists and community indecent assaulters were found to have poor empathy for their own victim, that is, more than one standard deviation outside the treated range. When rapists and peer indecent assaulters were given rape vignettes they were not found to differ significantly from rapists assessed post-treatment or normal adolescents who had been given these vignettes. It appeared, therefore, that for the majority of adolescent rapists, their victim empathy problems related primarily to their own victim rather than to rape victims in general. Despite this lack of overall difference, it still remained the case that 34 per cent of rapists were found to have poor empathy for their own victim.

The findings of this part of the study are in keeping with those previously described where sexual abusers have poorest empathy for their own victims compared with when they are asked to consider other victims of sexual abuse, as depicted in vignettes. 58 per cent of adolescent child abusers were found to have poor empathy for their own victims, with a considerable minority of child abusers also having poor empathy for child victims of sexual abuse as depicted in vignettes. In this regard a considerable proportion of child abusers appear to have general victim empathy deficits. In contrast, only one third of peer sexual aggressors were found, at the point of assessment, to have poor empathy for their own victims and relatively few showed general victim empathy deficits when assessed on rape vignettes. It appears, therefore, that the majority of rapists, by the time they enter treatment, accept their victim was distressed and harmed by the abuse they suffered. On average, adolescents referred to the ASAP had committed their assaults more than two years prior to their referral for assessment. This raises the question as to the extent to which the adolescent abusers were able to suspend empathy for their victims at the time they committed their assaults as opposed to the point at which assessment was taking place.

Cognitive distortions

The assessment and treatment of thinking errors and cognitive distortions associated with sexually abusive behaviour is one of the main components of adult sex offender treatment. However despite their perceived importance as a major contributor to sexual offending, there is surprisingly little empirical research in this area. This is particularly the case where adolescent abusers are concerned. The study of cognitive distortions and justifications raises a number of issues which have yet to be resolved. These include the variety of definitions used to describe the phenomena, the process which contributes to distorted thinking and the problems of designing assessment measures which are not vulnerable to faking and socially desirable responding. As to the definition of cognitive distortions, the term is sometimes used interchangeably with other terms such as maladaptive beliefs (Ward *et al.* 2000), justifications, minimisations and rationalisations (Nichols and Molinder 1984), and thinking errors, rape myths and excuses (Pollock and Hashmal 1991). Gibbs and Potter (1991) made a distinction between primary and secondary distortions whereby primary distortions were defined as consisting of underlying beliefs and assumptions which are relatively stable and guide behaviour across a range of situations. They contrasted these with secondary distortions which operate immediately prior to or following an antisocial act and which serve to reduce feelings of guilt and responsibility. Within the category of secondary distortions, they included blaming others and minimising or mislabelling the effects of sexual abuse. Murphy (1990) describes similar processes whereby sex offenders justify their behaviour by making it morally acceptable, or shift responsibility by devaluing victims or minimising victim harm and misattributing its cause.

The problem of designing measures to assess cognitive distortions which are not overly transparent and vulnerable to socially desirable responding presents a significant challenge. Even when assessment scales have been developed and found not to be especially prone to socially desirable responding in one context, this can change in other contexts or with other populations. For example, Bunby (1996) developed MOLEST and RAPE scales to measure cognitive distortions in men who sexually assaulted children and women respectively. When originally developed, the scales were standardised on intrafamilial child abusers and rapists who were (it is assumed) attending voluntarily a cognitive-behavioural treatment programme in a maximum security American prison. When examined, the scales were found to have good psychometric properties, not strongly correlating with measures of socially desirable responding and satisfactorily distinguishing between child abusers and other non-child abusing inmates. Both scales were also reported as useful in measuring treatment change. However, when Arkowitz and Vess (2003) used these measures in a new context, different results were obtained. The authors evaluated the MOLEST and RAPE scales with patients civilly committed to hospital under California's Sexual Violent Predator law. Unlike the original study group, none of these offenders was a voluntary participant in treatment. Moreover they were aware that their test results could become part of subsequent legal proceedings to determine their release or continued involuntary hospitalisation. Furthermore, the child abusers were extra- as opposed to intrafamilial abusers. When assessed on the MOLEST and RAPE scales, test scores were appreciably lower than found in the original Bunby sample, and the pattern of test results had changed so that test scores no longer adequately distinguished between rapists and child abusers. The researchers proposed a number of possible explanations for these results. Not only were there differences in the type of child abuser studied in each sample, but there were also significant differences in the context of the assessment. Whereas the original prison group studied were treatment volunteers and their release was not closely tied to treatment outcome, the hospital group were admitted for compulsory treatment and their test results could determine their release or continued involuntary hospitalisation. In such circumstances the authors concluded that these offenders would probably be highly motivated to present themselves in the best possible light, and this changed the pattern of their test scores.

In the ASAP study cognitive distortions were assessed using the Children and Sex questionnaire (Beckett *et al.* in preparation) adjusted for adolescents. This test was originally designed for use with adult child abusers and has two subscales measuring cognitive distortions and emotional congruence with children respectively. The cognitive distortion subscale consists of fifteen questions scored on a four-point Likert scale from *strongly agree strongly* to *strongly disagree*. There is also the option for respondents to answer *don't know* to the questions posed, for which they also receive a score. The original test questions were derived from interviews with paedophilic men who had a strong underlying sexual interest in children, and who were typically recidivist child sex abusers. The cognitive distortion scale embodies four core beliefs which were frequently expressed by the child abusers: that children are sexually knowledgeable and sophisticated, that they are sexually proactive with adults, able to consent to and not harmed by sexual contact with them. In this present study the Adolescent Children and Sex questionnaire was found to have good internal consistency (Cronbach's alpha 0.92) and adequate test-retest reliability (0.76 over a fourteen-day period).

Findings

As shown in Table 15.5, the mean cognitive distortion score for the mixed group of adolescent child abusers was not significantly different from non-offending adolescents. However, when intra- and extrafamilial adolescent child abusers were compared, a significant difference ($p > 0.05$) was found. Here 30 per cent of extrafamilial abusers compared with 19 per cent of intrafamilial abusers were found to have high levels of cognitive distortions, that is cognitive distortions of more than one standard deviation above the normal. This finding is similar to when the same scale was used with adult child abusers (Beckett *et al.* 1994). Here it was found that while the scale did not discriminate between normal subjects and a mixed group of adult child abusers, 33 per cent of adult child abusers were found to have high (more than one standard deviation above normal) cognitive distortions. Beech

Table 15.5 Children and sex questionnaire cognitive distortion scores

	N	Cognitive distortions (mean score)	% High* cognitive distortions
Normal adults	81	13.10(8.80)	7
Adult child abusers	59	15.06(13.30)	33
Normal adolescents	97	17.19(9.21)	9
Adolescent child abusers(mixed)	235	16.34(10.46)	21
Intrafamilial abusers	121	14.74(9.04)	19
Extrafamilial abusers	114	16.74(10.78)	30

Note. Figures in parentheses are standard deviations.
*More than 1 standard deviation above normal.

et al. (1999) found that adults with high cognitive distortions were typically extrafamilial child abusers with high actuarial risk of reconviction as measured by scales such as Static-99 (Hanson and Thornton 1999). Beech *et al.* (2002) subsequently reported that high levels of cognitive distortions were associated with increased risk of sexual recidivism when child abusers were followed up for a six-year period. For comparison purposes, ASAP adolescents were compared with adult child abusers who had been assessed in the previous study on the same cognitive distortions scale (Becket *et al.* 1994). No significant differences were found in cognitive distortion scores between adolescents and adult child abusers. However, when normal adolescents and adults were compared, adolescents were found to have significantly higher levels of cognitive distortions (p>0.05).

There are a number of possible explanations as to why the cognitive distortion scale failed to discriminate between normal and child abusing adolescents. First there were important differences in the context in which adolescent abusers and normal adolescents were assessed. Adolescent abusers were all assessed having been accused of sexually abusing a child. Whether they were being assessed in the context of criminal or child protection proceedings the outcome of the assessment, including psychometric assessment, would have potentially serious consequences, for example, the extent to which they were perceived as dangerous, whether or not they should be removed or reintegrated back into their family, and in some cases the type of sentence they might receive from courts. Under such circumstances, the pressure to fake good and, for example, not disclose underlying beliefs about children which might cause consternation would be considerable. In contrast, normal adolescents who were secondary school students were assessed in complete anonymity where there were no consequences for disclosing their beliefs about children. In such circumstances they might well be less likely to censure their beliefs about children. If this is the case it may be unrealistic to expect significant differences to emerge between adolescent abusers and normal adolescents. It is quite possible that if normal subjects were tested in non-anonymous conditions, for example, where they might expect feedback on test results, that significant differences might emerge between normal and sexually abusive adolescents on cognitive distortions and other scales which are vulnerable to socially desirable responding. Studies of adult abusers suggest that whereas the majority of pre-treatment child abusers minimise and to some extent justify their sexually abusive behaviour, it is only the more sexually entrenched abusers who have strong distortions of attitude and belief regarding children, the nature of their sexuality and the consequences of sexual contact with adults (Beech 1998). That only a minority of adult abusers appear to hold such views may help explain why cognitive distortions scales generally fail to discriminate child abusers from normal subjects. Similarly, it may well be that the majority of adolescent child abusers do not have deeply held cognitive distortions. Again, this may help to explain why significant differences were not found between adolescent abusers and normal subjects using the Children and Sex questionnaire or by a previous study investigating adolescent cognitive distortions (Hunter *et al.* 1991).

The study of adolescent cognitive distortions is, at the present time, in its infancy. As described above, even with adult abusers, we have yet to achieve a consensus as to the definition of cognitive distortions and how these might be reliably distinguished from arguably the more superficial processes of justifications, minimisations and victim blaming. Moreover, basic mapping of the nature and full extent of adolescent cognitive distortions and justifications has yet to take place. It is not inconceivable that the type of distortions and justifications made, particularly by younger adolescents, may be different from those seen in adults and older abusers. With regard to younger abusers cognitive distortions, where present, are probably less likely to be entrenched, though older adolescents may have cognitive distortions and justifications indistinguishable from adult abusers.

Although there were no significant differences found between normal and sexually abusive adolescents, a significant difference ($p > 0.05$) was found between normal adolescents and adults. There are a number of possible explanations for this difference. First, it may be that adolescents genuinely do have more distorted attitudes regarding children and their sexuality than the average adult. It may be that, as adolescents grow older and the age difference increases between them and children, these beliefs are gradually revised and thus distorted thinking is reduced. Second, the significant difference found might also be a consequence of sampling bias. While both normal adult and adolescent groups were tested in anonymous conditions, the adolescents were drawn from an unselected sample of secondary school students. The normal adult sample, however, consisted of men who had applied for jobs as prison officers in a private prison. As such, this group was self-selected and may have conceivably been more conservative or guarded regarding their attitudes and beliefs about children.

Despite the lack of difference between normal and abusive adolescents, a minority of the adolescent child abusers were found to have high levels of cognitive distortions. As such, these adolescents endorsed views such as: *not all sexual contact between children and adolescents causes harm; it is not always the adolescent's fault when sexual contact takes place with children; some children are interested in sexual contact with adolescents.* Because such beliefs, when held by adult child abusers, can be deeply entrenched and associated with elevated risks of recidivism (Beech 1998) it would seem prudent for adolescent treatment programmes to pay adolescents with high levels of cognitive distortions particular attention. With adult abusers, individuals with high cognitive distortions often present with significant socioaffective problems such as emotional loneliness and low self-esteem (Beckett *et al.* 1994; Beech *et al.* 2002). Because there is theoretical (Marshall 1989) and some, albeit equivocal, empirical evidence (Knight and Prentky 1993) that poor social competence in adolescents may increase risk of recidivism, it would seem particularly appropriate for treatment programmes to give especial priority to adolescents who present with a combination of high cognitive distortions and socioaffective problems such as poor social competence, low self-esteem and high emotional loneliness. However, despite grounds to be concerned about adolescents with high levels of cognitive distortions, there is as yet no empirical evidence that such adolescents are indeed at greater risk of sexual recidivism. This can only be determined through recidivism studies.

Conclusions

Whether viewed from the perspective of official criminal records (Home Office 2004) or community victimisation surveys, about one third of all sexual assaults in the UK are committed by young people aged 18 years or younger. Available evidence suggests that important distinctions exist between adolescent and adult offenders. Studies to date suggest most adolescents who sexually abuse will cease this behaviour by the time they reach adulthood, especially if they are provided with specialised treatment and supervision. Particularly for adolescent child abusers, poor social competency and deficits in self-esteem rather than paraphilic interests and psychopathic tendencies currently appear to offer the best explanation as to why they commit sexual assaults. The challenge is to develop measures to identify high-risk adolescent abusers, to develop treatment programmes which accurately target their criminogenic needs, and to evaluate the impact of treatment programmes through long-term follow-up.

Unlike with adult sex offenders, we do not have actuarial risk assessment scales to predict the likelihood of sexual recidivism in adolescent sexual abusers. A considerable amount of research will need to be undertaken before we are in a position to develop such actuarial scales, particularly if they are going to incorporate dynamic as well as static risk factors. This is because even in the more advanced field of predicting adult sexual recidivism, dynamic risk factors have only recently started to become reliably measured and tentatively incorporated into adult risk prediction scales. In the absence of actuarial risk prediction scales for adolescent sexual abusers, empirically guided risk assessment check lists have been developed for adolescent abusers. These include the ERASOR (Worling 2001) and J-SOAP (Prentky and Righthand 2001). However, because of the paucity of adolescent recidivism studies, such protocols draw heavily on what is known about adult sex offender recidivism. This chapter describes the problems of using adult static risk prediction scales with adolescent sexual abusers and the problems associated with developing measures of dynamic risk. However, without reliable measures of those dynamic factors which are the targets of treatment, we are constrained in our ability to target treatment effectively, to assess the impact of our interventions and to improve risk prediction.

Acknowledgement

The author wishes to acknowledge and express his gratitude to Sarah Brown and Constance Gerhold for their major contributions, as researchers, to the ASAP project.

Part 4

Practitioner issues

16 The personal and professional context to work with children and young people who have sexually abused

Simon Hackett

Introduction

What does it mean to you to be working with children and young people who have sexually victimised others? Do you enjoy your work? How and why do you find it rewarding? Do you like the young people you work with? How does what you do affect you? Has your world-view changed since you started practising in this field? Have your personal relationships been affected? Do you ever feel angry, distressed or overwhelmed when hearing the details of a young person's abusive behaviour? How do you cope with being immersed in a world which many other people would rather not think about?

These are the kind of questions I have asked myself frequently since starting work in this field. Maybe they have some degree of personal and professional resonance for you, though I suspect that there will be many other questions which have been raised in the course of your practice. This chapter is concerned with these kind of questions. In it, I seek to describe a framework through which practitioners can consider the professional and personal context to work with children and young people who have sexually abused others. The essential premise herein is that in order to be effective as practitioners we need to engage interpersonally with young people to empower change. We can only do this if we, in turn, are empowered by the framework of theory and knowledge we hold, and by the structures and remit of the organisations within which we practise.

Three key areas are therefore addressed in the chapter. First, I look at what is known about impact issues in work with sex offenders generally and in work with young people who have sexually abused in particular. Second, I offer some thoughts on coping with the work. Third, I examine the importance of empowering approaches in this field, including attention to issues of diversity and the importance of user perspectives.

The personal impact of work with young people who have sexually abused

Like many other people, my route into work with young people with harmful sexual behaviours happened as much by chance as by design. But 'it' (that is, the work and my struggles to integrate it into both my personal and professional experience) has come to represent an important element of who I am and what I do. In short, I feel privileged to be working in such an important field and to be making a contribution to the lives of some of the most damaged, and damaging, young people and their families. But making this contribution can come at a cost, both personally and professionally. Bengis (1997) suggests:

> Once treatment providers have chosen to work in sex offender treatment, we enter what I can best describe as a 'twilight world.' This world alters our perceptions of daily events

and, even more disturbingly, may change our inner lives – sometimes irrevocably. What we see when we walk down the street, what we think about in public places, what we fantasise, feel and/or fear often differs markedly from the experiences of others who do not experience the worlds in which we immerse ourselves.

(p. 31)

It is hardly surprising that work with sex offenders can impact upon practitioners in these complex and difficult ways. The highly charged and contentious social *context* within which sex offender work takes place means that the work is rarely straightforward and the *content* of the work, with its emphasis on dealing with the abuse of sexuality, means that it is not emotionally neutral. Sometimes, working in the field of sexual aggression can feel like our personal and professional boundaries are being pushed on all sides; by our clients, whose wide-ranging needs are projected on to us in the hope that we can make a difference for them; or by the anxiety and demands of the communities within which we practise and sometimes live. We are also often overwhelmed by the demands of the inadequate systems and structures within which we work. Finally, we can bombard ourselves with unrealistic expectations of the extent of our own influence on outcomes. Understanding the pressures on oneself, and maintaining appropriate boundaries without becoming over-enmeshed or distanced, can be a truly difficult balancing act.

There is evidence that professionals working with sex offenders can face difficulties at a societal level (Polson and McCullom 1995), with community criticism and ostracism as well as isolation and disapproval from other professional groupings documented (Barnard *et al.* 1989; The National Adolescent Perpetrator Network 1993). Additionally, a wide range of emotional responses to sex offender work are described in the literature, for example, anger and hatred (Haugaard and Reppucci 1988); sadistic feelings and retaliatory impulses (Mitchell and Melikian 1995); feeling psychologically victimised by young people who have abused, due to unresolved issues of victimisation from one's own past or an over-identification with victims (The National Adolescent Perpetrator Network 1993); fear and paranoia (ibid.); feeling 'dirtied' by the work (Hoghughi *et al.* 1997); and feeling powerlessness and desiring control (Erooga 1994).

As a result of the constant struggle to encourage young people to look critically at their gender-related attributions and cognitions which, in some cases, are hostile and reflect an underlying pro-abuse schema, both male and female workers can experience feelings of loss and grief regarding aspects of their gender. Ellerby *et al.* (1993) found that 84 per cent of the women therapists in their research felt that their boundaries had been invaded by clients, and 42 per cent described feeling sexualised by abusers. Male therapists reported these invasions much less frequently, 34 per cent and 16 per cent respectively. Fifty-eight per cent of all therapists said that they had felt 'unclean' after a session with a sex offender. In the same study, 73 per cent of female and 63 per cent of male practitioners reported having felt endangered or threatened by a client.

Such emotional responses have been linked to a range of behavioural responses, which have been termed 'burnout'. Burnout has been explained as the 'prolonged response to chronic emotional and interpersonal stressors on the job . . . defined by three dimensions of exhaustion, cynicism, and inefficacy' (Maslach *et al.* 2001: 397). Maslach and colleagues (2001) suggest that burnout is characterised by exhaustion which, in turn, prompts people to behave in a way so as to distance themselves emotionally and cognitively from their work. This can result in an inability to respond to the needs of users, including depersonalising them and failing to perceive their individual needs and qualities.

Bird Edmunds (1997b) investigated factors known to be associated with burnout in a sample of 289 sexual abuser treatment professionals using a standardised questionnaire. Respondents were almost equally split in terms of gender and represented a wide range of professional disciplines and roles. Almost half of the subjects studied had over fifteen years' experience of mental health work and a similar proportion had worked specifically with sexual abusers for between 3 and 8 years. Although this subgroup included those who worked with adults as well as young people, 41 per cent reported that they mainly worked with 10–20-year-olds. Bird Edmunds found that high numbers of these people – 85 per cent in total – retained a positive attitude towards their work and 97 per cent perceived themselves to be effective. Despite this, however, she found that over half of those surveyed reported increased fatigue and over a third indicated an increase in cynicism, sleep disturbances and preoccupation with work outside of work time. Approximately one quarter said they had difficulties in making decisions, or experienced depression or depressive episodes. Twenty per cent said they had become more insensitive to others, and 10 per cent had misused drugs or alcohol to cope with the emotional demands of the work. Interestingly, all of these findings applied in almost equal measure to both the male and female respondents. Bird Edmunds' study underlines the potential stress of sex offender work and suggests that burnout may be a risk for professionals working in this field. Significant as these findings are, however, it is important to stress that the majority of the respondents taking part did not exhibit burnout as defined by Maslach *et al.* (2001). Nevertheless, the findings from the study suggest that it may be particularly important to seek to identify factors that appear to heighten the risk of burnout in those working with sexual offenders.

Factors which may be relevant include the length of time a worker has contact with sex offenders (Lea *et al.* 1999) or the intensity of that contact. For example, Weekes and colleagues (1995) found that prison officers with more years of service experienced more job stress in dealing with sex offenders than colleagues with lesser levels of experience. This is also borne out by Farrenkopf (1992) who found that highly experienced mental health therapists who worked with sex offenders described clear symptoms of burnout. Farrenkopf recommended strategies for dealing with this by diversifying away from sex offender work or by taking a break from the intense focus of the work. Somewhat contradictorily, Bird Edmunds (1997a) found a different relationship between frequency of burnout symptoms and the amount of sexual abuser contact. Respondents reporting the greatest increases in cynicism (43 per cent), frustration (62 per cent) and fatigue (67 per cent) worked, on average, 11–20 client contact hours a week, with these percentages dropping for those who had even more client contact. This would appear to suggest that some workers may experience stress and incongruence between the different aspects of their work if they are not working routinely with sexual abusers.

What can we make of these findings? We might conclude that it is difficult to work with the occasional adolescent who has sexually abused amongst a general caseload of child welfare cases. It could be that non-specialists have received less training and are, therefore, less well equipped to deal with the particular challenges of working in this area. Equally, total immersion in the worlds of sex offenders over a protracted period of time may also pose a significant risk of burnout.

Sex, sexuality and the issue of workers' own victimisation experiences

A major area of potential impact relates to sex and sexuality. This is perhaps the most difficult area of impact to acknowledge. As Bengis says:

> Few practitioners work with sex abusers without becoming aware of the presence of new ideas, feelings, fantasies, impulses and urges related to this work. In spite of ourselves, we may discover inner imagery that simply will not go away or fantasies that parallel the acts described to us by our clients.
>
> (Bengis 1997: 31)

Bengis suggests that for the most part, we live with these occupational hazards of our work in isolation. We may worry about our own sexual identification, we can become too sensitised on sexual matters and we can become hyper-vigilant about the safety of our own or other children. In a survey of men working in the sexual abuse field (Hackett 1997), I found that the following impact issues relating to sex and sexuality were typical:

- Mistrust of others' sexual behaviour or motivations, especially in relation to those with access to children;
- Seeing sex and abuse in everything – projecting a sexual dimension on to non-sexual interactions;
- Hyper-awareness of one's own arousal patterns and fantasies leading, in some cases, to sexual dysfunction and interference in sexual relationships, or heightening the importance of sex in personal relationships;
- An inability to talk to one's partner about sex, about work or about the connections between the two;
- Over-sensitisation to sex, with sex becoming a way of self-soothing, coping with the stress of the work or 'ridding oneself' of particularly distasteful images from casework;
- Intrusive flashbacks to details of case work; and
- Feelings of sexual corruption; a sense of being dirtied by hearing and having to listen to such 'sordid' sexual material.

It is hardly surprising that these responses can occur. Work with young people who have sexually abused forces us to connect issues of sex, violence and children (as abusers) in a way which can be distressing and which can bring aspects of our sexuality sharply into focus. These are difficult issues to acknowledge and workers need both a safe forum and a sensitive approach from supervisors or external consultants if they are to reflect on such matters.

How do these findings impact on workers who have a personal experience of sexual abuse? This is a particularly contentious issue. A somewhat higher than expected incidence of childhood victimisation has been tentatively noted in research with caring professionals in general (Barter 1997), as well as with sex offender therapists. For example, Bird Edmunds (1997b) found that 56 per cent of sex offender therapists had been physically, sexually or emotionally abused at some point in their lives. Of these, 22 per cent reported psychological abuse, 11 per cent physical abuse and 21 per cent sexual abuse. However, it is important to note that research into the incidence and prevalence of abuse in professionals and non-professional groups is fraught with methodological problems, and it is well established that much sexual abuse never finds its way into official statistics or research. This means that it is difficult, if not impossible, to draw definitive conclusions about whether the higher than expected reported incidence of abuse in professionals is a reflection of their increased likelihood of having been abused, or merely a consequence of professionals' increased ability to disclose their experiences.

Nonetheless, a debate has ensued about the significance of workers' own victimisation histories and the impact of abuse upon a professional's ability to practise in the field. At times, survivors' motivation, commitment and competence to carry out work in this field have been called into question. For example, in outlining the debate on the 'wounded healer', Barter (1997) suggests that:

> [P]ossible problems taken into therapeutic relationships by 'wounded healers' include counter-transference biases which may be harmful; unresolved personal needs which may prevent appropriate attending to the needs of the client and unwitting or even intentional exploitation of therapeutic relationships in order to meet their own needs.
>
> (p. 118)

This kind of statement is easy to make but more difficult to evidence. For example, Bird Edmunds (1997a) compared burnout experiences of survivors and non-survivor therapists and found that the survivor group appeared to experience less fatigue and sleep disturbance, but more frustration and depression than the non-survivor group. Whilst these findings in no way suggest a causal link, the important message that emerges is the degree to which sexual abuser work can connect with workers' prior experiences, irrespective of their nature, and the importance of being sensitive to the impact of our own life experiences, whatever these are. As indicated by the figures of own abuse experiences, survivors play a major role in this field of work and should not be seen to be limited by their experience. Indeed, many workers have derived skills and strength in having survived their own abuse experiences which may help them to cope better with some facets of professional burnout than non-survivors.

Coping with the work

As I have set out above, literature and empirical research support the hypothesis that practitioners working with young people with harmful sexual behaviours may be subjected to a wide-ranging set of potential areas of personal impact across several key dimensions. As workers, we should accept the inevitability of a personal response of some nature (Morrison 1990), but it is likely that these impact issues will differ significantly from one person to another by virtue, for example, of their own support networks, their personal histories, their gender and their sexuality. Thus, we can conclude that impact and burnout are interactional phenomena, influenced by a complex set of variables both within the individual practitioner and the work environment. This highlights the need for workers to consider their own position in respect of their work across a number of interacting dimensions, including their own *backgrounds*, the *context or environment* in which they engage in the work, the dynamics within the *relationship* they have with individual users, as well as their responses to the work on *cognitive, behavioural* and *affective* levels. The questions set out in Table 16.1 may be important in exploring these inter-related areas.

The National Taskforce, a North American committee of leading practitioners and academics in this field, distinguishes between preventive and renewal strategies to avoid practitioner burnout (The National Adolescent Perpetrator Network 1993). *Preventive strategies* relate largely to the strengthening of a worker's personal and professional supports. *Renewal strategies* relate to the building into practice of ways of seeking help when stress occurs. Strategies include the constructive use of supervision, consultation or counselling. The report authors also advise workers to maintain professional exposure to non-sex offender clients. Whilst this is a useful way of maintaining a reality check and preventing the adoption of distortions from constant exposure to accounts of abuse, as discussed above there may also be problems created for some practitioners who are expected to work with sexually

Table 16.1 Questions to ask yourself to monitor your response to your work

Core influences:	In what way do my previous life and professional experiences influence my responses to young people and their families? How do my values, particularly in relation to sexuality and abuse, affect the way I work and make sense of my professional role? What are my previous experiences of practice in this field? How do they influence my approaches and responses?
The environment:	What is happening in my external life/personal life currently and how might this affect my work and vice versa? How does the environment I work in contribute to, or influence, the impact of the work on me?
The interpersonal exchange you have in your work:	What are the details of the interpersonal exchanges I have with my clients? What are the particular themes and struggles associated with my direct contact with young people?
Feelings domain:	What feelings are promoted in me as a consequence of the work: about me, my work and my world view? What patterns and links can I trace in the feelings that emerge?
Thoughts domain:	What particular scripts and schemas are being projected upon me? In what ways are my thoughts, beliefs and attitudes being changed, eroded or strengthened through the experience of the work?
Behaviour domain:	What is different now about my behaviour from when I first engaged in this work? To what degree are my behaviours appropriate and effective ways of coping? To what extent are my behaviours, thoughts and feelings congruent with each other?

aggressive behaviour infrequently and without a clear remit or focus. From my own experience of working with young people with harmful sexual behaviours across a variety of contexts, I think that the challenge for the practitioner is to find 'caseload congruence', to integrate work with young people with harmful sexual behaviours with a variety of other professional activities and to seek a helpful balance between these various aspects.

Maslach *et al.* (2001) have articulated a model for conceptualising and overcoming the core mechanisms involved in job burnout, which focuses on six key dimensions. They propose that the greater the mismatch between people and these six key domains of their work, the more likely it is that burnout will occur. In contrast, they suggest that the better the fit between the worker and these domains, the greater the individual's engagement with the job will be. This model has, therefore, direct relevance in helping both to prevent and to overcome burnout when it occurs. Table 16.2 summarises these six key domains, with the factors identified by Maslach and colleagues in the left-hand column, with my own thoughts in the right-hand column about the implications of these factors with specific reference to work with young people who have sexually abused.

As Maslach *et al.* (2001) point out, these six inter-relating factors are not merely a list summarising research findings from burnout studies, but provide an important conceptual framework which 'emphasizes the importance of looking at the person in context, in terms of his or her fit with the key domains of worklife' (p. 416). My attempt to reflect upon their implications in our specific field are also, therefore, merely suggestive. I would strongly

Table 16.2 Burnout factors and their implications for burnout avoidance

Maslach et al. *(2001) burnout factors*	*Recommendations for avoiding burnout in work with young people with harmful sexual behaviours*
Workload: • Excessive workload • Too many demands exhaust individual energy • Wrong kind of work, where people lack skills or inclination for certain type of work • Emotional work especially draining when people required to display emotions inconsistent with feelings	• Need for managed caseloads which reflect intensity of the work • Need for choice to opt into this area of work, as well as specific training to equip workers with appropriate skills • Need for explicit permission and space within agency (or therapeutic) supervision or consultation for workers to reflect on their emotional response to the work
Control: • Individuals have insufficient control over resources needed to do their work • Individuals have insufficient authority to pursue the work they believe to be most effective • Individuals' responsibilities exceed their authority • Individuals feel deeply committed to producing certain results but are distressed by lack of capacity to achieve results	• Agency attention needed to appropriate resources necessary for the work (physical, intellectual, emotional) • Attention within supervision given to issues of power, authority and responsibility to ensure personal and organisational balance • Importance of explicit remit and roles which clarify expectations, boundaries and responsibilities. Open discussion within teams and organisations about the division of, and balance between, powers
Reward: • Lack of appropriate rewards, financial and social (i.e. when hard work is not appreciated by others) or intrinsic (e.g. pride in the importance of the work) • Lack of recognition devalues work and worker • Lack of reward closely associated with feelings of inefficacy	• Stable (rather than perpetually uncertain) funding arrangements for projects, which provide foundation for worker satisfaction • Agency/team/ manager explicitly rewards good practice (financially or socially) • Appropriate use of praise within supervision
Community: • People lose a sense of connection with others in the workplace • Job isolation or lack of social support in the workplace which undermines sense of shared values and community • Chronic and constant negative feelings of frustration and hostility within the workplace which undermines sense of support	• Team ownership of work with young people who have sexually abused (even if carried out by only part of team) • Development of an explicit team/ agency value base in relation to the importance of the work • Overall environment and management style that fosters sense of peer identity and commonality within staff group • Learning led culture which is open to new ideas and new ways of doing things
Fairness: • Perceived unfairness exists in the workplace • Lack of mutual respect amongst work colleagues • Unfair treatment leads to emotional distress and exhaustion or fuels cynicism about the workplace	• Management clarity about decision making and consistency of treatment of workers/clients • Culture of openness and appropriate support/ challenge which can deal with perceived unfairness at the earliest opportunity without it festering

continued

Table 16.2 continued

Maslach et al. *(2001) burnout factors*	Recommendations for avoiding burnout in work with young people with harmful sexual behaviours
Values: • Conflict between values of individual and agency, e.g. where workers are asked to do something which they consider unethical or contrary to own values • Worker caught up in contradictory agency values (e.g. high-quality service provision, versus cost-cutting) • Mismatch between personal aspirations for own career and structure of organisation	• Clear agency/team value base about young people who have sexually abused and their families, as well as about the nature and importance of the work, and its process and content • Clear career development structure and opportunities for training and personal development

recommend that individual workers, supervisors, teams and agencies use the table to talk through their own contexts, experiences and needs.

Empowering approaches

The preceding part of this chapter identified a range of considerations relating to practitioners' own experiences of the work they undertake with young people who have sexually abused others. In this third section, I examine the other side of the same coin: that is the experience of users. First, I emphasise the findings of several key empirical studies about the importance of key worker characteristics in influencing intervention outcomes for users. Next, I go on to suggest that effective and ethical practice is founded not only on personal awareness and preparation, but also requires a commitment to valuing user perspectives, as well as sensitivity to issues of diversity.

The importance of worker interpersonal qualities and approach

One of the failings of earlier practice literature in relation to work with sex offenders in general, including young people who have abused, was the tendency towards combative and confrontational approaches (see, for example, Sheath 1990). Other and more recent literature (see, for example, Jenkins 1990; Marshall *et al.* 1999) advocates that a much more respectful and person-centred approach be adopted in work with adult sex offenders. A particularly important ingredient within this process is the quality of the relationship between the worker and the service user. As Blanchard (1995) points out:

> Because so many sex offenders have experienced dysfunctional and abusive primary relationships, an essential element of restoration lies in the healing power of interpersonal relationships – particularly the relationship with the therapist.
>
> (p. 10)

This point is perhaps all the more important in relation to work with young people, many of whom come into the intervention process with no prior experiences of positive, nurturing or caring relationships. Indeed, practitioners in the field are emphasising that holistic and child-focused interventions, which are designed to support young people's social and emotional growth, are essential (Hackett *et al.* in press, a). This is a powerful argument against the 'mechanisation of treatment' (Blanchard 1995) or the kind of stale and defensive approach where the worker opens the workbook at the correct page, the next treatment exercise or psychometric test is completed, but where the reality of the young person's external world is kept separate from the therapy session and both the practitioner and young person remain largely untouched by the whole experience. As workers we need to conceive of ourselves, not a piece of paper with a photocopied circle on it, as the most powerful therapeutic tool and best resource for young people:

> [T]herapeutic techniques and therapeutic relationships are not (and cannot be) mutually exclusive: they are inherently interrelated and inter-dependent.
>
> (Mahoney and Norcross 1993: 423)

Whilst some therapeutic interventions appear to demonstrate better outcomes than others, it is increasingly being recognised that some of the most important contextual influences on successful outcomes are the interpersonal characteristics of the person delivering the intervention and their approaches. For example, in relation to behavioural programmes, Alexander *et al.* (1976 cited Marshall *et al.* 1999) found that 60 per cent of the variance on outcomes measures was accounted for by therapist features. Marshall and colleagues (1999) have investigated these issues in the adult sex offender field and found a number of reliably identified worker characteristics to be linked with better outcomes, as listed in Table 16.3 below.

Relating specifically to work with young people with harmful sexual behaviours, the National Taskforce Report (The National Adolescent Perpetrator Network 1993) identifies a series of desirable personal characteristics of the practitioner. These include emotional wellbeing, respect for self and others and personal behaviour that is value-directed. Additionally, Blanchard (1995) states that one of the factors of importance for therapists is possessing congruence between one's thoughts, feelings and actions, as well as being authentic (being genuine, spontaneous and trustworthy) warm, compassionate and responsive.

Of course, the significance of 'worker attributes' should not be surprising to us in the sex offender field, for they are a direct reflection of the general processes and factors, the 'core

Table 16.3 Reliably identified worker characteristics linked to effective intervention outcomes (Marshall *et al.* 1999)

- Respectful
- Warm and friendly
- Sincere and genuine
- Rewarding and encouraging
- Confident
- Interested
- Non-confrontational challenge
- Non-collusive
- Appropriately self-disclosing
- Appropriate use of humour
- Communicates clearly
- Encourages active participation
- Encourages pro-social attitudes
- Asks open-ended questions
- Deals appropriately with frustrations and difficulties
- Spends appropriate time on issues

conditions' or 'therapeutic alliance', which have been advocated in the counselling and psychotherapy literature for several decades (see, for example, Howe 1993). Such factors appear to operate to influence outcomes independently of either overarching theoretical modality or specific therapeutic techniques employed in the work. In other words, it doesn't matter how well versed you are in cognitive behavioural therapy, but if you don't like the young people you work with, if you do not feel empathy for their difficulties, and if you find it impossible to offer them understanding, then you should not be doing the work. Marshall *et al.* (1999) conclude that:

> From the client's perspective, these features of the therapist translate into a number of characteristics. Clients do best . . . when they feel supported and are comfortable discussing personal problems without feeling attacked, and they do better when they perceive the [worker] as sympathetic, warm, understanding, empathic, and confident. In most studies, clients report that they desire advice and direction.
>
> (p. 44)

These factors are also highlighted in a small-scale study of 29 users conducted (Hackett and Masson in press) over nine sites in the UK. This found that young people who had sexually abused and their parents appreciated supportive interventions from workers that offered opportunities for them to gain both insight into the nature of their (or their child's) sexually abusive behaviour, and also, importantly, which helped them to deal with their own feelings about their problems. Regardless of the nature of the professional involved, or the service context, being able to talk and be heard therefore appear to be the most important consideration for users. At the same, many of the users in our research reported that they did not understand the professional process and many felt that they did not get clear information from professionals about what was going to happen in their case. It seems that the provision of clear information about professional processes and timescales is vital for users who are experiencing distress and uncertainty in the aftermath of the discovery of the abuse. Young people also reported examples where professionals had given false reassurances early on in the process of work with them. The message from users is straightforward: it is more damaging for assurances to be made which then turn out to be inaccurate than it is to have to face up to the painful reality and uncertainty of their situation from the outset. From the study it is clear that what users welcome is not so much specific techniques or approaches, but workers who are prepared to involve them in a meaningful way at all points in the professional process, who can understand their distress and respect the difficulty of facing up to the abuse and who can offer clarity and truthfulness.

The importance of attention to issues of power, diversity and empowerment

In a field where the abuse of power is a central issue, it is important for practitioners to assess and understand the various sources of their own power and examine how these various elements may conflict at times. Most important is that the individual is committed to the non-abusive use of personal power, which involves attention to:

- Personal acknowledgement of the existence of power imbalances within one's relationships with others;
- A readiness to focus on how one's own power is used and experienced;
- An ability to maintain critical openness about oneself and others;

- Recognition of others' 'difference' and a willingness to validate and value this in contact with others;
- Scrutiny of personal values and behaviour, with specific regard to sex, sexuality and gender.

Whilst workers benefit from a clear set of principles and ethics upon which to build practice (Hackett *et al.* 1998), principles in themselves are passive expressions of intent. Abramson (1996) describes the process of owning and mobilising principles into practice as 'knowing oneself ethically'. Having and using ethical self-knowledge is a cornerstone in building effective practice. In particular, it allows the practitioner to:

> move from an understanding of his or her own attitude toward fate and responsibility to an appreciation of why he or she believes that a particular client should be treated in a manner different from how another client is treated.
>
> (Abramson 1996: 198)

Abramson describes this process of gaining ethical self-knowledge as involving a number of distinct stages, which are summarised as:

- Understanding one's own world view;
- Knowing what makes one feel good about oneself and one's practice;
- Ascertaining and monitoring how one uses and prioritises ethical principles in practice.

Using Abramson's model, each stage poses a number of important questions to be considered by workers engaging with young people who display harmful sexual behaviours. The exercise set out in Table 16.4, adapted from Abramson's work, can be considered by the individual practitioner alone or within the context of supervision, co-work or consultation.

Working with young people to look at the nature of difference and oppression are important aspects of the *content* of intervention. If the message is that oppression is not to be tolerated and that sexual abuse is a fundamental expression of disrespect and oppressive behaviour, then the *delivery* also has to model this in every way. There is, for example, no way that we can begin to help our clients manage anger constructively, if the message they receive from us every time we meet is that, as powerful people, we are entitled to be angry and disrespectful towards them.

Of particular importance here is the need to see young people as individuals and to respect elements of diversity including those of gender, race, sexuality and disability. Elsewhere, I have argued that it is not incompatible to conceive of an approach to people who have abused their power which is sensitive to issues of empowerment and I have sought to outline some of the important dimensions of an anti-oppressive approach to sexual offenders (Hackett 2000). Recent research into the degree to which there is consensus amongst practitioners working with young people has further underlined the importance of approaches to young people which view them first and foremost as children in need, rather than as 'offenders' or 'perpetrators' and which stress the need to attend to difference and diversity (Hackett *et al.* in press).

Table 16.4 Developing ethical self-knowledge: an exercise for practitioners

---

Stage 1: Understanding my own world view:

• What do I know and recognise of myself in terms of race, ethnicity, gender, class, sexuality, disability status?
• What do I recognise of my own personal and value system, biases, experiences, stereotypes and agenda that are derived from my own personal and cultural history?
• How do these factors inform my perspectives on sexual violence, young people and their families?

Stage 2: Knowing what makes me feel good about my practice and myself:

• What is it about my work with young people who sexually abuse that generates self-esteem and self-approval in me?
• What is my image of a competent sex offender therapist/practitioner?
• What is my perception of a good therapist in terms of professional standards and ethics?
• What makes me feel a responsible member of the team/organisation that I work for?
• What is it about my work that makes me feel that I have done a good job or made a valid contribution: to my organisation, the community, victims of sexual abuse, young people who abuse?

Stage 3: Ascertaining and monitoring how I use and prioritise ethical principles in my practice:

• Where do I stand on issues such as autonomy, justice, victim/abuser rights?
• How important are these principles to me?
• How do I resolve conflicts that arise between these principles in my practice with young people, particularly in relation to empowerment and control?
• What is my view on the way that 'justice' is served/not served in relation to the sexual behaviour of young people? How does this influence my practice?
• How far are my judgements about what young people deserve from others and from me based on my own attributions of moral responsibility?
• When an individual young person's rights and needs come into conflict with the community's rights and needs, how do I resolve this? Under what circumstances am I more likely to sympathise with one or the other?

Conclusion

This chapter has discussed a range of impact issues relating to work with young people who sexually abuse others and has proposed a model of empowered practice. It is hoped these concepts will be used and further developed by those working in the field. Engaging with young people with sexual aggression problems remains a complex and challenging area. The practitioner's 'parallel journey', which often proceeds silently and unobserved alongside that of young people, frequently involves painful lessons and difficult experiences. Yet it can bring significant opportunities for new and heightened personal awareness and professional development. This chapter ends, therefore, with a plea that as we continue to develop our practice models and theoretical understandings, so we continue to share our experiences and learn from each other.

17 The responsibility avoidance syndrome

Unconscious processes in practitioners' therapeutic work with children and young people who sexually abuse

Nick Bankes

Don't it always seem to go,
You don't know what you've got 'til it's gone,
They paved paradise and put up a parking lot.
(Joni Mitchell, 'Big Yellow Taxi', 1970)

Introduction

This chapter, which is based on recent research (Bankes 2003), argues that when practitioners are working therapeutically with children and young people who sexually abuse, unconscious processes occur which affect the manner in which the therapy is carried out. It is also argued that these processes appear to suggest a recurring pattern of affective, communicative and behavioural responses by the practitioners, and a model, the 'responsibility avoidance syndrome', is proposed to explain this pattern. The psychodynamic concepts of counter-transference and projective identification are suggested as ways of understanding these unconscious processes. Finally, the implications of this analysis for practitioner training and supervision are discussed.

The original research involved videotaping practitioners' individual therapeutic sessions with young people who sexually abuse, the videotapes then being analysed using both qualitative and quantitative approaches. Subsequently, the practitioners participated in semi-structured interviews about the sessions with the researcher and these interviews were also analysed using both qualitative and quantitative analytic tools.

What do practitioners do in therapeutic sessions?

One of the most striking results from the research was that the practitioners spoke nearly twice as much as their clients and the majority of utterances by the clients were monosyllabic 'yeah's', 'dunno's' etc. The clients demonstrated a reluctance to engage in the work and the practitioners compensated for this by talking more, in an attempt to get the clients engaged.

In addition, on average, the practitioners interrupted their clients 29 times in an hour's session (nearly once every two minutes) and more than half of these interruptions were attempts by the practitioners to bring their clients back to the practitioners' agenda. For example:

Client:　　　　Like if I . . .

Practitioner:　(interrupting) By not coming here on a regular basis what that says to me is that, actually, you don't really want to change your behaviour at the minute. What you want to do is to continue to abuse little girls. Hmm?

There was a strong correlation between the frequency with which the practitioners interrupted their client and the degree to which the therapist was attempting to control the agenda of the session.

The clients' own interruptions largely demonstrated their attempts to convince their practitioner that they did not pose a risk of further sexually abusive behaviour. For example, in the following quote, the practitioner had been exploring with the client why he chose to attempt to initiate conversations with young female voluntary helpers in the prison and whether these young women resembled the victims of his sexual offences:

Practitioner:　I didn't say you shouldn't have had a conversation at all. What I said was . . . I was just exploring with you why you would have certain conversations with certain people and not others. I mean I'm not . . .

Client:　　　　(interrupting) I have a conversation with everybody, everybody: male, female, green, orange. It doesn't matter what, what colour they are, or what they are, I just have a conversation with everybody.

On the whole, silences were not allowed to develop in the sessions. The average length of silence was five seconds. The silences mostly appeared to take place when the practitioner was attempting to focus on the sexual abuse perpetrated by the client and could thus be interpreted as examples of the client attempting to resist the practitioner's agenda. The silences were usually 'broken' by the practitioners, indicating that the practitioners were experiencing a need or pressure to engage the clients in discussing their sexual abuse.

On average, the practitioners initiated new topics into the session more than twice as much as their clients and reintroduced topics which they had previously initiated in the session more than twice as much as their clients. In examining the content of these interventions it transpired that, in the overwhelming majority of cases, the topic which the practitioners sought to initiate or reintroduce into the sessions was, not unsurprisingly, the sexual abuse carried out by the client and/or the risk of them carrying out sexual abuse in the future.

Overall, the practitioners controlled the agenda of the sessions three times as much as their clients and approximately half of their agenda-setting focused on the sexual abuse perpetrated by the young person. Miller and Rollnick (1991) argue that the more the practitioner's agenda dominates the session the more the session is educative whereas the more the client's agenda dominates the session then the more the session is therapeutic. So, according to Miller and Rollnick, these sessions were educational rather than therapeutic.

There were a significant number of times when the practitioners did not respond to, or pick up on, what the client had just said. In nearly half of these non-responses the practitioners were attempting to return the session to the topic of sexual abuse. Non-responses frequently co-occurred with a practitioner interruption as can be seen in the following example:

Client:　　　　Hmm, I think my little brother or my little sister said, hmm, 'Oh, mum's got a new boyfriend now' or something like that. And, hmm, and she's started going 'Aw, I bet he's a bloke with a rich car, hmm, just to go after his money' and all that, and I didn't really like that so I stuck my fingers up at her and that's why she slapped me outside the car . . .

Practitioner: (interrupting) Right. OK. And how long . . . how long after that was it that you abused Sharon?

Practitioners frequently used what can be described as an 'interrogative' style of questioning – it seemed that the practitioner was attempting to trip the client up or elicit further, previously undisclosed, aspects of their abuse. For example:

Practitioner: 'Cos from what I can remember the police actually then went on and investigated it further and it actually came out that you actually put your penis inside of her vagina didn't you?

Practitioner: 'Cos the file that I've read is different from what you're telling me.

Practitioners frequently also specifically referred to the need for clients to accept responsibility for their abusive behaviour. The clients in the study, on the other hand, were usually reluctant to accept responsibility for their abusive behaviour.

Practitioner: Right. Let's . . . let's get down to . . . to where we were last week. Er, we talked about an awful lot last week. As well as (inaudible) (laughter) er, we . . . we talked quite a lot about you taking responsibility didn't we?

There were a significant number of communications that appeared to indicate that the practitioners were feeling 'victimised' either by their client or by the pressure from their own or other organisations to ensure that their clients did not abuse again. Most of these types of communications comprised instances of the practitioner being anxious about the fact that the client was not engaging in the therapeutic process. This was linked, then, to the practitioner's sense of feeling responsible for ensuring that the client did not abuse again because the client was not owning this responsibility. For example:

Practitioner: So if we're going to get on with this work, because you've been coming in a very long time now, and people are worried about your behaviour, you know that don't you? Particularly since this last thing happened. The thing when you were actually upstairs doing the vacuum cleaning, we were very worried about that because it's, it means that, mmm, the number of times it's happening now, that people think this is really getting very serious, what do we do? And they ask me what my, mmm, do I think that you're getting on with the work you need to: do you really want to stop this behaviour? And I don't know whether you do or not. There's lots of things I don't know, that I need to know in order to be able to say 'that's ok, it won't happen again', but I can't say that for sure but I have to be, I have to have a good idea about how you are stopping yourself from doing things that you shouldn't be doing, right, do you understand all that? So, mmm, there's no point in me doing all the work, I can do the writing but then you won't remember, you do have difficulty in remembering, so we must find a way that will help you to remember and help you not to have to come here anymore and help you to get on with your life in a way that you . . . you enjoyed before.

The practitioners sometimes used a rather 'persecutory' style of communication. The persecutory communications were invariably connected to the practitioners' sense that their clients were not accepting responsibility for their sexually abusive behaviour. For example:

Practitioner: The only thing I can do if you don't turn up is to write to Social Services to say Joe is a really, really high risk and he's going to abuse again. I have no doubt about that, OK?

They also used communications which indicated concern for their clients. For example, this practitioner made the following communication when her client began to cry:

Practitioner: Okay, that's fine, that's fine. You find it very difficult don't you to talk about it . . .

The practitioner then avoided mentioning the abuse for the remainder of the session.

Finally, the practitioners frequently employed a 'teaching' style of communication; that is, they sought to explain or encourage their client to understand by providing examples. Three quarters of the communications of this type were connected to the sexual abuse which the client had committed. So, for example:

Practitioner: So I can't tell what you're thinking right now. I can ask you and you can tell me, but I can't hear what your thoughts are. So what I will do is guess what your thoughts might have been and then I'll say to you 'Do you think that you might have been thinking this' and you'll say 'No, absolutely not, it's a load of rubbish' or 'Yeah, but it wasn't quite that; it was something else.' So that's what I do, I make assumptions and I would assume that when you saw Alice's photo it may also have brought back quite a . . . er, a few sexual feelings as well, Kevin. What do you think to that assumption?

And another example:

Practitioner: Now all men and all women and all boys of your age and all girls of your age wank or masturbate, yeah? Usually, what helps them to come, to have an orgasm, to get that feeling, is that they have to think about something sexually OK? And I wanted to ask you what you think about. Be honest about it.

The analysis of the videotapes, therefore, revealed various, regular communicative responses in the practitioners. The purpose of the subsequent research interviews with the practitioners was to determine whether these responses were being consciously employed by the practitioners or whether some were unconscious responses.

What do practitioners say about the work?

Prior to the semi-structured interviews with the researcher, the practitioners were provided with transcripts of their sessions. During this process of review and interview all of the practitioners in the study recognised their own unconscious processes operating in their work and how these were acted out in ways which, to varying degrees, were meeting their own unconscious needs and were, therefore, unhelpful to their clients. This was particularly evident when the practitioners were asked to comment on what they thought was going on for them in the short video clips of their sessions shown to them as part of the interview with the researcher. In other words, inviting the practitioners to reflect on their own practice gave them an insight into how they could improve their practice by paying more attention to these unconscious processes.

Practitioner: Who are these sessions for? That's the real question I think, I really need to think about that.

Practitioner: You know I've missed quite a lot there, I've missed a hell of a lot of what Kevin was saying and I think the agendas that I was carrying into those sessions were the all important ones really. I need to check that.

Practitioners' motivation for working with this client group was explored with them. All came to the work with a high degree of positive or optimistic feelings and nearly all those in this study came into this work by way of social work, rather than through psychotherapeutic, psychological or psychiatric disciplines. This is also the case for the majority of practitioners in the UK who work therapeutically with children and young people who sexually abuse and their families (Hackett *et al.* 2003). Half the practitioners acknowledged that their motivation for being involved in this type of work was also connected with personal issues from their own childhood. These included experiencing sexual abuse, feeling fearful of and protective towards a violent older brother and being fostered as a child. These practitioners also cited, as a motivating factor for working in this field, a desire to protect the victims or potential victims from their clients' abusive behaviour. The other half of the practitioners cited only professional development as their motivation for working in this field, in addition to their optimism.

The practitioners described the impact that working with children and young people who sexually abuse had on them. They reported that it caused them to experience feelings of hope/optimism, anxiety, a sense of the work being difficult, fear, sadness, feeling de-skilled, anger and feelings of responsibility for ensuring that the client did not abuse again. They also acknowledged that working with children and young people who sexually abuse impacted on them in ways which were specific to this client group. They spoke of their difficulty in working with the details of the clients' sexual abuse and the clients' resistance to doing this anyway. As discussed in Chapter 1, in cognitive behavioural therapeutic work with children and young people who sexually abuse, the client is expected to discuss in detail the sexual abuse they have perpetrated: this is part of their journey towards accepting responsibility for their abusive behaviour. It seems likely that this tension was at the root of the emotional impact of the work. The isolation of the work as well as a lack of guidelines, other than cognitive behavioural, for working therapeutically with young people who abuse and their families, compounded this tension and contributed towards the practitioners feeling 'de-skilled':

Practitioner: Probably the deeper part is about an insecurity to do with 'is this any good, is this having some effect?' And feeling responsible for having some dramatic effect on someone's behaviour, unrealistically but nevertheless a very real feeling.

Evidence of unconscious processes

The feelings the practitioners reported experiencing in working with this client group could be broken down into four categories: feelings of victimisation, of being persecutory, of rescuing and of withdrawing. What evidence was there, then, in the analysis of these practitioners' work, to support the assertion that these kinds of feelings were being translated into the processes that were taking place and affecting the way in which they carried out their task?

From the analysis of the videotaped sessions and the interviews with the practitioners there was a considerable amount of evidence to support the original research hypothesis that unconscious processes would be evident in the sessions and were being enacted by the practitioners. Interestingly, not only did practitioners themselves recognise these processes operating within their sessions when being interviewed by the researcher, but they also recognised many of those processes when they watched the videotapes. So, for example, based on the researcher's analysis of the videotapes, four of the practitioners had appeared to use an interrogative style of questioning in their sessions. When they were then interviewed, these same four practitioners self-critically volunteered this observation about their practice in the interview, although they had not been conscious of using this approach. It was only, therefore, through reflecting on their practice in the research interview, that this became apparent to them. This was not an approach that they felt was a beneficial therapeutic technique and they recognised that its use must have had an unconscious cause. All of the practitioners recognised their tendency to talk more than the client and to interrupt or be unresponsive to their client at inappropriate moments. The practitioners acknowledged that they had not been aware of doing these things at the time; hence they were not conscious of them.

Practitioner: I think now, I think that he was showing me a confused part of himself and a fragmented part of himself and an uncertain place inside himself but I missed that because I was too tied up in being brilliant.

In addition, although there was less evidence for this, other than what the practitioners reported, it seems possible to hypothesise that the enactment by the practitioners in the therapy of these unconscious processes was specific to, or at the very least more likely to take place in, work with children and young people who sexually abuse. Specifically, the practitioners' experience of feeling responsible for ensuring that their clients did not abuse again when their clients appeared unwilling to accept this responsibility themselves, caused them to behave in a variety of ways which they claimed was not typical of their work with other client groups. So, for example, they attempted to control the agenda of the sessions by ignoring or interrupting what the client was saying and tried to get the client to focus on their abusive behaviour. In the face of their clients' continued unwillingness to discuss their abusive behaviour, the practitioners felt victimised and this in turn caused them to behave in persecutory or rescuing ways or to attempt to emotionally detach themselves from the clients. There were numerous examples that highlighted how the themes of: feeling victimised; rescuing; persecuting; feeling de-skilled; the 'contaminating' effect of the work on the practitioner; the need to try harder; feeling responsible that the client does not abuse again; or feeling the need to emotionally distance themselves from the client, were all either specific to working with this client group or more intensely experienced in working with this client group.

Practitioner: I was completely pissed off with the young person and I'd had enough and I thought 'I'm doing all the work here' . . . thinking back on it, I know that I responded in exactly the way he had pushed and pushed and pushed to see how far he could push the boundaries. So I behaved like mum or I behaved like a teacher or any of these other people who have given him a negative response.

Practitioner: It has to be about me; it has to be about the way in which . . . I mean so many of these youngsters are in very, very dysfunctional, difficult families, or they're out of their families completely . . . and I'm sure it must be about maternal instinct and wanting to care for and parent them.

Practitioner: So you can actually feel quite strongly about something, more strongly than I usually do because of the nature of the intensity of the work.

There is a considerable degree of professional and societal concern about child sexual abuse. It would not be surprising, therefore, if the practitioners working to prevent child sexual abuse were to experience this as an additional pressure within their work, thus increasing the emotional intensity of their task. Remaining unaware of, or ignoring this increase in emotional intensity, appeared from the research study, however, to result in practice which was not necessarily in the clients' best interests but was, rather, an unconscious reaction to personal, societal and professional expectations.

The responsibility avoidance syndrome

The unconscious processes illustrated in this study are reminiscent of Karpman's drama triangle (Karpman 1968). Stephen Karpman analysed fairy tales to highlight how three 'roles' of victim, persecutor and rescuer are played out interchangeably in real life situations as well as in therapeutic relationships:

> In the Pied Piper, the hero begins as Rescuer of the city and Persecutor of the rats, then becomes Victim to the Persecutor mayor's double-cross (fee withheld), and in revenge switches to be the persecutor of the city's children. The mayor switches from Victim (of rats), to Rescuer (hiring the Pied Piper), to Persecutor (double-cross), to Victim (his children dead). The children switch from Persecuted Victims (rats) to Rescued Victims, to victims Persecuted by their Rescuer.
>
> (Karpman 1968: 40)

Karpman proposed that we unconsciously 'act out' the roles in the drama triangle in every-day life and he suggested that bringing these unconscious dynamics into conscious awareness through therapy enables us to step out of what he called an 'errant life script' (p. 39).

The various aspects of this victim, persecutor and rescuer dynamic were recognised by practitioners during the process of being invited to reflect on their work with the client in the videotape. This is admirably described by one of the practitioners in the following quotation:

Practitioner: I'd already begun to think of ways of working with him that would engage him. That would be in some ways fun for him. When I was feeling positive I really wanted to do that. *(Rescuer)*

Interviewer: Yes, what I'm picking up there is a sense of trying very hard?
Practitioner: Yeah, yeah, I think so. But then when he didn't turn up . . . I mean it's almost like . . . I remember somebody saying to me 'you've bought all the cakes but nobody has come to your party'. *(Victim)* So he did engage well but then he stopped coming and I'm sure in the middle sessions I didn't try as hard. Or I tried in a different way. I wasn't as taken in by him. I'd felt manipulated, so then the hard side of me kicked in if you like. Perhaps a bit of a more punitive side. *(Persecutor)*

The difference in the analysis of what the practitioners described in this study from Karpman's model is the centrality of the feeling of victimisation for practitioners who work with children and young people who sexually abuse. For example, it was the clients' feeling of being victimised by their practitioners, because their practitioners wanted them to discuss the sexual abuse, that caused them to resist their practitioners' agenda and this, in turn, caused the practitioners to feel victimised by their clients. One could also speculate that societal and professional concerns about the subject of child sexual abuse would heighten this sense of victimisation. The practitioner attempts to overcome these feelings of victimisation through either a persecutory or rescuing approach to the client, other professionals or the client's carer/s. In psychodynamic terms (which will be discussed more fully shortly) the practitioners' experience of feeling victimised was a countertransference reaction which was unconsciously acted out by the practitioner in a persecutory or rescuing manner.

Another difference from the Karpman model was the rather different way in which the practitioners acted out the countertransference reaction. Several of the practitioners referred to strategies which they used to emotionally distance or protect themselves from the anxiety of feeling victimised. These included feeling tired in sessions, finding it difficult or forgetting to write the session notes or even, in one case, cancelling sessions.

There does seem, then, to be a recurrent pattern in these unconscious processes which is similar to Karpman's model but which has additional aspects to it. This can be conceptualised as the 'responsibility avoidance syndrome'. The following figure, 17.1, overleaf, demonstrates this process.

In this model the practitioner comes to his or her work with the motivation to help the client change their abusive behaviour. The practitioner is hopeful of being able to effect change. They may have positive feelings towards the client and may also feel saddened by the client's own trauma. In order to effect this change the practitioner attempts to encourage the client to accept responsibility for their abusive behaviour: a cognitive behavioural therapeutic imperative. If the client is unwilling to accept this responsibility the practitioner feels that they are now left holding the responsibility. This causes the practitioner to feel they are not doing their job properly, with an associated fear that if the client abuses another person this will be due to their inadequacy as a practitioner. They compensate for this by trying harder with increasing attempts to control the agenda of the session.

From this point on, the practitioner and the client enter a spiral of avoidance: a mutual attempt to avoid accepting the responsibility for the abuse. The client feels guilty and unable to face the horror of their actions and feels victimised by their practitioner's attempts to make them do so, whilst the practitioner feels increasingly victimised by the client's reluctance to accept responsibility for their abusive behaviour. The more the practitioner attempts to impose this imperative on the client the more the client resists. Thus the practitioner increases their efforts to try harder, which are met with an increased hardening of the client's barriers to an acceptance of responsibility. The practitioner's increased efforts may be driven by angry

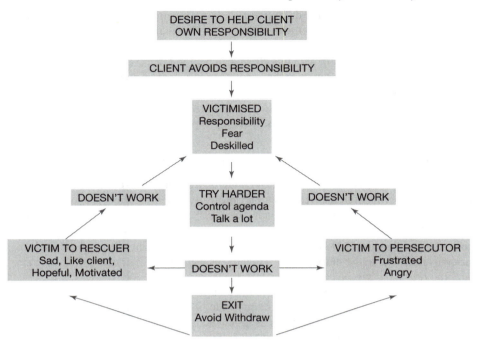

Figure 17.1 The responsibility avoidance syndrome.

or sad feelings. Accordingly s/he may either increase his or her persecutory or rescuing responses to the client. The following quotations illustrate this point:

Practitioner: So I thought to myself 'OK, we've said all we need to say about him coming here, it's now his responsibility' but I was carrying that around: that's something that's just struck me that I hadn't realised before, that I was carrying that responsibility. But looking at it retrospectively I think he's a kid that very good at allowing other people to take responsibility.

Practitioner: That leads to the despair sometimes, not necessarily to do with the young people, but to do with my practice I suppose: am I doing anything which is the slightest bit good? At other times it's quite clear to me. That's something I'm aware of: a process that I find that I feel devalued and I don't know where the root of that is other than myself so I'm projecting that out all over the place. I'm looking for somebody to be the one that's devaluing me; and also not being able to hear where there's clear evidence of things improving.

It is important to emphasise again the societal, political and professional context within which this work takes place. It has been mentioned earlier that there is a considerable degree of political, societal and professional concern about the subject of child sexual abuse. Practitioners who work therapeutically with children and young people who sexually abuse are essentially trying to prevent child sexual abuse. Several of the practitioners in this study referred to the pressures they experienced from external sources. For example, almost half felt that there were pressures from other agencies, or even within their own agency, to be effective in their work: to produce definitive risk assessments on the children and young people they were working with and then to cure them. These practitioners were also aware of the impossibility of achieving this. A third voiced their misgivings about the cognitive behavioural approach to working with this client group as an effective panacea that has to be adhered to. Yet all of the practitioners in this study felt motivated to attempt to help the young people they were working with. This complex melange of political, societal, professional and personal hopes, expectations and misgivings increased the emotional intensity of the processes, both conscious and unconscious, that they experienced in their work.

A psychodynamic understanding of the unconscious processes

The unconscious processes described throughout this chapter can be conceptualised as instances of countertransference reactions and projective identification, terms which are drawn from psychodynamic and psychoanalytic theory, the only therapeutic discipline which has a rich and in-depth narrative for describing unconscious processes in therapy.

Laplanche and Pontalis (1973) define countertransference as: 'The whole of the analyst's unconscious reactions to the individual analysand – especially to the analysand's own transference' (p. 92).

Laplanche and Pontalis go on to acknowledge that there is a considerable amount of disagreement within the psychoanalytic community as to how broadly or narrowly the concept is defined and the consequent implications as to how to deal with it. This lack of agreement may be understood, in part, in the context of the fact that Freud never really fully developed the concept. In fact Freud made only four references to countertransference in all his writings.

Since the middle of the twentieth century there has been a growing acknowledgement that the narrow classical definition is less useful than the broader definition: i.e. the totality of the therapist's response to the client including conscious and unconscious feelings, thoughts and behaviour.

The concept of projective identification was originally developed by Melanie Klein (1988) as taking place between an infant and its mother. Klein believed that the very earliest development of the child's ego is driven by the experience of birth as persecutory (separation anxiety). This is its first experience of the external world. The child in its first few months of life is unable to differentiate between itself and the external world. The child is, however, able to experience itself in relation to part-objects, crucially the mother's breast. The breast becomes an object of gratification and frustration – the 'good' and 'bad' breast. Because the child is unable to integrate good and bad within its fragile ego at this stage, a process of splitting occurs. The child projects alternately its inner feelings of rage (bad) or contentment (good) on to the mother's breast. Equally the child introjects a sense of goodness or badness from the mother's breast. Klein proposed that: 'The good breast – external and internal – becomes the prototype of all helpful and gratifying objects, the bad breast the prototype of all external and internal persecutory objects' (Klein 1988: 63).

Projective identification takes place when the mother experiences the rage or contentment which the child projects into her as though they are her own feelings. Like countertransference, the concept of projective identification has been considerably developed since Klein first outlined the process (see, for example, Ogden 1979). In psychotherapeutic terms it is now understood to be an unconscious process between individuals whereby one person splits off and projects into another person that which they cannot tolerate within themselves, making the other person experience what has been projected into them. So, for example, with a client who is passive but who makes the practitioner feel angry with their passivity, it is possible that the client has split off and projected their own unbearable inner rage into the practitioner.

These concepts can be used as a way of understanding or giving meaning to the unconscious processes that were observed in the videotapes and commented on by the practitioners in the interviews with the researcher. One of the practitioners explained that the interview had made them realise that distressing experiences from their own childhood had been acted out in the session. This can be described as an unconscious enactment of this practitioner's *countertransference*. In another case the client's passive aggressive resistance to the practitioner's attempts to encourage him to take responsibility for his abusive behaviour and the practitioner's subsequent feelings of helplessness and doubt in his/her own efficacy as a practitioner could be understood as an unconscious enactment of a *projective identification*.

It may be helpful to consider an anonymised case example from my own practice in order to understand these processes more fully.

'Fred', a white Caucasian boy of 17, was accused of sexually abusing four girls aged between 4 and 9 over a six-month period. Fred lived with foster carers and had been in care since he was 13. He had befriended a group of children in the neighbourhood. He played 'games' with the children – turning them upside down so their dresses fell down. The girls said that he would then touch their vaginas inside their knickers.

Fred was brought up primarily by his father and paternal grandmother. His mother left the matrimonial home when Fred was 3 and he had had no contact with her since then. There was a history of anger/violence towards his father. For example, he remembered that when he was 3 or 4 he had thrown a toy at his father in temper. He described his relationship with his father as 'we always wind each other up'. The dynamic between Fred and his father was subsequently replayed with me and other professionals. He transferred his way of relating to his father on to other authority/parental figures in his world. This was his *transference*.

In addition, in order to defend himself against fears of rejection, Fred *projected* that unwanted part of himself into others and then attacked those others as they represented 'badness', the 'bad' part of himself which he had not been able to tolerate or integrate. Fred could not face or tolerate his inner sense of hopelessness, uselessness (because this implied being rejected) so he *projected* it into me. He imagined me to be useless to him, our encounters were hopeless, of no use.

The difference between *projection* and *transference* is that projection is about what Fred could not bear in himself so that he preferred to believe that it existed in others. Transference however is about how he related to others based on significant past relationships and included the defence mechanism of projection.

Professionals reported feeling 'wound up' by Fred. I also experienced this: our sessions were frequently characterised by a battle of wills between us. This caused me to feel a strong desire to reject and/or punish him. This was my *countertransference*.

If the worker identifies with (or introjects) the projection then a process of *projective identification* is going on. Projective identification is a specific form of countertransference. So, with Fred, my feelings of frustration, hopelessness and uselessness were a projective identification. Like Fred, in order to defend against these feelings I became angry, felt wound up, got into a battle of wills with him and felt a strong desire to reject and/or punish him.

The 'responsibility avoidance syndrome' (Figure 17.1) can be conceptualised as demonstrating processes of projective identification. Those aspects of the client's personality which, unconsciously, he cannot tolerate are split off and projected into the practitioner. The practitioner experiences this unwanted part of the client as though it belonged to or originated in the practitioner. The most likely source of the aspect of the client, which the client cannot tolerate, is a sense of self-loathing. At one level this could be a sense of self-loathing regarding their abusive behaviour. At a deeper level it is more likely that the self-loathing is connected to the client's past trauma or lack of secure attachments which, in turn, lead to their low self-esteem and subsequent abusive behaviour. What is experienced, then, by the practitioners as a sense of responsibility for ensuring that the client does not abuse again is, we can speculate, a projective identification: the client projects the unwanted, self-loathing aspect of themselves into the practitioner who experiences this as being victimised. The 'battle of wills' and competitiveness between clients and practitioners seen in some of the sessions are examples of the unconscious manoeuvres employed within the therapeutic session to, on the clients' side, project the 'split-off' and unwanted 'badness' into the practitioners and, on the practitioners' side, to defend themselves against the projected 'badness'.

Campbell (1994) compares this process to a re-enactment in the therapeutic situation of the adolescent abuser's unconscious identification with their own abuser as a defence against vulnerability, helplessness, confusion and shame that caused the adolescent to abuse in the first place. The circularity of this process is neatly summed up in the following quotation by one of the practitioners.

Practitioner: It is a bit like he pushes his vulnerability on to me. So it is a kind of cycle thing and so it goes round between us like that. But then I think it is why I am so aware of the feeling, because I am not wanting to push it back. I want to take it from him but then if I take it wholeheartedly from him, I'm vulnerable and I'm not sure how helpful that is to him or to me. So yes it's quite a grappling thing.

Campbell illustrates this point with a case example where he describes the adolescent client's apparent desire to 'compete with and defeat' (p. 318) the practitioner. Similarly, Hodges *et al.* (1994) suggest that the young sexual abusers who were part of their study experienced 'intense feelings of guilt and self-hate' (p. 289) but that the very intensity of these feelings 'made it almost unbearable for the boys to be in touch with them' (p. 289). As a result they re-enacted their feelings in the therapy by projecting them into the practitioner.

The massive projection of hostility, mingled with something deadly, was experienced in the countertransference. Without word or deed the practitioners used to experience overwhelming feelings of threat and the need to get away from him. Feeling trapped she would feel sadistic towards him.

(p. 302)

Recognising these kinds of unconscious processes in our work with clients is important because this can help practitioners to:

*   determine whether their feelings and reactions to clients are their own, induced by their clients, or a mixture of the two;
*   understand the inner world of their clients; and
*   apply brakes to their own acting-out of these feelings.

Similarly, clients can be helped to:

*   understand their own processes – what they are doing, why others respond to them in the way they do, where their feelings of hurt, anger, pain, for example, belong, how they are

constantly repeating patterns of relating in the here and now which actually belong to unresolved issues related to past relationships;

- (within a safe and containing environment) work through these unresolved issues and learn that there can be more positive outcomes;
- integrate (re-introject) the 'bad' aspects of themselves in a modified, less feared form.

Implications for practitioners training and supervision

This chapter has described a recurring pattern of unconscious processes which takes place in practitioners' therapeutic work with children and young people who sexually abuse and a model, conceptualised as the 'responsibility avoidance syndrome', has been proposed. It is suggested that the concepts of countertransference and projective identification provide a useful way of understanding these processes. The remainder of the chapter now discusses the implications of this analysis for the training and supervision of practitioners who work therapeutically with children and young people who sexually abuse and for those who train and supervise them.

The specialist training which qualified professionals undertake for this type of work typically comprises three-to-five-day training courses run by private and voluntary organisations who specialise in work with children and young people who sexually abuse. Perhaps the most well-known of these organisations are the Lucy Faithfull Foundation and G-Map. The content of these specialist courses predominantly draws on cognitive behavioural theory although, more recently, attention has begun to focus on the developmental stage of the child or young person and attachment theory (see, for example, Ryan 1999a). The National Organisation for the Treatment of Abusers (NOTA) is a charitable organisation in the UK for practitioners working with people who sexually abuse, including children and young people. NOTA hosts a three-day conference every year and a glance at the titles of the keynote speeches, workshops and seminars also illustrates the predominance of cognitive behavioural theory, with titles and course descriptions suggesting that consideration of psychodynamic theory or unconscious processes is largely absent in these training events.

At the qualifying level, it is also the case that most courses pay little attention to psychodynamic and psychoanalytic approaches. For example, as regards social work (social workers making the majority of workers in this field), the basic social work training in the UK from the early 1990s until 2003/4 was the Diploma of Social Work (DipSW), since which a three-year degree has been introduced. On both these kinds of courses, psychodynamic theory and an understanding of unconscious processes in the social worker/client relationship receive only token consideration in the curricula (Yelloly and Henkel 1995; Jordon 2000).

My own social work training predated even the DipSW and was the Certificate of Qualification in Social Work (CQSW). Prior to the introduction of a more standardised curriculum on the CQSW by the awarding body (firstly CCETSW, now the GSCC), such courses had a relatively free hand as to the content. The course that I undertook was predominantly informed by psychodynamic theory. I found it difficult to grasp fully the meaning of many of the concepts and how they could be applied to my work as a social worker. However this difficulty diminished as I began to realise that what I was experiencing, particularly what I was feeling, in my work with clients had unconscious meaning and that this meaning became clearer the more I allowed myself to contemplate the experience rather than react to it without contemplation. The latter strategy, I realised, was driven by my own unconscious need to 'do something' in order to rid myself of the discomfort I was experiencing with the client. It also became clearer to me through my own therapy that experiences in my own childhood were sometimes being unconsciously reactivated in my relationships with clients. These were my 'blind spots', my Achilles' heel. Through a process of reflecting on the meaning of these experiences I became able to differentiate between my blind spots and those of the clients. Thus the psychodynamic concepts being taught on my CQSW course became clearer to me by way of these experiential processes. This helped me to help my clients without unconsciously acting out my countertransference reactions.

Given, then, the hypothesis that the unconscious processes discussed in this chapter do actually take place, remain largely unconscious and affect practitioners' interventions with their clients to the detriment of the therapeutic task, incorporating psychodynamic theory into basic qualifying training, as well as post-qualifying specialist training in therapeutic work with children and young people who sexually abuse, would seem to be essential. However, a purely intellectual understanding of these concepts is insufficient. A full understanding of these concepts is only possible if they are gained experientially as well as intellectually. As the epistemological philosopher Michael Polanyi (1958) points out, a purely intellectual and scientific understanding of the mechanics of how to ride a bicycle will not enable one to ride a bike. This is a skill that must be learned experientially. Similarly, in the field of social work training, Yelloly and Henkel (1995) proposed that the complexities of working with clients are 'almost never amenable to standardised or prescribed responses' (p. 8) but that the skills required by social workers to deal with these complexities were best acquired experientially and understood through reflective practice.

Understanding the complex phenomena of unconscious processes in work with children and young people who sexually abuse cannot be achieved during a specialist post-qualifying training course of a few days' duration. However, if the participants on such a course already had a good understanding of these phenomena from their basic social work or other pre-qualifying training, then the way in which these processes are played out in work with children and young people who sexually abuse would be more readily understood.

Reflective practice and evidence-based practice?

An understanding of the concepts of countertransference and projective identification is not, in itself, a guarantee that these unconscious processes will not be enacted within therapy with children and young people who sexually abuse. This understanding has to be continuously and rigorously applied. Indeed this continuous and rigorous application provides the practitioner with ongoing and enriching learning opportunities. This is best achieved by way of adopting a combination of reflective practice, taking on board the fact of unconscious processes within therapeutic work, and evidence-based approaches as illustrated by, for example, cognitive models of work.

Within the fields of social work and other professional training, however, there is a debate which contrasts reflective practice with evidence-based practice (Yelloly and Henkel 1995; Chapman and Hough 1998; Jordon 2000; Sheldon and Chilvers 2000). This is mirrored by the debate in academic arenas contrasting empirical and quantitative research with descriptive and qualitative research (Miles and Huberman 1994). In similar vein, Jones and Joss (1995) propose several different typologies of professionalism. Within these they describe the 'technical expert', who advocates a prescriptive approach, and the 'reflective practitioner', who advocates a contemplative approach. It is interesting to note that the authors' distinction between these two approaches does not consider the possibility of an integration of the two. In this sense, although Jones and Joss are supporting the notion of reflective practice, they are, in fact, describing this preference as though they are technical experts. In all these debates, the authors all appear to take an either/or position which seems unnecessarily simplistic.

In contrast, it is argued here that a reflective practitioner approach within social work and in other professional disciplines can be integrated with an evidence-based practice approach. Central to this argument is one's definition of what constitutes 'evidence' or 'knowledge'. Philosophers and researchers have been contemplating this question since Plato did in *The Republic* (Annas 1981) and whilst it is beyond the scope of this chapter to consider these epistemological questions in any depth, I would invite the reader to consider the work, previously referred to, by Michael Polanyi (1958), who argued that the discovery of 'new' knowledge is a dynamic, organic and heuristic process. A reflective practice approach necessarily implies a commitment to the possibility of the existence of the unseen and the unknown (Polanyi's heuristic impulse) and, therefore, the possibility that such an approach can be informed by an evidence-based approach and vice versa.

Familiarity with reflective practice and evidence-based practice approaches, as well as an understanding of the concepts of countertransference and projective identification, have implications for the supervision of the practitioners who are working therapeutically with children and young people who sexually abuse. This aspect is explored in the following section.

Supervision

All of the practitioners involved in the research study expressed the view that it had been a useful exercise for them in terms of increasing their insight into their own practice. The interviews with the researcher, in particular, were seen as especially valuable, one practitioner mentioning that the research interview had been like a good clinical supervision session. This was not an intentional aspect of the research but was, nevertheless, an interesting finding. First, it indicates that a simple semi-structured interview format can help practitioners become aware of aspects of their therapeutic work of which they had previously been unaware. Second, it suggests that reviewing short segments from videotaped therapeutic sessions can assist in this process. This supports the practice of videotaping therapeutic sessions for the purpose of review in supervision. Paying attention to how the practitioners experienced their work at an emotional level, and inviting them to reflect on this, enabled the practitioners to find a deeper and richer meaning to their experience.

This leads me to suggest that those who supervise practitioners who work therapeutically with children and young people who sexually abuse should be thoroughly familiar, intellectually and experientially, with the psychodynamic principles underpinning unconscious processes, as well as with reflective and evidence-based practice approaches. The recent interest in 'emotional intelligence' (see, for example: Morrison 1997; Saarni 1997; Salovey and Sluyter 1997; Goleman 1998; Taylor *et al.* 1999; Bar-on and Parker 2000; Sternberg 2000) is a testament to the importance of emotions and how they can unconsciously influence behaviour. However, these texts tend to use the discourse of cognitive behavioural, empirical and quantitative research theory to support their arguments, thereby missing the opportunity to integrate these theoretical orientations with psychodynamic theory and qualitative research methods.

Conclusion

The implication for practitioners who work therapeutically with children and young people who sexually abuse that arises from the research study described in this chapter is the importance of integrating psychodynamic concepts, particularly those of countertransference and projective identification, with their other theoretical orientations. Not to do so will lead to practitioners carrying out their therapeutic work in a counter-therapeutic manner, such as emotionally detaching themselves from the client or adopting a persecutory or rescuing approach. It is also quite likely that these practitioners will be meeting their own needs through their work rather than their clients' needs. Campbell (1994) and Hodges *et al.* (1994) comment, from their own clinical experience as psychotherapists, on the potentially destructive impact of unconscious processes such as countertransference reactions and projective identification in psychotherapeutic assessments of adolescents who sexually abuse.

The emotional impact, both conscious and unconscious, of this field of work on practitioners should not be underestimated. The day-to-day experiences of feeling helpless, de-skilled, confused, angry, anxious, fearful, sad, responsible for the client not abusing again must take their toll, not only in the therapeutic sessions, but also, in the longer term, on practitioners' psychological health. The way to avoid this is for practitioners to heighten their awareness that these feelings indicate the possibility that unconscious processes are taking place.

Apart from recognising these feelings as indicators of possible unconscious processes, there are also behavioural and communicative indicators, which the research study illustrated, which might signify the possibility of unconscious processes taking place in the practitioners' work. Examples of these behavioural and communicative indicators are:

* talking more than the client;
* not allowing silences to develop and breaking the silences;
* interrupting the client;
* controlling the agenda of the session;
* not responding to clients' inputs other than discussion of their sexual abuse;
* boundary violations;
* an interrogative style of questioning;
* a tendency towards using the sessions to educate the clients as opposed to creating a therapeutic dialogue;
* avoiding sessions or write-ups of sessions;
* health disturbances.

The affective, behavioural and communicative indicators that have been illustrated in this chapter are not necessarily, in themselves, indicative of unconscious processes. They are merely clues to alert the practitioner, and their supervisor, to reflect on their practice for the possible existence and meaning of unconscious processes. If particular styles of intervention are, or become, habitual for practitioners, either in a general sense or with a particular client, this may be the practitioner's preferred conscious style. However, it may also be an unconscious enactment of a countertransference, particularly if it is a reaction to a specific client. It behoves the practitioner, therefore, with their supervisor, to reflect on their feelings, thoughts and behaviour in their sessions and to contemplate their meaning. For example, providing the client with knowledge may be best achieved by means of an educative session and this could well be conceptualised as part of the therapeutic process of change. In such an instance, however, the practitioner should be clear that this is what they are undertaking for that session and still be alert to other possible indicators of unconscious processes such as interrupting the client.

There are currently, in the UK, suggestions that an accreditation body should be created which would produce guidelines for post-qualifying training and therapeutic interventions for work with people who sexually abuse, including children and young people. The issues outlined in this chapter should, I believe, be taken into account if and when such a body is created. Similarly, pre-qualifying training for social workers and other professionals could usefully consider how to empower new professionals to be more attuned to unconscious processes in their work with clients and their impacts.

References

Abassi, K. and Jamal, S. (2002) 'South Asian adolescent sex offenders: Effective assessment and intervention work', in M. Calder (ed.) *Young People who Sexually Abuse: Building the Evidence Base for your Practice*, Lyme Regis: Russell House Publishing.

Abel, G., Becker, J., Cunningham-Rathner, J., Kaplan M. and Reich, J. (1984) *The Treatment of Child Molesters,* New York: Columbia University.

Abel, G., Becker, J.V., Cunningham-Rathner, J., Rouleau, J., Kaplan, M. and Reich, J. (1986) *The Treatment of Child Molesters – A Manual*, available from SBC-Tm, 722 West 168th Street, Box 17, New York, NY 10032.

Abramson, M. (1996) 'Reflections on knowing oneself ethically: Toward a working framework for social work practice', *Families in Society: The Journal of Contemporary Human Services*, April: 195–202.

Advisory Group on Youth Crime (2000) *It's a Criminal Waste: Stop Youth Crime Now*, London: The Stationery Office.

Ageton, S. (1983) *Sexual Assault among Adolescents*, Lexington, MA: Lexington Books.

Alexander, J.F., Barton, C., Schiavo, S., Parsons, B.V. (1976) 'Systems-behavioral intervention with families of delinquents: therapist characteristics, family behaviour and outcome', *Journal of Consulting and Clinical Psychology*, 44: 656–664.

Alexander, M.A. (1999) 'Sexual offender treatment efficacy revisited', *Sexual Abuse: A Journal of Research and Treatment*, 11, 2: 101–116.

Alexy, E.M. (2003) 'Pornography in the lives of sexually reactive children and adolescents', unpublished doctoral thesis, University of Pennsylvania.

Alvarez, A. (1990) 'Child sexual abuse –The need to remember and the need to forget', in J. Ouston (ed.) *The Consequences of Child Sexual Abuse*, Occasional Papers No. 3. [Association for Child Psychology and Psychiatry, St. Saviour's House, 39/41 Union Street, London, SE1 1 SD.]

Alvarez, A. and Phillips, A. (1998) 'The importance of play: A child psychotherapist's view', *Child Psychology and Psychiatry Review*, 3, 3: 99–103.

Anderson, T. (1987) 'The reflecting team: Dialogue and meta dialogue in clinical work', *Family Process*, 26: 415–428.

Andrews, D. (1995) 'The psychology of criminal conduct and effective treatment', in J. McGuire (ed.) *What Works: Reducing Reoffending: Guidelines from Research and Practice*, Chichester: Wiley.

Annas, J. (1981) *An Introduction to Plato's Republic*, Oxford: Clarendon Press.

Anthony, E.J. (1974) 'The syndrome of the psychologically invulnerable child', in E.J. Anthony and C. Koupernik (eds) *The Child in His Family: Children at Psychiatric Risk, Vol. 3*, New York: Wiley.

APA Task Force (1999) *Dangerous Sex Offenders: A Task Force Report of the American Psychiatric Association*. Washington, DC: American Psychiatric Association.

Araji, S. (1997) *Sexually Aggressive Children – Coming to Understand Them,* Thousand Oaks, CA: Sage.

Arkowitz, S. and Vess, J. (2003) 'An evaluation of the Bumby RAPE and MOLEST scales as measures of cognitive distortions with civilly committed sexual offenders', *Sexual Abuse: A Journal of Research and Treatment*, 15: 237–249.

Ashfield, S., Bradshaw, H. and Henniker, J. (2004a) 'You must be mistaken: Research into young females who sexually abuse', Presentation at Nexus Conference, Working with Adolescent Sex Offenders: Towards a Therapeutic Approach Within a Judicial Context, 6/7 November 2004.

Ashfield, S., Bradshaw, H. and Henniker, J. (2004b) 'You must be mistaken: Research into young females who sexually abuse', Manchester: AIM and Lucy Faithfull Foundation. Available from authors in pdf format.

Audit Commission (1998) *Misspent Youth '98. The Challenge for Youth Justice*, London: Audit Commission Publications.

Awad, G. and Saunders, E.B. (1989) 'Male adolescent sexual assaulters', *Journal of Interpersonal Violence*, 6: 446–460.

Bacon, R. (1988) 'Counter transference in a case conference,' in G. Pearson, J. Treseder, M. Yelloly (eds) *Social Work and the Legacy of Freud*, London: Macmillan.

Bandura, A. (1969) *Principles of Behaviour Modification*, New York: Holt, Rinehart and Winston.

Bankes, N. (2002) 'I'm sorry I haven't a clue: Unconscious processes in practitioners who work with young people who sexually abuse', in M. Calder (ed.) *Young People Who Sexually Abuse: Building the Evidence Base for your Practice*, Lyme Regis: Russell House Publishing.

Bankes, N. (2003) 'Unconscious processes in practitioners who work therapeutically with children and young people who sexually abuse', unpublished doctoral thesis, University of Sussex.

Barak, A. and Fisher, W.A. (2002) 'The future of Internet sexuality', in A. Cooper (ed.) *Sex and the Internet. A Guidebook for Clinicians*, New York: Brunner Routledge.

Barbaree, H., Marshall, W. and Hudson, S. (eds) (1998) *The Juvenile Sex Offender*, New York: Guilford Press.

Barker, M. and Morgan, R. (1993) *Sex Offenders: A Framework for the Evaluation of Community-Based Treatment*, London: Home Office.

Barnard, M., Fuller, S., Robbins, E. and Shaw, M. (1989) *The Child Molester*, New York: Plenum Press.

Bar-on, R. and Parker, J. (eds) (2000) *Handbook of Emotional Intelligence*, San Francisco, CA: Jossey-Bass.

Barter, S. (1997) 'Social work students with personal experiences of sexual abuse: Implications for Diploma in Social Work programme providers', *Social Work Education*, 16, 2: 113–132.

BASW (2004) 'Rough Justice: BASW's response to the Home Office Report: Youth Justice – the Next Steps', *Professional Social Work*, February: 13.

BASW (2005) 'Response to YJB Consultation on strategy for the secure estate for juveniles', available at www.basw.co.uk (accessed on April 12 2005).

BBC News (24/04/2005) Available online from: http:newsvole.bbc.co.uk/mpapps/pagetools/print/news.bbc.co.uk/2/htp

Becker, J. (1988a) cited in A. Bentovim and B. Williams (1998) 'Children and adolescents: Victims who become perpetrators', *Advances in Psychiatric Treatment*, 4: 101–107.

Becker, J. (1988b) 'The assessment of adolescent perpetrators of childhood sexual abuse', in *Understanding, Assessing and Treating Juvenile and Adult Sex Offenders: A Special Issue of the Irish Journal of Psychology*, 9, 1: 68–81.

Becker, J. (1990) 'Treating adolescent sexual offenders', *Professional Psychology Research and Practice* 21: 362–365.

Becker, J. (1998) 'What we know about the characteristics and treatment of adolescents who have committed sexual offenses', *Child Maltreatment*, 3, 4: 317–329.

Becker, J. and Abel, G. (1985) 'Methodological and ethical issues in evaluating and treating adolescent sex offenders', in E.M. Odey and G.D. Ryan (eds) *Adolescent Sex Offenders: Issues in Research and Treatment*, Rockville, MD: NI Mt, Department of Health and Human Services (Publication No ADM-85–1396).

Becker, J.V. (1994) 'Offenders: characteristics and treatment', *Future of Children: Sexual Abuse of Children*, 4: 176–197.

Becker, J.V. and Hunter, J.A. (1993) 'Aggressive sex offenders', *Journal of the American Academy of Child and Adolescent Psychiatry*, 2: 477–487.

Becker, J.V. and Hunter, J.A. (1997) 'Understanding and treating child and adolescent sexual offenders', in T.H. Ollendick and R.J. Prinz (eds) *Advances in Clinical Child Psychology*, New York: Plenum.

Becker, J.V. and Kaplan, M. (1988) 'The assessment of adolescent sex offenders', *Advances in Behavioral Assessment of Children and Families*, 4: 97–118.

Becker, J.V., Kaplan, M.S., Tenke, C.E. and Tartaglini, A. (1991) 'The incidence of depressive symptomatology in juvenile sex offenders with a history of abuse', *Child Abuse Neglect*, 15: 531–536.

Beckett, R. (1994a) 'Cognitive-Behavioural Treatment of Sex Offenders', in T. Morrison, M. Erooga and R. Beckett (eds) (1994) *Sexual Offending Against Children: Assessment and Treatment of Male Abusers*, London: Routledge

Beckett, R. (1999) 'Evaluation of adolescent sexual abusers', in M. Erooga and H. Masson (eds) *Children and Young People who Sexually Abuse Others: Challenges and Responses*, London: Routledge.

Beckett, R., Beech, A., Fisher, D. and Fordham, A.S. (1994) *Community-Based Treatment For Sex Offenders: An Evaluation Of Seven Treatment Programmes*, London: Home Office.

Beckett, R.C. (1998) 'Community treatment in the UK', in W.G. Marshall, S.M. Hudson, T. Ward and Y.M. Fernandez (eds) *Sourcebook of Treatment Programs for Sexual Offenders*, New York: Plenum Press.

Beckett, R.C., Brown, S., Gerhold, C. and Beech, A.R. (in preparation) 'Assessing victim empathy in adult and adolescent rapists'.

Beech, A. and Griffin, H. (2003) 'Greater Manchester sample of adolescents who have sexually harmed', Manchester: Youth Justice Trust (unpublished).

Beech, A., Fisher, D. and Beckett, R. (1999) *STEP 3: An Evaluation of the Prison Sex Offender Treatment Programme*, London: Home Office Publications Unit [50 Queen Anne's Gate, London SW1H 9AT].

Beech, A.R. (1998) 'A psychometric typology of child abusers', *International Journal of Offender Therapy and Comparative Criminology*, 42: 319–339.

Beech, A.R. and Hamilton-Giachritsis, C. (2005) 'Relationship between therapeutic climate and treatment outcome in group-based sexual offender treatment programs', *Sexual Abuse: A Journal of Research and Treatment*, 7, 7: 127–141.

Beech, A.R., Friendship, C., Erikson, M. and Hanson, R.K. (2002) 'The relationship between static and dynamic risk factors and reconviction in a sample of UK child abusers', *Sexual Abuse: A Journal of Research and Treatment*, 14: 155–167.

Bengis, S. (1986) *A Comprehensive Service Delivery System with a Continuum of Care for Adolescent Sexual Offenders*, Orwell, VT: Safer Society Press.

Bengis, S. (1997) 'Personal and interpersonal issues for staff working with sexually abusive youth', in S. Bird Edmunds (ed.) *Impact: Working with Sexual Abusers*, Brandon: Safer Society Press.

Bengis, S., Brown, A., Freeman-Longo, R., Matsuda, B., Ross, J,. Singer, K. and Thomas, J. (1999) *Standards of Treatment for Youth in Sex Offence-Specific Programmes*, Orwell, VT: National Offence-Specific Residential Standards Task Force.

Bentovim, A. (1991) 'Children and young people as abusers', in A. Hollows and H. Armstrong (eds) *Children and Young People as Abusers*, London: National Children's Bureau.

Bentovim, A. (1992) 'Family violence: Explanatory models to describe violent and abusive families' in D. Campbell and R. Draper (eds) *Trauma Organised Systems. Physical and Sexual Abuse in Families,* Systemic Thinking and Practice Series, London: Karnac Books.

Bentovim, A. (1998) 'Family systematic approach to work with young sex offenders', *Irish Journal of Psychology*, 19, 1: 119–125.

Bentovim, A. and Bingley-Miller, L. (2001) *The Family Assessment*, Brighton: Pavilion.

Bentovim, A. and Williams, B. (1998) 'Children and adolescents: Victims who become perpetrators', *Advances in Psychiatric Treatment*, 4: 101–107.

Berg, I.K. (1994) *Family Based Service: A Solution Focused Approach*, New York: Norton.

Berkowitz, R. and Leff, J. (1984) 'Clinical teams reflect family dysfunction', *Journal of Family Therapy*, 6, 2: 79–90.

Bird Edmunds, S. (ed.) (1997a) *Impact: Working with Sexual Abusers*, Brandon: Safer Society Press.

Bird Edmunds, S. (1997b) 'The personal impact of working with sex offenders' in S. Bird Edmunds (ed.) *Impact: Working with Sexual Abusers*. Brandon: Safer Society Press.

Blanchard, G. (1995) *The Difficult Connection: The Therapeutic Relationship In Sex Offender Treatment*, Orwell, VT: Safer Society Press.

Blechman, E.A. and Vryan, K.D. (2000) 'Prosocial family therapy: A manualised preventive intervention for juvenile offenders', *Aggression and Violent Behaviour*, 5, 4: 343–378.

Blues, A., Moffatt, C. and Telford, P. (1999) 'Working with adolescent females who sexually abuse: Similarities and differences', in M. Erooga and H. Masson (eds) *Children and Young People Who Sexually Abuse Others: Challenges and Responses*, London: Routledge.

Blumstein, A. and Cohen, J. (1987) 'Characterizing criminal careers', *Science*, Aug., 237: 985–991.

Blumstein, A., Cohen, J. and Farrington, D.P. (1988) 'Criminal career research: It's value for criminology', *Criminology*, 26: 1–35.

Boer, D.P., Hart, S.D., Kropp, P.R. and Webster, C.D. (1997) *Manual for the Sexual Violence Risk – 20*. Burnaby, BC: The Mental Health, Law & Policy Institute, Simon Fraser University.

Bolger, K. and Patterson, C. (2003) 'Sequelae of child maltreatment: Vulnerability and resilience', in S. Luthar (ed.) *Resilience and Vulnerability. Adaptation in the Context of Childhood Adversities*, Cambridge: Cambridge University Press.

Bonta, J. (1995) 'The responsivity principle and offender rehabilitation', *Forum on Corrections Research*, 7, 3: 34–37.

Borduin, C.M., Henggeler, S.W., Blaske, D.M. and Stein, R.J. (1990) 'Multisystemic treatment of adolescent sexual offenders', *International Journal of Offender Therapy and Comparative Criminology*, 34: 105–113.

Borduin, C.M., Mann, B.J., Cone, L.T., Henggeler, S.W., Fucci, B.R., Blaske, D.M. and Williams, R.A. (1995) 'Multisystemic treatment of serious juvenile offenders: Long-term prevention of criminality and violence', *Journal of Consulting and Clinical Psychology*, 63: 569–578.

Bourke, M.L. and Donohue, B. (1996) 'Assessment and treatment of juvenile sex offenders: An empirical review', *Journal of Child Sexual Abuse*, 5, 1: 47–70.

Braswell, L. (1991) 'Involving parents in cognitive-behavioral therapy with children and adolescents', in P.C. Kendall (ed.) *Child and Adolescent Therapy: Cognitive-Behavioral Procedures*, New York: Guilford Press.

Braswell, L., Koehler, C. and Kendall, P.C. (1985) 'Attributions and outcomes in child psychotherapy', *Journal of Social and Clinical Psychology*, 3: 458–465.

Brearley, P.C. (1982) *Risk in Social Work*, London: Routledge, Kegan and Paul.

Bremer, J.F. (1998) 'Challenges in the assessment and treatment of sexually abusive adolescents', *Irish Journal of Psychology*, 19: 82–92.

Bridge Child Care Development Service, The (2001) *Childhood Lost: Part 8 Case Review, Overview Report DM*, Hay-on-Wye: The Bridge Publishing House Limited.

Britton, R. (1981) 'Re-enactment as an unwitting professional response to family dynamics', in S. Box, B. Copley, J. Magagna and E. Moustaki (eds) *Psychotherapy With Families: An Analytic Approach*, London: Routledge and Kegan Paul.

Brown, L.M. and Gilligan, C. (1992) *Meeting at the Crossroads: Women's Psychology and Girls' Development*, New York: Ballantine Books.

Browne, K.D. and Hamilton-Giachritsis, C. (2005) 'The influence of violent media on children and adolescents: A public health approach', *Lancet*, 365: 702–710.

Bunby, K.M. (1996) 'Assessing the cognitive distortions of child molesters and rapists: Development and validation of the molest and rape scales', *Sexual Abuse: A Journal of Research and Treatment*, 8: 37–54.

Burck, C. and Daniel, G. (1995) *Gender and Family Therapy*, London: Karnac Books.

Burck, C. and Speed, B. (1995) *Gender, Power and Relationships*, London: Routledge.

Burnham, J. (1986) *Family Therapy: First Steps Towards a Systemic Approach*, London: Tavistock Publications.

Burnham, J., Moss, J., Debelle, J. and Jamieson, R. (1999) 'Working with families of young sexual abusers: Assessment and intervention issues', in M. Erooga and H. Masson (eds) *Children and Young People who Sexually Abuse Others: Challenges and Responses* (1st edn), London and New York: Routledge.

Burr, V. (1995) *An Introduction to Social Constructionism*, London: Routledge.

Burton, D.L. and Meezan, W. (2005) 'Revisiting recent research on social learning theory as an etiological proposition for sexually abusive male adolescents', in M. Calder (2005) (ed.) *Children and Young People who Sexually Abuse. New Theory, Research and practice Developments*, Lyme Regis: Russell House Publishing.

Burton, D.L., Nesmith, A.A. and Badten, L. (1997) 'Clinician's views on sexually aggressive children and their families: A theoretical exploration', *Child Abuse and Neglect*, 21, 2: 157–170.

Calder, M.C. (2002) (ed.) *Young People Who Sexually Abuse: Building the Evidence Base for your Practice*, Lyme Regis: Russell House Publishing.

Calder, M.C. (ed.) (2005) *Children and Young People who Sexually Abuse. New Theory, Research and Practice Developments*, Lyme Regis: Russell House Publishing.

Calder, M.C., Hanks, H. and Epps, K.J. (1997) *Juveniles and Children who Sexually Abuse: A Guide to Risk Assessment*. Lyme Regis: Russell House Publishing.

Cameron, K.A., Salazar, L.F., Bernhardt, J.M., Burgess-Whitman, N., Wingwood, G.M. and DiClemente, R.J. (in press) 'Adolescents' experience with sex on the web: Results from online focus groups', *Journal of Adolescence*.

Campbell, D. (1994) 'Breaching the shame shield: Thoughts on the assessment of adolescent child sexual abusers', *The Journal of Child Psychotherapy*, 20, 3: 309–326.

Campbell, J. and Lerew, C. (2002) 'Juvenile sex offenders in diversion', *Sexual Abuse: A Journal of Research and Treatment*, 14, 1: 1–17.

Cantwell, H.B. (1995) 'Sexually aggressive children and societal response', in M. Hunter (ed.) *Child Survivors and Perpetrators of Sexual Abuse: Treatment Innovations*, Thousand Oaks, CA: Sage.

Carpenter, D.R., Peed, S.F. and Eastman, B. (1995) 'Personality characteristics of adolescent sexual offenders: A pilot study', *Sexual Abuse: A Journal of Research and Treatment*, 7: 195–203.

Carr, A. (1989) 'Counter transference to families where child abuse has occurred', *Journal of Family Therapy*, 11, 1: 87–97.

Carr, A. (2004) *Internet traders of child pornography and other censorship offenders in New Zealand*. Available online at http://www.dia.govt.nz?pubforms.nsf/URL/entirereport.pdf/$file/entirereport.pdf

Carrell, S. (1993) *Group Exercises for Adolescents: A Manual for Therapists*, Thousand Oaks, CA: Sage.

Carson, C. and AIM Project (2002) *Guidelines for Identifying and Managing Sexually Problematic/Abusive Behaviour in Schools and Nurseries*, Manchester: AIM Project.

Carson, C. and Education Leeds (2005) 'Ongoing work on developing tools for managing children and young people, including those with autism, with sexual behaviour problems in school settings', Carol Carson, PO Box 14, Pudsey, LS28 7ZQ.

Carson, C. and Leeds Education Department (1996) 'G.E.S.T. Project on developing assessment criteria and intervention strategies for Primary School aged children with sexually inappropriate/abusive behaviours', unpublished document, Leeds Education Department.

Cauce, A.M., Stewart, A., Rodriguez, M.D., Cochran, B. and Ginzler, J. (2003) 'Overcoming the odds? Adolescent development in the context of urban poverty', in S. Luthar (ed.) *Resilience and*

Vulnerability. Adaptation in the Context of Childhood Adversities, Cambridge: Cambridge University Press.

Cavanagh-Johnson, T. (1988) 'Child perpetrators – children who molest other children: Preliminary findings', *Journal of Child Abuse and Neglect*, 12: 219–229.

Cavanagh-Johnson, T. (1989), 'Female child perpetrators – children who molest other children', *Journal of Child Abuse and Neglect*, 13: 571–585.

Cavanagh-Johnson, T. (1999) *Understanding Your Child's Sexual Behaviour: What's Natural and Healthy*, Oakland, CA: New Harbinger Publications.

Cavanagh-Johnson, T. and Doonan, R. (2005) 'Children with sexual behaviour problems: What have we learned in the last two decades?', in M. Calder (ed.) *Children and Young People who Sexually Abuse. New Theory, Research and Practice Developments*, Lyme Regis: Russell House Publishing.

Cavanagh-Johnson, T. and Gil, E. (1993) *Sexualised Children, Assessment and Treatment of Sexualised Children and Children Who Molest*, Rockville, MD: Launch Press.

Cawson, P., Wattam, C. Brooker, S. and Kelly, G. (2000) *Child Maltreatment in the United Kingdom. A Study of the Prevalence of Child Abuse and Neglect*, London: NSPCC.

CBS News, Porn in the USA Sept. 5, 2004, Available online at http://www.cbsnews.com/stories/2003/11/21/60minutes/main585049.shtml

Cecchin, G. (1987) 'Hypothesizing – circularity – neutrality revisited: An invitation to curiosity', *Family Process*, 26: 405–413.

Cellini, H.R. (1995) 'Assessment and treatment of the adolescent sexual offender', in B.K. Schwartz and H.R. Cellini (eds) *The Sex Offender: Vol. 1. Corrections, Treatment and Legal Practice*, Kingston, NJ: Civic Research Institute.

Centre for Residential Child Care, The (1995) *Guidance for Residential Workers Caring for Young People who have been Sexually Abused and those who Abuse Others*, Social Work Services Inspectorate, The Scottish Office: Glasgow.

Chaffin, M. (2003) 'Working with young people who have sexual behaviour problems: Lessons from research on risk and resilience', paper presented at G-Map conference 'Working holistically with young people who sexually harm', June 2003.

Chaplin, T.C., Rice, M.E. and Harris, G.T. (1995) 'Salient victim suffering and the sexual responses of child molesters', *Journal of Consulting and Clinical Psychology*, 63: 249–255.

Chapman, T. and Hough, M. (1998) *Evidence Based Practice: A Guide to Effective Practice*, London: Home Office Publications.

Child-Wise Monitor (2002) Available online at: http://www.ecpat.org/media-releases.html

Christodoulides, T.E., Richardson, G., Graham, F., Kennedy, P. J. and Kelly, T.P. (2005) 'Risk assessment with adolescent sex offenders', *Journal of Sexual Aggression*, 11: 37–48.

Cicchetti, D. and Rogosch, F.A. (1997) 'The role of self-organization in the promotion of resilience in maltreated children', *Development and Psychopathology*, 5: 629–647.

Clare, I. (1993) 'Issues in the assessment and treatment of male sex offenders with mild learning disabilities', *Sexual and Marital Therapy*, 8: 167–180.

Clark, P. and Erooga, M. (1994) 'Groupwork with men who sexually abuse children', in T. Morrison, M. Erooga and R.C. Beckett (eds) *Sexual Offending Against Children: Assessment and Treatment of Male Abusers*, London: Routledge.

CNBC (2004) Thompson, M.J. Porn profits go mainstream. April 13. Available online at: http://moneycentral.msn.com/content/CNBCTV/Articles/TVReports/P80813.asp

Coolican, H. (1996) *Research Methods and Statistics in Psychology,* London: Hodder and Stoughton.

Cooper, A. and Griffin-Shelley, E. (2002) 'Introduction. The Internet: The next sexual revolution', in A. Cooper (ed.) *Sex and the Internet. A Guidebook for Clinicians*, New York: Brunner-Routledge.

Corder, B.F., Whiteside, L. and Haizlip, T.M. (1981) 'A study of the curative factors in group psychotherapy with adolescents', *International Journal of Group Psychotherapy*, 31: 345–354.

Cortoni, F. and Marshall, W. (2001) 'Sex as a coping strategy and its relationship to juvenile sexual history and intimacy in sexual offenders', *Sexual Abuse: A Journal of Research and Treatment*, 13, 1: 27–43.

Cowburn, M. (1996) 'The black male sex offender in prison: Images and issues', *The Journal of Sexual Aggression*, 2, 2: 122–142.

Craissati, J. and McClurg, G. (1997) 'The challenge project: A treatment program evaluation for perpetrators of child sexual abuse', *Child Abuse and Neglect*, 21, 7: 637–648.

Crittenden, P.M. and Claussen, A.H. (eds) (2000) *The Organisation of Attachment Relationships: Maturation, Culture and Context.* New York: Cambridge University Press.

Cullen, J.E. and Seddon, J.W. (1981) 'The application of a behavioural regime to disturbed young offenders', *Personality and Individual Differences*, 2: 285–292.

Curtis, N.M., Ronan, K.R. and Borduin, C.M. (2004) 'Multisystemic treatment: A meta-analysis of outcome studies', *Journal of Family Psychology*, 18: 411–419.

Daily Herald (24 April 2005). Available online at: http://www.newutah.com/print.php?sid=53417.

Daily Mail (21 April 2005) p. 24. Available online at http://www.communitycare.co.uk/AccessSite/articles/article.asp?liSectionID=4&liarticleID=49007.

Dallos, R. and Draper, R. (2001) *An Introduction to Family Therapy, Systemic Theory and Practice*, Buckingham: Open University Press.

Davis, G.E. and Leitenberg, H. (1987) 'Adolescent sex offenders', *Psychological Bulletin*, 101, 3: 417–427.

Davis, M. (1983) 'Measuring individual differences in empathy: Evidence for a multidimensional approach', *Journal of Personality and Social Psychology*, 44: 113–126.

de Shazer, S. (1988) *Clues: Investigating Solutions in Brief Therapy*, New York: Norton.

DeBell, M. and Chapman, C. (2003) *Computer and Internet use by Children and Adolescents in 2001*, Washington, DC: US Department of Education, National Center for Education Statistics.

Deblinger, E. and Heflin, A.H. (1996) *Treating Sexually Abused Children and their Non-offending Parents: A Cognitive Behavioural Approach*, Thousand Oaks, CA: Sage.

Department of Health (1991a) *The Children Act 1989 Guidance and Regulations: Volume 4, Residential Care*, London: HMSO.

Department of Health (1991b) *Working Together under the Children Act 1989. A Guide to the Arrangements for inter-agency co-operation for the protection of children from abuse*, London: HMSO.

Department of Health (1995) *Child Protection: Messages from Research*. London: HMSO.

Department of Health (1999) *Working Together to Safeguard Children*, London: DOH.

Department of Health (2000) *Framework for the Assessment of Children in Need and their Families*, London: DOH.

Department of Health and Social Security (DHSS) (1988) *Diagnosis of Child Sexual Abuse: Guidance for Doctors*, London: HMSO.

Department of Health, Social Services and Public Safety (2003) *Co-operating to Safeguard Children*, Belfast, available at www.dhsspsni.gov.uk

DeRisi, W.J. and Butz, G. (1975) *Writing Behavioural Contracts*, Champaigne, IL: Research Press.

DfES (2003) *Every Child Matters*, London: The Stationery Office.

DfES (2004a) *Every Child Matters: Next Steps*, London: The Stationery Office.

DfES (2004b) *Every Child Matters: Change for Children in Schools*, London: DfES.

DfES (2004c) *Safeguarding Children in Education 2004*, London: DfES.

DfES (2005) *Excellence and Enjoyment: Social and Emotional Aspects of Learning (S.E.A.L.)*, London: DfES.

Dimmock, B. and Dungworth, D. (1985) 'Beyond the family: Using network meetings with statutory child care cases', *Journal of Family Therapy*, 7, 1: 45–68.

Dolan, M., Holloway, J., Bailes, S. and Kroll, L. (1996) 'The psychosocial characteristics of juvenile sex offenders referred to an adolescent forensic service in the UK', *Medicine, Service and the Law*, 36: 343–352.

Doshay, L.J. (1943) *The Boy Sex Offender and Later Career*, Montclair, NJ: Patterson Smith.

Doughty, D. and Schneider, H. (1987) 'Attribution of blame in incest among mental health professionals', *Psychological Reports*, 60: 1159–1165.

Douglas, T. (1995) *Survival In Groups: The Basics Of Group Membership*, Buckingham: Open University Press.

Duane, Y., Carr, A., Cherry, J., McGrath, K. and O'Shea, D. (2002) 'Experiences of parents attending a programme for families of adolescent child sex abuse perpetrators in Ireland', *Child Care in Practice*, 8, 1: 46–57.

Duboust, S. and Knight, P. (1995) *Group Activities for Personal Development*, Bicester: Winslow Press.

Durlak, J., Furnham, T. and Lampman, C. (1991) 'Effectiveness of cognitive-behavioral therapy for maladapting children: A meta-analysis', *Psychological Bulletin*, 110, 2: 204–214.

Dwivedi, K.N. (1993) (ed.) *Groupwork with Children and Adolescents: A Handbook*, London: Jessica Kingsley.

Dziuba-Leatherman, J. and Finkelhor, D. (1994) 'How does receiving information about sexual abuse influence boys' perceptions of their risk?', *Child Abuse and Neglect*, 18: 557–568.

Ebersole, S. (2000) 'Uses and gratifications of the web among students', *Journal of Computer-Mediated Communication*, 6: 1–16.

Edleson, J. (1997) 'Charging battered mothers with failure to protect is often wrong', APSAC *Advisor*, 10: 2–3.

Eldridge, H. and Still, J. (1995) 'Apology and forgiveness in the context of the cycles of adult male sex offenders who abuse children', in A.C. Salter (ed.) *Transforming Trauma: A Guide to Understanding and Treating Adult Survivors of Child Sexual Abuse*, London: Sage.

Elkins, I.J., Iacono, W.G., Doyle A.E. and McCue, M. (1997) 'Characteristics associated with the persistence of antisocial behaviour: Results from recent longitudinal research', *Aggression and Violent Behaviour*, 2, 2, 101–124.

Ellerby, L., Gutkin, B., Smith, T. and Atkinson, R. (1993) 'Treating sex offenders: The impact on clinicians', Poster presentation, 12th Annual Conference of the Association for the Treatment of Sexual Abusers, Boston, MA.

Elliot, D.S. (1994) 'The developmental course of sexual and non-sexual violence: Results from a national longitudinal study', presentation at the 13th Annual Research and Treatment Conference of the Association of Sexual Abusers, San Francisco, CA.

Elliot, D.S., Dunford, F.W. and Huzinga, D. (1983)' The identification and prediction of career offenders utilizing self-reported and official data', unpublished manuscript, Boulder, CO: Behavioural Research Institute.

Elliott, C.E. and Butler, L. (1994) 'The Stop and Think Group: Changing sexually aggressive behaviour in young children', *The Journal of Sexual Aggression*, 1: 15–28.

Elliott, M. (1993) (ed.) *Female Sexual Abuse of Children: The Ultimate Taboo*, London: Longmans.

Emerick, R.L. and Dutton, W.A. (1993) 'The effect of polygraphy on the self-report of adolescent sexual offenders: Implications for risk assessment', *Annals of Sex Research*, 6: 83–103.

Epps, K. (1999) 'Looking after young sexual abusers: Child protection, risk management and risk reduction', in M. Erooga and H. Masson (eds) *Children and Young People who Sexually Abuse Others: Challenges and Responses*, London: Routledge.

Epps, K. and Fisher, D. (2004) 'A review of the research literature on young people who sexually abuse', in G. O'Reilly, W.L. Marshall, A. Carr and R. Beckett (eds) *The Handbook of Clinical Intervention with Young People who Sexually Abuse*, Hove: Psychology Press.

Epps, K.J. (1997) 'Managing risk', in M. Hoghughi, S. Bhate and F. Graham *Working with Sexually Abusive Adolescents*, Thousand Oaks, CA: Sage.

Erooga, M. (1994) 'Where the professional meets the personal', in T. Morrison, M. Erooga, and R.C. Beckett, *Sexual Offending Against Children Assessment and Treatment of Male Abusers*, London: Routledge.

Erooga, M. and Masson, H. (eds) (1999) *Children and Young People who Sexually Abuse Others: Challenges and Responses*, London: Routledge.

Evans, J. (1998) *Active Analytic Psychotherapy for Adolescents*, London: Jessica Kingsley.

Evans, T. and Harris, J. (2004) 'Street-level bureaucracy, social work and the (exaggerated) death of discretion', *British Journal of Social Work*, 34: 871–895.

Fahlberg, V.I. (1991) *A Child's Journey through Placement*, London: BAAF.

Faller, K.C. (1987) 'Women who sexually abuse children', *Violence and Victims*, 2: 263–267.

Farmer, E. (1998) 'Fostering and residential care for sexually abused and abusing children', paper presented at the British Association for the Study and Prevention of Child Abuse and Neglect National Study Day, Services for Children in Need with Practical Solutions to Help Them, Bristol, England, March.

Farmer, E. and Pollock, S. (1998) *Sexually Abused and Abusing Children in Substitute Care*, Chichester: John Wiley.

Farmer, E. and Pollock, S. (1999) 'Mix and match: Planning to keep looked after children safe', *Child Abuse Review*, 8: 377–391.

Farrenkopf, T. (1992) 'What happens to therapists who work with sex offenders?' *Journal of Offender Rehabilitation*, 8, 3–4: 217–223.

Farrington, D.P. (1973) 'Self-reports of deviant behaviour: Predictive and stable?', *Journal of Criminal Law and Criminology*, 64: 99–110.

Farrington, D.P. and Hawkins, J.D. (1991) 'Predicting participation, early onset and later persistence in officially recorded offending', *Criminal Behaviour and Mental Health*, 1: 1–33.

Farrington, D.P., Ohlin, L.E. and Wilson, J.Q. (1986) *Understanding and Controlling Crime*, New York: Springer.

Fawcett, B., Featherstone, B. and Goddard, J. (2004) *Contemporary Child Care Policy and Practice*, Basingstoke: Palgrave Macmillan.

Fehrenbach, P.A., Smith, W., Monastersky, C. and Deisher, R.W. (1986) 'Adolescent sexual offenders: Offender and offence characteristics', *American Journal of Orthopsychiatry*, 56: 225–233.

Fergusson, D.M. and Lynskey, M.T. (1996) 'Adolescent resilience to family adversity', *Journal of Child Psychology and Psychiatry*, 37: 281–292.

Fernandez, Y.M. and Marshall, W.L. (2003) 'Victim empathy, social self-esteem and psychology in rapists', *Sexual Abuse: A Journal of Research and Treatment*, 15: 11–26.

Fernandez, Y.M., Marshall, W.L., Lightbody, S. and O'Sullivan, C. (1999) 'The child molester empathy measure', *Sexual Abuse: A Journal of Research and Treatment*, 11: 17–31.

Fine, M. (1988) 'Sexuality, schooling and adolescent females: Missing the discourse of desire', *Harvard Education Review*, 58, 1: 29–52.

Finkelhor, D. (1979) *Sexually Victimised Children*, New York: Free Press.

Finkelhor, D. (1984) *Child Sexual Abuse: New Theory and Research*, New York: Free Press.

Finkelhor, D. (1986) *A Source Book on Child Sexual Abuse*, New York: Free Press.

Finkelhor, D. and Browne, A. (1985) 'The traumatic impact of child sexual abuse: An update.' *American Journal of Orthopsychiatry*, 55: 530–541.

Finkelhor, D. and Jones, L.M. (2004) 'Explanations for the decline in child sexual abuse cases', OJJDP Bulletin: Crimes Against Children Series, Washington, DC: OJJDP.

Finkelhor, D., Mitchell, K.J. and Wolak, J. (2000) 'Online victimization: A report of the nation's youth', Washington, DC: National Center for Missing and Exploited Children. Available online from http://www.missingkids.com/en_US/publications/NC62.pdf

Flaskas, C. (2002) *Family Therapy beyond Postmodernism,* London: Brunner-Routledge.

Ford, M.E. and Linney, J.A. (1995) 'Comparative analysis of juvenile sexual offenders, violent nonsexual offenders, and status offenders', *Journal of Interpersonal Violence*, 10: 56–70.

Forth, A.E., Kosson, D.S. and Hare, R.D. (1994) 'The Psychopathy Checklist: Youth Version', unpublished test manual.

Franklin, B. and Petley, J. (1996) 'Killing the age of innocence: Newspaper reporting of the death of James Bulger', in J. Pilcher and S. Wagg (eds) *Thatcher's Children*, London: Routledge.

Freeman-Longo, R.E., Bays, L. and Bear, E. (1996) *Empathy and Compassionate Action: Issues and Exercises – A Guided Workbook for Clients in Treatment*, Burlington, VT: Safer Society Press.

Freidberg, R.D. and McClure, J.M. (2002) *Clinical Practice of Cognitive Therapy with Children and Adolescents: The Nuts and Bolts*, New York and London: Guilford Press.

Freud, S. (1905) 'Three essays on the theory of sexuality. I. The sexual aberrations', in J. Strachey (ed.) *The Standard Edition of the Complete Psychological Works of Sigmund Freud*, London: Hogarth Press and Institute of Psycho-analysis.

Friedrich, W.N. (1997) *CSBI: Child Sexual Behaviour Inventory. Professional Manual.* Odessa, FL: Psychological Assessment Resources.

Friendship, C., Mann, R. and Beech, A. (2003) 'Evaluation of a national prison-based treatment program for sexual offenders in England and Wales', *Journal of Interpersonal Violence*, 18: 744–759.

Fromuth, M.E., Jones, C.W. and Burkhart, B.R. (1991) 'Hidden child molestation: An investigation of perpetrators in a non-clinical Sample', *Journal of Interpersonal Violence*, 6, 3: 376–384.

Furby, L., Weinrott, M.R. and Blackshaw, L. (1989) 'Sex offender recidivism: A review', *Psychological Bulletin*, 105: 3–30.

Furniss, T. (1991) *The Multi-professional Handbook of Child Sexual Abuse: Integrated Management, Therapy and Legal Intervention*, London: Routledge.

Garland, J.A. (1992) 'The establishment of individual and collective competency in children's groups as a prelude to entry into intimacy, disclosure and bonding', *International Journal of Group Psychotherapy*, 42, 3: 395–405.

Garmezy, N. (1983) 'Stressors of childhood', in N. Garmezy and M. Rutter (eds) *Stress, Coping, and Development in Children*, New York: McGraw-Hill.

Garmezy, N. (1985) 'Stress-resistant children: The search for protective factors', in J.E. Stevenson (ed.) *Recent Research in Developmental Pathopathology: Journal of Child Psychology and Psychiatry Book Supplement No. 4*, Oxford: Pergamon Press.

Garmezy, N. (1991) 'Resilience in children's adaptation to negative life events and stressed environments', *Pediatric Annals*, 20: 459–466.

Gendreau, P. and Andrews, D.A. (1990) 'What the meta-analysis of the offender treatment literature tells us about "what works"', *Canadian Journal of Criminology*, 32: 173–184.

Gendreau, P., Little, T. and Goggin, C. (1996) 'A meta-analysis of the predictors of adult offender recidivism: What works', *Criminology*, 34: 575–607.

George, E., Iveson, C. and Ratner, H. (2001) *Problem to Solution*, London: Brief Therapy Press.

Gibbs, J.C. and Potter, G. (1991) 'Aggression replacement training in the context of positive peer culture', paper presented at the meeting of the Ohio Council for Children with Behavioral Disorders, Columbus, OH.

Gilbert, N. (1988) 'Teaching children to prevent sexual abuse', *The Public Interest*, 93: 3–15.

Gilgun, J. (1999) 'CASPARS: Clinical assessment instruments that measure strengths and risks in children and families', in M. Calder (ed.) *Working with Young People who Sexually Abuse: New Pieces of the Jigsaw*, Lyme Regis: Russell House Publishing.

Gilgun, J. (2003) Personal communication.

Gilligan, C. (1982) *In A Different Voice: Psychological Theory and Women's Development*, Cambridge, MA: Harvard University Press.

Gilligan, C., Lyons, N.P. and Hammer, T.J. (eds) (1990) *Making Connections: The Relational Worlds of Adolescent Girls at Emma Willard School.* Cambridge, MA: Harvard University Press.

Gilligan, R. (2000) 'Adversity, Resilience and young people: The protective value of positive school and spare time experiences', *Children and Society*, 14: 37–47.

Glasgow, D., Horne, L., Calam, R. and Cox, A. (1994) 'Evidence, incidence, gender and age in sexual abuse of children perpetrated by children: Towards a developmental analysis of child sexual abuse', *Child Abuse Review*, 3: 196–210.

Glasser, M. (1979) 'Some aspects of the role of aggression in the perversions', in L. Rosen (ed.) *Sexual Deviations*, Oxford: Oxford University Press.

GMC (1997) *Confidentiality In Duties of a Doctor, Guidance from the General Medical Council*, General Medical Council, 178–202 Great Portland Street, London WIN 6JE.

Goldner, V. (1988) 'Generation and gender: Normative and covert hierarchies', *Family Process*, 27: 17–31.

Goldner, V. (1990) 'Love and violence: Gender paradoxes in volatile attachments', *Family Process*, 29, 4: 343–364.

Goleman, D. (1998) *Working with Emotional Intelligence*. New York: Bantam Books.

Graham, F., Richardson, G. and Bhate, S. (1997) 'Assessment', in M. Hoghughi, S. Bhate and F. Graham (1997) *Working with Sexually Abusive Adolescents*, Thousand Oaks, CA: Sage.

Green, L. and Masson, H. (2002) 'Adolescents who sexually abuse and residential accommodation: Issues of risk and vulnerability', *British Journal of Social Work*, 32: 149–168.

Greenfield, P.M. (2004a) 'Developmental considerations for determining appropriate Internet use guidelines for children and adolescents', *Applied Developmental Psychology*, 25: 751–762.

Greenfield, P.M. (2004b) 'Inadvertent exposure to pornography on the Internet: Implications of peer-to-peer file sharing networks for child development and families', *Applied Developmental Psychology*, 25: 741–750.

Griffin, H. (2003) *Greater Manchester Sample of Adolescents who have Sexually Harmed*, Manchester: Greater Manchester AIM Project.

Griffin, S., Williams, M., Hawkes, C. and Vizard, E. (1997) 'The Professional Carers Group supporting group work with young sexual abusers', *Child Abuse and Neglect*, 21, 7: 681–690.

Gruber, E. and Grube, J.W. (2000) 'Adolescent sexuality and the media: A review of current knowledge and implications', *Western Journal of Medicine*, 172: 210–214.

Guardian, The (1998) See extensive coverage of the trial of four 10 year old boys accused of raping a female classmate in the school toilets: 16 January, 6 February.

Haaven, J.L. and Coleman, E.M. (2000) 'Treatment of the intellectually disabled sex offender', in R.D. Laws, S.M. Hudson and T. Ward (eds) *Remaking Prevention with Sex Offenders: A Sourcebook*, Thousand Oaks, CA: Sage Publications.

Hackett, S. (1997) 'Men protecting children? A study of male social workers' experiences of working in child sexual abuse', unpublished MA thesis, University of Manchester.

Hackett, S. (2000) 'Sexual aggression, diversity and the challenge of anti-oppressive practice', *Journal of Sexual Aggression*, 5, 1: 4–20.

Hackett, S. (2001) *Facing the Future: A Guide for Parents of Young People Who Have Sexually Abused*, Lyme Regis: Russell House Publishing.

Hackett, S. (2004) *What Works for Children and Young People with Harmful Sexual Behaviours?* Nottingham: Barnardos.

Hackett, S. and Masson, H. (in press) 'Young people who have sexually abused: What do they (and their parents) want from professionals?' *Children and Society*.

Hackett, S., Masson, H. and Phillips, S. (2003) 'Mapping and exploring services for children and young people who have sexually abused: Final Report. Durham/Huddersfield: University of Durham and University of Huddersfield, available from h.c.masson@hud.ac.uk and on Youth Justice Board website at http://www.youth-justice-board.gov.uk/Publications/Scripts/prodView.asp?idproduct=267&ep=

Hackett, S., Masson, H. and Phillips, S. (in press) 'Exploring consensus in practice with youth who are sexually abusive: Findings from a Delphi Study of Practitioner Views in the United Kingdom and the Republic of Ireland' *Child Maltreatment*.

Hackett, S., Print, B. and Dey, C. (1998) 'Brother Nature?: Therapeutic intervention with young men who sexually abuse their siblings', in A. Bannister (ed.) *From Hearing to Healing: Working with the Aftermath of Child Sexual Abuse, Second Edition,* Chichester: Wiley.

Hackett, S., Telford, P. and Slack, K. (2002) 'Groupwork with parents of children who have sexually harmed others', in M.C. Calder (ed.) *Young People who Sexually Abuse: Building the Evidence Base for Your Practice*, Lyme Regis: Russell House Publishing.

Hagan, M.P. and Cho, M.E. (1996) 'A comparison of treatment outcomes between adolescent rapists and child sexual offenders', *Journal of Offender Therapy and Comparative Criminology*, 40, 2: 113–122.

Hagan, M.P., Gust-Brey, K.L., Cho, M.E. and Dow, E. (2001) 'Eight-year comparative analyses of adolescent rapists; adolescent child molesters and other adolescent delinquents, and the general population', *International Journal of Offender Therapy and Comparative Criminology*, 45, 3: 314–324.

Haley J. (1980) *Leaving Home*, New York: McGraw-Hill.

Hall, G.C. (1995) 'Sexual offender recidivism revisited: A meta-analysis of recent treatment studies', *Journal of Consulting and Clinical Psychology*, 63, 5: 802–809.

Hamlin, B., Keep, J. and Ash, K. (2000) *Organisational Change and Development: A Reflective Guide for Managers, Trainers and Developers*, London: Financial Times Pearson Group.

Hammen, C. (2003) 'Risk and protective factors for children of depressed parents', in S. Luthar (ed.) *Resilience and Vulnerability. Adaptation in the Context of Childhood Adversities*, Cambridge: Cambridge University Press.

Hanson, C.L., Henggeler, S.W., Haefele, W.F. and Rodick, J.D. (1984) 'Demographic, individual and family relationship correlates of serious and repeated crime amongst adolescents and their siblings', *Journal of Consulting and Clinical Psychology*, 52: 528–538.

Hanson, R.K. (1997) 'The development of a brief actuarial risk scale for sexual offense recidivism', *User Report No 1997–04*, Ottawa, ON: Department of the Solicitor General of Canada.

Hanson, R.K. (2000) *Risk Assessment*, Beaverton, OR: Association for the Treatment of Sexual Abusers.

Hanson, R.K. and Bussière, M.T. (1996) 'Predictors of sexual offender recidivism: A meta-analysis', *User Report No 1996–04*, Ottawa, ON: Department of the Solicitor General of Canada.

Hanson, R.K. and Bussière, M.T. (1998) 'Predicting relapse: A meta-analysis of sexual offender recidivism studies', *Journal of Consulting and Clinical Psychology*, 66: 348–362.

Hanson, R.K. and Harris, A.J.R. (2000a) 'Where should we intervene? Dynamic predictors of sex offense recidivism', *Criminal Justice and Behavior*, 27: 6–35.

Hanson, R.K. and Harris, A.J.R. (2000b) 'The Sex Offender Need Assessment Rating (SONAR): A method for measuring change in risk levels', *User Report No 2000–01*, Ottawa, ON: Department of the Solicitor General of Canada.

Hanson, R.K. and Harris, A.J.R. (2001) 'A structured approach to evaluating change among sexual offenders', *Sexual Abuse: A Journal of Research and Treatment*, 13: 105–122.

Hanson, R.K. and Scott, H. (1995) 'Assessing perspective-taking amongst sexual offenders, non-sexual criminals and non-offenders', *Sexual Abuse: A Journal of Research and Treatment*, 7: 259–277.

Hanson, R.K. and Thornton, D. (1999) 'Static-99: Improving actuarial risk assessments for sex offenders', *User Report No 1999–02*, Ottawa, ON: Department of the Solicitor General of Canada.

Hanson, R.K. and Thornton, D. (2000) 'Improving risk assessments for sexual offenders: A comparison of three actuarial scales', *Law and Human Behavior*, 24: 119–136.

Hanson, R.K., Gordon, A., Harris, A.J.R., Marques, J.K., Murphy, W., Quinsey, V.L. and Seto, M.C. (2002) 'First report of the collaborative outcome data project on the effectiveness of psychological treatment of sex offenders', *Sexual Abuse: A Journal of Research and Treatment*, 14, 2: 169–194.

Hardy, K.V. and Laszloffy, T.A. (1995) 'The cultural genogram: Key to training culturally competent family therapists', *Journal of Marital and Family Therapy*, 21, 3: 227–237.

Harnett, P. (1997) 'The attitudes of female and male residential care workers to the perpetrators of sexual and physical abuse, *Child Abuse and Neglect*, 21, 9: 861–868.

Hart, G. (2000) 'Extent of regretted sexual intercourse among young teenagers in Scotland: A cross-sectional survey', *British Medical Journal*, 320: 1243–1244.

Haugaard, J. and Reppucci, N. (1988) *The Sexual Abuse of Children: A Comprehensive Guide to Current Knowledge and Intervention Strategies*, San Francisco, CA: Jossey-Bass.

Hawkes, C., Jenkins, J.A. and Vizard, E. (1997) 'Roots of sexual violence in children and adolescents', in V.P. Varma (ed.) *Violence in Children and Adolescents*, London: Jessica Kingsley.

Hayashino, D.S., Wurtele, S.K. and Klebe, K.J. (1995) 'Child molesters: An examination of cognitive factors', *Journal of Interpersonal Violence*, 10: 106–116.

Heiman, M.L., Lieblum, S. Cohen-Esquilin, S. and Melendes Pallitto, L. (1998) 'A comparative study about normal sexual behaviors', *Child Abuse & Neglect*, 22, 4: 290–304.

Hendrick, H. (1997) *Children, Childhood and English Society 1880–1990*, Cambridge: Cambridge University Press.

Hendrick, H. (2003) *Child Welfare: Historical Dimensions, Contemporary Debates*, Bristol: The Policy Press.

Henniker, J. (2001) *AIM Project Policies and Procedures*, Manchester: Greater Manchester AIM Project.

Henniker, J. and Foster, J. (2000) *Research Findings about Young People who Sexually Abuse in Greater Manchester*, Manchester: Greater Manchester AIM Project.

Henniker, J., Print, B. and Morrison, T. (2002) 'An inter-agency assessment framework for young people who sexually abuse: Principles, processes and practicalities', *Child Care in Practice*, 8, 2: 114–126.

Herbert, M. (1991*) Clinical Child Psychology: Social Learning, Development and Behaviour*, Chichester: Wiley.

Himelein, M.J. and McElrath, J.A.V. (1996) 'Resilient child sexual abuse survivors: Cognitive coping and illusion', *Child Abuse and Neglect*, 20, 8: 747–758.

HM Inspectorate of Probation (1998) *Exercising Constant Vigilance: The Role of the Probation Service in Protecting the Public from Sex Offenders. Report of a Thematic Inspection of the Work of the Probation Service with Sex Offenders*, London: Home Office.

HM Inspectorate of Probation (2004) *Joint Inspection of Youth Offending Teams. The First Phase, Annual Report 2004*, London: Home Office

Hobbs, C.J. and Wynne, J.M. (1993) 'The evaluation of child abuse', in C.J. Hobbs and J.M. Wynne (eds) *Child Abuse, Clinical Paediatrics, International Practice and Research*, 1, 1: 1–29.

Hodges, J., Lanyado, M. and Andreou, C. (1994) 'Sexuality and violence: Preliminary clinical hypotheses from psychotherapeutic assessments in a research programme on young sexual offenders', *Journal of Child Psychotherapy*, 20, 3: 283–308.

Hoghughi, M., Bhate, S. and Graham, F. (1997) *Working with Sexually Abusive Adolescents*, Thousand Oaks, CA: Sage.

Holmes, R.N. (1983) *The Sex Offender*, Springfield, IL: Charles C. Thomas.

Home Office (1997) *No More Excuses: A New Approach to Tackling Youth Crime in England and Wales*, Home Office Juvenile Offenders Unit, Cmnd 3809, London: The Stationery Office.

Home Office (2003a) *MAPPA Guidance*, London: Home Office.

Home Office (2003b) *Youth Justice, the Next Steps*, London: Home Office.

Home Office (2004) *Criminal Statistics, England and Wales 2003/2004*, London: Home Office.

Home Office (2004a) *Youth Justice – The Next Steps: Summary of Responses and the Government's Proposals*, London: Home Office.

Home Office (2004b) *Every Child Matters: Change for Children in the Criminal Justice System*, London: Home Office.

Horner, G. (2004) 'Sexual behavior in children: Normal or not?' *Journal of Paediatric Health Care*, 18: 57–64.

House of Lords and House of Commons Joint Committee on Human Rights (2003) *10th Report of the Joint Committee on Human Rights – The UN Convention on the Rights of the Child*, London: The Stationery Office.

Howard League for Penal Reform (2004) Independent inquiry into the treatment of children in penal custody, chaired by Lord Carlile of Berriew, QC (on-going).

Howe, D. (1993) *On Being a Client. Understanding the Process of Counselling and Psychotherapy*, London: Sage.

Hunter, J. (2000) *Understanding Juvenile Sex Offenders: Research Findings and Guidelines for Effective Management and Treatment*, Richmond, VA: The Virginia Department of Criminal Justice.

Hunter, J., Aurelio, J., Malamuth, N. and Becker, J. (2003) 'Juvenile sex offenders: Towards the development of a typology', *Sexual Abuse: Journal of Research and Treatment*, 15, 1: 27–48.

Hunter, J.A. and Becker, J.V. (1994) 'The role of deviant sexual arousal in juvenile sexual offending: etiology, evaluation and treatment', *Criminal Justice and Behaviour*, 21: 132–149.

Hunter, J.A. and Figueredo, A.J. (1999) 'Factors associated with treatment compliance in a population of juvenile sexual offenders', *Sexual Abuse: A Journal of Research and Treatment*, 11: 49–68.

Hunter, J.A., Becker, J.V., and Kaplan, M.S. (1991) 'The reliability and discriminative utility of the adolescent cognitions scale for juvenile sex offenders', *Annals of Sex Research*, 4, 3–4: 281–286.

ICD-10 Classification of Mental and Behavioural Disorders (1992) *Clinical Descriptions and Diagnostic Guidelines*, Geneva: World Health Organisation.

Irish Examiner (2004) (22 January) Available online at: http://archives.tcm.ie/irishexaminer/2004/01/22/story779427727.asp

Ishi, K. (2004) 'Internet use via mobile phone in Japan', *Telecommunications Policy*, 28, 1: 43–58.

James, A. and Jenks, C. (1996) 'Perceptions of childhood criminality', *British Journal of Sociology*, 47, 2: 315–331.

James, A.C. and Neill, P. (1996) 'Juvenile sexual offending: One-year period prevalence study within Oxfordshire', *Child Abuse and Neglect*, 20: 477–485.

Jenkins, A. (1990) *Invitations to Responsibility – The Therapeutic Engagement of Men Who Are Violent and Abusive*, Adelaide: Dulwich Centre Publications.

Jenkins, A., Joy, M. and Hall, R. (2003) 'Forgiveness and child sexual abuse: A matrix of meanings', in *Responses to Violence: A collection of papers relating to child sexual abuse and violence in intimate relationships*, Adelaide: Dulwich Centre Publications.

Jenks, C. (1996) *Childhood*, Key Ideas Series, London: Routledge.

Jones, S. and Joss, R, (1995) 'Models of professionalism', in M. Yelloly and M. Henkel (eds) *Learning and Teaching in Social Work*, London and Bristol, PA: Jessica Kingsley Publishers.

Jones, D.P.H. and Ramchandani, P. (1999) *Child Sexual Abuse: Informing Practice From Research*, Oxford: Radcliffe Medical Press.

Jones, L.M. and Finkelhor, D. (2003) Putting together the evidence on declining trends in sexual abuse: A complex puzzle', *Child Abuse & Neglect*, 27: 133–135.

Jones, L.M., Finkelhor, D. and Kopiec, K. (2001) 'Why is sexual abuse declining? A survey of state child protection administrators', *Child Abuse & Neglect*, 25, 9: 1139–1158.

Jordan, J.V., Kaplan, A.G., Miler, J.B., Stiver, I.P. and Surrey, J.L. (1991) *Women's Growth In Connection: Writings From The Stone Centre*, New York: Guilford Press.

Jordon, B. (2000) *Social Work and the Third Way: Tough Love as Social Policy*, London and New York: Sage.

Jung, C. (1933) *Modern Man in Search of a Soul*, New York: Harcourt Brace.

Justice, R. and Justice, B. (1993) 'Child abuse and the law: How to avoid being the abused or the abuser', *Transactional Analysis Journal*, 23, 3: 139–145.

Kahn, T.J. and Chambers, H. (1991) 'Assessing reoffence risk and juvenile sexual offenders', *Child Welfare*, 70, 3: 333–346.

Kanuga, M. and Rosenfeld, W.D. (2004) 'Adolescent sexuality and the Internet: The good, the bad and the URL', *Journal of Pediatric Adolescent Gynecology*, 17: 117–124.

Karpman, S. (1968) 'Fairy tales and script drama analysis', *Transactional Analysis Bulletin*, 7, 26: 39–43.

Kaufman, K.L., Holmberg, J.K., Orts, K.A., McCrady, F.E., Rotzien, A.L., Daleiden, E.L. and Hilliker, D.R. (1998) 'Factors influencing sexual offenders' modus operandi: An examination of victim-offender relatedness and age', *Child Maltreatment*, 3: 349–361.

Kaufman, K.L., Wallace, A., Johnson, C. and Reader, M. (1995) 'Comparing female and male perpetrators' modus operandi: Victim's reports of sexual abuse', *Journal of Interpersonal Violence*, 10, 3: 322–333.

Kavoussi, R., Kaplan, M. and Becker, J. (1988) 'Psychiatric diagnoses in juvenile sex offenders', *Journal of the American Academy of Child and Adolescent Psychiatry*, 27: 241–243.

Kendall, P.C. (1991) 'Guiding theory for therapy with children and adolescents', in P.C. Kendall (ed.) *Child and Adolescent Therapy: Cognitive-Behavioral Procedures*, New York: Guilford Press.

Kendall, P.C. (1993) 'Cognitive behavioural therapies with youth: Guiding theory, current status and emerging development', *Journal of Consulting and Clinical Psychology*, 61: 235–247.

Kendall, P.C. and Braswell, L. (1985) *Cognitive-Behavioural Therapy for Impulsive Children*, New York: Guilford Press.

Kendall, P.C., Panichelli-Mindel, S.M. and Gerow, M.A. (1995) 'Cognitive-behavioural therapies with children and adolescents', in H.P.J. van Bilsen, P.C. Kendall and J.H. Slavenberg (eds) *Behavioural Approaches for Children and Adolescents, Challenges for the Next Century*, New York: Plenum Press.

Kendal-Tackett, K.A., Williams, L.M. and Finkelhor, D. (1993) 'Impact of sexual abuse on children: A review and synthesis of recent empirical studies', *Psychological Bulletin*, 113: 164–180.

Kennedy, E. (2004) 'Child and adolescent psychotherapy: A systematic review of psychoanalytic approaches'. Commissioned by the Child Psychotherapy Steering Group of the North Central London Strategic Health Authority. Available from: www.nclondon.nhs.uk or from: laura.painter@ enfield.nhs.uk

Kennel, R. and Agresti, A. (1995) 'Effects of gender and age on psychologists' reporting of child sexual abuse', *Professional Psychology: Research & Practice*, 26, 6: 612–615.

Kenny, D., Keogh, T. and Seidler, K. (2001) 'Predictors of recidivism in Australian juvenile sex offenders: Implications for treatment', *Sexual Abuse: A Journal of Research and Treatment*, 13, 2: 131–148.

Kilbrandon Report (1964) *Report of the Committee on Children and Young Persons, Scotland*, Cmnd 3065, London: HMSO.

Klein, M. (1946) 'Notes on some schizoid mechanisms', in Masud R. Khan (ed.) *Envy and Gratitude and Other Works (1946–1963) The Writings of Melanie Klein, Volume III*, The International Psycho-Analytical Library No. 104, London: Hogarth Press and Institute of Psychoanalysis.

Klein, M. (1988) *Envy and Gratitude and Other Works*, London: Virago Press.

Knight, R.A. and Prentky, R. (1993) 'Exploring characteristics for classifying juvenile sex offenders', in H.E. Barbaree, W.L. Marshall and S.M. Hudson (eds) *The Juvenile Sex Offender*, New York: Guilford Press.

Knight, R.A. (1997) 'A unified model of sexual aggression: Consistencies and differences across noncriminal and criminal samples', paper presented at the 16th Annual Meeting of the Associated for the Treatment of Sexual Abusers, Arlington, VA.

Knight, R.A. (1999) 'Validation of a typology for rapists', *Journal of Interpersonal Violence*, 14, 3: 303–330.

Knight, R.A. (2004) 'Comparisons between juvenile and adult offenders', in G. O'Reilly, W.L. Marshall, A. Carr and R.C. Beckett (eds) *The Handbook of Clinical Intervention with Young People who Sexually Abuse*, London: Brunner-Routledge.

Knight, R.A., Prentky, R. and Cerce, D.D. (1994) 'The development, reliability, and validity of an inventory for the multidimensional assessment of sex and aggression', *Criminal Justice and Behaviour*, 21, 1: 72–94.

Kobayashi, J., Sales, B.D., Becker, J.V., Figueredo, A.J. and Kaplan, M.S. (1995) 'Perceived parental deviance, parent–child bonding, child abuse, and child sexual aggression', *Sexual Abuse: A Journal of Research and Treatment*, 7, 1: 25–43.

Kolb, D. (1988) 'The Process of Experiential Learning', in D. Kolb (ed.) *Experience as the Source of Learning and Development*, London: Prentice Hall.

Kubik, E.K., Hecker, J.E. and Rightland, S. (2002) 'Adolescent females who have sexually offended: Comparisons with delinquent adolescent female offenders and adolescent males who sexually offend', *Journal of Child Sexual Abuse*, 11, 3: 63–83.

Ladwa, T.U. and Sanders, R. (1999) 'Juvenile sex abusers: Perceptions of social work practitioners', *Child Abuse Review*, 8: 55–62.

Lamb, S. (2001) *The Secret Lives of Girls: What Good Girls Really Do – Sex Play, Aggression and Their Guilt*, New York: Free Press.

Laming, H. (2003) *The Victoria Climbié Inquiry*, London: The Stationery Office.

Lane, S. (1978) 'Treatment design developed at Closed Adolescent Treatment Centre, Denver, CO', quoted in G. Ryan, S.R.N. Lane and J.M.A. Davis (1987) 'Juvenile sex offenders: development and correction', *Child Abuse and Neglect*, 2: 385–395.

Lane, S. (1991) 'The sexual abuse cycle', in G. Ryan and S. Lane (eds) *Juvenile Sexual Offending: Causes, Consequences and Correctiosn* (1st edn), Lexington, MA: Lexington Books.

Lane, S. (1997) 'The sexual abuse cycle', in G. Ryan and S. Lane, (eds) *Juvenile Sexual Offending Causes, Consequences and Corrections* (2nd edn), San Francisco, CA: Jossey-Bass.

Lane, S. and Zamora, P. (1978) 'Syllabus materials from inservice training – Closed Adolescent Treatment Centre', cited in G. Ryan and S. Lane (1991) *Juvenile Sexual Offending: Causes, Consequences and Corrections* (1st edn), Lexington, MA: Lexington Books.

Lane, S. and Zamora, P. (1982, 1984) cited in S. Lane (1997) 'The sexual abuse cycle', in G. Ryan and S. Lane (eds) *Juvenile Sexual Offending – Causes, Consequences and Corrections* (2nd edn), San Francisco, CA: Jossey-Bass.

Lane, S. with Lobanov-Rostovsky, C. (1997) 'Special populations: Children, females, the developmentally disabled, and violent youth', in G. Ryan and S. Lane *Juvenile Sexual Offending: Causes, Consequences and Corrections* (2nd edn), San Francisco, CA: Jossey-Bass.

Langevin, R. and Curnoe, S. (2004) 'The use of pornography during the commission of sexual offenses', *International Journal of Offender Therapy and Comparative Criminology*, 48: 572–586.

Langevin, R., Wright, P. and Handy, L. (1988) 'Empathy, assertiveness, and defensiveness among sex offenders', *Annals of Sex Research*, 1: 533–547.

Långström, N. and Grann, M. (2000) 'Risk for criminal recidivism among young sex offenders', *Journal of Interpersonal Violence*, 15: 855–871.

Laplanche J. and Pontalis J.-B. (1973) *The Language of Psycho-Analysis*, translated by Donald Nicholson-Smith, New York: Norton.

Laws, D.R. (1986) 'Prevention of relapse in sex offenders', paper presented at the NIMH Conference at the 12th Annual Meeting of the International Academy of Sex Research, Amsterdam.

Le Doux, J.E. (1994) 'Emotion, memory and the brain', *Scientific American,* June: 50–57.

Lea, S., Auburn, T. and Kibblewhite, K. (1999) 'Working with sex offenders: The perceptions and experiences of professionals and paraprofessionals', *International Journal of Offender Therapy and Comparative Criminology*, 43, 1: 103–119.

Lee, D.G. and Olender, M.B. (1992) 'Working with juvenile sex offenders in foster care', *Community Alternatives: International Journal of Family Care*, 4: 63–75.

Levene, K.S., Augimeri, L.K. Pepler, D.J., Walsh, M.M., Webster, C.D. and Koegl, C.J. (2001) *Early Assessment Risk List for Girls*, Earl-21G Consultation Edition, Toronto, ON: Earlscourt Child and Family Centre.

Lewis, D.O., Shankok, S.S. and Pincus, J.H. (1979) 'Juvenile male sexual assaulters', *American Journal of Psychiatry*, 136 (suppl. 9): 1194–1196.

Limentani, A. (1989) *Between Freud and Klein. The Psychoanalytic Quest for Knowledge and Truth*, London: Free Association Books.

Lipsky, M. (1980) *Street-level Bureaucracy: The Dilemmas of Individuals in Public Service*, New York: Russell Sage Foundation.

Little, L. and Hamby, S. (1996) 'Impact of a clinician's sexual abuse history, gender, and theoretical orientation on treatment issues related to child sexual abuse', *Professional Psychology: Research & Practice*, 27, 6: 617–662.

Livingstone, S. and Bober, M. (2005) 'UK children go online', available from: http://www.children-go-online.net

Loeber, R. (1990) 'Development and risk factors of juvenile antisocial behaviour and delinquence', *Clinical Psychology Review*, 10: 1–41.

Longo, R.E. (2004) 'Young people with sexual behaviour problems and the Internet', in M. Calder (ed.) *Child Sexual Abuse and the Internet: Tackling the New Frontier*, Lyme Regis: Russell House Publishing.

Longo, R.E., Brown, S.M. and Orcutt, D.P. (2002) 'Effects of Internet sexuality on children and adolescents', in A. Cooper (ed.) *Sex and the Internet. A Guidebook for Clinicians*, New York: Brunner-Routledge.

Loughlin, B. (1992) 'Supervision in the face of no cure – working on the boundary', *Journal of Social Work Practice*, 6, 2: 111–116.

Lovell, E. (2002) *'I think I might need some more help with this problem . . .' Responding to children and young people who display sexually harmful behaviour*, London: NSPCC.

Lush, D., Boston, M. and Grainger, E. (1991) 'Evaluation of psychotherapy with children: Therapists' assessments and predictions', *Psychoanalytic Psychotherapy*, 5, 3: 191–234.

Luthar, S. (1999) *Poverty and Children's Adjustment*, Newbury Park, CA: Sage.

Luthar, S. and Zelazo, L.B. (2003) 'Research on resilience. An integrative review', in S. Luthar (ed.) *Resilience and Vulnerability. Adaptation in the Context of Childhood Adversities*, Cambridge: Cambridge University Press.

Luthar, S., Cicchetti, D. and Becker, B. (2000) 'The construct of resilience: A critical evaluation and guidelines for future work', *Child Development*, 71, 3: 543–562.

MacKinnon, C.A. (1995) 'Vindication and resistance: A response to the Carnegie Mellon study of pornography in Cyberspace', *Georgetown Law Journal*, 83: 1959–1967.

Madell, D. and Muncer, S. (2004) 'Back from the beach but hanging on the telephone? English adolescents' attitudes and experiences of mobile phones and the Internet', *CyberPsychology & Behavior*, 7, 3: 359–367.

Mahoney, M.J. and Norcross, J.C. (1993) 'Relationship styles and therapeutic choices: A commentary', *Psychotherapy*, 30: 423–426.

Malamuth, N.M. (1993) 'Pornography's impact on male adolescents', *Adolescent Medicine*, 4: 563–576.

Malamuth, N.M. (2000) 'Pornography and sexual aggression: Are these reliable effects and can we understand them?' *Annual Review of Sex Research*, 11: 26–91.

Malamuth, N.M. and Brown, L.M. (1994) 'Sexually aggressive men's perception of women's communications: Testing three explanations', *Journal of Research and Treatment*, 7: 259–277.

Malamuth, N.M., Heavey, C.L. and Linz, D. (1993) 'Predicting men's antisocial behaviour against women: The interaction model of sexual aggression', in G.C. Nagayama Hall, R. Hirschman, J.R. Graham and M.S. Zaragoza (eds) *Sexual Aggression: Issues in Etiology and Assessment, Treatment and Police*, Washington, DC: Hemisphere.

Malamuth, N.M., Sockloskie, R.H., Koss, M.P. and Tanaka, J.S. (1991) 'Characteristics of aggressors against women: Testing a model using a national sample of college students', *Journal of Consulting and Clinical Psychology*, 59: 670–681.

Malan, D. (1979) *Individual Psychotherapy and the Science of Psychodynamics,* London: Butterworth-Heinemann.

Malekoff, A. (2004) *Group Work with Adolescents: Principles and Practice*, New York: Guilford Press.

Manocha, K. and Mezey, G. (1998) 'British adolescents who sexually abuse: A descriptive study', *The Journal of Forensic Psychiatry*, 9, 3: 588–608.

Marlatt, G.A. and Gordon, J.R. (eds) (1985) *Relapse Prevention: Maintenance Strategies in the Treatment of Addictive Behaviours*, New York: Guilford Press.

Marshall, W., Anderson, D. and Fernandez, Y. (1999) *Cognitive Behavioural Treatment of Sexual Offenders*, Chichester and New York: Wiley.

Marshall, W., Barbaree, H. and McCormick, J. (1998) 'The development of deviant sexual behaviour among adolescents and its implications for prevention and treatment', *Irish Journal of Psychology*, 19, 1: 208–225.

Marshall, W., Jones, R., Ward, T., Johnston, P. and Barbaree, H. (1991) 'Treatment outcomes with sex offenders', *Clinical Psychology Review*, 11: 463–485.

Marshall, W.L. (1989) 'Invited essay: Intimacy, loneliness and sexual offenders', *Behaviour Research and Therapy*, 27: 491–503.

Marshall, W.L. and Barbaree, H.E. (1990) 'Outcome of comprehensive cognitive-behavioural treatment programmes', in W.L. Marshall, D.R. Laws and H.E. Barbaree (eds), *Handbook of Sexual Assault: Issues, Theories and the Treatment of the Offender*, London: Plenum Press.

Marshall, W.L. and Maric, A. (1996) 'Cognitive and emotional components of generalized empathy deficits in child molesters', *Journal of Child Sexual Abuse*, 5: 101–111.

Marshall, W.L., Anderson, D. and Fernandez, Y. (1999) *Cognitive Behavioural Treatment of Sexual Offenders*, Chichester: Wiley.

Marshall, W.L., Hudson, S.M. and Hodkinson, S. (1993) 'The importance of attachment bonds in juvenile sexual offending', in H.E. Barbaree, W.L. Marshall and S.M. Hudson (eds) *Juvenile Sex Offending*, New York: Guilford Press.

Marshall, W.L., Hudson, S.M. and Ward, T. (1992) 'Sexual deviance', in P.H. Wilson (ed.) *Principles and Practice of Relapse Prevention*, London: Guilford Press.

Marshall, W.L., Jones, R., Hudson, S.M. and McDonald, E. (1993) 'Generalised empathy in child molesters', *Journal of Child Sexual Abuse*, 2: 61–68.

Marshall, W.L., O'Sullivan, C. and Fernandez, Y.M. (1996) 'The enhancement of victim empathy among incarcerated child molesters', *Legal and Criminological Psychology*, 1: 95–102.

Marshall, W.L., Serran, G.A. and Cortoni, F.A. (2000) 'Childhood attachments, sexual abuse, and their relationship to adult coping in child molesters', *Sexual Abuse: A Journal of Research and Treatment*, 12, 1: 17–26.

Maslach, C., Schaufeli, W.B. and Leiter, M.P. (2001) 'Job burnout', *Annual Review of Psychology*, 52: 397–422.

Masson, H. (1995) 'Children and adolescents who sexually abuse other children: Responses to an emerging problem', *Journal of Social Welfare and Family Law*, 17, 3: 325–336.

Masson, H. (1997/1998) 'Issues in relation to children and young people who sexually abuse other children: A survey of practitioners' views', *Journal of Sexual Aggression*, 3, 2: 101–118.

Masson, H. (2004) *Children and Young People who Sexually Abuse Others: Policy and Practice Developments since the early 1990s*, BASW Expanding Horizons in Social Work and Allied Professions, Birmingham: Venture Press.

Masson, H. and Erooga, M. (1989) 'The silent volcano – Groupwork with mothers of sexually abused children', *Practice Journal*, 3, 1: 24–41.

Masson, H. and Hackett, S. (2003) 'A decade on from the NCH report (1992): Adolescent sexual aggression policy, practice and service delivery across the UK and Republic of Ireland', *Journal of Sexual Aggression*, 9: 109–124.

Masson, H. and Morrison, T. (1999) 'Young sexual abusers: Conceptual frameworks, issues and imperatives', *Children and Society*, 13: 203–215.

Masson, J. (1992) *The Assault on Truth. Freud and Child Sex Abuse*, London: Fontana.

Masten, A. (2001) 'Ordinary magic: Resilience processes in development', *American Psychologist*, 53: 205–220.

Masten, A. and Garmezy, N. (1985) 'Risk, vulnerability, and protective factors in developmental psychopathology', in B. Lahey and A. Kazdin (eds) *Advances in Clinical Child Psychology*, New York: Plenum Press.

Masten, A. and Powell, J. (2003) 'A resilience framework for research, policy, and practice', in S. Luthar (ed.) *Resilience and Vulnerability. Adaptation in the Context of Childhood Adversities*, Cambridge: Cambridge University Press.

Matthews, R. (1987) *Female Sexual Offenders: Treatment and Legal Issues*, Minneapolis, MN: PHASE and Genesis II for Women.

Matthews, R., Hunter, J.A. and Vuz, J. (1997) 'Juvenile female sexual offenders – Characteristics and treatment issues', *Sexual Abuse – A Journal of Research and Treatment*, 9, 3: 187–199.

Matthews, R., Matthews, J.K. and Spelz, K. (1989) *Female Sexual Offenders an Exploratory Study*, Brandon, VT: Safer Society Press.

Mayer, A. (1992) *Women Sex offenders – Treatment and Dynamics*, Holmesbeach SLA: Learning Publications Inc.

Maynard, C. and Wiederman, M. (1997) 'Undergraduate students' perceptions of child sexual abuse: Effects of age, sex and gender-role attitudes', *Child Abuse and Neglect*, 21, 9: 861–868.

McDougall, J. (1990) *Plea for a Measure of Abnormality*, London: Free Association Books.

McGoldrick, M. (1998) (ed.) *Revisioning Family Therapy. Race, Culture and Gender in Clinical Practice*, New York and London: Guilford Press.

McKinnon, L.K. and Miller, D. (1987) 'The New Epistemology and the Milan Approach. Feminist and socio-political considerations', *Journal of Marital and Family Therapy*, 13, 2: 139–155.

McNamee, S. and Gergen, K.J. (eds) 1992) *Therapy as Social Construction* Thousand Oaks, CA: Sage.

Menzies, L. (1970) *The Functioning of Social Systems as a Defence Against Anxiety*, London: Tavistock Institute of Human Relations.

Mezey, G., Vizard, E. and Hawkes, C. (1990) 'A community treatment programme for convicted child sex offenders: A preliminary report', *Journal of Forensic Psychiatry*, 1: 12–25.

Middleton, D., Beech, A. and Mandeville-Norton, R. (2005) 'What sort of person could do that? – Psychological profiles of Internet pornography users', in E. Quayle and M. Taylor (eds) *Viewing Child Pornography on the Internet: Understanding the Offence, Managing the Offender, Helping the Victim*, Lyme Regis: Russell House Publishing.

Milan, M.A. (1987) 'Basic behavioural procedures in closed institutions', in E.K. Morris and C.J. Braukmann (eds) *Behavioural Approaches to Crime and Delinquency: A Handbook of Application, Research and Concepts*, New York: Plenum Press.

Miles, M. and Huberman, A. (1994) *Qualitative Data Analysis* (2nd edn), London and New York: Sage.

Miller, A. (1984) *Thou Shalt Not Be Aware. Society's Betrayal of the Child*, London: Pluto Press.

Miller, J.B. and Stiver, I.P. (1997) *The Healing Connection: How Women Form Relationships in Therapy and in Life*. Boston, MA: Beacon Press.

Miller, W.R. and Rollnick, S. (1991) *Motivational Interviewing: Preparing People to Change Addictive Behavior*, New York and London: Guilford Press.

Milloy, C.D. (1994) *A Comparative Study of Juvenile Sex Offenders and Non-sex Offenders,* Olympia, WA: Washington State Institute for Public Policy.

Mintzer, M. (1996) 'Understanding Countertransference reactions in working with adolescent perpetrators of sexual abuse', *Bulletin of the Meninger Clinic*, 60, 2: 219–227.

Mir, B. and Okotie, E. (2002) *Study of the Experiences of Black and Asian Young People whose Behaviour is Sexually Harmful to Others*, Greater Manchester: AIM Project.

Mitchell, C. and Melikian, K. (1995) 'The treatment of male sex offenders: Countertransference reactions', *Journal of Child Sexual Abuse*, 4, 1: 87–93.

Mitchell, K.J., Finkelhor, D. and Wolak, J. (2003) 'The exposure of youth to unwanted sexual material on the Internet. A national survey of risk, impact and prevention', *Youth & Society*, 34, 3: 330–350.

Moffitt, T.E. (1993) 'Adolescence – limited and life-course-persistence antisocial behaviour: A developmental taxonomy', *Psychological Bulletin*, 100: 674–701.

Morgan, A. (2000) *What is Narrative Therapy? An Easy to Read Introduction*, Adelaide: Dulwich Centre Publications.

Morrison, T. (1990) 'The emotional effects of child protection on the worker', *Practice*, 4, 4: 253–271.

Morrison, T. (1994) 'Learning together to manage sexual abuse: Rhetoric or reality?', *Journal of Sexual Aggression*, 1, 1: 29–44.

Morrison, T. (1997) 'Emotionally competent child protection organisations: Fallacy, fiction or necessity?' in J. Bates, R. Pugh and N. Thompson (eds) *Protecting Children: Challenges and Changes*, Aldershot: Arena Publications.

Morrison, T. (1998) 'Managing risk: Learning our lessons', NOTA Conference, September 1997, *NOTA News* 25.

Morrison, T. (1999) 'Is there a strategy out there? Policy and management perspectives on young people who sexually abuse others', in M. Erooga and H. Masson (eds) *Children and Young People who Sexually Abuse Others: Challenges and Responses*, London: Routledge.

Morrison, T. (2000) 'Preparing services and staff to work with young people who sexually abuse; context, mandate; pitfalls and frameworks', in W. Marshall, R. Beckett, A. Carr and G. O'Reilly (eds) *Handbook of Clinical Intervention*, London: Wiley.

Morrison, T. (2001a) 'Surveying the terrain: Current issues in the prevention and management of sexually abusive behaviour by males', *Journal of Sexual Aggression*, 7, 1: 19–39.

Morrison, T. (2001b) *Staff Supervision in Social Care*, Brighton: Pavilion Publishing.

Morrison, T., O'Callaghan, D., Print, B., Quayle, J. and Wilkinson, L. (2005) *Comprehensive Assessment and Intervention Guides for Work with Young People who Sexually Harm*, Manchester: Greater Manchester AIM Project.

Morrison, T. and Wilkinson, L. (2003) *Initial Assessment of the Parents/Carers of Young People who Sexually Abuse Others*, Manchester: Greater Manchester AIM Project.

Morrison, T. and Wilkinson, L. (2005) *Comprehensive Assessment and Treatment Guide for the Families of Young People who Sexually Abuse Others*, Manchester: Greater Manchester AIM Project.

Morrison, T., Erooga, M. and Beckett, R. (1994) *Sexual Offending Against Children. Assessment and Treatment of Male Abusers*, London: Routledge.

Muncie, J. (2004) *Youth and Crime*, 2nd edn, London: Sage.

Murphy, W.D. (1990) 'Assessment and modification of cognitive distortions in sex offenders', in W.L. Marshall, D.R. Laws and H.E. Barbaree (eds) *Handbook of Sexual Assault: Issues, Theories and Treatment of the Offender*, New York: Plenum Press.

Murphy, W.D., DiLillo, D., Haynes, M.R. and Steere, E. (2001) 'An exploration of factors related to deviant sexual arousal among juvenile sex offender', *Sexual Abuse: A Journal of Research and Treatment*, 13, 2: 91–103.

Myers, S. (2002) *Early Evaluation of the Training Programme and Practitioner's Response to AIM*, Manchester: Greater Manchester AIM Project.

NACRO (2003a) *Counting the Cost: Reducing Child Imprisonment*, London: NACRO.

NACRO (2003b) *A Failure of Justice: Reducing Child Imprisonment*, London: NACRO.

National Adolescent Perpetrator Network (1993) 'The Revised Report from the National Task Force on Juvenile Sexual Offending' (Special report edition), *Juvenile & Family Court Journal*, 44, 4: 1–121.

National Children's Home (1992) *Report of the Committee of Enquiry into Children and Young People who Sexually Abuse Other Children*, London: NCH.

Net Ratings Australia (2005) Kidsonline@home 'Internet use in Australian Homes'. Available online at: http://www.netalert.net.au?02010-kidsonline@home---Internet-use-in-Australia-homes---April-2005.pdf

Newton, C. and Wilson, D. (2003) *Creating Circles of Friends: A Peer Support and Inclusion Workbook*, Nottingham: Inclusive Solutions.

Nichols, H.R. and Molinder, I. (1984) *Manual for the Multiphasic Sex Inventory*, available from Nichols and Molinder, 437 Bowes Drive, Tacoma, WA 98466.

North West Treatment Associates (1988) in A. Salter (1988) *Treating Child Sex Offenders and Victims – A Practical Guide*, Beverly Hills, CA: Sage.

NOTA National Committee on Adolescents Who Sexually Harm (2003) *Response to Protecting the Public – Strengthening Protection against Sex Offenders and Reforming the Law on Sexual Offences* (2002, Cm 5668, TSO), available from www.nota.co.uk

O'Callaghan, D. (1999) 'Young abusers with learning disabilities: Towards better understanding and positive intervention', in M. Calder (ed.) *Working with Young People who Sexually Abuse: New Pieces of the Jigsaw*, Lyme Regis: Russell House Publishing.

O'Callaghan, D. (2002) *AIM Initial Assessment of Young People with Learning Difficulties who Sexually Abuse Others*, Manchester: Greater Manchester AIM Project.

O'Callaghan, D. and Print, B. (1994) 'Adolescent sexual abusers: Research, assessment and treatment', in T. Morrison, M. Erooga and R.C. Beckett (eds) *Sexual Offending Against Children Assessment and Treatment of Male Offenders*, London: Routledge.

O'Callaghan, D., Print, B. and Quayle, J.D. (2004) *The G-MAP Group Treatment Programme Handbook: An Adapted Programme for Low Risk Young People Who Have Sexually Harmed*, Manchester: Produced for AIM Project, Building 3, Quay's Reach, South Langworthy Road, Salford M50 2PU.

Ogden, T. (1979) 'On projective identification', *International Journal of Psychoanalysis*, 60: 357–373.

Ogden, T. and Halliday-Boykins, C.A. (2004) 'Multisystemic treatment of antisocial adolescents in Norway: Replication of clinical outcomes outside of the US', *Child and Adolescent Mental Health*, 9, 2: 77–83.

O'Hagan, K. (1997) 'The problem of engaging men in child protection work', *British Journal of Social Work*, 27, 1: 25–42.

Olafson, E., Corwin, D. and Summit, R. (1993) 'Modern history of child sexual abuse awareness – Cycles of discovery and suppression', *Child Abuse & Neglect*, 17, 1: 7–24.

Olsson, C., Bond, L., Burns, J., Vella-Brodrick, D. and Sawyer, S. (2003) 'Adolescent resilience: A concept analysis', *Journal of Adolescence*, 26: 1–11.

Openshaw, D., Graves, R., Erickson, S., Lowry, M., Durso, D., Agee, L., Todd, S., Jones, K. and Scherzinger, J. (1993) 'Youthful sexual offenders: A comprehensive bibliography of scholarly references, 1970–1992', *Family Relations*, 42: 222–226.

O'Reilly, G. (2001) 'Adolescents who sexually abuse others', in K. Lalor (ed.) *The End of Innocence: Child Sexual Abuse in Ireland*, Dublin: Oak Tree Press.

O'Reilly, G., Marshall, W.L., Carr, A. and Beckett, R. (2004) (eds) *The Handbook of Clinical Intervention with Young People who Sexually Abuse*, Hove: Psychology Press.

O'Reilly, G., Sheridan, A., Carr, A., Cherry, J., Donohoe, E., McGrath, K., Phelan, S., Tallon, M. and O' Reilly, K. (1998) 'A descriptive study of adolescent sexual offenders in an Irish community-based treatment programme', *Understanding, Assessing, and Treating Juvenile and Adult Sex Offenders, A Special Issue of the Irish Journal of Psychology*, 19, 1: 152–167.

Parents Plus (2002) 'Families and adolescents programme manual', a video-based parenting guide to handling conflict and getting on better with older children and teenagers (aged 11–15), C/o Department of Child and Adolescent Psychiatry, Mater Hospital, North Circular Road, Dublin 7, Ireland.

Patterson, G.R. (1982) *A Social Learning Approach: Vol. 3 Coercive Family Process*, Eugene, OR: Castalia Publishing.

Pavlov, I.P. (1927) *Conditional Reflexes*, London: Oxford University Press.

Perkins, D., Hammond, S.M., Coles, D. and Bishopp, D. (1999) *An Evaluation of Sex Offender Treatment Programmes*, London: High Security Psychiatric Commissioning Board, Department of Health.

Perry, B.D. (1994) 'Neurobiological sequelae of childhood trauma: PTSD in children', in M. Murray (ed.) *Catecholamines in Post-Traumatic Stress Disorder: Emerging Concepts*, Washington, DC: American Psychiatric Press.

Perry, G. and Orchard, J. (1992) *Assessment and Treatment of Adolescent Sex Offenders*, Sarasota, FL: Professional Resource Press.

Pithers, W. (1999) 'Empathy: Definition, enhancement and relevance to the treatment of sexual abusers', *Journal of Interpersonal Violence*, 14: 257–284.

Pithers, W.D. (1990) 'Relapse prevention with sexual aggressors: A method for maintaining therapeutic gain and enhancing external supervision', in W.L. Marshall, D.R. Laws and H.E. Barbaree (eds) (1990) *Handbook of Sexual Assault: Issues, Theories, and Treatment of the Offender*, New York: Guilford Press.

Pithers, W. and Gray, A. (1996) 'Utility of relapse prevention in treatment of sexual abusers', in *Sexual Abuse. A Journal of Research and Treatment*, 8, 3.

Pithers, W.D., Beal, L.S., Armstrong, J. and Petty, J. (1989) 'Identification of risk factors through clinical interviews and analysis of records', in D.R. Laws (ed.) *Relapse Prevention with Sex Offenders*, New York: Guilford Press.

Pithers, W.D., Kashima, K. Cummings, G.F., Beal, L.S. and Buell, M. (1988a) 'Relapse prevention of sexual aggression', in R. Prentky and V. Quinsey (eds), *Human Sexual Aggression: Current Perspectives*, New York: New York Academy of Sciences.

Pithers, W.D., Kashima, K.M., Cumming, G.F. and Beal, L.S. (1988b) 'Relapse prevention: A method of enhancing maintenance of change in sex offenders', in A. Salter (ed.) *Treating Child Sex Offenders and their Victims*, Thousand Oaks, CA: Sage.

Polanyi, M. (1958) *Personal Knowledge – Towards a Post-Critical Philosophy*, London: Routledge.

Pollack, N.L. and Hashmal, J.M. (1991) 'The excuses of child molesters', *Behavioural Sciences and the Law*, 9: 53–59.

Polson, M. and McCullom, E. (1995) 'Therapist caring in the treatment of sexual abuse offenders: Perspectives from a qualitative case study of one sexual abuse treatment program', *Journal of Child Sexual Abuse*, 4, 1: 21–43.

Prentky, R. and Knight, R. (1991) 'Identifying critical dimensions for discriminating amongst rapists', *Journal of Consulting and Clinical Psychology*, 59: 643–661.

Prentky, R.A. and Knight, R.A. (1993) 'Age of onset of sexual assault: Criminal and life history correlates', in G.W. Hall, R. Hirschman, J. Graham and M. Zaragoza (eds) *Sexual Aggression: Issues in Aetiology, Assessment and Treatment*, Abingdon: Taylor & Francis.

Prentky, R. and Righthand, S. (2001) 'Juvenile Sex Offender Assessment Protocol (J-SOAP): Manual', Unpublished document.

Prentky, R., Harris, B., Frizzell, K. and Righthand, S. (2000) 'An actuarial procedure for assessing risk with juvenile sex offenders', *Sexual Abuse: A Journal of Research and Treatment*, 12, 2: 71–93.

Prentky, R.A., Knight, R.A. and Lee, A.F.S. (1997) 'Risk factors associated with recidivism among extra familial child molesters', *Journal of Consulting and Clinical Psychology*, 65, 1: 141–149.

Preston-Shoot, M. and Agass, D. (1990) *Making Sense of Social Work: Psychodynamics, Systems & Practice*, Basingstoke: Macmillan.

Print, B., Morrison, T. and Henniker, J. (2001) 'An inter-agency assessment framework for young people who sexually abuse: Principles, processes and practicalities', in M. Calder (ed.) *Juveniles and Children who Sexually Abuse: Frameworks for Assessment* (2nd edn), Lyme Regis: Russell House Publishing.

Print, B., Morrison, T. and Henniker, J. (2002) 'A model for an initial assessment of young people who have sexually abused', in *Working with Young People who Display Sexually Inappropriate and Abusive Behaviour*, Manchester: Greater Manchester AIM Project.

Print, B., O'Callaghan, D. and Quayle, J. (2005) *Comprehensive Assessment and Treatment Manual for Young People who Sexually Abuse Others*, Manchester: Greater Manchester AIM Project.

Prochaska, J. and Di'Clemente, C. (1983) 'Stages and processes of self-change of smoking: Towards an integrative model of change', *Journal of Consulting and Clinical Psychology*, 51: 390–395.

Prochaska, J. and Di'Clemente, C. (1986) 'Towards a comprehensive model of change', in W. Miller and N. Heather (eds) *Treating Addictive Behaviours*, New York: Plenum Press.

Proctor, E. and Flaxingon, F. (1996) 'Community based Interventions with sex offenders organised by the Probation Service: A survey of current practice', Association of Chief Officers of Probation.

Quayle, E. (2004) 'The impact of viewing on offending behaviour', in M.C. Calder (ed.) *Sexual Abuse and the Internet: Tackling the New Frontier*, Lyme Regis: Russell House Publishing.

Quayle, E. and Taylor, M. (2001) 'Child seduction and self-representation on the Internet', *CyberPsychology & Behavior*, 4: 597–608.

Quayle, E. and Taylor, M. (2002) 'Child pornography and the Internet: Perpetuating a cycle of abuse', *Deviant Behavior*, 23, 4: 331–362.

Quayle, E., Vaughan, M. and Taylor, M. (2006) 'Sex offenders, Internet child abuse images and emotional avoidance: The importance of values', *Aggression and Violent Behavior*, 11: 1–11.

Quinsey, V.L., Harris, G.T., Rice, M.E. and Harris, G.T. (1995) 'Actuarial prediction of sexual recidivism', *Journal of Interpersonal Violence*, 10: 85–105.

Rasmussen, L.A. (1999) 'Factors related to recidivism among juvenile sexual offenders', *Sexual Abuse: A Journal of Research and Treatment*, 11: 69–85.

Reder, P. (1983) 'Disorganised families and the helping professions: Who's in charge of what?', *Journal of Family Therapy*, 5, 1: 23–36.

Reder, P. (1986) 'Multi-Agency Family Systems', *Journal of Family Therapy*, 8, 2: 139–151.

Reynolds-Mejia, P. and Levitan, S. (1990) 'Countertransference issues in the in-home treatment of child sexual abuse', *Child Welfare*, 69, 1: 53–61.

Rice, M.E., Chaplin, T.C., Harris, G.T. and Coutts, J. (1994) 'Empathy for the victim and sexual arousal among rapists and nonrapists', *Journal of Interpersonal Violence*, 9: 435–449.

Rich, S. (1998) 'A developmental approach to the treatment of adolescent sexual offenders', *Irish Journal of Psychology*, 17, 1: 102–118.

Richardson, G., Bhate, S. and Graham, F. (1997) 'Cognitive-based practice with sexually abusive adolescents', in M. Hoghughi, S. Bhate and F. Graham (eds) *Working with Sexually Abusive Adolescents*, Thousand Oaks, CA: Sage.

Roberts, J. (1998) 'Fathering trust', *Community Care*, 27: 9–15.

Roberts, W. and Strayer, J. (1994) 'Empathy, emotional expressions and prosocial behaviour', Cariboo College, Kamloops, BC: manuscript submitted for publication.

Robinson, S.L. (2005) 'Considerations for the assessment of female sexually abusive youth', in M. Calder (ed.) *Children and Young People who Sexually Abuse: New Theory, Research and Practice Developments*, Lyme Regis: Russell House Publishing.

Rogers, C. (1951) *Client-Centred Therapy*, Boston, MA: Houghton Mifflin.

Ronen, T. (1992) 'Cognitive therapy with young children', *Child Psychiatry and Human Development*, 23, 1: 19–30.

Ronen, T. (1997) *Cognitive Developmental Therapy with Children*, Chichester and New York: Wiley.

Roosa, M. (2000) 'Some thoughts about resilience versus positive development, main effects versus interactions, and the value of resilience', *Child Development*, 71, 3: 567–569.

Ross, J. and Loss, P. (1987) *Assessment Factors for Adolescent Sexual Offenders,* New London, CT: Ross, Loss and Associates.

Ross, J. and Loss, P. (1991) 'Assessment of the juvenile sex offender', in G. Ryan and S. Lane (1991) *Juvenile Sexual Offending – Causes, Consequences and Corrections*, Lexington, MA: Lexington Books.

Rowe, J. and Lambert, L. (1973) *Children who Wait*, London: Association of British Adoption Agencies.

Russell, M.N. (1995) *Confronting Abusive Beliefs: Group Treatment for Abusive Men*, Thousand Oaks, CA: Sage.

Rutter, M. (1987) 'Psychosocial resilience and protective mechanisms', in J. Rolf, A. Masten, D. Cichetti, K. Nuechterlein and S. Weintraub (eds) *Risk and Protective Factors in the Development of Psychopathology*, New York: Cambridge University Press.

Rutter, M. (1999) 'Resilience concepts and findings: implications for family therapy', *Journal of Family Therapy*, 21: 119–144.

Ryan, G. (1996) 'Goals of group process: The struggle for safety', paper presented at NOTA Conference, Chester, England.

Ryan, G. (1999a) 'The treatment of sexually abusive youth. The evolving consensus', *Journal of Interpersonal Violence*, 14, 4: 422–436.

Ryan, G. (ed.) (1999b) *Web of Meaning – A Developmental-Contextual Approach in Sexual Abuse Treatment*, Brandon, VT: Safer Society Press.

Ryan, G. and Lane, S. (1991) *Juvenile Sexual Offending – Causes, Consequences and Corrections*, Lexington, MA: Lexington Books.

Ryan, G. and Lane, S. (1997) *Juvenile Sexual Offending: Causes Consequences and Corrections* (2nd edn), San Francisco, CA: Jossey-Bass.

Ryan, G., Miyoshi, T., Metzner, J., Krugman, R. and Fryer, G. (1996) 'Trends in a national sample of sexually abusive youths', *Journal of the American Academy of Child and Adolescent Psychiatry*, 35: 17–25.

Saarni, C. (1997) 'Emotional competence and self-regulation in childhood', in P. Salovey and D. Sluyter (eds) *Emotional Development and Emotional Intelligence: Implications for Educators*, New York: Basic Books.

SAFT (2003) 'Children's study – investigating online behaviour', Available at: http://www.ncte.ie/InternetSafety/Publications/d1736.PDF

Salovey, P. and Sluyter, D. (eds) (1997) *Emotional Development and Emotional Intelligence: Implications for Educators*, New York: Basic Books.

Salter, A.C. (1988) *Treating Child Sex Offenders and Victims: A Practical Guide*, Thousand Oaks, CA: Sage.

Saunders, E.B. and Awad, G.A. (1988) 'Assessment, management and treatment planning for male adolescent sexual offenders', *American Journal of Orthopsychiatry*, 58: 571–579.

Saunders, E.B., Awad, G.A. and White, G. (1986) 'Male adolescent sexual offenders: The offender and the offense', *Canadian Journal of Psychiatry*, 31: 542–549.

Scharff, J.S. and Scharff, D.E. (1994) *Object Relations Therapy of Physical and Sexual Trauma*, London: Jason Aronson Inc.

Schoenwald, S.K., Ward, D.M., Henggeler, S.W., Pickrel, S.G. and Patel, H. (1996) 'Multisystemic therapy treatment of substance abusing or dependent adolescent offenders: Costs of reducing incarceration, inpatient and residential placement', *Journal of Child and Family Studies*, 5: 431–444.

Schwartz, B.K. (1992) 'Effective treatment techniques for sex offenders', *Psychiatry Annals*, 22: 315–319.

Scottish Executive (2004) 'Getting it right for every child. Consultation pack on the Review of the Children's Hearings System, available at www.scotland.gov.uk/consultations/education/chhp-01.asp (accessed 12 April 2005).

Scottish Executive (2005) *Youth Justice in Scotland. A Progress Report for all those Working with Young People who Offend*, Edinburgh: Scottish Executive.

Scottish Office (1998) *Protecting Children – A Shared Responsibility. Guidance on Inter-Agency Co-operation*, Edinburgh: Scottish Office.

Scottish Office (2000) *Scottish Executive's Response to the Advisory Group Report on the Youth Crime Review*, London: The Stationery Office.

Scram D.D., Milloy, C.D. and Rowe, W.E. (1991) *Juvenile Sex Offenders: A Follow-up Study of Reoffence Behaviour*, Olympia, WA: Washington State Institute for Public Policy.

Segal, Z.V. and Stermac, L.E. (1990) 'The role of cognition in sexual assault,' in W.L. Marshall, D.R. Laws and H.E. Barbaree (eds) *Handbook of Sexual Assault: Issues, Theories and Treatment of the Offender*, New York: Plenum Press.

Selekman, M.D. (1993) *Pathways to Change: Brief Therapy Solutions for Difficult Adolescents*, London: Guilford Press.

Seto, M. and Eke, A. (2005) 'The criminal histories and later offending of child pornography offenders', *Sexual Abuse: A Journal of Research and Treatment*, 17, 2: 201–210.

Shaw, J., Campo-Bowen, A.E. and Applegate, B. (1993) 'Young boys who commit serious sexual offences: Demographics, psychometrics, and phenomenology', *Bulletin of American Academic Psychiatry Law*, 21: 399–408.

Shaw, J.A. (1999) 'Sexually aggressive behaviour', in J.A. Shaw (ed.) *Sexual Aggression*, Washington, DC: American Psychiatric Press.

Shaw, J.A., Applegate, B. and Rothe, E. (1996) 'Psychopathology and personality disorders in adolescent sex offenders', *American Journal of Forensic Psychiatry*, 17, 4: 19–37.

Shaw, T., Funderburk, J.R. and Schlank A.M. (1999) 'Cognitive-behavioural treatment strategies and the integrated model for adolescent perpetrators of sexual abuse', in J.A. Shaw (ed.) *Sexual Aggression*, Washington, DC: American Psychiatric Press.

Sheath, M. (1990) 'Confrontative work with sex offenders: Legitimised nonce-bashing?', *Probation Journal*, 37, 4: 159–162.

Sheinberg, M. and Fraenkel, P. (2001) *The Relational Trauma of Incest*, New York: Guilford Press.

Sheldon, B. and Chilvers, R. (2000) *Evidence-Based Social Care: A Study of Prospects and Problems*, Lyme Regis: Russell House Publishing.

Sheldrick, C. (1999) 'Practitioner review: The assessment and management of risk in adolescents', *Journal of Child Psychiatry and Psychology*, 40: 507–518.

Sheridan, A., McKeown, K., Cherry, J., Donohhoe, E., McGrath, K., O'Reilly, K., Phelan, S. and Tallon, M. (1998) 'Perspectives on treatment outcome in adolescent sexual offending: A study of a community-based treatment programme', *Irish Journal of Psychology*, 19, 1: 168–180.

Sinason, V. (1997a) 'The learning disabled (mentally handicapped) offender', in E.V. Welldon and C. Van Velsen (eds) *A Practical Guide to Forensic Psychotherapy*, London: Jessica Kingsley Publishing.

Sinason, V. (1997b) 'Stress in the therapist and the Bagshaw Syndrome', in V. Varma (ed.) *Stresses in Psychotherapists*, London: Routledge.

Sinclair, I., Wilson, K. and Gibbs, I. (2004) *Foster Placements: Why They Succeed and Why They Fail*, London: Jessica Kingsley.

Sipe, R., Jensen, E. and Everett, R. (1998) 'Adolescent sexual offenders grown up: Recidivism in young adulthood', *Criminal Justice and Behaviour*, 25, 1: 109–124.

Skinner, B.F. (1953) *Science and Human Behaviour*, London: Collier Macmillan.

Skuse *et al.* (1997) cited in A. Bentovim and B. Williams (1998) 'Children and adolescents: victims who become perpetrators', *Advances in Psychiatric Treatment*, 4: 101–107.

Slattery, G. (2003) *Working with Young Men: Taking a Stand against Sexual Abuse and Sexual Harassment in Responses to Violence*, Adelaide: Dulwich Centre Publications.

Smallbone, S. (2005) 'Attachment insecurity as a predisposing and precipitating factor for sexually abusive behaviour by young people', in M. Calder (ed.) *Children and Young People who Sexually Abuse. New Theory, Research and Practice Developments*, Lyme Regis: Russell House Publishing.

Smallbone, S.W. and Milne, L. (2000) 'Associations between trait anger and aggression used in the commission of sexual offenses', *International Journal of Offender Therapy and Comparative Criminology*, 44, 5: 606–617.

Smallbone, S.W., Wheaton, J.W. and Hourigan, D. (2003) 'Trait empathy and criminal versatility in sexual offenders', *Sexual Abuse: A Journal of Research and Treatment*, 15: 49–60.

Smith, G. (1994) 'Parent, partner, protector: Conflicting role demands for mothers of sexually abused children' in T. Morrison, M. Erooga and R. Beckett (eds) *Sexual Offending Against Children: Assessment and Treatment of Male Abusers*, London: Routledge.

Smith, R. (2003) *Youth Justice: Ideas, Policy, Practice*, Cullompton: Willan Publishing.

Soothill, K. (1997) 'Rapists under 14 in the news', *The Howard Journal*, 36, 4: 367–377.

Spaccarelli, S., Bowden, B., Coatsworth, J.D. and Kim, S. (1997) 'Psychosocial correlates of male sexual aggression in a chronic delinquent sample', *Criminal Justice and Behavior*, 24: 71–95.

Speed, B. (1991) 'Reality exists OK? An argument against social constructivism and social constructionism', *Journal of Family Therapy*, 13: 395–408.

Spence, S.H. and Donovan, C. (1998) 'Interpersonal problems', in P. Graham (ed.) *Cognitive Behaviour Therapy for Children and Families*, Cambridge and New York: Cambridge University Press

Spivak, G. and Shure, M.B. (1974) *Social Adjustment of Young Children: A Cognitive Approach to Solving Real Life Problems*, San Francisco, CA: Jossey-Bass.

Sprenger, P. (1999) 'Phone fight on the last frontier', Wired News Online, http://www.wired.com/news/news/technology/story/19340.html

Steadman, H.J., Monahan, J., Robbins, P.C., Applebaum, P.S., Grisso, T. and Klassen, D. (1993) 'From dangerousness to risk assessment: Implications for appropriate research strategies', in S. Hodgins (ed.) *Crime and Mental Disorder*, Newbury Park, CA: Sage.

Steen, C. and Monnette, B. (1989) *Treating Adolescent Sex Offenders in the Community*, Springfield, IL: Thomas Books.

Stermac, L. and Segal, Z.V. (1989) 'Adult sexual contact with children: An examination of cognitive factors', *Behavior Therapy*, 20: 573–584.

Stermac, L. and Sheridan, P. (1993) 'The developmentally disabled adolescent sex offender', in H.E. Barbaree, W.L. Marshall and S.M. Hudson (eds) *The Juvenile Sex Offender*, London and New York: Guilford Press.

Sternberg, R.J. (ed.) (2000) *Handbook of Human Intelligence* (2nd edn), New York: Cambridge University Press.

Stoller, R.J. (1975) *Perversion: The Erotic Form of Hatred* (Maresfield Library), London: Karnac Books.

Strasburger, V. (2004) 'Children, adolescents, and the media', *Current Problems in Adolescent Health Care*, 34: 54–113.

Surrey Children's Services (1998) 'Placement Review Report' (unpublished).

Suzuki, L.K. and Calzo, J.P. (2004) 'The search for peer advice in cyberspace: An examination of online teen bulletin boards about health and sexuality', *Applied Developmental Psychology*, 25: 685–698.

Swenson, C.C., Henggeler, S.W., Schoenwald, S.K., Kaufman, K.L. and Randall, J. (1998) 'Changing the social ecologies of adolescent sexual offenders: Implications of the success of multisystemic therapy in treating serious antisocial behavior in adolescents', *Child Maltreatment*, 3, 4: 330–338.

Taylor, G.J., Parker, J.D.A. and Bagby, R.M. (1999) 'Emotional intelligence and the emotional brain: Points of convergence and implications for psychoanalysis', *Journal of the American Academy of Psychoanalysis*, 27, 3: 339–354.

Taylor, M. and Quayle, E. (2003) *Child Pornography: An Internet Crime*, Hove: Psychology Press.

Taylor, M. and Quayle, E. (2004) 'Abusive images of children', in S. Cooper, MD; A. Giardino, MD, PhD, V. Vieth, JD and N. Kellogg, MD (eds) *Medical and Legal Aspects of Child Sexual Exploitation*, St Louis, MO: GW Medical Publishing.

TES Cymru (2005) 'Web picture dangers. Warning as schoolgirls post indecent photos on internet for "a bit of fun"', 9 March.

Thompson, S. (1990) 'Putting a big thing into a little hole: Teenage girls' account of sexual initiation', *Journal of Sex Research*, 27: 341–361.

Thornton, D. (2002) 'Constructing and testing a framework for dynamic risk assessment', *Sexual Abuse: A Journal of Research and Treatment*, 14: 139–153.

Thornton, D. and Travers, R. (1991) *A Longitudinal Study of Criminal Behaviour of Convicted Sex Offenders,* proceedings of the Prison Psychologists Conference, HM Prison Service, London: Home Office.

Tolman, D.L. (1991) 'Adolescent girls, women and sexuality: Discerning dilemmas of desire', in C.A. Gilligan, G. Rogers and D.L. Tolman (eds) *Women, Girls and Psychotherapy: Reframing Resistance*, Binghamton, NY: Haworth Press.

Tolman, D.L. (1994) 'Daring to desire: Culture and bodies of adolescent girls', in J.M. Irvine (ed.) *Sexual Cultures and the Construction of Adolescent Identities*, Philadelphia, PA: Temple University Press.

Tolman, D.L. (1999) 'Female adolescent sexuality in relational context: Beyond sexual decision making', in N.G. Johnson, M.C. Roberts and J. Worell (eds) *Beyond Appearance: A New Look at Adolescent Girls*, Washington, DC: American Psychological Association.

Tolman, D.L. (2001) 'Female adolescent sexuality: An argument for a developmental perspective on the new view of women's sexual problems', in E. Kaschak and L. Tiefer (eds) *A New View of Women's Sexual Problems*, Binghamton, NY: Haworth Press.

Tolman, D.L. (2002) *Dilemmas of Desire: Teenage Girls Talk about Sexuality*, Cambridge, MA: Harvard University Press.

Travis, A. (2004) 'Crime strategy: Five-year plan pins hopes on street policing', London, *The Guardian*, 20 July, p. 4.

Trowell, J., Kolvin, I., Weeramanthri, T., Sadowski, H., Berelowitz, M., Glaser, D. and Leitch, I. (2002) 'Psychotherapy for sexually abused girls: Psychopathological outcome findings and patterns of change', *British Journal of Psychiatry*, 180: 234–247.

Tutt, N. (1999) 'Dealing with young offenders: A view at the millennium', *Community Care*, 2–8 December: i–viii.

UK Periodic Report (1999) 'United Kingdom's Second Periodic Report to the UN Committee on the Rights of the Child', London, available at www.cypu.gov.uk/corporate/index.cfm

UK Update Paper (undated) 'Update Paper on the UN Convention on the Rights of the Child, London', available at www.cypu.gov.uk/corporate/index.cfm

United Nations Committee on the Rights of the Child (2002) *Consideration of Reports Submitted by State Parties under Article 44 of the Convention – Concluding Observations of the Committee on the Rights of the Child: United Kingdom of Great Britain and Northern Ireland*, New York: United Nations, reference CRC/C/15Add.188.

United Nations Convention on the Rights of the Child (1989) Available at www.unicef.org/crc/fulltext.htm

US Center for Disease Control and Prevention (2002) Available at http://www.cdc.gov/node.do/id/0900f3ec8000ec28

Utting, Sir W. (1997) *People Like Us*, London: The Stationery Office.

Vance, J.E. (2002) 'Risk and protective factors as predictors of outcome in adolescents with psychiatric disorder and aggression', *Journal of the American Academy of Child and Adolescent Psychiatry*, 41, 1: 36–43.

Vick, J., McRoy, R. and Matthews, B.M. (2002) 'Young female sex offenders', *Journal of Sexual Abuse*, 11, 2: 19.

Vizard, E. (1997) 'Adolescents who sexually abuse', in E.V. Welldon and C. Van Velsen (eds) *A Practical Guide to Forensic Psychotherapy*, London: Jessica Kingsley Publishing.

Vizard, E., Monck, E. and Misch, P. (1995) 'Child and adolescent sex abuse perpetrators: A review of the research literature', *Journal of Child Psychology and Psychiatry*, 36: 731–756.

Vizard, E., Wynick, S., Hawkes, C., Woods, J. and Jenkins, J. (1996) 'Juvenile sexual offenders: assessment issues', *British Journal of Psychiatry*, 168: 259–262.

Von Eye, A. and Schuster, C. (2000) 'The odds of resilience', *Child Development*, 71, 3: 563–566.

Ward, L.M. (2003) 'Understanding the role of entertainment media in the sexual socialization of American youth: A review of the empirical research', *Developmental Review*, 23: 347–388.

Ward, T. and Mann, R. (2004) 'Good lives and the rehabilitation of offenders: A positive approach to treatment', in A. Linley and S. Joseph (eds) *Positive Psychology in Practice*, London: Wiley.

Ward, T., Hudson, S. and McCormack, J. (1997) 'Attachment style, intimacy deficits and sexual offending', in B. Schwartz and H. Cellini (eds) *The Sex Offender: New Insights, Treatment Innovations and Legal Developments, Vol. 2*, Kingston, NJ: Civic Research Institute.

Ward, T., Keenan, T. and Hudson, S.M. (2000) 'Understanding cognitive, affective and intimacy deficits in sexual offenders: A development perspective', *Aggression and Violent Behaviour*, 5: 41–62.

Ward, T., Louden, K., Hudson, S.M. and Marshall, W.L. (1995) 'A descriptive model of the offense chair for child molesters', *Journal of Interpersonal Violence*, 10: 452–472.

Watkins, C.E. (1997) *Handbook of Psychotherapy Supervision*, London: Wiley.

Watzlawick, P., Weakland, J. and Fisch, R. (1974) *Change: Principles of Problem Formation and Problem Resolution*, New York: Norton Press.

Way, I. (2005) 'Empathy, emotional intelligence and alexithymia: Implications for research and practice with young people with sexually abusive behaviours', in M. Calder (ed.) *Children and Young People who Sexually Abuse. New theory, Research and Practice Developments*, Lyme Regis: Russell House Publishing.

Webster-Stratton, C. (1990) 'Long-term follow-up of families with young conduct problem children: from pre-school to grade school', *Journal of Clinical Child Psychology*, 19, 2: 144–149.

Weekes, J.R., Pelletier, G. and Beaudette, D. (1995) 'Correctional officers: How do they perceive sex offenders?' *International Journal of Offender Therapy and Comparative Criminology*, 39: 55–61.

Weinrott, M. (1996) *Juvenile Sexual Aggression: A Critical Review*. Boulder, CO: Institute of Behavioural Science, University of Colorado.

Wenet, G. and Clarke, T. (1986) *Juvenile Sex Offender Decision Criteria, The Oregon Report on Juvenile Sex Offenders*, State of Oregon: Department of Human Resources, Children Services Division.

White, M. (1989) *Selected Papers*, Adelaide: Dulwich Centre Publications.

White, M. (1991) *Deconstruction and Therapy*, Adelaide: Dulwich Centre Newsletter No 3.

White, M. (2002) *Addressing Personal Failure*, Adelaide: Dulwich Centre Newsletter No 3.

White, M. and Epston, D. (1990) *Narrative Means to Therapeutic Ends*, London: Norton Publications.

Wight, D., Henderson, M., Raab, G., Abraham, C., Buston, K., Scott, S., Hart, G., (2000) 'Extent of regretted sexual intercourse among young teenagers in Scotland: A cross sectional survey', *British Medical Journal,* 320: 1243–1244.

Wilkinson, L. (2005) *Comprehensive Assessment and Intervention Guide for Children under 10 Years with Problematic Sexual Behaviour and their Families*, Manchester: Greater Manchester AIM Project.

Wilkinson, L. and Carson, C. (2003) *AIM Initial Assessment of Children under 10 Years with Problematic Sexual Behaviour*, Manchester: Greater Manchester AIM Project.

Will, D. (1994) 'A treatment service for adolescent sex offenders', *Psychiatric Bulletin*, 18: 742–744.

Will, D. (1999) 'Assessment issues', in M. Erooga and H. Masson (eds) *Children and Young People who Sexually Abuse*, London: Routledge.

Wilson, C. (1998) 'Are battered women responsible for protection of their children in domestic violence cases?', *Journal of Interpersonal Violence*, 13: 289–293.

Wilson, D. and Andrews, C. (2004) 'Internet traders of child pornography and other censorship offenders in New Zealand: Updated statistics' (November 2004). Available online from: http://www.dia.govt.nz/puforms.nsf/URL/profilingupdate.pdf/$file/profilingupdate.pdf

Wolak, J., Finkelhor, D. and Mitchell, K.J. (2005) *Child-Pornography Possessors Arrested in Internet-Related Crimes: Findings from the National Juvenile Online Victimization Study*, Washington, DC: National Center for Missing and Exploited Children.

Wolak, J., Mitchell, K.J. and Finkelhor, D. (2003) 'Escaping or connecting? Characteristics of youth who form close online relationships', *Journal of Adolescence*, 26: 105–119.

Wolf, N. (1997) *Promiscuities: The Secret Struggle For Womanhood*, New York: Random House.

Wolf, S.C. (1984) 'A multifactorial model of deviant sexuality', paper presented at the Third International Conference on Victimology, Lisbon.

Wolfe, D.A., Werkerle, C., Reitzel-Jaffe, D., Grasley, C., Pittman, A. and MacEachran, A. (1993) 'Interrupting the cycle of violence: Empowering youth to promote healthy relationships', in D.A. Wolfe, R.S. McMahon and R.D. Peters (eds) *New Directions in Prevention and Treatment across the Lifespan*, Thousand Oaks, CA: Sage.

Wolfe, F.A. (1987) 'Twelve female sexual offenders', presentation to 'Next Steps in Research on the Assessment and Treatment of Sexually Aggressive Persons (Paraphiliacs)', St Louis, MO.

Woods, J. (1997) 'Breaking the cycle of abuse and abusing: Individual psychotherapy for juvenile sex offenders', *Clinical Child Psychology and Psychiatry*, 2, 3: 379–392.

Worling, J.R. (1995) 'Sexual abuse histories of adolescent male sex offenders: Differences on the basis of the age and gender of their victims', *Journal of Abnormal Psychology*, 104: 610–613.

Worling, J.R. (2001) 'Personality-based typology of adolescent male sexual offenders: Differences in recidivism rates, victim-selection characteristics, and personal victimization histories', *Sexual Abuse: A Journal of Research and Treatment*, 13: 149–166

Worling, J.R. and Curwen, T. (2001) *The 'ERASOR': Estimate of Risk of Adolescent Sexual Offense Recidivism, Version 2.0*, Toronto, ON: SAFE-T Programme.

Yelloly, M. and Henkel, M. (eds) (1995) *Learning and Teaching in Social Work: Toward Reflective Practice*, London and Bristol: Jessica Kingsley Publishers.

Youth Justice Board (2000) *ASSET Form*, London: Youth Justice Board.

Youth Justice Board (2004a) *Differences or Discrimination*, London: Youth Justice Board.

Youth Justice Board (2004b) (1st edn) *Key Elements of Effective Practice: Young People who Sexually Abuse*, London: Youth Justice Board.

Youth Justice Board (2004c) *Reader – Young People who Sexually Abuse*, ECOTEC Research and Consultancy Ltd and Nottingham Trent University on behalf of the Youth Justice Board.

Zillmann, D. (2000) 'Influence of unrestrained access to erotica on adolescents' and young adults' dispositions toward sexuality', *Journal of Adolescent Health*, 27S: 41.

Zolondek, S., Abel, G., Northey, W. and Jordan, A. (2001) 'The self-reported behaviors of juvenile sex offenders', *Journal of Interpersonal Violence*, 16, 1: 73–85.

Index